Words of Passage

Words of Passage

National Longing and the
Imagined Lives of Mexican Migrants

HILARY PARSONS DICK

University of Texas Press ❧ *Austin*

Requests for permission to reproduce material from this work should be sent to:
Permissions
University of Texas Press
P.O. Box 7819
Austin, TX 78713–7819
utpress.utexas.edu/rp-form

♾ The paper used in this book meets the minimum requirements of ANSI/NISO Z39.48–1992 (R1997) (Permanence of Paper).

Library of Congress Cataloging-in-Publication Data

Names: Dick, Hilary Parsons, author.
Title: Words of passage : national longing and the imagined lives of Mexican migrants / Hilary Parsons Dick.
Description: First edition. | Austin : University of Texas Press, 2018. | Includes bibliographical references and index.
Identifiers: LCCN 2017031820
    ISBN 978-1-4773-1401-2 (cloth : alk. paper)
    ISBN 978-1-4773-1402-9 (pbk. : alk. paper)
    ISBN 978-1-4773-1403-6 (library e-book)
    ISBN 978-1-4773-1404-3 (non-library e-book)
Subjects: LCSH: Mexico—Emigration and immigration. | Mexico—Emigration and immigration—Social aspects. | Uriangato (Mexico)—Emigration and immigration. | Mexicans—Migrations.
Classification: LCC JV7401 .D53 2018 | DDC 305.868/72073—dc23
LC record available at https://lccn.loc.gov/2017031820

doi:10.7560/314012

For my grandparents Laura, Mac, James, and Geneva:
Through you, I have been able to see this world

Contents

Acknowledgments

This is a book of journeys, including my own from a September over two decades ago when I began work on my PhD to the completion of this book—these words of passage. At this journey's beginning I was unsure if I—a child not of scholars, but of blue-collar laborers, homemakers, government workers, and businessmen—would even complete the degree, let alone realize the career that I have been blessed so far to have. I have accumulated debts, in some ways immeasurable, for the generosity that has been shown to me as I picked my way carefully from then to now. But, even so, thanks are to be given.

My first thanks go, as ever, to the families whose lives are at the center of this book. Without their care, their gift of time and words, there would be no book, no journey of which to tell. *A ustedes les doy todas las gracias por su apoyo, cariño y ayuda.* Though I must use pseudonyms for many of the people who helped me in my research, I acknowledge the friends I met on both sides of the border, particularly Luis Castro, Sahara Lou Grande Ferrer, Carlos Guzmán, Manuel Lombera, Elaine Marnel, Juan Carlos Navarro, Loretta Perna, Howard Porter, Guillermo Rivera, Sister Jane and Father Frank, the families of La Vista Linda, Linda and family, Marisol and family, and all the people referred to in this book, especially Elena and her family and my host family in Uriangato. In their fervent striving I found echoed the passion, stoicism, wit, compassion, and hard work of the laborers in my family: people who taught me that it is not only migrants who can be displaced from the lives that they feel compelled to lead but many, many people who never leave home.

The field research upon which this book is based was generously funded by a Fulbright–García Robles grant and by two Mellon Foundation Population Studies grants, administered through the Mexican Migration Project of Princeton University and La Universidad de Guadalajara. I also received support from several departments and programs at the University of Pennsylvania, where I completed my PhD—especially its Center for Programs in Contemporary Writing, Department of Anthropology, Ethnohistory Program, and Latin American and Latino/a Studies Program. In developing the ideas that became the basis of this book, I benefited from postdoctoral fellowships at the Center for Latin American Studies and Department of Anthropology at the University of Chicago and the Center for the Humanities at Temple University. During my tenure as a visiting assistant professor at Haverford College, I enjoyed the support of their Department of Anthropology. Since I began my position at Arcadia University in 2011, I have yearly received a Professional Development Grant, which has allowed me to present aspects of this book at several conferences and to hire research assistants. During 2016 I was the fortunate recipient of a Wenner-Gren Hunt Postdoctoral Fellowship to complete this book.

I am deeply grateful for the support I received over the years from my dissertation committee and many other mentors. I must begin by thanking my primary dissertation advisor, Greg Urban, whose work inspired me to enter graduate school at the University of Pennsylvania (Penn) and whose kindness, wisdom, and advocacy have sustained me throughout my career. I have also been the beneficiary of generous, discerning, and in many cases ongoing guidance from the other members of my dissertation committee: Asif Agha, Miguel Díaz-Barriga, Gautam Ghosh, and Douglas S. Massey. Each of these scholars has pushed me in ways that collectively led to this book. I give particular thanks to Asif Agha, whose works-in-progress seminar at Penn helped lay the foundation for several chapters, and to Douglas S. Massey for allowing me to participate in the Mexican Migration Project and connecting me with his partners in Mexico, especially Jorge Durand. Since my very first semester at Penn, Douglas has believed in my work, even though it falls outside the considerable reach of his scholarship. I must also thank Nancy Farriss, who was a key supporter during my PhD training and whose work helped me to remember, always, the central importance of spiritual life in the politics of Latin America. I have been blessed at various points to receive counsel from several other scholars: Warren Breckman, John Comaroff, Ann Farnsworth-Alvear, Kesha Fikes, Victor Garcia, Laura González Martínez, Kathleen Hall, Rebecca Huss-Ashmore, Norma Mendoza-Denton, Julia Paley, Luis Miguel Rionda,

Roger Rouse, Peter Stallybrass, Bonnie Urciuoli, Amanda Weidman, and Stanton Wortham.

After completing my PhD, I spent several years as a postdoctoral fellow and visiting professor at institutions where I was fortunate to meet wonderful mentors and colleagues: Bryn Mawr College, the University of Chicago, Temple University, and Haverford College. Here I must first acknowledge Michael Silverstein. Starting during my graduate training and carrying on into the present I, like many of my peers from Penn, have benefited immeasurably from the mentoring and support of Michael Silverstein, whose scholarship undergirds this project and so many others in our field. Though he has had no obligation to do so, Michael has repeatedly found time to provide incisive feedback on my work. During my time at the University of Chicago, I also received support from members of the Center for Latin American Studies and Department of History, particularly Dain Borges, Emilio Kourí, and Mauricio Tenorio-Trillo, all incomparable historians whose work has provided invaluable perspective on the enduring nature of the processes described in this book. Since my fellowship, I have had the privilege of participating in the Michicagoan Faculty Seminar. Through this experience, I have received feedback from fellow seminar participants, especially Richard Bauman, Susan Gal, Judith Irvine, Webb Keane, Alaina Lemon, John Lucy, Bruce Mannheim, and Barbra Meek. I am particularly grateful to Susan Philips, who took the time to respond carefully to several book chapters. When I held my fellowship at Temple University, I was blessed by the mentorship and encouragement of Peter Logan. At Haverford College, Maris Boyd Gillette and Laurie Kain Hart gave me much-needed support at a low point in my job search.

I am also indebted to the intellectual challenge from my scholarly peers. In the early years of my dissertation project, Deborah Lattanzi Shutika played a pivotal role in introducing me to people in my Pennsylvania field sites. I must particularly acknowledge the following people, who have not only responded to multiple versions of my book chapters and articles but have been a source of emotional support during times both challenging and celebratory: E. Summerson Carr, Michele Koven, Alejandro Paz, Jennifer Riggan, and Kristina Wirtz. I have also received astute and compassionate counsel from Jillian Cavanaugh and Shalini Shankar, who provided perceptive comments on the book and helped me navigate the process of book publishing. Extra thanks to Shalini for help with the book's title. I also thank Michael Cepek, who championed this book and convinced me to reach out to the University of Texas Press. And I acknowledge Lynnette Arnold. Though I began as an external member of Lynnette's dissertation committee, she has become a friend and co-author; working with her has deeply enriched this project. And many other people have been friends and insightful interlocutors over the years, including Christopher Ball, Yarimar Bonilla, M. Bianet Castellanos, Sonia Das, David Divita, Aiden Downey, Paja Faudree, Michael Hesson, Jenny Jacobs, Paul Kockelman, Carmen Lamas, Michael Lempert, Adrienne Lo, Constantine Nakassis, Sabina Perrino, Angela Reyes, Jonathan Rosa, Stephen Scott, Robin Shoaps, Ruti Talmor, Lorrin Thomas, Matt Tomlinson, Jessica Winegar, Yanna Yannakakis, and Rihan Yeh.

In fall 2011 I joined the distinguished faculty at Arcadia University. I am grateful for my Arcadia colleagues, who have helped me build a sustaining career at the university and beyond: Samer Abboud, Roland Adjovi, Jonathan Church, Amy Cox, Maryam Deloffre, Ana Maria Garcia, Warren Haffar, Geoff Haywood, Angela Kachuyevski, Doreen Loury, Dina Pinsky, Anita Washington, and Amy Widestrom. I also acknowledge Sandra Crenshaw, John R. Hoffman, Nataliia Shablia, Charu Varma, and Anna Wagner for their support of my research. I must especially thank Jennifer Riggan, my fellow anthropologist at sea, and Peter Siskind, who as our department chair has steadfastly protected our time for scholarship.

Over the past several years, I have been privileged to work with magnificent undergraduate research assistants (RAs), who have updated my research, copyedited my writing, assisted with translations, and in some cases become co-authors. Danielle Diverde, Nicole Edwards, Margaret Keenan, Sean Lanning, Camilo López Delgado, Alison Martinez-Davis, Bryan Mier, Jake Nightlinger, Claudia Segura, and Veronica Willig all made important contributions to this book. Their responses gave me the confidence that *Words of Passage* would be appealing to people other than scholars, for which I am enormously grateful. I also acknowledge the contributions of Emily Brown, Hannah Cohen, Nancy Dennehy, Sarah Guyer, Elise Harry, Kate Heath, Amanda Joachim, Le'ah McCray, Kayla Mueller, Jennifer Samson, and Robin Young.

I have been honored to present aspects of this book to the Departments of Anthropology at New York University, Northwestern University, Notre Dame University, Temple University, University of Chicago (Semiotics Workshop), and Wake Forest University. Thank you to Christopher Ball, Margaret Bender, Grace Cooper, Sonia Das, Paul Garrett, Elina Hartikainen, Shalini Shankar, Michael Silverstein, and

Gabe Tusinski for the invitations and to Susan Blum, Alex E. Chávez, Bambi Schieffelin, and the other faculty—and students—of each department for their insights. I also thank Sarah Jo Cohen at Temple University for her consideration of this project.

My editor at the University of Texas Press, Casey Kittrell, found wonderful readers who gave me penetrating responses that improved the book considerably. Casey's own guidance—and patience!—has been invaluable. I am thankful for the support of Angelica Lopez-Torres and the copyediting work of Amanda Frost and Kathy Lewis. Thanks also to Sandra A. Spicher for creating an excellent index. I am grateful for the feedback I received from my anonymous reviewers at the University of Texas Press, whose insights made *Words of Passage* a much better book. I am delighted to thank publicly Valentina Napolitano, one of my anonymous reviewers who later shared her identity with me. I am a longtime admirer of her work and am indebted to her for her thoughtful review of this book.

Limited portions of this book have appeared in *American Anthropologist*, *American Ethnologist*, *A Companion to Diaspora and Transnationalism Studies*, *Language & Communication*, and the *Journal of Linguistic Anthropology*. For chapters 1 and 2, Wiley allowed me to draw on my article "Imagined Lives and Modernist Chronotopes in Mexican Nonmigrant Discourse," *American Ethnologist* 37(2): 275–290. With the permission of Wiley, parts of chapter 2 are also informed by my article "Una Gabacha Sinvergüenza/A Shameless White-Trash Woman: Moral Mobility and Interdiscursivity in a Mexican Migrant Community," *American Anthropologist* 119(2): 223–235. Chapter 3 takes inspiration from my article "Diaspora and Discourse: The Contrapuntal Lives of Mexican Nonmigrants," in *A Companion to Diaspora and Transnationalism*, edited by Ato Quayson and Girish Daswani (Malden, MA: Wiley-Blackwell), pp. 412–427; and from "From South to North and Back Again: Making and Blurring Boundaries in Conversations across Borders," *Language & Communication* (in press), which I co-authored with Lynnette Arnold. Some of the analysis in chapter 4 was developed from my article "No Option But to Go: Poetic Rationalization and the Discursive Production of Mexican Migrant Identity," *Language & Communication* 30(2): 90–108, with permission from Elsevier. I was granted permission from Wiley to draw from my article "Making Immigrants Illegal in Small Town USA," *Journal of Linguistic Anthropology* 21(s1): e35–e55 for the book's conclusion.

Finally, I must thank my family and nonacademic friends. I cannot name all of my community of friends in Philadelphia and beyond, but you know who you are—please know that you help me get back to it every day. I give special thanks to the members of the El Grupo Caminero—Alfredo, David, Santiago, Primitivo, and Fernando: this is the night, now and forever. I acknowledge Sally Carton, who helped me traverse the perplexing pathways of the heart, which wound like a labyrinth to these words of passage. I am grateful to my parents Donald and Trudy Dick: thank you for your faith in me, even when you had no idea what I was doing. Thank you to my brother John and my sister-in-law Janet—for your support and for blessing me with my nieces Janet Elizabeth and Heidi Catherine. Many thanks, also, to my Aunt Kathryn, Uncle Norm, Aunt Anne, Uncle Richard, and cousins Sam, Brooks, and Chad; to my parents-in-law John and Rosie as well as my sisters-in-law and brothers-in-law Meghan and Marco and Mary Rose and Ryan; and to my "modern family": Bridget, Ewen, Billie, and Miller—you all make me feel at home everywhere. Eternal gratitude to my grandparents: Laura, Mac, James, and Geneva, to whom this book is dedicated. Finally, my whole heart goes to my husband, Sean Graham Ward, and my stepson, Emerson Wallace Ward: you make everything possible, everything worth doing. Thank you for putting up with me during the long night of this book.

Technical Note: Methodology and Methods

Words of Passage is based on multi-sited ethnography, which adapts the classical features of qualitative fieldwork—a researcher's long-term engagement with a location that cultivates familiarity with local language and sociocultural life—to the exploration of processes that unfold across multiple sites (Burawoy et al. 2000; Dick and Arnold 2017b; Hannerz 2003; Marcus 1995). This type of ethnography places at its center analysis of the interconnections between the present and various historical, imaginative, and geographical "beyonds." As such, it involves research in two or more locations linked by a practice, such as migration. My research involved over twenty-four months of continuous fieldwork between June 2000 and September 2002, first in small towns in Chester County, Pennsylvania, and then in Uriangato, Guanajuato, Mexico. My period of intensive fieldwork was book-ended by several preliminary field trips to both locations in 1997 and 1999 and numerous follow-up research trips between 2003 and 2005. Since that time I have maintained informal contact with the people with whom I grew the closest, in particular the members of my host family. However, the period of my formal research terminated in 2005.

Therefore my ethnographic research offers a window onto a period just before three significant changes related to Mexico-US migration and the political economy that links these countries. First is the mass deportations that began in 2006 under George W. Bush's Operation Endgame, a process that accelerated under Barack Obama, who deported more undocumented immigrants than any other US president, and continues apace under Donald J. Trump. During the decades that most shaped the migration of my research participants—the 1970s to the early 2000s—the US government did not engage in mass deportations, as it had done before and has done since. Because migrants from Mexico make up the largest percentage of undocumented migrants in the United States—and because they are the focus of US anti-immigrant politics (Chávez 2015; De Genova 2005; Dick 2011b)—mass deportations affect Mexican migrant communities to a greater degree than other groups. The current period of mass deportations heralded a new era of immigration policy crackdowns. Since 2006, there has been a wave of state and municipal anti-immigrant laws (Varsanyi 2010), colloquially described as policies of "self-deportation." Such policies seek to make conditions so unbearable for undocumented migrants that they opt to leave. In addition, they promote the criminalization of Mexican migrants, or anyone perceived to be Mexican, regardless of legal status (Dick 2011b, 2012). These crackdowns have left migrants and their relations in fear of separation. Rather than encouraging "self-deportation," they have in fact encouraged, however unwittingly, an existing trend toward the settlement-oriented migration of families, as people chose to "shelter in place." Nearly half of US households headed by undocumented migrants contain children who are US citizens, many of whom have never been to their parents' country of origin (Hernández-León and Zúñiga 2016; Passel and Cohn 2009). This makes the prospect of returning the family to Mexico complicated and undesirable, even as conditions of life worsen for migrants in the United States.

The recent immigration policy crackdowns have coincided with the second major change that has occurred since my research period ended: an intensification of the Drug War in Mexico. This war has led to a dramatic increase in violence in certain parts of Mexico, including Michoacán, a state that borders Guanajuato and is a mere twenty minutes south of Uriangato. This conflict has spilled over into Uriangato, which, though not the site of the extensive violence seen elsewhere, has experienced assassinations of those involved in the drug trade. I have not returned to Uriangato in over ten years due to concern for my safety. Because of the increase in violence, many migrants are also reticent to return to Mexico and, indeed, are motivated to bring their family to the United States, despite the immigration crackdowns. Finally, these changes happened in concert with a third transformation: the stagnation of the US economy, which—though a long-term trend—was made sharply worse by the Great Recession of 2008. This economic slowdown has served to legitimate and justify immigration crackdowns, often in the name of protecting jobs for "American workers," as we see in the rhetoric of Donald J. Trump. And it has helped bring Mexico-US migration to a net zero, even putting it in negative numbers for some years (Gonzalez-Barrera 2015). Together these changes have produced new dimensions of migration that this book cannot address, such as the challenges faced by Mexican public schools as they seek to integrate the children of migrants, many of whom have limited or no ability to speak Spanish (Hernández-León and Zúñiga 2016).

In part because my ethnographic research terminated before these changes took hold, this book cannot be and is not an ethnography of the processes that shape contemporary migration between Mexico and the United States. But even if my research could be revealing of these processes, I would still not make them the focus of this book. As I explain in the introductory chapter, *Words of Passage* addresses a lacuna in the study of Mexico-US migration: how the production of representations of migration has long been central to nation-building and the production of inequality in Mexico. That is, I am more concerned with the ways migration shapes nonmigratory processes, especially the forms of national belonging and socioeconomic mobility to which working-class people in Mexico have access. For this reason, even though I conducted dual-sited fieldwork, this ethnography is focused on Mexico and how migration shapes the social world in Uriangato. Representations of migrants have played a key role in informing the production of "proper Mexicanness" (Mexicanidad) since at least the late nineteenth century for both state actors and people in Mexico's migrant communities. This process shapes people's access to the resources that allow for mobility. These representations have enduring features that have not disappeared in the intervening years since my ethnographic research ended.

Thus the data presented in this work continue to be relevant to understanding how such representations shape Mexicanidad. Indeed, as I argue in chapters 3 to 5, forms of diasporic belonging, which are only furthered by the contemporary period of immigration crackdowns and families separated by a fear of moving across the US-Mexico border, are a distinguishing feature of "being Mexican" for working-class people. Overall, then, *Words of Passage* is a study of mobility and its politics understood holistically, as pertaining not only to geographical movements—"migration"—but to social and imaginative mobility as well (cf. Berg 2015). This is an underconsidered and important perspective, especially as the physical and social mobility of people across the globe is increasingly politicized and problematized, as discussed in the conclusion.

A Note on Terminology

During my graduate studies, I was often asked if my project focused on "documented" or "undocumented" migrants—or whether I looked at settlement-oriented "immigration" or seasonal "migration." I always resisted answering these questions or placing them at the center of my research because they presuppose and help legitimate boundaries between groups and processes that do not exist empirically (De Genova 2002). Over the course of their lifetimes, migrants may move in and out of migratory and "immigratory" patterns (cf. Hondagneu-Sotelo 1994). They could spend twenty years as seasonal migrants, returning to Mexico every year for a few months, then spend another twenty years as immigrants, living principally in the United States, and finally decide to retire in Mexico. In much the same way, migrants can move in and out of legal statuses. They may begin migrating illegally then be legally contracted as guest workers, only to return to undocumented status later (cf. Ngai 2004). And this is only one of many possible scenarios. In a given community of Mexican migrants, any number of migratory patterns and legal statuses will be unfolding in close proximity. Some people return to Mexico each year for several weeks and thus follow a more migratory (seasonal) pattern, while others return once every four years and thus follow a more immigratory (settlement-oriented) pattern. Movement patterns are rarely definitive, as they exist in dynamic tension with ever-shifting life trajectories and geopolitics. For this reason, and in keeping with the terminological tradition of contemporary studies of global mobility (e.g., Basch et al. 1994; Berg 2015; Smith 2006; Urry 2007), I refer to cross-border movements as "migration" to convey the sense of open-ended dynamism.

In terms of US legal status, there is no such thing as a bounded group of documented migrants who live apart from undocumented migrants (De Genova 2005; Dick 2011b). Rather, their lives are intertwined and mutually informing. Mexican nationals with US legal permanent residency inhabit the same social space with temporary guest workers, naturalized citizens, US citizens by birth, and undocumented migrants— often within a single household. A nuclear family with three children could have a US citizen father, a mother in the United States on a temporary spousal permit, a child without documents, a child with legal permanent residency, and a child born in the United States. Such sociolegal complexity is not uncommon; indeed, 4 million US-born children lived in such "mixed status" households in 2008 (Passel and Cohn 2009).

When we consider that the majority of Mexican migrants who now have US legal status either used to be undocumented or have spouses or parents who were once undocumented, the supposedly sharp division between documented and undocumented becomes duller still. Indeed, many of the migrants I worked with in Chester County fit this profile. Initially a migration largely of undocumented sojourner migrants, this migration became a "mixed status" family migration in the early 1990s. This change was a result of the Immigration Reform and Control Act of 1986, which gave US legal status to millions of Mexican families (Durand and Massey 2003) but was not accessible to all families, as I explain in chapter 4. Moreover, studies of policy crackdowns have shown over and over that they affect not only undocumented migrants but anyone who fits the ethnoracial and linguistic profile of an unauthorized migrant, regardless of actual legal status (Balderrama and Rodríguez 1995; De Genova 2005; Dick 2011b; Ngai 2004). Thus, despite the frequent claims of anti-immigrant policy makers that they "have no problem with legal immigrants," their policies have a negative impact on people of all statuses, including citizens. Therefore, while I address US legal status where relevant, this book intentionally resists the reification of the divide between "documented" and "undocumented," representing these statuses and their effects as interwoven.

Methodological Approach

As intimated above, the methodology that centrally undergirds *Words of Passage* is dual-sited ethnography—first in Chester County and then in Uriangato. Although in recent decades multi-sited ethnography has been acknowledged as essential to the study of migration (see the discussion in Dick and Arnold 2017b), there are still very few works based on research in both the sending country and receiving country (but see Abrego 2014; Gamio 1930; Hirsch 2003; Lattanzi Shutika 2011; Smith 2006). Yet this methodological approach has several concrete benefits. Conducting field research in Chester County allowed me to use a method that George Marcus (1995: 106) calls "follow the people," which involves developing a network of social relations that piggybacks on the networks of migrants. My connections with transnational families helped me build the foundation of a research and social life in Uriangato. The people I lived with in Uriangato are the relatives of a family I worked with in Chester County. As with many newly arrived migrants in the United States who receive support from more long-term migrants (cf. Hondagneu-Sotelo 1994; Massey et al. 1987), relatives of my research participants in Pennsylvania helped me get oriented to the routines of life in Uriangato. Moreover, my relationships with people in Chester County helped make my presence in Uriangato comprehensible, helping me gain an audience with people who became not only research participants but friends. Building a life out of relationships with families was central to forestalling negative readings of my presence as a gringa (Dick 2017). As I explain in chapter 2, rooting my research in family allowed me to enact a respectable womanhood that mitigated against prevalent stereotypes about immoral US women.

But I centered my research in family life for more than practical reasons. Family relations play a central role in shaping migration processes (Abrego 2014; Castellanos 2010; Chávez 2017a; Hirsch 2003; Hondagneu-Sotelo 1994; Massey et al. 1987; Rouse 1991, 1992, 1995; Smith 2006). *Words of Passage* further elaborates, in particular, scholarship that examines the role of family-internal difference in migration. Early research on family networks (e.g., Massey et al. 1987) entails a cooperative model of households that does not attend to power differentials inside families. Subsequent research has highlighted, for instance, that gender difference shapes access to networks and other family resources (Castellanos 2010; Goodson-Lawes 1993; Hirsch 2003; Hondagneu-Sotelo 1994; Rouse 1992). This research shows that migration typically emerges through family conflict, in which potential migrants contend with family members' resistance to their migration. Gender plays a crucial role in determining the degree of resistance to their migration desires, a pattern that I found replicated in people's talk of migration (see chapter 4). Beyond this, as chapters 2-5 show, the cultivation of family life is foundational to how Uriangatenses understand and enact national belonging and thus is the key social arena in which these processes unfold.

Another driving methodological principle of my work was a commitment to giving back to the people who participated in my research. Anthropology and sociocultural studies of language have a long-standing tradition of engaging in reciprocal research relationships that make research useful to research participants (Bucholtz et al. 2014). Most Uriangatenses have a strong desire to learn English, so the main way I gave back was by offering free English as a Second Language (ESL) classes, having worked as an ESL teacher between college and graduate school. In Chester County my ESL teaching consisted of several night classes for adults, which I ran through my field research in Pennsylvania. I was also an in-home English tutor for several stay-at-home mothers. I taught the formal classes in the basement of an affordable housing office that worked largely with Mexican migrants. In the fall of 2000 I began to work at the housing office as a grant writer and administrator who helped the office's credit counselor in his work educating migrants about the US mortgage and credit markets. In addition to this work, I volunteered at a Catholic mission that aids Mexican migrants and on a committee to create a Mexican community center. Through my volunteer work I also developed relationships with social service workers and local business and government leaders. Perhaps most significantly, my volunteer work allowed me to meet a core group of seven families whom I visited several times a week. I became close to these families, engaging in a range of activities from formal interviews to everyday socializing. It was the relatives of these families who helped me build my life in Uriangato.

In Uriangato I continued to give back by offering free ESL classes, which I designed at the behest of parents who wanted their children to learn English. Many Uriangatense parents see the acquisition of English as key to their children's future mobility, whether as migrants or in the local textile industry. The English language learning centers in Uriangato are cost prohibitive for the working-class families whose lives are at the heart of this ethnography. Using the materials that I had developed for my classes in Chester County, I ran two free weekly classes for children in the neighborhood where I lived in Uriangato. At the request of one of the fathers I knew, who worked as a security guard at Uriangato's technical institute where his son was a student, I also taught an advanced English conversation class to twenty college-aged students. This enabled me to build social relations with middle-class students and teachers, whose perspectives on migration helped me discern the uniquely working-class experience of migration, detailed throughout this book.

Beyond teaching, I also took on an informal role in the neighborhood advising mothers on their right to receive child support from their spouses in the United States. While in Chester County, I had learned from Mexican consular officials that Mexico and the United States have a bilateral agreement that allows Mexican consulates to garnish the wages of delinquent migrant fathers and send them to their spouses in Mexico. I helped several mothers apply for and receive support through this program. In fact, I became so well known for this work on the block where I lived that my friends teased me as I was getting ready to return to the United States that I should stay and open up an office offering this service.

Methods of Data Collection

My methods of data collection and analysis involved a combination of participant observation, captured in daily field notes, survey and ethnographic interviews, and a linguistic anthropological approach to the close textual analysis of discourse as interaction. Between 2000 and 2005 I compiled thirty field-note journals, which I subsequently typed up and organized by theme. In Chester County my ability to conduct the classical participant observation that Clifford Geertz (1998) famously described as "deep hanging out" was circumscribed by the rhythm of life for migrants: long work hours and the social isolation typical of US suburbia. While I was able to engage in a range of activities with people—and especially with the families I came to know well—my ability to participate in and observe people's lives was contained within my volunteer work and my weekly experiences with the families at the center of my research. In contrast, my research in Uriangato was conducted in the context of more classical participant observation, with its deep hanging out. As such, my ethnographic experience in Uriangato was more fluid and full time than it was in Chester County. I lived with a family in the neighborhood where my research was grounded, and my participant observation was based in both the mundane routines and extraordinary events of my friends and research participants.

In Chester County and in Uriangato my interview work took two forms: open-ended ethnographic interviews lasting one to two hours and thirty-minute survey interviews, which were conducted in partnership with the Mexican Migration Project (MMP), discussed in chapter 2 (see also Dick 2006b). With a few exceptions, all interviews were conducted in Spanish, my second language. In Chester County I completed 30 ethnographic interviews between 2000 and 2001 and 17 MMP interviews in 2003. In Uriangato I completed 48 ethnographic interviews and 170 MMP interviews between 2001 and 2002. All of my ethnographic interviews were audio-recorded and subsequently transcribed and translated by me, in a few cases with the support of my undergraduate research assistants at Arcadia University. A majority of the survey interviews were not audio-recorded; instead, information was noted by hand on the MMP survey questionnaire. I received permission from the MMP to audio-record these interactions, however, if interviewees agreed; I was able to record roughly 20 percent of the survey interviews.

In my interview work, I primarily engaged migrants and their relations, although in each locale I also conducted ethnographic interviews with government officials, social service workers, and employers, who provided me information about the history and political economies of both locations. My ethnographic interviews with migrants and their relations were almost always conducted with people I knew well and involved a series of questions evaluating life in Mexico and the United States, which I had developed inductively through my informal conversations with research participants. I enlisted the help of close friends who gave me feedback on the questions, letting me know if my Spanish was comprehensible and resonant with the ways Uriangatenses talk about migration. By contrast, the MMP survey interviews were—by design—conducted with people I did not know and followed a protocol developed by the MMP, which asks a series of questions about work and migration history and the educational and income level of households (see Dick 2006b; Massey et al. 1987 for a description). For some households that I met through the survey, I came to know members of those families well. I did both a survey interview and a subsequent ethnographic interview with some people, which led to some interesting results discussed elsewhere (Dick 2006b).

Part of the design of the MMP survey is to conduct follow-up interviews in the United States with the family members of people interviewed in Mexico, which meant contacting people at addresses provided by their relations in Uriangato. In contrast to my experience in Uriangato, where I discovered—to my surprise—that people were very willing to participate in the survey interviews, people in Chester County were quite reticent do so. Migrants in the United States are much more vulnerable to state intervention if they share information about their lives, so they were understandably wary of speaking with a person from the United States with whom they had no prior relationship. I was able to hire and train "Verónica," a woman whom I had met in Uriangato who had subsequently migrated to Pennsylvania. She and I had become close friends, and her help with the MMP interviews proved invaluable. She aided me in contacting households and attended all interviews, which helped people trust that I was not working for the US government or otherwise occupying some unsavory social role. Indeed, in my research, I needed to navigate carefully around a number of unflattering social positions, a process discussed at length in chapter 2.

Interviews

I began my fieldwork intending to audio-record naturally occurring discourse, understood to be produced through interactions in which local meanings are created (Koven 2014: 509; Potter 2002; Urban 1991, 1996). I had originally planned for the interviews to supplement recordings of naturally occurring talk. But, although people were willing to be recorded in the context of an interview, I was unable to get permission to record interactions outside the interview frame. When it was time to socialize, it was time to put the recorder away (see chapter 2). To insist on recording noninterview talk would have risked my being read as a gringa,[1] who only cares about work and does not understand the importance of sociality—a loaded framing that I had to avoid lest I be barred from social relations altogether, which would have made any kind of research impossible. I was not willing to take that risk, both as a practical concern and, more importantly, out of respect for the people who had graciously welcomed me into their lives. As a result, all of my recorded data are from interview interactions.

This research constraint forced me to think carefully about the place of interviews in the local "communicative ecology" (Shoaps 2009: 465; see also Briggs 2007) and about what kind of data interviews provide. Since the seminal critiques of the social science interview by Charles Briggs (1986) and Elliot Mishler (1986), qualitative researchers have turned a critical lens on this practice, spotlighting that interviews can occlude the perspectives of research participants and reinscribe power inequities (Koven 2014). Moreover, interviews can be unfamiliar forms of interaction that grate against the speech genres of our research participants, inhibiting collection of accurate information and/or violating norms of appropriate behavior (Briggs 1986; Dick 2006b; Koven 2014). As a result, some qualitative researchers eschew interviews because they are assumed to be unavoidably nonegalitarian and artificial (e.g., Potter 2002). By contrast, methods that allow the collection of naturally occurring data are favored, because they can make research more egalitarian and facilitate capturing data that exemplify the practices under study. Greg Urban, my dissertation supervisor, for example, got permission from his research participants to spend the majority of his field research with a tape recorder hanging from his neck, running continually. Thus, he was able to record a range of spontaneous interactions, from routine talk to sessions of myth telling.

As a scholar whose intellectual home is linguistic anthropology, my inability to record noninterview interactions was alarming. Documenting interactions in field notes makes it difficult to complete the kind of careful textual analysis necessary for understanding how language and other semiotic practices not only reflect but also shape the social world—a underlying aim in nearly all sociocultural studies of language, including this book. In addition, interviews are ill suited for capturing certain kinds of exchanges. A project focused on the discursive analysis of religious rituals, for instance, would be very limited if the only recorded data were interview-elicited reports on such happenings. Yet I had to accept the limitations on my research and make the most of my interview data. This has proven much more productive than I initially imagined possible. My research aimed primarily to capture migrants' and nonmigrants' discourse about migration, which explains who migrates and positions actors with respect to "right" and "wrong" ways of migrating. Interview exchanges are well suited for this kind of meta-discursive rationalization, as illustrated in chapters 4 and 5.

Moreover, as I show through the interactional analysis of interviews in these chapters, such exchanges often co-occur with breakthroughs to "natural exchanges," such as interruptions or narratives of personal experience (De Fina and Perrino 2011; Perrino 2011). Interviews are shaped by prior and anticipated discourse and by the social lives in which they are embedded, so they can be revealing of these processes (Briggs 2007; De Fina and Perrino 2011; Koven 2014; Perrino 2011). Sensitivity to these discursive relationships makes it possible to conduct interviews in ways that are interactionally recognizable and sensitive to power differentials (Briggs 1986). Furthermore, interviews are not necessarily foreign to local communicative ecologies: they can themselves be naturally occurring. Indeed, as I argue in chapter 2, the migrant enclaves of Chester County and Uriangato are "interview societies" (Briggs 2007: 552): social milieus in which interviews are familiar interactions recognized as sites for the production of consequential information.

Nonetheless, it bears emphasizing that *Words of Passage* is not an "interview-based study." Its insights are not derived from my interviews alone but from the triangulation of these data with other kinds of information. Because I am able to situate my recorded data inside of my participant observation and involvement with the lives of Uriangatenses over many years, I am able to analyze my interviews inside these relationships and the other interactions that I recorded in field notes. Indeed, I not only developed the questions in my ethnographic interviews out of the propositions and framings of everyday talk about migration but also carefully coordinated analysis of the interviews with the resonant themes of such discourse, which I surmised from processing my field notes. When I transcribed the recorded interviews, I organized them not only by theme but by certain discursive practices that I noticed recurring, such as the gendered patterns of pronominal usage discussed in chapters 4 and 5. This allowed me to track the overarching patterns in Uriangatense migration discourse and calibrate it with the noninterview talk that I had documented in field notes, showing robust similarities between the talk of migration recorded in interviews and discourse from other interactions (Dick 2017).

Moreover, I was able to share portions of the interviews with my research participants (always being careful not to identify speakers, by using pseudonyms and decontextualizing the discourse excerpts) and—subsequently—with two of my undergraduate research assistants—Camilo López Delgado and Bryan Mier, who are native speakers of Spanish—to ascertain their interpretations of the interactions and coordinate/revise my own accordingly (cf. Koven 2007). I also document the similarities and differences between interview discourse and discourse produced by state-actors and journalists. Between 2000 and 2005 I built a database of local and national newspaper articles and speeches of government officials related to migration, which supports my analysis in chapters 1 and 2. Finally, this book considers more than people's talk of migration. It imbricates analysis of such talk not only with related forms of discourse (in particular immigration and economic policy) but with other semiotic practices that inform Mexicanidad, especially home construction (chapter 3) and the Catholic cult of the saints (chapter 5).

Naming and Protecting Identities

Because migrants—especially Mexican migrants in the United States—are often subject to state surveillance and other kinds of monitoring, which can be devastating for family networks, it is important to take measures to protect their identities. In accordance with the Mexican Migration Project (MMP) protocol, the survey data I collected in Uriangato were randomized: each household was assigned a number and was sorted by an Excel program; no other identifying feature was assigned to these homes. The survey data I collected in Pennsylvania came from people related to members of the MMP households in Uriangato, though they were similarly de-identified with a number. Once the surveys were completed, I returned them to the MMP. The information was compiled into aggregate statistical data, stored by the MMP. As mentioned above, I received permission from the MMP to record some of the survey interviews but gathered no names during these recordings, identifying the household only by its number. Consent for all research interactions, including interviews, was obtained orally. Asking people to sign consent forms—especially in the United States, where people are often wary of "official exchanges" signaled by documents because of concerns about legal status—would have presented an insurmountable barrier to research. For my qualitative data (both my field notes and ethnographic interviews), I assigned each research participant a pseudonym. For public or historical figures, I use actual names; all other names in this book are pseudonyms. Moreover, to protect my research participants in the United States, I do not name any particular town but refer to the site in aggregate as "Chester County." People residing in Mexico are much less vulnerable to direct threats to their well-being from the government or fellow residents as a result of migration, so I have not changed the name of the city where I concentrated my research there. Moreover, because it is necessary to describe the political economic history of Uriangato, which distinguishes it from similar cities in Mexico, it would be immediately identifiable even with a pseudonym. However, I have changed the name of the neighborhood where I grounded my life and research and conducted the MMP survey, calling it "La Libertad." I have also altered all street names and other salient details about the particular locations of households. Finally, out of respect for my relationships with the people with whom I grew closest, I chose to base the extended analysis of conversations in chapters 4 and 5 on interactions with people with whom I was not as close. To do an analysis of a conversation with a close friend felt like a violation of intimacy—though the perspectives of these people, in particular the members of my host family and my friend Elena and her family, inform every aspect of this book and appear narratively throughout.

Translation and Transcription Conventions

I compiled the majority of the translations of my recorded data by myself. The material analyzed in chapter 5 was translated in collaboration with my research assistants Camilo López Delgado and Bryan Mier. For transcriptions of my recordings, I used the following conventions, which are standard in the field (e.g., Du Bois 2007).

Transcription Key

Symbol	Meaning
A	Don Arturo (chapter 4)
B	Belén (in italics) (chapter 5)
C	Doña Cecilia (in italics) (chapter 4)
H	Hilary (in bold) (chapters 4 and 5)
M	Magdalena (chapter 5)
R	Rigoberto (chapter 5)
—	Interruption
{ }	Interpolations
[ ]	Simultaneous speech
. . .	Pause
Ø	Discourse pattern not found

Words of Passage: Imagined Lives, Migration Discourse, and National Belonging

We can't imagine our lives without the unlived lives they contain.
(PHILLIPS 2013: XIII)

Vignette One

It is a day in early August 2002 and air space is shut down over Mexico City. Pope John Paul II is leaving, having completed what would be his final trip to Mexico. Before flying off, the pope's plane circles the national capital for fifteen minutes, while an estimated 1 million people on the ground hold up mirrors to reflect the day's brilliant sun toward the aircraft as a sign of affection: *un recuerdo* (a parting gift of remembrance) for their adored pope. With John Paul II aged eighty-two and increasingly feeble, many suspect that this will be their final farewell to a pontiff who included Mexico on his very first papal trip outside of Italy in 1979 and visited the country five times during his papacy. This fifth visit was especially significant because during it John Paul II canonized Juan Diego, the first Native American saint in the church pantheon. The Virgin of Guadalupe, patron saint of Mexico, appeared to Juan Diego in 1531, telling him to build a church at Tepeyac, on the outskirts of what is today Mexico City, where a massive basilica now stands in honor of the Virgin and the country's Catholic essence.

Scenes of the pope's departure and much of his visit were broadcast live on television in Mexico. No matter what home I was visiting in Uriangato, the Mexican seat of my fieldwork on migration between this small city and Pennsylvania, the television was sure to be on during his trip. As people kept tabs on the pope during the course of their daily obligations, this coverage filled the hours with a sense of the heavenly beyond and Mexico's place in it. On the day of the pope's departure I visited with Don Arturo and Doña Cecilia,[1] a couple I had come to know well. When I arrived, they were glued to the screen. Doña Cecilia pulled up a chair, inviting me to watch with them. Don Arturo reminded me that John Paul II and Mexico enjoyed a special relationship: this pope liked to visit the country—perhaps more than any other—because Mexicans understand how to be Catholic better than any other *raza* (race-nation) in the world. I heard many people make this claim, especially as we talked about migration. "Being Mexican" has long been bound up with being Catholic—even, or perhaps especially, for those who imagine sojourning in El Norte (the North: the United States). Since at least the early nineteenth century Mexican Catholicism—emblematized in the relationship between the Virgin of Guadalupe and Juan Diego—has been mobilized as a sign of the country's God-given sovereignty, especially in moments of encounter with imperial incursions from the outside, first Spain then later the United States. The pope's recognition that Mexico is more successfully Catholic and, as such, more moral than any other nation is an endorsement of particular value for Uriangatenses. Therefore it is not surprising people would emphasize this to me, a sojourner from the United States.

Vignette Two

It is Christmas time in Uriangato. Laden with decorations, the houses illuminate the night with sparkle and flash. The daily masses at the main cathedral overflow to the sidewalk with congregants. After mass they stroll across the street to the town square to take in the open-air arts and culture events that happen nightly throughout December. El Día de Los Reyes Magos (The Day of the Wise Men: Epiphany), the day the wise men visited the newborn baby Jesus, is fast approaching. In Mexico this is when children receive Christmas gifts (Santa Claus is seen as a silly gringo invention). About halfway through December the quotidian soundscape of radio programs that blasts out of homes, business, and passing vehicles from dawn to dusk becomes punctuated with advertisements hawking Día de los Reyes promotions. Parents who cannot provide Los Reyes (as Christmas gifts are called) are forced to confront the emotional bite of poverty in the disappointment of their children. The year I lived there, the municipal government collected gifts for poor children—but only those in the municipality's rural villages.

In radio announcements, government officials spoke over a maudlin background of children's voices tinged with sadness, describing *las comunidades* (the rural communities) as locations of financial desperation, where raggedy youth are taken care of by loving parents, too poor to deliver Los Reyes. They pleaded with urban residents to do their civic duty by donating gifts.

Like many government programs, the gift drive construed poverty as a rural problem, eliding the need of urban residents, as Sara, my friend and neighbor in Uriangato, found out. Sara is a *mujer abandonada* (abandoned woman): her husband left her when he migrated to the United States and pays no child support for the son they had together. She struggles even to buy food and pay basic bills, so she was in distinct need of some Los Reyes charity. One afternoon during the Christmas season I was talking to her about a policy that allows Mexican women to collect child support from errant fathers in the United States. This policy was administered through the municipal offices of Desarrollo Integral de Familias (DIF: Integrated Family Development), the government office also responsible for the Three Kings gift drive. At my mention of DIF, Sara launched angrily into a story about her most recent trip to the office, where she collects *dispensas*—the Mexican equivalent of food stamps. While they were there, Sara's son spied a red ball brought in for the drive. But when she asked for it—"¡para Los Reyes! (for the Kings!)"—her request was denied. "They wouldn't even give me that one stupid ball," she said with venom. This denial came not because she is not poor enough (she had to demonstrate her need to receive *dispensas*) but because she is an urban dweller. For Sara, this story is typical of the ways her government and community fail her, something she imagines would be different were she to go *al otro lado* (to the other side: the United States)—a place where life is hard, she tells me, but at least it is fair.

Vignette Three

On Thursday, December 13, I am awoken at 3:30 A.M. by the sound of weeping. Having been at a late night mass for the feast day of the Virgin de Guadalupe, I'm frustrated to be stirred so shortly after falling asleep, thinking that it must be one of the children awakened by a bad dream. The sound persists, and soon there is a loud knocking on my bedroom door. It is María, one of the daughters-in-law of my host family: "Se murió mi suegra (My mother-in-law died)." We both start to cry—Doña Lupe, her mother-in-law, my host mother, was a kind soul who had graciously welcomed me into her home, even though she was already ill when I arrived three months before. We hug for a long, bracing beat. Then, drawing in breaths of courage, we walk together to Doña Lupe's bedroom. There we sit around Doña Lupe: her children who live in town (she had eight in all, three in the United States), their spouses, her grandchildren, her sister, her husband, and me—stunned and crying. Her eldest daughter and principal caretaker leads the mourning with repeated laments:

> ¡Ay Mama, no puede ser!
> (Oh Momma, it cannot be!)
> ¿Ay Mama, por qué no me dijiste nada?
> (Oh Momma, why didn't you tell me anything {was wrong}?)
> ¿Ay Dios, por qué hiciste esto?
> (Oh God, why did you do this?)

Eventually one of Doña Lupe's sons breaks our trance of early mourning to set up for the viewing.

The viewing is held from about eight in the morning on Thursday until late in the afternoon on Friday. We close the street in front of the house, making this a space of grief and communion, where people sit on folding chairs we have placed for them. Someone has gotten out word of the family's loss, and friends and relatives from all over Uriangato come to pay their respects. Every few hours when one of the women from the neighborhood visits to say the Rosary a call goes out: "We're going to pray!" Each time we gather around the body and ask for the Virgin's guidance—for us, for Doña Lupe's departing soul. Several large pots of food and hot drinks arrive late Thursday afternoon, sent by relatives and friends. The daughters-in-law and I serve the mourners, while the preteen boys of the family offer the men cigarettes and brandy. The neighbors make note of the relatives who have come in from the rancho (rural town) where Doña Lupe and her husband grew up and started their family. The women's tattered rebozos (shawls) and the men's dusty cowboy hats make them stand out.

Although the rancho is only forty minutes away, people in the city are more likely to go to the United States than to visit it: so far apart are these worlds imagined by people in this working-class neighborhood, where most residents are, nevertheless, related to people from the ranchos.

But no moment arrests the attention of the block more than the arrival of Doña Lupe's migrant children: two sons who live in Pennsylvania and a daughter who lives in Michigan. I am buying soda from a convenience store near the house, chatting with some neighbors, when a cry echoes down the street: "¡Han llegado los muchachos! [The kids have arrived!]" Everyone turns to watch as the three return migrants—all people in their thirties with families of their own—run to the house from the taxi that dropped them off down the block. Their mother's passing has brought them home, making them children again. Doña Lupe is laid out in the garage and the gate is open, framing a sorrowful scene of homecoming that we stand silently to witness. The returning siblings fall on each other at the casket, the daughter crying "¡Mama!, ¡Mama!" the sons quietly shaking, tearful beside her. After they have had time to say good-bye, the coffin is closed for the burial mass and internment. We walk in the street to the church behind the station wagon with her coffin. We are about fifty in all. More gather at the church. After mass is said, we walk behind Doña Lupe to the graveyard. The next day we begin the Novena—the nine days of Rosary prayer and Bible readings that help ensure Doña Lupe's soul will make it to heaven. We gather around an ashen cross on the floor where her coffin had been, surrounded by flowers and candles. The Novena will end on December 23. Then we will have a final mass in honor of her passing soul, while the rest of the world celebrates *las fiestas* of Navidad (the Christmas season).

This is an ethnography of the imagined lives of Mexican migrants—whether the lives people imagine for themselves in migration or the types of persons migrants are envisioned to be—and the ways they shape national belonging and resource access in a part of Mexico with ties to the United States. My exploration of this process is grounded in five years of dual-sited ethnographic research during the early 2000s.[2] This research took me to the industrial city of Uriangato, in the Mexican state of Guanajuato, and to several towns in Pennsylvania, home to mushroom farms worked by migrants from Uriangato and its neighboring municipalities. As illustrated in the opening vignettes, Uriangatenses live their lives in the company of remembered, returned, or imagined fellows, so that the unfolding of the present is refracted through a prism of possible counterpoint lives as yet (and perhaps forever) unlived—found not only in the United States but in other places "beyond here": in the ranchos, in heaven.

Therefore the imagined lives I explore are about more than migration, as they elucidate and intervene in a range of processes not directly related to movements to El Norte. The significance of a pope's visit to Mexico is brought into relief by images of the morally corrupted lives of migrants. A woman understands the denial of her poverty against a backdrop of support that she assumes would await her if she went north. The burial of a mother cannot be completed without the return of her migrant children, a return that captivated my neighbors because it displayed the power of the Mexican family, even across a geopolitical border.

Counterpoint lives matter, in part, because they form a measuring stick against which people evaluate their immediate world. As Adam Phillips (2013: xiii) puts it in the epigraph to this chapter, "We can't imagine our lives without the unlived lives they contain." Counterpoint lives help actors determine whether the life they possess is as it should be or, more often than not, how that life should be something different. This process is highlighted and made especially pressing in contexts of migration. That migration creates a "double consciousness" in which people's present world is shaped by counterpoint lives inhabitable elsewhere is a phenomenon that has been remarked upon by a number of scholars (e.g., Appadurai 1996; Gupta 1992; Larkin 2002; Ong 1999, 2000; Werbner 2013). Yet few have systematically examined the imagination of counterpoint lives as a practice that reveals how such refraction becomes consequential in particular contexts. In offering just such a systematic account, *Words of Passage* shows that the imagined lives of Mexican migrants play a central role in the creation of Mexicanidad (Mexicanness)—right and wrong ways to be Mexican—for Mexican state institutions and people in Uriangato.

This is especially true in the working-class neighborhood where I grounded my research, which I call "La Libertad." Thus the production of the imagined lives of migrants is about more than the evaluation of individual trajectories. It is a social and political process that orders how people are hailed to be members of the Mexican nation-state: what is called *interpellation* (Althusser 2001; Butler 1993, 1997; Carr 2011). The central insight of *Words of Passage*, then, is that counterpoint lives are an interpellative practice through which Uriangatenses are called to be and see themselves as Mexican. This process constrains access to belonging and resources and, as such, helps order social inequality.

During my fieldwork, I built social relations and did research with local government officials, social workers, and educators who work with migrants on both sides of the border, but this ethnography focuses primarily on the experiences of people directly involved in migration between Uriangato and the United States, especially southern Pennsylvania. By this I mean both migrants and their loved ones and neighbors who do not migrate. There is a robust literature examining how Mexican migrants develop and maintain a sense of national belonging—of still "being Mexican"—while creating lives rooted in the United States (e.g., Baquedano-López 2001; Farr 2006; Gálvez 2009; Lattanzi Shutika 2011; Mendoza-Denton 2008; Smith 2006). But being Mexican is a practice in which people in Mexico's migrant-sending communities must also engage—it is not something given just by virtue of living in the country. Yet scant attention has been paid to the process of being Mexican for such *nonmigrants*: people connected to the practice of migration who themselves either have not migrated or have tried migration briefly and rejected it. This process has a lot to tell us about how migration reflects upon and orders social worlds long before, and even without, actual movements abroad (cf. Berg 2015). Therefore this book focuses on the relatively underexamined perspectives of nonmigrants.

As this suggests, *Words of Passage* is not principally a study of migration itself, at least not as such study has been developed in the social sciences over the last several decades. While this book addresses some of the processes that shape migration from Uriangato, it is not centrally concerned with the factors that initiate, perpetuate, or otherwise inform patterns of Mexico-US migration—a subject thoroughly addressed in the existing literature (e.g., Alarcón 1992, 2011; Durand 1994; Hirsch 2003; Hondagneu-Sotelo 1994; Lopez 2015; Massey et al. 1987; Smith 2006), including work on migration between Guanajuato and Pennsylvania (Lattanzi Shutika 2011). In different ways literature in this vein tends to treat migration as a countervailing force to the nation-state that either reveals its failures or pushes against it, generating potentially distinct forms of political organization (Alonso 1994; Basch et al. 1994; De Genova 2005; Malkki 1992, 1995; Schmidt Camacho 2008; Wimmer and Glick-Schiller 2002). *Words of Passage* shows that migration practices, and most centrally the imagination of lives in migration, are integral to nation-state building in Mexico, not a sign of its failure.

Examining the imagined lives of migrants from the perspective of nonmigrants reveals the fundamental role such imaginings play in the *variegation* of national belonging, the way some people are incorporated into the nation-state by virtue of always being marginal to it (Biolsi 2005; Bonilla 2015; Herzfeld 1997; Kelly and Kaplan 2001; Ong 1999; Simpson 2014). Attention to these lives shows that being Mexican is not the same prospect for everyone. Rather, people are called to be members of the polity in ways that make them into unequal kinds. As such, interpellation not only informs a person's affective sense of "belonging" to a place but also the constraints on such belonging and who can and cannot access the resources associated with full membership in a polity (cf. Carr 2011), processes which are often heightened in contexts of migration (Abrego 2014; Basch et al. 1994; Berg 2015; De Genova 2005; Dick 2011b; Hall 2002; Ngai 2004; Smith 2006). In focusing on such constraints, *Words of Passage* spotlights interpellation into the nation as a process that foments marginalization and dislocation, producing national *longing* as much as—or more than—belonging.

As such, the imagination of lives is not a fanciful practice. It is a sociopolitical process that plays a central role in constructing migration, national (be)longing, and resource access in Mexico and in the transnational political economy that connects Mexico and the United States. Therefore the stakes are high for working-class Uriangatenses as they render their present world against the backdrop of the lives they imagine beyond here. While there is a robust literature on how Mexican migrants are positioned within and resist US projects of variegation (Chávez 2015, 2017a, 2017b; Coutin 2005, 2007; Coutin and Pease Chock 1995; De Genova 2005; Dick 2011b; Gálvez 2006, 2007, 2009; Mehan 1997; Mendoza-Denton 2008; Santa Ana 2002), much less attention has been paid to the ways people engage Mexican state-building practices (but see Schmidt Camacho 2008).[3] In examining boundaries of belonging in Mexico, I highlight the affective and material consequences (be)longing has for a range of activities—from building a home to crossing a national border. As such, being Mexican is not just about expressing an "identity": a process highlighted in the literature on migration and belonging (e.g., Farr 2006; Lattanzi Shutika 2011; Smith 2006). It is a project of social differentiation and political critique (cf. Chávez 2015, 2017a, 2017b; Flores and Rosa 2015; Mendoza-Denton 2008; Rosa 2014, 2016). Therefore this book offers a unique perspective on migration, showing that the imagination of cross-border lives has long been central to the construction of who can successfully lay claim to Mexicanidad and its associated resources, irrespective of actual movements abroad.

Being properly Mexican is a fraught process for working-class people in La Libertad, a place with active migration pathways to the United States. Visions of Mexicanidad produced by state institutions have long figured migrants and working-class people as simultaneously representing the essence of Mexico's cultural uniqueness and also as the country's greatest barriers to progress (Dick 2010a; Lomnitz 2009; Schmidt Camacho 2008; Walsh 2004). Mexican state institutions have used such modernist visions to justify the variegation of national belonging so that some people (not only migrants and working-class people but also women, Indigenous groups, and rural people) are positioned as impeding Mexico's advancement and denied access to the full rights of citizenship (see chapter 1). Consider the story of Sara above.

The DIF Christmas gift drive replicated visions of Mexicanidad produced by state institutions, which often figure poverty as a rural phenomenon. These visions tell a story of linear advance from country to town, from poverty to wealth, from past to future: a moral geography that calls rural people to emblematize Mexico's poverty while erasing the needs of urban people of limited means, whose poverty exposes the failures of progress in Mexico. By denying Sara's gift request, DIF hailed her as someone who can manage progress on her own, thereby positioning her inability to do so as her failing—as evidence of her improper Mexicanidad. The imagination of lives beyond here therefore provides a measuring stick against which actors can evaluate and potentially transform life across multiple domains, from the here-and-now to relationships with their government to transnational experiences in the United States. And, as Sara's story suggests, the practices through which people construct the imagined lives that inform being Mexican are fundamentally discursive, born in the social and interactional practices through which people depict counterpoint lives and link actual lives to them.

Migration Discourse, Social Imaginaries, and Ethico-moral Life

And above, in the light
Of the star-lit night,
Swift birds of passage wing their flight . . .

O, say not so!
Those sounds that flow
In murmurs of delight and woe
Come not from wings of birds.

They are the throngs
Of the poet's songs,
Murmurs of pleasures, and pains, and wrongs,
The sound of winged words.

In this 1845 poem "Birds of Passage" Henry Wadsworth Long-fellow depicts the sounds of migratory birds in flight as being like the words that beat in a poet's mind, murmuring of "pleasures, and pains, and wrongs." Around the time when this poem was published, the phrase "birds of passage" was becoming popular in the United States as a way to refer to temporary labor migrants—first those from eastern and southern Europe and later those from Asia and Mexico.[4] These sojourner migrants came to the United States with the aim of saving money and returning home. Such seasonal mobility typified Mexico-US migration for most of its nearly 130-year history. While other migrations had become the subject of public concern prior to the "birds of passage" era, such as the early and mid-nineteenth century migration of Germans who settled in the United States (Schmid 2001), temporary migrants seemed to arouse new suspicions. Their lack of rootedness was taken by some as a sign of their inherently untrustworthy natures (cf. Malkki 1992, 1995). Even today policy makers tend to depict seasonal migration as exceptional, as a sign of the failures of state building and economic "progress" and also as a harbinger of moral decline at home and abroad.

Economist Michael J. Piore (1979) took on these imagined lives of migrants in his seminal work *Birds of Passage: Migrant Labor and Industrial Societies*, arguing that the movement of labor is not aberrant but integral to industrial capitalism (see also Sassen 1988). As *Words of Passage* reveals, depictions of migrants are also integral to the visions of national belonging that organize who can and cannot lay claim to full membership in a polity and its associated resources, not only in migrant-receiving societies but in migrant-sending ones as well. Therefore it is not only the migrants themselves whose lives are used to shape the variegation of national belonging but also the words of passage through which images of migrants and their pleasures, pains, and wrongs become recognizable and take flight.

While Uriangatenses produce the imagined lives that undergird processes of interpellation into Mexicanidad through several overlapping semiotic practices, including homebuilding and participation in the Catholic cult of the saints (see chapters 3 and 5), the most central of these is *migration discourse* (Dick 2010a). This term refers to talk and writing that summon up or presuppose the figures of personhood, rhetorical themes, forms of spatial reference, or logical propositions that people associate with the causes and consequences of migration. Migration discourse can take the form of overt rationalizations about migration, as when people state why they do or do not want to migrate or a scholar makes an argument about the factors that initiate migration. But, as suggested above, migration discourse can also be elliptical, emerging in the course of activities that seemingly have little to do with migration, such as Pope John Paul II's final visit to Mexico. As I show in chapter 1, figures of migration—whether as corrupted degenerates or as national heroes—have long informed the production of national identity in Mexico, as they have in US national imaginings as well. So migration discourse is never only about migration. It is also about the promises, possibilities, and failures of home—of lives both actualized and as yet unlived. This book focuses on these lives and their consequences.

Migration discourse is generated across multiple arenas, from the channels of media to the chambers of government to the halls of academia. It is also a routine part of life in the neighborhood where I centered my ethnographic research in Mexico (Dick 2010a). It flows through conversations between family members separated by migration. It animates sidewalk gossip sessions. It imbricates actually unfolding happenings in Uriangato with migration, refracting them through visions of life abroad, which render those happenings uniquely Mexican by contrast. Although the migration discourse produced in these different arenas generates distinct impacts and terrains of distribution, it nevertheless has one important feature in common: it is organized around the production of *imaginaries*. This term refers to visions of the social world, within which actors posit themselves as certain kinds of agents who "traverse a social space and inhabit a temporal horizon, entertain certain beliefs and norms . . . , and exist among other agents" (Gaonkar 2002: 10; see also Salazar 2010; Taylor 2004). The depiction of Mexico as an exemplary Catholic nation that is morally superior to the United States is an imaginary of particular significance to working-class Uriangatenses. As I show below, the (re)production and resistance of this imaginary is a lynchpin of the processes of interpellation that create the variegation of Mexicanidad. In the next section I explore this imaginary, first unpacking anthropological work on imaginaries and how *Words of Passage* contributes to this work.

Discursive Production of Mexican Imaginaries of Moral Mobility

The concept of the social imaginary—and a broader interest in the imagination—has emerged as a productive way for anthropologists to

think through how actors create and transform large-scale social formations, like the nation-state, and social processes, such as mobility (Crapanzano 2004; Dave 2012; Gaonkar 2002; Mittermaier 2011; Salazar
2010, 2011).[5] Within this larger body of work is a nascent but important literature that employs the concept of the imaginary to understand
how cultural depictions of migrants inform nation-state formation, with
a particular focus on migration between Latin America and the United
States (e.g., Hallett 2012; Hallett and Baker-Cristales 2010; Schmidt
Camacho 2008). This work elegantly documents depictions of migrants—or "migrant imaginaries"—produced by state actors and other
elites (newspaper writers, artists, and so on) as part of their crafting who
does and does not belong within the nation.

As this suggests, the concept of the "imaginary" is cousin to the analytic "imagined community" crafted by Benedict Anderson (1991) in his
treatise on modern nationalism. Anderson examines the processes that
allow people to envision affinity with co-citizens, most of whom they
never meet, what Michael Warner (2002) calls "stranger sociability."
The national imagined community is a paradigmatic social imaginary,
but it is not the only one. As suggested in the work on migrant imaginaries, the stranger sociability rendered from other bases of collectivity, such as transnational migrant networks, often exists in tension with
the sociability of the nation-state (cf. Appadurai 1996, 2001; Eisenlohr
2006; Ferguson 2006; Gupta 1992; Hallett and Baker-Cristales 2010;
Paz 2015; Schmidt Camacho 2008). Moreover, the anthropology of nationalism shows that, in contrast to Anderson's theory, which depicts
the national community as an egalitarian fellowship, social differentiation is at the heart of nation-state building (Bauman and Briggs 2003;
Benhabib 2002; Eisenlohr 2006; Herzfeld 1997; Kelly and Kaplan 2001;
Lomnitz 2001b; Ong 1999; Paz 2015): a finding that *Words of Passage*
strongly underscores. Therefore the concept of an imaginary is more
productive for thinking through and outside the nation, enabling us
to push against what Andreas Wimmer and Nina Glick-Schiller (2002:
302) call "methodological nationalism": the idea that the nation-state is
the natural container of analysis. Methodological nationalism produces
scholarship that elides the pragmatics that make possible the nation-
state's emergence and continued salience, keeping us from interrogating how national belonging matters, who gets to say why it matters, and
what practices enable us to lay claim to it.

Building on this literature, *Words of Passage* situates the work of the
imagination in concrete quotidian practices that enact collective be-

longing, inequality, and resource allocation in Uriangato—from side-walk gossip sessions to government-run Christmas gift drives. These practices are shaped but not determined by nationally and transnationally circulating migration discourse. Collectively, work on imaginaries has sidelined the important role that language practices play in imaginative processes. Yet most of the imagining in what we call imaginaries happens discursively, both as visions of the social world are reproduced across time and space and also in particular instances of talk and writing about the subjects of our imagination. The salience of even the most seemingly private acts of imagination, such as dreams, is created through the articulation and social sharing of discourse (cf. Graham 1995; Urban 1996; Wirtz 2007). Therefore the discursive analysis of imaginaries mandates attention. I respond to this mandate by combining two approaches to the study of discourse—one drawn from the work of Michel Foucault, the other from contemporary sociocultural studies of language in linguistic anthropology and sociolinguistics. This combined approach enables me to theorize and empirically ground the ways imaginaries are produced and when, how, and to whom they become consequential.

The Foucauldian approach, often described as "genealogical," tracks the emergence of politically interested regimes of warrants and expertise that allow some, and not others, to make assertions about the social world (cf. Asad 2003; Dick 2011b; Hill 2008; Winegar 2006; Wirtz 2013, 2014). Chapter 1 highlights this approach, as it follows the cycles of re-incarnation experienced by particular visions of Mexicanidad from the late nineteenth century to the present—visions that directly contribute to who can and cannot lay claim to being "properly Mexican." Every chapter combines a sensitivity to such genealogies with the analysis of discourse as it is conceptualized in sociocultural studies of language. Work informed by this approach examines the "actual material presence . . . of language-in-use" (Hill 2008:32) and the interaction between actors involved in such use, linking them to broader historical, political economic, and cultural processes (e.g., Carr 2011; Carr and Lempert 2016; Eisenlohr 2006; Irvine and Gal 2000; Lempert 2012a; Shankar 2015; Silverstein and Urban 1996; Urban 2001; Wirtz 2014; Wortham and Reyes 2015).

Careful attention to actual language use is evinced in chapters 4 and 5, in which I explore how conversations about migration comment on and contribute to major demographic shifts in migration and the processes of religious nationalism in Mexico. The sociocultural approach to language, then, shines a light on how the subjectivities of actual people are forged in exchanges that entail multiple domains, from the intimacy of family life to transnational political economies (cf. Chávez 2017a, 2017b; Dick and Arnold 2017a), an intricate process too easily glossed over by scholarship that does not analyze actual language use. As this suggests, Foucauldian and linguistic-anthropological discourse does not describe absolute differences in kind. They are an analytical distinction used to understand how, on the one hand, moments of interaction draw on broader processes; it is difficult to ascertain the relevance of any particular interaction without situating it inside of such processes. On the other hand, this distinction illuminates that widely circulating processes depend on discrete moments of interaction for their (re)creation (Dick 2011b; Lempert 2013; Wirtz 2014; Wortham and Reyes 2015).

In taking this integrative approach to the study of discourse, this book makes several contributions to the study of imaginaries. It moves beyond the description of extant imaginaries to help illuminate how they are produced and re-created across time and space. This aspect of my analysis shows that in Mexico the imagination of lives in migration is part of an enduring practice of imagining beyond here that has long helped order people's interpellation into Mexicanidad. Since at least the late nineteenth century Mexican state institutions have forwarded imaginaries of national belonging mandating that Mexicans progress economically in a moral way signaled by the preservation of "traditional Mexican practices," especially those associated with Catholicism. I call these imaginaries of _moral mobility._ The central conceit of such _state-endorsed_ imaginaries (where "state-endorsed" refers to practices, policies, events, and so on produced or authorized by state actors) is that Mexico needs to "progress" to be socioeconomically mobile but do so in a religiously grounded, communally oriented way coded as "moral." So being properly Mexican is about integrating morality and mobility, treating them as checks for each other. In such imaginaries, the United States is Mexico's foil: the immoral dark to Mexico's Catholic light. Therefore, in this vision of Mexicanidad, being Mexican is rendered in explicit contrast to life in the "beyond here" of the United States through allegiance to a vision of nation rooted in links to Catholicism and its heavenly beyond.

This imaginary is used not only to distinguish between Mexican and US people but also between "good" and "bad" Mexicans, generating a hierarchy of belonging in which some people are citizens but not full members of the polity. State-endorsed visions have long fashioned certain groups—including working-class people—as representing both the authentic essence of "true Mexico," with the responsibility to maintain its traditional morality, and the country's greatest impediments to progress, as their "backward" ways constrain Mexico's mobility. State actors have repeatedly used such imaginaries to justify the variegation of belonging and resource access by positing people's inability to progress socioeconomically as a moral failure that indicates they are not yet ready for full inclusion in the polity (see chapter 1). State-endorsed imaginaries of moral mobility circulate into Uriangato via multiple channels—the media, policy implementation—through which they hail working-class people to be Mexican in ways that perpetually reproduce their exclusion from belonging and the rights of citizenship (see chapter 3).

Therefore, while elite imaginaries are of relevance to Uriangatenses, *Words of Passage* moves beyond an exclusive focus on them. This is the second contribution to the study of imaginaries: examining the interaction between elite and nonelite imaginaries. As discussed above, most of the work on migrant imaginaries documents elite visions of social life. It does not consider carefully enough how they work their way into or refract the perspectives of migrants and their nonmigrant relations, who—after all—produce their own visions of national belonging. Uriangatenses respond to state-endorsed calls to Mexicanidad in their migration discourse, their homebuilding practices, and their participation in the Catholic cult of the saints. Analysis of these activities shows that most of the Uriangatenses accept the idea that to be Mexican is to progress in a way that is more moral than US-style progress. Yet they also critique the terms of state-endorsed imaginaries, as they produce their own visions of belonging that serve as a critical commentary on the barriers to mobility that constrain working-class lives in Mexico. This interpellative response not only allows working-class Uriangatenses to endeavor to achieve belonging and resource access in Mexico writ large; it also shapes how they engage their immediate world. For example, it is especially difficult for working-class women to be properly Mexican because both state-endorsed and Uriangatense imaginaries of moral mobility figure female respectability as rooted in practices of enclosure and cloistering. This makes women's mobility always potentially immoral—a framing used to constrain women's access to family resources as much as nation-state ones (cf. Hondagneu-Sotelo 1994; Molyneux 2006; Wright 2006).

Another signal contribution that this book makes to the study of imaginaries is to draw on the analytical tools developed in sociocultural

studies of language to examine how language and related semiotic practices create forms of inequality (e.g., Agha 2007a; Bucholtz and Hall
2004; Gal and Woolard 2001; Hastings and Manning 2004; Kroskrity
2000). Such scholarship includes concern with the relationship between
language and nation building (e.g., Bauman and Briggs 2003, Eisenlohr
2006; Irvine and Gal 2000; Paz 2016; Woolard 1990, 2016; Woolard and
Schieffelin 1994; Yeh 2012, 2017) and between language and processes of
globalization, including migration (e.g., Arnold 2016; Blommaert 2010,
2013; Chávez 2015; 2017b; Coupland 2010; Das 2016; Dick 2011a; Farr
2006; García-Sánchez 2014; Heller 2007; Jacquemet 2005; Koven 2004,
2007, 2013a, 2013b, 2016; Koven and Simões Marques 2015; Mendoza-
Denton 2008; Reyes and Lo 2009; Paz 2009, 2015; Perrino 2015). Although this work is primarily focused on detailing how language beliefs and practices produce forms of hierarchical social difference, it also
helps illuminate the mechanisms through which imaginaries take form
and are (re)created across sociohistorical and interactional contexts.

One such mechanism pertains to the language practices that allow actors to conjure possible worlds beyond here, enabling a "virtual
space time travel" (Lempert and Perrino 2007: 208) that draws the beyond into the present in ways that are consequential to the immediate
interaction and the formation of collectivities (e.g., Blommaert 2015;
Das 2016; Dick 2010a; Eisenlohr 2006; Urban 1996; Wirtz 2014, 2016;
Woolard 2016). This consequentiality is generated through the historical production and interactional accomplishment of social indexicality:
how language and other semiotic practices create, point to, and enact
cultural images of personhood (Agha 2007b; Dick 2010a, 2011b; Koven
2013a, 2013b; Irvine and Gal 2000; Silverstein 1976, 1979; Wirtz 2014;
Woolard 2016). As this suggests, images of personhood and their associated semiotic forms are often not treated as value neutral. Rather,
they are situated inside of indexical orders (Silverstein 2003), which render some images more valuable, more "correct" than others (see also
Agha 2007a; Blommaert 2010; Irvine and Gal 2000).

Finally, *Words of Passage* builds a theory of social imaginaries that situates their production in actual moments of interaction. Beyond establishing the recurring features of state-endorsed and Uriangatenses'
imaginaries of moral mobility, this book examines the discursive practices (most particularly the production of images of personhood in migration discourse) that allow Uriangatenses to (re)create imaginaries.
Through such practices, actors create points of interconnection between the present and worlds beyond here, making them available for

contemplation and taking stances on which imagined lives are desirable (Dick 2010a). For example, in the second opening vignette, Sara evaluates DIF's failure to recognize her economic need against the backdrop of the life she imagines living in the United States, where she believes the government distributes resources fairly—a common proposition of Uriangatense migration discourse, especially among women (see chapters 4 and 5).

When people engage in migration discourse, they not only address their present interlocutors to particular ends—for example, to display need and express a desire to migrate, as did Sara in talking to me. They also critically reflect on the processes that shape inclusion and access in Mexico and in the transnational political economy that connects Mexico to the United States. Sara's story is as much a political commentary on the failures of institutional care and inclusivity in Mexico as it is a way to display her need and desire. Through such activities people construe themselves and others as recognizable social types (as deserving, properly Mexican, and so forth)—processes fundamental to understanding how people come to recognize, take up, and/or transform state-endorsed interpellation. Thus, the discursive analysis of imaginaries not only reveals how imaginaries are generated and maintained. It also helps illuminate how imaginaries enter into people's lives and how, in turn, people critique and revise them in ways that potentially alter the social boundaries that state-endorsed imaginaries generate and legitimate.

In developing this theory of social imaginaries, this book also contributes to the study of social indexicality a sensitivity to circulation, revision, and contestation. I show that the boundaries of national belonging are rendered through the discursive production of what does and does not count as being properly Mexican across and between multiple interactional arenas—from the historical production of state-endorsed visions of Mexicanidad to the parsing of people's evolving allegiances to Mexico in discussions of migration in the homes of Uriangato. I track how the indexical orders that undergird social imaginaries move across contexts, producing similarities and resonances over time and space but also points of contention and friction—a process relatively underconsidered in sociocultural studies of language (Blommaert 2013; Carr and Lempert 2016; Wirtz 2014; Wortham and Reyes 2015).

A hallmark of Mexican nationalism is its simultaneous vibrancy—people actively contemplate and work on being Mexican—and contestation. There are profound fissures in what being Mexican means, evinced in state-endorsed variegation of belonging and also in differences in how people take up their interpellation. These fissures point to unresolved tensions in Mexican nation building, which I explore in chapters 1, 3, and 5 (cf. Gálvez 2009; Lomnitz 2001a, 2001b, 2008, 2009; Napolitano 2016: 127, 136; Yeh 2017). As recent work on migrants and imaginative labor in language has shown (e.g., Chávez 2015; Eisenlohr 2006; Mendoza-Denton 2008; Paz 2009; Yeh 2012), we must track exactly such processes of resonance and friction in order to understand how imaginaries shape actors' responses to state-endorsed interpellation. But, unlike these works, *Words of Passage* offers a full theory of "imaginative work" that considers these processes from the important perspectives of the migrant-sending county and the nonmigrants who are connected to the practice of migration, though they remain "at home."

In so doing, I offer a multimodal analysis that coordinates the consideration of migration discourse with other social semiotic practices important to processes of interpellation into moral mobility. In particular, I consider the symbolic loading of homebuilding and the spatial layout of La Libertad (chapter 3) and examine working-class people's participation in the Catholic cult of the saints (chapter 5). As I show, these practices work in concert with migration discourse to imbricate the presuppositions and perspectives of imaginaries of moral mobility into the built environment of Uriangato and the hearts of its people. But they also reveal cracks and imperfections in these imaginaries: it is harder for some to be properly Mexican than for others; people disagree on what Mexicanidad means and why it matters to enact and reproduce it; and so forth. Therefore *Words of Passage* not only illuminates why imaginaries produced by state institutions in Mexico have emerged at key moments in history. I also consider how working-class Uriangatenses revise these imaginaries in dialogue with other homegrown imaginaries that potentially move beyond Mexico, interweaving life in the here-and-now with life in the United States and also in heaven.

As I show throughout, these processes have long been imbricated with migration discourse. Moreover, in connecting interpellation into Mexicanidad with processes of resource distribution and access in Uriangato and Mexico more widely, I show that language practices do more than create social indexicality. They also serve as forms of appeal, persuasion, and protest (cf. Duchêne and Heller 2011; Hastings and Manning 2004), through which actors seek to reimagine the nation. In examining the dynamics of belonging and resource distribution in Uriangato it becomes evident that the interpellative calls of imaginaries of moral mobility matter, in part, because they not only reveal the terms of who can lay claim to national belonging but also construe what it means to live right, period. That is, imaginaries are integral to the creation of ethico-moral life. What does it mean to be a good person or a bad one? Through what practices do we create such ethico-moral personhood and signal it to others? Imaginaries of national belonging matter to the creation of ethico-moral life in Uriangato, as is evident in the construal of authentic Mexicanidad as a state of being "more moral" than people from the United States. It is also apparent in the ways that the boundaries of inclusion and exclusion in Mexico (who can readily lay claim to being properly Mexican and who cannot) are rendered through depictions of ethico-moral personhood.

Moral Mobility and the Politics of Ethico-moral Life

Words of Passage makes two main interventions into the anthropology of morality and ethics, both of which are supported by its discourse-analytic approach to imaginaries. First, it maintains a sense of fluidity and complexity in conceptualization of these terms. There is a long-standing tendency in anthropology to posit morality as the normative (existing and familiar) ideas about what constitutes right and wrong in particular contexts and ethics as the practices through which people construct themselves as right with respect to those norms (Daswani 2010, 2013b; Fassin 2012a, 2012b; Good 2012; Lambek 2010; Mahmood 2005; Robbins 2007). Indeed, some argue that that these terms need to be treated as referring to distinct processes, so that "morals" are associated with the habitual and unreflexive enactment of norms and "ethics" with conscious moments of choice and creativity (e.g., Dave 2012; Zigon 2007, 2008, 2011). Such arguments build on an enduring intellectual tradition that associates morality with the reproduction of tradition—with uncritical normativity—and ethics with freedom and the possibility of change (Robbins 2007). The study of ethics has emerged in recent years as the preferred analytical focus in anthropology because it turns attention to the ways people can resist normativity. But this viewpoint is too absolute in its distinctions, too hermetically sealed.

The beliefs and practices to which the terms "morality" and "ethics" refer are often so thoroughly overlapping that absolute distinctions between them do not hold up in practice (Fassin 2012a, 2012b; Keane 2010, 2014). For this reason I favor the term "ethico-moral." Morality and ethics mutually depend on the simultaneous interaction of normativity and open-ended interaction, both of which are processual. The establishment of moral norms requires interaction to be produced, and ethical practice has its own norms of interaction. Furthermore, we rarely orient ourselves to a single set of ethico-moral norms when evaluating right and wrong. People usually reckon with and combine multiple ethico-moral frameworks (Blommaert 2013; Collier and Ong 2005; Dick 2017; Zigon 2011). Attention to such complexity reveals that tradition and freedom are not opposites. As Saba Mahmood (2005) has persuasively argued, the tendency to treat these as dichotomous is a product of Western concepts of personhood and collectivity, which envision political transformation as a process of resisting—becoming "free from"—norms (see also Keane 2007).

Certainly resisting norms can constitute a form of political transformation (e.g., Dave 2012). But enactment of norms can also be part of transformational creativity (Abu-Lughod 1986; Agha 2007a; Dick 2010b; Lester 2005; Mahmood 2005). As I show in chapter 5, for example, women often use normative traditions of pious suffering as a modality of critique. Throughout this book, I attend to the ongoing dynamism between extant norms and creative process in the production of the imaginaries that undergird right and wrong in Uriangato. This means paying attention to reflexivity: the ability to step outside of and critically evaluate unfolding events and our place(s) inside them (Keane 2010, 2014).

Existing scholarship on ethico-moral life spotlights the importance of conscious moments of reflection (Collier and Ong 2005; Zigon 2011). Such moments—whether they involve intimate flashes of self-awareness or the public proclamations of experts—are important to understanding the assembly of right and wrong. However, a discourse analytic approach opens up an equally important source of reflexivity, which is underconsidered in the cultural anthropology of morality and ethics: the implicit forms of positioning and critique entailed in language practices. Such *semiotic reflexivity* refers broadly to the ways people use language and other signs to typify and appraise the social world and encompasses conscious and also less overt forms of evaluation (Dick 2017; Hill 1995; Keane 2010, 2014; Lazar 2015; Lempert 2013: 376; Shankar 2015). Thus, semiotic reflexivity is not encompassed by explicitness; it is also evinced in more implicit forms of "standing apart" (Keane 2010: 69). For example, patterns of pronoun use play a role in the enactment of gendered forms of respectable personhood in Uriangato. These patterns exist largely below the conscious awareness of speakers but nevertheless help position some as ethico-morally right and others as wrong, in ways that directly contribute to processes of national belonging and resource access (see chapters 4 and 5).

Both the conceptualization of ethico-moral character and the practices through which people can successfully enact themselves as possessing such a character are not uniform across members of the polity but are distinct for people in different groups. As intimated above, state-endorsed imaginaries of moral mobility in Mexico have consistently figured working-class people and migrants as having questionable ethico-moral character and thus as needing to engage in moral improvements before they can fully access the rights and privileges of national-belonging (see chapter 1). This is a familiar strategy of nation-building, which collectively blames poverty on the poor and then uses that poverty to justify the delay of the rewards of full belonging—a strategy of citizenship variegation that has taken on particularly acute force during the neoliberal era (Fennel 2015; Muehlebach 2012; Paley 2001; Wacquant 2009). Such figuration constrains not only who can and cannot readily realize proper Mexicanidad but also who can and cannot make authoritative claims about what constitutes right and wrong in particular contexts. This process is deeply bound up with discursive practices, including the cultivation of expertise about nation and migration, which influences what can and cannot be constituted an "authoritative account" and whose migration discourse is and is not heard (cf. Carr 2011; Hill and Irvine 1993; Paz 2009), a highly gendered process explored in chapters 2, 4, and 5.

As this suggests, *Words of Passage* moves beyond an exclusive focus on self-discipline, which characterizes much recent anthropological work on ethico-moral life. Scholarship in this vein draws on Aristotelian "virtue ethics," which considers how an individual cultivates a personal character that is most appropriately suited to a situation (Robbins 2007). It takes inspiration from Foucault's adaptation of virtue ethics in his analysis of the "techniques of the self" that allow an individual to embody moral norms (Dave 2012; Foucault 1990, 1997; Hirschkind 2006; Lester 2005; Mahmood 2005: 30; Zigon 2008: 42). This scholarship tends to examine the microrituals in which people engage as they place themselves in compliance with or push against the virtues that represent "living a good life" in a given context (Fassin 2012a, 2012b; Zigon 2008: 23–24), such as Saba Mahmood's (2005) work on the cultivation of piety in Egypt or Jarrett Zigon's (2011) analysis of the production of morality in Russian drug rehabilitation programs.

Such work offers insight into how individuals use competing norms of ethico-moral life to make themselves right in the face of moral conflict. This work has a certain political perspective, as it considers how individuals critique their positioning within broader political economic regimes, but it falls short of showing how ethico-moral work makes possible those very social formations (cf. Anderson 2011). Yet notions of right and wrong are used not only to govern the self but to interpellate whole groups of people into formations that move well beyond the individual (cf. Anderson 2011; Carr 2011; Fassin 2012a, 2012b; Garcia 2014; Mittermaier 2011), like the nation-state or the universal Catholic communion.[6]

Therefore the second main intervention I make into the broader literature on morality and ethics is to hold the political dimensions and consequences of ethico-moral life at the center of analysis. In keeping with both Foucauldian and sociocultural studies of discourse in anthropology, I conceive of "the political" holistically, as pertaining not only to the formal workings of governance but to the wider processes that produce social differentiation and its associated relations of power, which make governance legitimate and legible in the first place. One way I hold the political at the center of analysis is by examining the historical emergence of notions of right and wrong in state-endorsed imaginaries of moral mobility. Through this, I show how the ethico-moral loading of social imaginaries plays a central role in the variegation of national belonging and resource access in Mexico. Responses to the interpellative calls of imaginaries are a form of ethico-moral work through which people enact themselves as right kinds of Mexicans, so how individuals "make themselves right" is salient in this context as well. But this is also part of a political process regarding who can demand full inclusion in the nation-state and access to its resources (cf. Dave 2012).

For instance, by using migration discourse to highlight that their inability to achieve moral mobility is the product of a lack of opportunity in Mexico (see chapter 3), working-class Uriangatenses are effectively saying: our poverty is a result not of our moral failings but of the failures of Mexico's political economy. Because state-endorsed imaginaries of moral mobility are also about relationships with the United States, working-class Uriangatenses signal their critical awareness of the history of entanglements between Mexico and the United States when they take up the terms of those imaginaries. These entanglements have bound these countries into a single framework of relations—forged by international development projects, by the (mis)management of the common border, and by countless reams and reels of migration discourse, produced by policy makers and nation builders, scholars and pundits, journalists and media producers. Such imbrications give ethico-moral life its shape and significance (cf. Lempert 2013). Therefore ethico-moral life is part of not only the everyday politics of social boundary-making but also the geopolitics of nation-states. Hence this book is not only a story of the ways discursively rendered acts of imagining inform national belonging in Mexico. It also reveals how such acts help people construe, navigate, and re-imagine this framework of relations—one that has marginalized not only working-class Mexicans and migrants but Mexico itself.

As this suggests, *Words of Passage* focuses both on the creation of boundaries and on acts of crossing them, considering the possibility of change engendered by such crossing (cf. Dave 2012; Mittermaier 2011). The discursive analysis of imaginaries illuminates the potential that beyond-here offers, with "the licit and illicit desires it triggers, the plays of power it suggests, the dread it can cause . . . [as well as] the exaltation, the thrill of the unknown, it can provoke" (Crapanzano 2004: 14). Throughout the book I highlight that the production of imaginaries generates both restriction and exclusion and also transformation toward a tomorrow when those who are now positioned as outside can one day belong. While enactments of Mexicanidad have long been imbricated with imagining a life beyond here, the salience and palpability of such lives were amplified by political economic changes of the late twentieth century—in particular the onset of large-scale migration out of urban Uriangato and the industrialization of the municipality. These changes have made the realities and possibilities of life elsewhere more available and consequential to Uriangatenses, especially those involved in migration. They also set the stage for how working-class Uriangatenses take up and transform the interpellative call of state-endorsed imaginaries of moral mobility.

Migration Comes to Uriangato:
Industrialization and Newly Imagined Lives

Uriangato is a municipality in the central Mexican state of Guanajuato. As there are no counties in Mexico, municipalities are the next level of government after state governments. States vary widely in how many municipalities they have: from as few as 5 (Baja California) to as many as

570 (Oaxaca). Guanajuato has 46. Each municipality is administratively autonomous. Citizens elect a *presidente municipal* (mayor) who heads a municipal council, which is responsible for public services and the supervision of local industry (Boehm de Lameiras 1987). The influence of municipal governments in state and federal politics is roughly equivalent to that of US cities of comparable size. Uriangato and its neighboring municipalities Moroleón and Yuriria are among the wealthiest and most influential municipalities in the state because of the textile industry that spans these three cities (see also Lattanzi Shutika 2011).[7] Like other municipalities of its size, Uriangato has an urban center, known as the *cabecera municipal* (county seat), which houses the municipal government and oversees the urban center as well as the municipality's rural communities, known as *localidades* (localities) or more commonly as ranchos. Uriangato has jurisdiction over twenty-three ranchos. During the early 2000s, municipal Uriangato had a population of roughly 53,000, the majority of whom lived in the urban center, with 46,000 in its *cabecera municipal* and 7,000 in its ranchos (Aranda Ríos 2000: 25). According to the 2010 Mexican Census, Uriangato's total population reached nearly 60,000, and the proportions of urban to rural population were the same.

Although Guanajuato has been a migrant-sending state since the late nineteenth century, large-scale migration out of urban Uriangato did not begin until the 1970s. The initiation of this migration was closely intertwined with another major change that also began in the 1970s: the transformation of Uriangato from a rural outpost to a thriving manufacturing center. These changes echoed political economic shifts occurring across Mexico and between Mexico and the United States during the late twentieth century, which helped spark a dramatic uptick in Mexican migration overall (Hondagneu-Sotelo 1994; Massey et al. 1987). Indeed the industrialization of Uriangato was spurred by national development efforts. In the 1960s and 1970s the Mexican government invested heavily in the industrialization of agricultural production and the creation of manufacturing centers (Fernández-Kelly 1983; Hewitt de Alcántara 1976; Hondagneu-Sotelo 1994; Iglesias Prieto 1999; Messing 2007). The industrialization effort reduced the number of small-scale farms and displaced many people from traditional forms of labor by decreasing both the economic feasibility of small-scale farming and the amount of labor needed for farming enterprises (Hondagneu-Sotelo 1994; Massey et al. 1987).

The shift toward industrial agricultural had a profound effect on

Uriangato's economy, which before the establishment of the textile industry relied on agriculture and its associated industries, such as the trade in farm supplies (seeds, fertilizer, etc.). As a result, many former agricultural workers began to migrate to Mexico's major textile production centers, especially Mexico City. The ties established by this internal migration are observable among my research participants, friends, and neighbors in Uriangato: my social network in Uriangato reached about 150 people at its height. Roughly a quarter of these people were born in Mexico City, were related to people from Mexico City, and/or had spent time working there.

Uriangato's textile industry was begun in the mid-1970s by internal migrants who had worked in textile factories in Mexico City (cf. Lattanzi Shutika 2011).[8] Early textile entrepreneurs drew on a tradition of weaving in the area, first manufacturing bedspreads and sweaters. When these endeavors proved fruitful, some factory owners bought cloth manufactured by their former employers in Mexico City to produce a wider range of products, including clothing, which now makes up the majority of output. This expansion was successful: people from all over Guanajuato and the neighboring state of Michoacán began to buy clothing in Uriangato, and clothing stores in other cities placed orders for Uriangato's products. Industrialists in Mexico City, not only from Mexican companies but from companies based in the United States, Japan, and Italy, began providing loans for factories to expand production. By the late twentieth century Uriangato had hundreds of factories of various sizes with an array of aims, from producing yarn and cloth to designing and sewing clothing to packaging and shipping goods. Today the city's downtown streets are draped with rows of clothing and animated by the constant rhythm of sewing machines. And work in the textile industry—as a sewer, weaver, or salesperson—is the principal employment option for Uriangatenses. A robust consumer culture has also emerged, generating additional economic opportunities, as shoppers create incentives for the expansion of the service industry (hotels, restaurants, etc.).

Overall, the textile industry grants Uriangato a degree of prosperity relative to other Mexican cities of its size. At the beginning of this century the national average salary in Mexico was 80 pesos per day (about 8 US dollars). In Uriangato it was more than double that amount at 200 pesos (20 US dollars) per day. According to the United Nations Human Development Index, in 2010 Uriangato had the sixth highest quality of life of municipalities in the state of Guanajuato, surpassed only by Celaya, León, Moroleón, Irapuato, and Guanajuato City (all major manufacturing centers), and it was eighth highest in terms of the index of human development. Uriangato is widely known as a place with an abundance of work, which draws workers not only from the immediate ranchos, municipalities, and states but from places as far away as Oaxaca. This history of movement is particularly evident in La Libertad. Until the 1970s this neighborhood was not a residential area but an *ejido* (communally owned farmland). As small-scale farming became untenable, many *ejidatarios* (people who have plots of land in an *ejido*) sold their land to migrants from other parts of Mexico who could not afford houses in already established parts of town. Instead they purchased plots in La Libertad and similar areas on the city's outskirts and built houses piece by piece, as I discuss in chapter 3 (cf. Lopez 2015). Therefore many of the families in the neighborhood, including the family with whom I lived, have their roots elsewhere, either in the immediate ranchos or in other states (cf. Castellanos 2010; Napolitano 2002).

Migration into the city from the rural surroundings helped spark migration out of urban Uriangato to the United States. Many of the rural families who moved into urban Uriangato in the 1970s already had experience with US migration. Throughout Mexico in the mid to late twentieth century both US-bound and internal migration in Mexico was typically initiated in rural communities, which are the first to feel the impact of the labor displacements caused by industrialization. Indeed it was extremely rare for someone to migrate to the United States from urban Uriangato before the influx of migrants from the rural communities in the 1970s. In contrast, according to data published by Consejo Nacional de Población (CONAPO: Mexico's census bureau) in 2005, an average of 52 percent of households in urban Uriangato have migration experience—a figure that reaches 85 percent in La Libertad (Dick 2006b). When urban families in La Libertad built connections with rural families, they began to have access to migrant networks, which helped make US migration plausible. Migrant networks encourage and facilitate future migration (Hondagneu-Sotelo 1994; Massey et al. 1987; Smith 2006). Having a father-in-law who lives in the United States makes migration a less daunting prospect, because this relationship brings with it obligations (e.g., a migrant's father-in-law is obliged to provide a place to stay and help in looking for work) [Massey et al. 1987; Hirsch 2003; Hondagneu-Sotelo 1994; Smith 2006].

The presence of families with loved ones in the United States also changed standards of living in poorer parts of urban Uriangato. Uriangatense families with migrant members generally have larger, more finely appointed homes and greater disposable income (cf. Hirsch 2003; Lattanzi Shutika 2011; Lopez 2015). The desire for the goods available to families with migrant members encourages desires for socioeconomic mobility through a process economists call "relative deprivation": the idea that people do not experience poverty on an absolute scale but in comparison to their immediate relations (Reichert 1982; Stark and Taylor 1991). When the standard of living increases for some, the previous standard of living becomes unacceptable, motivating others within the same community to aspire to the new standard. The internal migration of rural people with decades-long practices of US migration showed that migration could speed up access to economic resources. US-bound migration out of urban Uriangato therefore became part of the effort to accelerate the processes of mobility that were encouraged but also thwarted by the industrialization of the town. Work in the textile industry for all but a few managers and owners is typically "under the table" and inconsistent, so that at some times of the year people work overtime and at others they have no work at all. Working-class people have gotten a taste of the increased standards of living afforded by the industry, but their desires to improve their socioeconomic position have quickly outpaced the opportunities available to them locally (see chapter 3).

While these transformations were happening in Uriangato, the US and Mexican national economies were becoming more mutually dependent than ever, which increased migration from Mexico (Durand and Massey 2003; Hondagneu-Sotelo 1994; Lopez 2015; Massey et al. 1987; Wortham et al. 2002). Take the case of the mushroom industry in southern Chester County, Pennsylvania, where many Uriangatenses work.[9] In the late 1970s canned mushrooms produced by multinational companies with plants in Taiwan and Mexico began to threaten the competitiveness of farms in Chester County, forcing small-scale farms to consolidate. Between 1979 and 1987 the number of farms shrank from 387 to 137: a loss of 250 farms in less than ten years (Baurers 1993). By the mid-1990s there were only 80 mushroom farms in the region, all of which were industrial-sized (Anders 1993). In the 1990s, as US farmers began to compete with multinational companies with plants in Mexican states (including a Green Giant plant in Guanajuato), they had increasing incentives to hire laborers from Mexico.

This late twentieth century labor recruitment built on a history of Mexican migration into Chester County, which began in the 1970s (see also Garcia 2005; Lattanzi Shutika 2011). The first influx of Mexican migrants to Chester County consisted of men from Uriangato, Moroleón, and Yuriria who were already working in Chicago. I interviewed a few of them, who told me they learned of the mushroom industry through Puerto Ricans, who at the time were the majority of mushroom workers. These workers were engaged in a dispute with farm owners over pay and working conditions. Puerto Ricans, being US citizens, were empowered to unionize—in stark contrast to the Mexican migrants, many of whom were in the United States without authorization. When farm owners realized that Mexican laborers were willing to work longer hours for less pay and were unable to organize because of their lack of legal status, they began to recruit them.[10] Migrants told me growers would ask if they could invite relatives to work on the farms and would advertise work openings on radio stations in Uriangato. Before the decade was out, people were migrating directly to Chester County from Uriangato—and Puerto Rican mushroom workers had been replaced by Mexican workers.

The processes of industrialization and migration that took hold of Uriangato at the end of the twentieth century created active links between the urban center and multiple beyond-heres, from rural communities to Mexico City to the United States. These links are fostered by (and inspire) the imagination of life beyond here, as migration out of the urban center was sparked by ideas about the social trajectories that could be realized through movements away from here, modeled by the homes, lifestyles, and migration discourse of people with preexisting migration experience. Thus, the imagination of lives in migration took on new importance in the late twentieth century. Uriangatenses became increasingly linked to possible lives in other parts of Mexico as they or their relations moved to Mexico City and returned, participating in a textile industry with connections to places as far away as Japan. Moreover, people in the city began to be inspired to migrate north by seeing their own lives in contrast both to those of rural people who migrated and to the new lifestyles they envisioned might come along with such migration.

At the same time, changing standards of living altered the kinds of lives people felt they could—and should—realize, a process bound up with the evaluation and enactment of the imaginaries of moral mobility. Building a bigger house, for instance, is not just about wanting to live in more comfortable surroundings. It is also a way people signal they are trying to improve themselves both economically and morally—that they are becoming better Mexicans by living in finer circumstances. Although these changes were happening for everyone in Uriangato, they were experienced especially by the working-class people who formed the majority of textile workers and new migrants, for whom their positioning within imaginaries of moral mobility has always been fraught.

Being Working-Class in Mexico: Ethnographic Parameters and Protagonists

As intimated above, *Words of Passage* focuses on the variegation of national belonging for working-class people connected to the practice of migration. The overwhelming majority of people in Uriangato are part of the relatively unmarked racial category of mestizo (see chapter 1). Therefore, while racial difference always undergirds the construction of social differentiation, the central and most overt axis of such differentiation in Uriangato is socioeconomic class—and gender (see chapter 2). Designating people as "working-class" involves placing them within a socioeconomic status demarcated by certain economic indicators. But it is also a political process that produces social boundaries (Mendoza-Denton 2008; Urciuoli 1993, 1996). In many ways, I explore the politics of being working-class throughout this book—both the processes that constrain people's socioeconomic prospects and the forms of representation that work to define "working-class" in Mexico. In this section I outline the practical and ideological features of this sociopolitical status.

Mexico, like many other Latin American countries, has a high degree of income inequality (Ffrench-Davis 2005). Indeed the top 1 percent of earners in Mexico own 43 percent of the country's wealth (OXFAM 2016). Mexico is the fourth wealthiest country in the world by Gross Domestic Product (GDP), but over 50 percent of its population lives in poverty, defined as not being able to meet basic needs (OXFAM 2016). As a result, the majority of its population is either poor or working-class; the middle class is very small. These patterns have endured throughout Mexico's history and are reflected in the state of Guanajuato. Although the state is home to several thriving industries, the average daily income across the state is among the lowest in the country, according to Mexico's National Commission on the Minimum Wage. Though Uriangato enjoys a greater level of prosperity relative to other Mexican cities of its size, work for most people is unstable and unauthorized, "off the books," which places laborers in precarious economic and legal circumstances (see chapter 3).

In terms of economic indicators, being working-class means earning enough income to live above—though often just barely above—the poverty line. Mexico's Office of Social and Human Development defines poverty as living at or below the *línea de bienestar* (wellness line): people in this category are sometimes (though not always) able to meet basic nutritional, health care, and shelter needs but do not have additional income for schooling, transportation, or other resources that would facilitate mobility. Working-class people can meet basic needs and engage in a moderate level of mobility: building comfortable housing, sending children to secondary school, and starting businesses of their own, though usually only when they have access to US-bound migration—a point to which I return below.

In Uriangato people's self-designations mirror state-endorsed definitions as well as the political economy of class mobility in Mexico. Reflecting the reality of income inequality, people rarely refer to a "middle class" but talk in terms of a dichotomous contrast between "rich" and "poor." Working-class Uriangatenses describe themselves as occupying an interstitial status between these opposites, often saying they are *los que están más o menos bien* (people who are doing more or less well). They are not poor—they generally do not worry about meeting their basic needs—but they are also not rich. Unlike the rich, they have to fight hard for every scrap of mobility they get. In neighborhoods like La Libertad with high rates of US-bound migration, class designations are closely imbricated with migration. Being "working-class" in Uriangato is as much about relationships and experience with transnational migration as it is about someone's position within the political economy of the municipality or Mexico more broadly.

In Uriangato and Pennsylvania—as in other migrant-sending and receiving areas—people involved in migration form a subgroup who tend to live in particular neighborhoods and work in specific sectors of the economy. Most middle- and upper-class people in Uriangato either have never been to the United States or have only gone as tourists, and they generally do not have close relationships with anyone who has migrated. Consequently, even though Uriangato is a small city where people live in physical proximity, those in migrant-sending neighborhoods imaginatively and sociopolitically occupy a world apart, where migration experience shapes everything from family dynamics to the ways people respond to state-endorsed interpellation into Mexicanidad. Therefore I refer to the communities where migrants and their relations live as "migrant enclaves" (cf. Portes and Wilson 1980).[11]

Migrant enclaving in the United States creates evident social boundaries marked by language and demographics. In urban Uriangato, however, enclaving is subtly rendered, largely demarcated by how people talk about migration—that is, by their migration discourse, an activity that is also part of how class in Uriangato is signaled. For instance, working-class Uriangatenses frequently and readily assert that "those who are more or less doing well" are the people who must migrate to the United States to be socioeconomically mobile in Mexico (cf. Dick 2010a, 2013). By contrast, the "rich" are those who achieve mobility in Mexico and therefore do not need migration, while the "poor" are those who do not have access to the resources that would make migration possible. In other words, working-class migration discourse construes movements to the United States as part and parcel of life as working-class people, a sign of their relative mobility vis-à-vis the poor and also of the barriers to class mobility and of divisions marked by access to resources in Mexico. Thus, a critical class awareness is expressed through migration discourse (cf. Chávez 2015, 2017a, 2017b; Mendoza-Denton 2008).

As this suggests, being working-class is also part of the visions of Mexicanidad that have been produced since the late nineteenth century. As I discuss in chapter 1, state discourses of "progress" evinced in economic development policy create, legitimate, and rely on cultural images of the Mexican working-class (variously referred to as *la clase popular, el pueblo, el pelado*): a group posited as emblematic both of Mexico's potential for political economic "advancement" and of its failure to advance (see also Lomnitz 2009; Schmidt Camacho 2008). The Uriangatenses I know sometimes take up these images and their associated descriptors to assert their class identity and/or to critique their positioning in state-endorsed imaginaries. But more often than not, they describe themselves as *más o menos bien*. This descriptor is part of the social imaginary of Uriangatense society (discussed in chapter 3), which is written into the built environment of the municipality. Within this imaginary, working-class people see themselves in contrast not only to the urban rich and poor but also to people from the ranchos—the country people, who are both poor and backward, not urbane. As such, their lives represent a particular positioning within an expressly urban landscape, often posited as a form of "awakening" from the forms of naiveté and ignorance that they associate with the countryside (cf. Mendoza-Denton 2008; Napolitano 2002; Rouse 1992). But their positioning is, at the same time, a form of marginalization in which they are integral to the industrial economy but not fully integrated into it, as they are denied full access to its benefits and resources.

Migration discourse helps create and enact class status, as evidenced by the fact that middle- and upper-class people engage this subject in different ways than do working-class people. When I talked to middle-class and upper-class people, they often would blithely accuse migrants of being too lazy to work harder in Mexico, too "impatient and greedy" because they wanted wealth now, and "too selfish" to think of the impact migration would have on their families. In many migrant-sending societies, it is not uncommon for people who live outside migrant enclaves to view migrants with disdain and suspicion, accusing them of "giving up" on their country (cf. Koven 2013b, 2016; Lattanzi Shutika 2011; Zentella 1990). The migration discourse of middle-and upper-class Uriangatenses replicates more widely circulated state-endorsed imaginaries of moral mobility, which question the ethico-moral character of migrants and working-class people (as noted above). Thus, migration discourse is a social index—a sign that displays class status.

Rihan Yeh (2012) has found a similar pattern in her study of the discursive formation of "publics" in northern Mexico. Yeh shows that the way people engage the Mexican state in discourse about the politics related to undocumented migration and the drug trade (either by showing solidarity with state authority by supporting law enforcement or by turning a critical eye on Mexico's carceral state) helps construe them respectively either as middle- or upper-class people who are fully included in the Mexican polity or as marginalized working-class or poor people who are in league with Mexico's "criminal element" and thus not fully a part of the county. Middle- and upper-class people distinguish their cross-border movements from undocumented migration; as border residents, they have access to visas that allow them to travel into the United States for brief periods, so—they make it a point to assert—their activities are legal and within the fold of proper national belonging (Yeh 2012). Similarly, in Uriangato the ability to assert that people should and can be socioeconomically mobile in Mexico without migrating to the United States is a statement of class privilege that occludes the barriers to mobility faced by working-class people. Blaming migrants' inability to be mobile in Mexico on the failures of their character, in turn, makes them ineligible for full belonging and its rights of access to resources.

Working-class migration discourse is distinguished not only by the themes and propositions of their talk of migration but also by the patterns of spatial reference in such talk, especially a marked use of the terms *aquí* (here) and *allá* (there). *Aquí* and *allá* are *deictics*: referential indexes, signs whose semantic meaning is "constituted by the speech event itself" (Silverstein 1976: 17)—what "here" and "there" refer to can only be ascertained through reconstruction of the original utterance. But speakers in working-class migration discourse use *aquí* and *allá* to signal when to shift focus between the world of Mexico and the world of the United States. In so doing, they give these words relatively stable referents (Dick 2010a; Dick and Arnold 2017a). If speakers in Uriangato are engaging in migration discourse with other speakers familiar with this usage, they can say something like "I want to go there": people will know without further contextualization that they mean "there—the United States." In talk of migration, working-class speakers consistently ground description of their life in a stationary present "here" of Mexico, imbricating it with the possibility of movement to the "there" of the United States and imbuing the present with the possibilities of the beyond (Dick 2010a). This semantically stabilizing use of "here" and "there" is strange to middle- and upper-class Uriangatenses. When I used the terms in this way with such speakers, they would balk at my vagueness, saying with amusement and surprise: "There?: There where?!" Then they would correct me, assuming that as a non-native speaker of Spanish I was displaying my lack of skill in the language. Even when I clarified such usage, they often would reject it as "incorrect" or "ignorant"—yet more evidence of the moral failings of working-class people.

The stabilized use of "here"/"there" references Mexico and the United States—not Uriangato or any particular place to which Uriangatenses move, either in the United States or in the other countries to which Mexicans migrate. Whenever speakers clarify the referents of "here" or "there" in talk of migration, they say "aquí/allá en México" (here/there in Mexico) or "aquí/allá en los Estados Unidos" (here/there in the United States), depending on the country in which they are located. The contrast between Mexico and the United States is the core dichotomy against which people evaluate themselves, their country, and their socioeconomic and geopolitical mobility. This contrast itself is evidence of the ways relationships with the United States shadow life in Mexico. This process relies on the production and circulation of migration discourse not only by people in migrant enclaves but also by state actors and nation-builders, as I show in chapter 1. Working-class people's use of "here"/"there" as stable referents thus signals both their class status in Mexico—their awareness of the barriers to class mobility "at home"—and the framework of relationships that links Mexico and the United States. So in their migration discourse working-class Uriangatenses critically engage not only their class position in Mexico but their position within the transnational political economy that links these two countries asymmetrically, spotlighting their exploitation and vulnerability (see chapters 3 and 4).

Imaginative Practices: A Chapter Overview

Above I have unpacked the unique contributions of *Words of Passage*, detailed the local history of migration and industrialization, and sketched the outlines of what being working-class means in Uriangato. Here I outline the content of the book's chapters, detailing how each chapter adds to the exploration of the imagined lives of migrants and their political economic and ethico-moral consequences.

Chapter 1 (So Far from God: State-Endorsed Imaginaries of Moral Mobility in Mexico) documents the discourse history that has generated the key features of state-endorsed imaginaries, showing that they have consistently positioned migrants and working-class people as just beyond the fold of full national belonging. This chapter examines Mexican state-endorsed discourses of progress, especially development policies, which serve as a principal point of encounter between state institutions and working-class Uriangatenses. I explain the emergence of religious nationalism in Mexico and the ways it is complicated by the interrelated processes of industrialization and migration. I argue that Mexican development policies are an interpellative process that calls working-class people to be certain kinds of members of the polity, wherein the realization of moral mobility is posited as the natural opposite of life in the United States. As such, this chapter addresses the central role the United States has played as a foil of national belonging in Mexico. It also explores the ways being "working-class" is co-constructed in concert with notions of race and gender—and in critical dialogue with images of Mexicanidad produced in the United States.

Chapter 2 (Private Eyes, Good Girls: Authoritative Accounts and the Social Life of Interviewing) explores my interpellation into locally salient forms of female personhood through an analysis of the social life of the interviews I conducted. In particular, I explore the process of discourse circulation that shaped how people encountered and received my interviews, as part of making sense of my presence in Uriangato. The chapter argues that my interviews were a point of encounter between authoritative accounts of migration (produced by Mexican and ᵀ ᵀˢ scholars of migration as well as the media) and working-class Uriangatense migration discourse, which is generally marginalized as nonauthoritative. These interviews allowed me to perform an ethico-moral personhood, while also enabling my research participants to project their accounts of migration into the wider world of authoritative discourse, to which they perceived me to have access. Through my analysis of the social life of my interviews, I discuss the ethico-moral dimensions of local concepts of "public" and "private" and the salient semiotic practices through which "authority" is discursively produced and recognized in Uriangato. As I show, these processes are distinctly gendered, so that being able to speak authoritatively is a different prospect for men than for women.

Chapter 3 (Diaspora at Home: Homebuilding and the Failures of Progress) shows the ways working-class Uriangatenses both replicate and invert state-endorsed imaginaries of moral mobility. The ethnographic focus of the chapter is on homebuilding, both the discursive construal of Mexico as home and the acquisition of a place of residence. This chapter examines how migration discourse interacts with social semiotic practices in nondiscursive modalities, such as the symbolic loading of styles of home construction. Homebuilding is not only the central site where Uriangatenses endeavor to progress while remaining "morally Mexican"; it is also a driving motivator for migration. Homebuilding reveals people's desire to "progress" and also their inability to do so in Mexico: I describe this subjectivity as a "diaspora at home." Therefore this chapter spotlights the difficulties working-class people have in responding to the interpellative call of the Mexican state. I explore the moral geography that differentiates Mexico and the United States and urban and rural Mexico, showing that these distinctions help erase urban poverty and need. Both state-endorsed and Uriangatense imaginaries of moral mobility work to position working-class people as in between recognizable categories of belonging, as they are neither authentically "traditional" nor sufficiently "modern."

Chapter 4 (Possibility and Perdition: Discursive Interaction and Ethico-Moral Practice in Traditionalist Talk of Migration) is the first of two chapters that examine ethico-moral practice in specific interactions. I analyze a recorded conversation with a man who briefly migrated in the 1970s, Don Arturo, and his wife, Doña Cecilia, who has never migrated. This chapter argues that the discursive production of migration histories allows working-class people to negotiate the ethico-moral double-bind of the incomplete, diasporic interpellation in Mexico discussed in chapter 3, while also confronting more immediate conflicts in Uriangato, such as those created by the increasing migration of families. I show that ethico-moral practice is an intersubjective activity that allows people to move between entanglements across different arenas of belonging—from family, to neighborhood, to nation—and, when successful, produces not only ethico-moral selves but communities. This chapter also continues the discussion of gender, authority, and belonging in Uriangato. Tracking differences in patterns of pronoun use, I demonstrate that Don Arturo favors the use of the general second-person singular "you" in reference to himself. This enables him to link his migration with the assertion of general truths, thus positioning himself as an expert on migration. By contrast, Doña Cecilia uses pronouns to refer to actual people, especially herself and her family, performing an ethical self as a "woman of family." Through the analysis of conversational turn taking, I demonstrate that Doña Cecilia plays a pivotal role in enabling the ethical work of our conversation.

Chapter 5 (Saints and Suffering: Critical Appeal in Relationships with the Divine Beyond) continues the consideration of ethico-moral life and gender. The ethnographic focus of this chapter is on the practices that allow Uriangatenses to maintain relationships with Catholic saints, especially the Virgin Mary. Saintly relationships are a central practice through which working-class Uriangatenses in general and women in particular enact moral mobility. Participation in the cult of Mary is a fulfillment of the mandates of official national imaginings. To be sure, the Virgin of Guadalupe is the central figure of Mexican Catholic nationalism: her image is iconic of "Mexicanness" both at home and abroad. But her image is also used to critique the failures of the Mexican nation-state. The mobility entailed in pilgrimage is a key foil for the morally dangerous mobility of migration to the United States. Consequently, relationships with the saints help people realize their dreams of "progress"—including migration—while cultivating a virtuous ethico-moral character. As such, they allow working-class people and migrants to resist their positioning within state-endorsed imaginaries as immoral.

Furthermore, relationships with the saints are a form of appeal for resources previously denied. That is, these relationships involve not only the expression of forms of belonging but modalities of request and critique. Saintly relationships are distinguished by a process of obligation-fulfillment that comment on people's relationships with their government. Many working-class Uriangatenses see their government as failing their obligations to poor and working-class people: the system works only for the rich. In contrast, the cult of the saints posits a world that roots being Mexican in the practice of an imaginary in which the observation of social hierarchies leads to the fulfillment of obligations—a kind of social contract they argue their government does not realize for the poor and working-class. Thus, saintly relationships present an alternative basis for national belonging—one that is especially potent for working-class women.

CHAPTER 1

So Far from God: State-Endorsed Imaginaries of Moral Mobility in Mexico

In the 1870s a debate was raging among Mexico's power brokers over whether to build a rail link that would connect Mexico and the United States. In the nineteenth century railroads were key facilitators of industrialization and central icons of modernization and "progress" (Dick and Arnold 2017a; Massey et al. 1987; Ngai 2004; Sánchez 1993; Walsh 2004). Development of Mexico's rail system had been halted by decades of political turmoil, including violent conflict between Mexico's ruling parties, the 1840s war with the United States, and an invasion by the French in the 1860s. By the 1870s Mexican lawmakers and business leaders were anxious to resume railway expansion. Many elites, however, were concerned about foreign intervention, especially the imperial ambitions of the United States. Because of these anxieties, then Mexican president Sebastián Lerdo de Tejada argued against the rail link with the United States, asserting that Mexico's national sovereignty was too fragile to withstand the onslaught of US business interests that would come with it. He asserted that Mexico needed a geographical buffer to safeguard its sovereignty from intervention, a position he summed up in the tidy phrase: *Entre la debilidad y la fuerza, el desierto* (Between weakness and strength, the desert) (Lomnitz 2009: 105). Lerdo's position, however, did not become Mexico's future. Lerdo—and with him supporters of protectionist development—was ousted in the 1876 coup that installed infamous dictator Porfirio Díaz in the Mexican presidency until 1910.

In Díaz's estimation, the expansion of Mexico's railroad system would serve as a public display of the country's ability to modernize after decades of conflict. He oversaw a dramatic increase in rail construction, aggressively pursuing rail links with the United States (Tenorio-

Trillo 1996: 33). The first transnational rail link was forged in 1884 in Piedras Negras and was soon followed by links in Matamoros, Ciudad Juárez, and Laredo. By 1890 the Mexican railroad system was connected directly or indirectly to all continental US states (Cardoso 1980: 14–17; Massey et al. 1987: 41). Díaz argued for these links by countering Lerdo's protectionist arguments with his own punchy formulation, which continues to epitomize Mexico's complex relationship with the United States: *¡Pobre México!—tan lejos de Dios y tan cerca de los Estados Unidos* (Poor Mexico!—so far from God and so close to the United States) (Lomnitz 2009: 105). Today this phrase is generally used to refer to Mexico's political and economic disadvantages in comparison to the United States—the idea of being "so far from God" indicates that Mexico has been left not to God's mercy but to the mercy of US political economic power. During the Porfiriato (as Díaz's almost forty-year rule is called) this phrase had a different valence, however—one that reveals a vision of national belonging that has informed state-endorsed imaginaries of moral mobility since this period.

Díaz claimed Mexicans were "far from God" because their history of political conflict proved they had not yet become virtuous people who could handle full citizenship (Lomnitz 2009). Thus, Mexico needed a period of patrimonial incursion from foreign interests that would allow it to develop into a country capable of managing its sovereignty. Díaz argued that the rail links would facilitate this incursion (Sánchez 1993: chapter 1). Díaz's policies—not only the expansion of the railroad but also his facilitating of massive increases in US and European investment—generated an imaginary of moral mobility that combined the values of nineteenth-century positivist progress (the adoption of open markets, scientific rationality, and technology) with a neocolonialist mentality that characterized Mexico's polity as incapable of achieving progress without authoritarian leadership and influence from more "advanced" societies. The production of this imaginary is evinced in the public relations campaign the Díaz administration mounted abroad. In exchanges with foreign politicians and industrialists, Mexican diplomats argued Díaz had the "firm hand" needed to transform Mexico from an "unstable and unsanitary" land into a modern nation distinguished by "order and progress" (Tenorio-Trillo 1996: 35–36).

Within the Porfirian imaginary, access to legitimate national belonging was limited to wealthy propertied males. Díaz put the brakes on mid-nineteenth century efforts to expand citizenship. He claimed

Mexico should focus instead on creating a strong central state that could support the cultivation of the nation's morality. Such cultivation would putatively develop Mexico's people to a point where they were ready for the responsibility of citizenship (Lomnitz 2001a: 307–309, 311, 316–317). This imaginary emerged in dialogue with large-scale migration to the United States, which began during this period. Ideas about US-bound migration informed both state-endorsed imaginaries of belonging and also countervailing imaginaries produced by migrants and other transnational actors.

The initiation of large-scale US migration was fostered by the Mexico–US rail links. The railways created an infrastructure that simultaneously encouraged US firms to set up plants in Mexico, a nineteenth-century version of "outsourcing" (Gonzalez 2004: chapter 3), and facilitated the recruitment of Mexican labor to work in the United States (Massey et al. 1987: 41; Ngai 2004: 64; Sánchez 1993: chapters 1 and 2; Walsh 2004). As migrants built lives that connected the United States and Mexico, they created their own imaginaries of moral mobility, which—not unlike those explored later in this book—complicated elite visions of national belonging in Mexico (Schmidt Camacho 2008: 9). Cross-border life sparked political organizing that brought together US dissidents in Mexico, Mexican migrants, and Mexican American activists in the United States, who championed solidarity between all working-class laborers (Schmidt Camacho 2008; Torres Pares 1990; Walsh 2004: 123). In order to undo the premise of equality upon which such transnational imaginaries relied, Díaz represented Mexico and its people as not on an equal footing with foreign actors, as needing their intervention. His policies not only legitimated and circulated this representation but helped institute dependency on the United States and other foreign powers, allowing Mexico's wealthy to benefit along with foreign investors, at the expense of Mexico's poor and disenfranchised (Dick and Arnold 2017a; Lomnitz 2009; Sánchez 1993).

In this chapter I detail the history of state-endorsed imaginaries of moral mobility in Mexico.[1] This history takes a brief detour from my ethnographic focus on working-class Uriangatenses to address how imaginaries generated or supported by state institutions have naturalized citizenship variegation: the processes through which national belonging is rendered unequal, so that not all citizens of a country are understood to be full members of the polity (Biolsi 2005; Ong 1999). These imaginaries have played a central role in constraining national belonging in Mexico by interpellating migrants, working-class people, and other marginalized groups (the rural, the Indigenous) to "be Mexican" in ways that construct them as ethico-morally suspect and therefore not yet ready for the rights of citizenship and the material resources associated with it—a process of hailing to the nation-state that is distinctly classed, raced, and gendered. These visions of Mexicanidad mandate consideration because they help form and justify the political economic and imaginative gauntlets through which working-class people must pass to lay claim to being properly Mexican—and therefore help further illuminate what being working-class means in Mexico.

My analysis of state-endorsed imaginaries of moral mobility is organized around key moments in Mexican nation building, which involved US migration and other encounters with the United States. I begin with the Porfiriato because this is when the federal government first endeavored to conglomerate Mexico's regions, states, and municipalities into a cohesive nation tied to a central state (Fitzgerald 2009; Sánchez 1993: chapter 1). In so doing, federal officials promoted a vision of national unity in which being Mexican became bound up with ethico-moral differences between the United States and Mexico, ratifying the ideal of moral mobility in economic development and citizenship policy. State-endorsed imaginaries of moral mobility have changed since the Porfiriato; later imaginaries, for example, took aim at the neocolonialist character of Porfirian moral mobility, arguing against the dependencies it created. This critique sparked the 1910 Revolution, which ousted Díaz. Despite these changes, however, post-Porfirian imaginaries unfolded in dialogue with those of the Porfiriato (Benjamin and Ocasio-Meléndez 1984; O'Toole 2003). They are connected by discourse genealogies created over the course of the twentieth century, as I illustrate by distilling the continuities between Porfirian imaginaries and those produced during two other periods of political transformation: the postrevolutionary era of the early to mid-twentieth century and the current neoliberal period, which began in the 1980s.

Three interrelated features persist across state-endorsed imaginaries during these periods, each of which is introduced in the opening story. First is the idea that Mexico becomes distinct as a nation-state by virtue of not being like the United States. Second is a tendency to formulate Mexico's present, to draw on the eloquent phrasing of Claudio Lomnitz (2009: 105), as "a perpetual state of becoming, as a kind of prelude . . . to true national sovereignty." This formulation extends to *algún futuro* (a distant future), the moment when Mexico is developed enough (morally, politically, economically) to grant full belonging to its people (Lomnitz 2001b; Trejo and Jones 1998). Third is an understanding of "progress" that draws on the familiar contrast between tradition and modernity (Dick 2010a).

The concepts of tradition and modernity are rooted in Enlightenment thought, which imagined "tradition" as a static thing from the past or from places that still live in the past, while "modernity" points toward change, renewal, and departures from tradition (Bauman and Briggs 2003). As is typical of modernist frameworks, state-endorsed imaginaries of moral mobility construe modernity and tradition in these ways. At the same time, however, these imaginaries mandate that Mexico's people distinguish themselves from people in the United States by cultivating an ability to integrate progress and tradition. This mandate creates a paradoxical form of interpellation: being traditional and being modern involve the realization of incompatible moral imperatives, creating a double-bind of belonging: how can a person progress and remain traditional at the same time? As I show below, this double-bind—while characteristic of Mexican belonging in general—is heightened for working-class and other "marginal" peoples in Mexico, who are framed as having flawed ethico-moral characters and therefore as outside the boundaries of proper Mexicanidad (cf. Roth-Gordon 2017; Wirtz 2014).

In tracing the production and reproduction of the key features of imaginaries of moral mobility across several moments of national transformation, this chapter illuminates the processes that have constructed citizenship and national belonging in Mexico as issues of morality. As such, it offers insight into how ethico-moral frameworks are used to create and govern particular populations (cf. Fassin 2012a, 2012b). Understanding these political dimensions of ethico-moral life involves recognizing that ethics and morality are not inherent to any particular social arena, topic, type of practice, or kind of person; rather, they are contingent and potentially fraught interactional accomplishments that are only semistable (Lempert 2013; Zigon 2011). In later chapters I explore this point through analysis of the ways ethico-moral stakes are made intersubjectively recognizable and interactionally relevant in particular instances of talk. In this chapter I turn attention to a different issue—the history of moralizing mobility in Mexico.

Political economic development need not take on an ethico-moral tinge, though it often does—and not only in Mexico (Fennel 2015; Muehlebach 2012; Wacquant 2009). This raises the questions of when, how, and why such moralizing happens and what are its consequences:

how does moralizing order the management of not just individual selves but whole collectivities? Such questions matter because they make mobility an ethico-moral problem that justifies potent processes of social differentiation that have not only made "Mexico" a distinct—and often unequal—entity vis-à-vis the United States but also have rendered different kinds of "Mexicans" in ways that legitimate inequality within the nation-state.

Tracing the history of moralizing mobility necessitates paying attention to what linguistic anthropologists call *interdiscursivity*: the practices through which people create relationships between talk or writing produced at different times and places and hence between the people who produced that discourse (Silverstein 2005—see also Bauman 2004; Bauman and Briggs 1990; Briggs and Bauman 1992; Dick 2017; Silverstein and Urban 1996; Wortham and Reyes 2015). Such relationships can be both textual and genealogical (Dick 2011b; Wirtz 2013). Textual interdiscursivity refers to the ways instances of talk or writing come to resemble each other, as when someone quotes another person. My importation of Díaz's phrase *¡Pobre México!—tan lejos de Dios y tan cerca de los Estados Unidos* is an example of textual interdiscursivity, which creates points of connection among this chapter, the moment when Díaz uttered this phrase, and the many subsequent times it has been repeated.

By contrast, as I discuss in the book's introduction, the term "genealogical" refers to the broad ideological similarities between distinct instances of discourse. This type of interdiscursivity is exemplified in the fact that state-endorsed imaginaries in the Porfirian, postrevolutionary, and neoliberal periods replicate a set of preconditions for making claims to and about national belonging. This process of replication has over time helped create the parameters of belonging: in order to be properly Mexican, people must negotiate the mandates of moral mobility. Thus, the genealogical approach means exploring the conditions that have permitted moral mobility to emerge as the central marker of Mexicanidad and not, for instance, the imaginaries promoted by transnational workers' coalitions mentioned in the introduction. By tracing the genealogical links among Porfirian, postrevolutionary, and neoliberal imaginaries, I show that they collectively produce what Kristina Wirtz (2013) aptly describes as an *interdiscursive web*, in which similar framings of belonging and exclusion are replicated across diverse and sometimes only indirectly related contexts, from museums to poverty alleviation protocols. Such webs produce a social milieu in which certain forms of belonging become naturalized, while others become abnormal.

Below I trace the genealogical connections among Porfirian, post-revolutionary, and neoliberal imaginaries through a consideration of the key figures of "authentic Mexicanness" in each, paying special attention to images of personhood to which working-class people are called. Thus, as this analysis reveals, interdiscursivity is a central dynamic of interpellation. Louis Althusser (2001), who first developed the concept of interpellation, uses it to refer to a power-laden process of call-and-response that "speaks to us as individuals and as it were calls us by name" (Jameson 2001: xiv). Take Althusser's paradigmatic example of a police officer calling "Hey, you there!" (Althusser 2001: 117ff.). In responding to this call, the "you" hailed by the officer is transformed into someone subject to the authority of the state. Examples of this kind of literal call follow in the chapter's analysis of interdiscursivity. As imaginaries of moral mobility are codified into state policy, they sometimes directly beckon members of the polity in distinct ways that constitute them as certain kinds of Mexicans. But this chapter considers more than such direct interpellation.

Building on Judith Butler's (1993, 1997) expansion of the concept, which argues that many kinds of practices can interpellate beyond literal calls and responses, this chapter also illuminates how state-endorsed imaginaries hail people to be certain kinds of Mexicans by creating an environment in which moral mobility becomes a normalized way of orienting to the world and being properly Mexican. In other words, interpellative practice can be traced in habituated social worlds and the ways people accept or reject them—worlds that centrally rely on the construction, circulation, and institutionalization of imaginaries, populated by images of personhood in which actors are meant to see themselves reflected.

I organize my analysis of interdiscursivity around an unpacking of discourse about economic development produced by leading political figures in Mexico in each period examined. Development programs have long been a central site for the production of state-endorsed imaginaries of moral mobility. "Development programs" is an umbrella term that covers a range of efforts to increase economic output and stability, from railroad construction to poverty alleviation initiatives. Development discourses often help create the social hierarchies that variegate national belonging and generate asymmetries between nation-states (e.g., Escobar 1995; Ferguson 2006; Kelly and Kaplan 2001). Development programs have not only helped order how Mexico and its people are envisioned by articulating the concept of uniquely "Mexican progress," which has always been integrated with ideas about migration and therefore the production of migration discourse and relationships with the United States. They are also a key mode of interaction through which these imaginaries enter into working-class Uriangatenses' lives, calling them to be Mexican in particular ways.

In focusing on elite discourse, I do not mean to imply that imaginaries of moral mobility are exclusively a top-down phenomenon. Throughout Mexican history the construction of national imaginaries has relied on interdiscursive relationships between the pressures, perspectives, and interests of elites and nonelites (Faudree 2013: 51). Indeed the rest of this book explores how working-class Uriangatenses respond to, resist, contribute to, and potentially transform elite visions of Mexicanidad. In this chapter, however, I focus on some of Mexico's key power brokers because their rendering of moral mobility helped define the state-endorsed imaginaries of their time. These imaginaries serve as points of orientation around which contemporary processes of interpellation revolve. I begin this analysis by fleshing out the foundational imaginary of moral mobility that emerged during the Porfiriato. I then establish the genealogical links between Porfirian and later imaginaries, which cumulatively have created a social milieu that calls working-class people to be Mexican in ways that (re)create the moral double-binds that marginalize them from full national belonging.

I then examine the replication and revision of features of Porfirian imaginaries: first, in the postrevolutionary imaginaries produced by leading nation-builders José Vasconcelos, Samuel Ramos, and Manuel Gamio, who wrote works of lasting impact on state-endorsed imaginaries of moral mobility (Alonso 2004; Lomnitz 2001b; Walsh 2004). Finally, I consider how state-endorsed imaginaries of the current neoliberal period interdiscursively respond to and recombine the imaginaries of both the Porfiriato and the postrevolutionary period. But, first, I further unpack the concept of "national belonging," highlighting that the variegation of such belonging is not an exclusive feature of the Mexican state but part of nation-state building more broadly.

National Belonging, Citizenship, and the Imagination of the Nation-State

The terms "national belonging" and "citizenship" point to related but distinct statuses. I use "citizenship" to refer to the status of being a rights-bearing member of a nation-state who has, among other things, the right to take certain political actions, such as voting or running for political office. By contrast, I use the term "national belonging" to refer to a person's ability to lay claim to legitimate membership as being someone who exemplifies the core qualities of the nation and who most deserves to be there and enjoy its resources.[2] While these statuses sometimes overlap, they are not necessarily coterminous. On the one hand, it is often the case that some people are understood to belong to a nation but do not have citizenship (Biolsi 2005; Ong 1999). For example, Mexican women did not win universal suffrage, a central feature of rights-bearing citizenship, until the 1950s (Lomnitz 2001b: 315; Olcott 2005). But that did not mean that women born and raised in the country did not have national belonging—they were viewed as being Mexican, though in a distinct way from their male counterparts. Women at every class level were depicted as needing the patronage of males and being unable to handle rights on their own.

On the other hand, some people who are citizens do not have national belonging. This point has been made extensively in the literature on migrant incorporation into receiving societies, which shows that migrant groups who do not resemble the dominant image of a "real" member of the host country are positioned as outsiders, regardless of legal status (Benhabib 2002; De Genova 2002, 2005; Dick 2011a, 2011b; Silverstein 2000, 2004; Stephen 2004, 2007). For instance, Uriangato has a growing population of South Korean migrants. There are now Korean families living in Uriangato with children born in Mexico who are therefore citizens. These children grow up speaking Spanish, attending local schools, and so forth. Nevertheless, it would be difficult to find a non-Korean Uriangatense who would call children of Korean descent Mexican. Given these complexities of belonging, I am not primarily interested in the history of rights-bearing citizenship in Mexico, though I address points related to it where relevant. While Uriangatenses care about rights-bearing citizenship, their attachments to Mexico—and the ways those attachments inform social life between Uriangato and Pennsylvania—are not only about legal rights. They are also about who gets to lay claim to full belonging (cf. Lattanzi Shutika 2011; Stack 2012a, 2012b). This process is informed by the variegation of Mexicanidad in state-endorsed imaginaries of moral mobility, which shape who can and cannot access rights and resources in the first place.

In rooting this exploration in my analysis of imaginaries and the means of their production and circulation, I take inspiration from Benedict Anderson's seminal theory of nationalism. Anderson (1991) famously describes the nation-state as an "imagined community," arguing that the power of nationalism to shape social life rests in the processes that allow it to become a commonsensical way of apprehending community (Anderson 1991: 5–6; Lomnitz 2001c: 329; Woolard 2004: 64). In emphasizing the imagined quality of nation-states, Anderson (1991:6) is not trying to dismiss them as merely "invented" and "ideological." He recognizes that all communities are the products of human invention—and that imaginative processes are essential to understanding how and why people form attachments to and make sacrifices for social formations like the nation-state. Therefore, he urges, we must work to understand how national communities are imagined and to what ends.

While Anderson's urging drives *Words of Passage*, his theory of nationalism ultimately cannot explain when or why national attachments matter because he decides at the outset what the salient types of imagining are. Extrapolating from Walter Benjamin's seminal (1968) work on art and European concepts of time, Anderson claims that the national imagined community became both plausible and appealing because of a shift in the understanding of time that made possible forms of egalitarian togetherness, which he argues come to replace older forms of imagined community that are not egalitarian, especially religious ones (Anderson 1991: 22, 24–25). Subsequent work, however, has shown both that Anderson misconstrues Benjamin's theory and also that few—if any—actual nation-states emerged under the conditions described by Anderson (Eisenlohr 2004; Lomnitz 2001c; Woolard 2004: 62). Rather, the nation-state is most often formulated in concert with other imaginaries, including religious ones, and almost always involves processes of variegation—not egalitarianism (Alonso 1994; Bauman and Briggs 2003; Eisenlohr 2004; Herzfeld 1997; Kelly and Kaplan 2001; Lomnitz 2001c; Silverstein 2000; Williams 1989; Woolard 2004). With these insights in mind, I turn to how the three key features of state-endorsed imaginaries of national belonging established during the Porfiriato (Mexico is not the United States; full belonging must be delayed to a distant future; and Mexicans must negotiate tradition and progress) have worked to variegate the national belonging of working-class people and migrants in Mexico.

Porfirian Imaginaries of Moral Mobility

Porfirian imaginaries of moral mobility, like those of following periods, are ordered by what I have described elsewhere as a *modernist chronotope*:

a spatiotemporal framing that contrasts a future-oriented, forward-moving "modern realm" of industrial development with an unchanging, now-oriented "traditional realm" of custom, religion, and morality (Dick 2010a). These framings also undergird the working-class Uriangatenses' imaginaries of moral mobility, the production of which is part of the uptake of state-endorsed interpellation (see chapter 3). Imaginaries of moral mobility, then, are incarnations of widespread modernist frameworks, which invariably craft modernity by placing it in contrast to tradition (Bauman and Briggs 2003). As a result of European colonialism, such frameworks took hold in many places in the eighteenth and nineteenth century and are still salient for people in a striking array of contemporary contexts (Bauman and Briggs 2003; Donham 1999; Roth-Gordon 2017; Winegar 2006; Wirtz 2014). Work on the semiotics of lives in migration suggests that modernist frameworks are a primary way people make sense of and link their lives to global processes (Arnold 2016; Dick 2011a; Divita 2014; Eisenlohr 2006; Good 2012; Koven 2013a, 2016; Mendoza-Denton 2008).

During the Porfiriato, the anchoring contrast of imaginaries of moral mobility—between modernity and tradition—was mapped onto geographic spaces and the people who inhabited them, enabling certain kinds of claims about the social world and making others less plausible, as often happens with such frameworks (Dick and Arnold 2017a; Gal 2016; Irvine and Gal 2000). Porfirian imaginaries figured the United States as a land of modernity and its people as the bearers of modernity's qualities (rationality, science, capitalist productivity, individualism) and Mexico as the land of tradition and its people as the bearer of its qualities (irrationality, backwardness, spirituality, communitarian sociality). This framework helped justify policies that sold off Mexico's land and natural resources to US investors, who putatively were better equipped to shepherd the country into modernity (Lund 2008), while making the egalitarian visions of transnational workers' organizations seem nonsensical.

As this suggests, Porfirian imaginaries helped delineate the parameters of national belonging—a process made possible through *fractal recursivity* (Irvine and Gal 2000): the projection of an opposition salient in one domain into another domain (see chapter 3). Within Porfirian imaginaries, the contrasts between the United States/modernity and Mexico/tradition were projected onto different parts of Mexico. Urban Mexico and rural Mexico became posited as different in ways similar to the United States and Mexico, so that urban Mexico became associated with modernity and progress and rural Mexico with tradition and stagnation. Similarly, within urban contexts the modernity-tradition contrast was projected onto class, so that upper-class people became synonymous with the qualities of modernity and urbanity and poor and working-class people with the qualities of tradition and rurality.

Díaz used these projections across domains to reanimate debates over Mexican citizenship from the early nineteenth century. Those debates had depicted nonelites as occupying various positions on a continuum of moral poverty—from *la plebe* (the unruly masses who would never be functioning citizens) to *el pueblo* (the docile popular classes), whose greatest asset was that they were obedient to the wealthy, under whose tutelage they might one day learn to be proper citizens (Lomnitz 2001b: 307–309, 311).[3] Thus, the interpellation of people of limited means—primarily through their subordination to patrons, such as the heads of haciendas (large farm holdings)—involved calling upon them to see themselves as in need of instruction by putative superiors (Sánchez 1993: chapter 1). Consequently, Díaz put off citizenship for many Mexicans until after that tutelage, facilitated by Mexico's wealthy and foreign elites. That is, his imaginary of moral mobility depended on a kind of "social tense" in which present marginalization was "legitimated by imagined futures" (Rosa 2016: 108), in this case that distant time when all of Mexico would be developed: a framing that persists into the neoliberal period.

Although Díaz welcomed US investors, he did not see the United States as an example for the moral development of his people. Rather, it was to Europe that he turned for this purpose. This appeal to Europe for moral instruction is evinced in the migration discourse—and immigration policy—of the Porfiriato. Díaz fostered migration into Mexico from northwestern Europe, offering land and tax exemptions to people from this region to incentivize their immigration (Tenorio-Trillo 1996: 35–36). Via the further recursion of the modernity/tradition contrast, Díaz's immigration policy construed southern and eastern Europe as backward, just like the rural or the urban poor in Mexico. Therefore they were considered undesirable candidates for recruitment to the project of modernizing Mexico. By contrast, Díaz argued that northeastern European immigrants would improve the "Mexican race" by inculcating its people into their styles of progress, represented as more gentile than the forms of progress typified by the individualism of the United States (Tenorio-Trillo 1996: 35–36). Through such inculcation, the inferiority of Mexico's people would be diluted and Mexico's political economic and moral development would be hastened.

Comparable pro-European immigration policies were implemented in other parts of Latin America during this period, pointing to a widespread and racialized policy regime that proposed the presence of lighter-skinned Europeans as necessary for successful nation-building (Clark 1998; Roth-Gordon 2017; Stepan 1991; Walsh 2004: 122; Wirtz 2014). Indeed Porfirian immigration policy carried on the racial project of the Spanish colonial era, which had construed both Indigenous and "mixed race" people as inferior to people of European descent (Alonso 2004; Young 1995). But it also solidified the idea of *moral* mobility, positing that "Mexican progress" should involve pursuing development in a way distinguished by a greater valuation of quality of life, family, and community, modeled by the traditions of Europe, and in explicit contrast to life in the United States.

Díaz's aggressive pursuit of foreign involvement in Mexico produced a level of prosperity previously unseen in the country, but it also created a dramatic income inequality, as the bulk of this wealth was distributed to foreign investors and a handful of Porfirian elites (Chasteen 2001: chapter 6). As people across the class spectrum witnessed Mexico's wealth flow into the hands of foreigners and Díaz's people, they became increasingly dissatisfied. This dissatisfaction sparked the Mexican Revolution (1910–1920), which ousted Díaz and generated a new nationalism that was anti-imperialist and anti-interventionist. During the early twentieth century, similar projects of nation building were occurring across Latin America (Chasteen 2001: chapter 7). In Mexico new nationalism unfolded in most immediate interdiscursive relationship with Porfirian imaginaries of moral mobility. In the discussion below I engage how postrevolutionary nation builders reconstituted such imaginaries, focusing on representations of working-class people and migrants.

Postrevolutionary Reformation of Porfirian Imaginaries of Moral Mobility

In countering Porfirian imaginaries, postrevolutionary nation builders did not reject the concept of moral mobility. Rather, they revised its tenets by repudiating foreign tutelage and inverting what Porfirian elites had imagined as the source of Mexico's development. During the Porfiriato, elites proposed two parallel tracks of development, both of which called for an abandonment of the "traditionally Mexican." One involved a movement toward the economic standards of the United

States; the other involved a movement toward the moral refinements of Europe. Conversely, postrevolutionary visions claimed that Mexico had within it the qualities needed to realize moral mobility. The cultivation of singularly Mexican traditions and forms of personhood, nation builders opined, would protect Mexico from the imperial press of outside interests, allowing the country to realize its sovereignty at last (Lomnitz 2008). As a result, identifying the features of *lo mexicano* (that which makes Mexico a unique entity) became a national imperative. Postrevolutionary elites realized this imperative through the creation of a veritable intellectual industry focused on discovering the "Mexican national character" (Lester 2005: 287). This became a profoundly compelling project that continues in the writings of later twentieth century intellectuals, most notably Octavio Paz (e.g., Paz 1994; see also Joseph and Henderson 2002: 9), and has proven difficult to shed, even for those who are critical of it (e.g., Bartra 1992; see Lomnitz 2001a and Tenorio-Trillo 1993 for discussion).

Postrevolutionary imaginaries of moral mobility produced a paradoxical form of interpellation for marginalized groups (Indigenous people, peasants, women, working-class laborers). These groups became positioned in state-endorsed imaginaries as the essence of Mexicanidad. It was their job to preserve the traditionalism considered fundamental to Mexico's uniqueness and sovereignty. Thus, they were called on by the nation in new ways that brought them further into the fold of the national polity than they had been during the Porfiriato. As part of this, nation builders expanded Mexican citizenship, advancing the promise of the Revolution: the state would distribute "the fruits of Mexican modernity" more equitably; no longer would they be hoarded by elites (Stack 2012a: 874; see also Faudree 2013: chapter 1). Therefore what marginalized groups might expect for responding to the call of national belonging changed. If before they could expect "patronage" from putative superiors who mediated their relationships with the state, now they could anticipate more direct relationships with state institutions, through which they could make claims on Mexico's fruits, assuming that they played their part of embodying Mexicanidad (cf. Lomnitz 2001b, 2008). And therein lies the paradox of belonging for working-class and other marginalized people.

If this period saw an increase in the prestige of *lo mexicano*, nevertheless the prerevolutionary idea that Mexicanidad was somehow morally flawed continued. Consequently, postrevolutionary imaginaries of moral mobility continued the variegation of national belonging, leaving marginalized groups vulnerable to exclusion. Such imaginaries positioned "traditional people" not only as the essence of Mexico but also as the central barriers to the realization of Mexico's progress. Therefore postrevolutionary imaginaries of moral mobility created a double-bind of belonging for Mexico's marginalized people: they were to keep the torch of tradition alive—never be too "advanced" lest Mexico lose its sovereign character—but also to change and progress. Any failure to do so would be blamed on their inability to improve, read as a sign of their immorality. This double-bind was used by government actors to justify the co-optation of marginalized groups into the apparatus of the state, so that the state "celebration" of tradition was a way to control potential opposition.

Below I explore in turn three dimensions of postrevolutionary imaginaries created out of the search for *lo mexicano*. These are the dimensions that most affected the lives of working-class people and migrants, and they all have strong genealogical connections to the Porfirian and contemporary neoliberal periods. First is the elevation of Spanish-Indigenous racial and cultural mixing (*mestizaje*) as the main source of Mexico's strength and potential for greatness (Stepan 1991: 145). Second is the transformation in the role working-class people play in Mexico's political economic advancement, illustrated in discourse about a common working-class figure: *el pelado* (the working-class urban scoundrel). Third is a new mandate migrants to the United States were given in fostering Mexico's development. My exploration of each dimension is organized around analysis of the discourse of central figures in the intellectual industry that produced the Mexican national character in the postrevolutionary period.

La Raza Cósmica (The Cosmic Race): Mestizaje, Racialized Nationalism, and Ambiguous Whiteness

The elevation of *mestizaje* in the early twentieth century is perhaps the prime example of how postrevolutionary nation builders upended Porfirian moral mobility, while nevertheless reproducing the ways it had variegated national belonging. In contrast to the mestizo nationalism of the early twentieth century, the racial ideologies of the Porfiriato treated racial hybridity as a form of moral corruption and a source of Mexico's inferiority. This vision emerged interdiscursively with US national imaginaries, which posited the United States as a primarily white country. There is a long history of associating "real America" with whiteness (Balderrama and Rodríguez 1995; Dick 2011b; Haney-López 2006). Porfirian elites associated the superiority of the United States with its whiteness, posited as the opposite of Mexican *mestizaje*, which the country was to purify (Stepan 1991). Therefore postrevolutionary mestizo imaginaries were in critical dialogue with both Porfirian and US racial frameworks, creating alignments between the United States, whiteness, imperialism, and immorality, projecting an image of the "proper Mexican" as a mestizo who is morally superior to US people.

One of the most influential authors of postrevolutionary mestizo imaginaries was José Vasconcelos (1882–1959), known for his still-controversial 1925 work *La raza cósmica* (The Cosmic Race) (Vasconcelos 1997; see also Alonso 2004; Stepan 1991: 145–153; Tenorio-Trillo 1996). More than any other work of Mexican nationalism, *La raza cósmica* distilled the concept of moral mobility—that Mexico's political economic development depended on integration of tradition and modernity—into a highly reproducible vision. This work endures as a key point of orientation for *lo mexicano*, even for people who critique it (Gallo 2006). Vasconcelos argued that the racial mixing of the European with a soupçon of the Indigenous would produce a new "cosmic race" that would eventually supersede the "Anglo-race" of the United States. He elaborated the extant view of the United States as morally corrupt, describing its people as "crassly pragmatic, arrogant, shallow, aggressive, and lacking in spirituality" (Vasconcelos as quoted in Joseph and Henderson 2002: 15; see also Martínez 2001). As Vasconcelos explained, "[w]ith his 'practical talents,' the Anglo-Saxon might excel at industry, but his accomplishments would be transcended by the 'Iberoamerican mestizo' with his superior aesthetic and spiritual sensibility" (Alonso 2004: 465).

This contrastive North/South vision was forwarded by many Latin American intellectuals in the early twentieth century as part of this period's new nationalism (Roth-Gordon 2017; Wirtz 2014). For example, influential Uruguayan essayist José Enrique Rodó's 1900 work *Ariel* (Rodó and Castro Morales 2000), which influenced Vasconcelos's thinking, depicts the United States as the materialistic Caliban of William Shakespeare's *The Tempest* and Latin America as the refined, moral Ariel. Building on Rodó's vision, Vasconcelos forecast a revolutionary future not only for Mexico but for the entire region. In realizing this future, Vasconcelos argued, Mexico would play a leading role, spearheading Latin America's spiritual triumph over the United States (Schmidt 1976: 181–186).

Mestizo imaginaries of moral mobility, such as that forwarded by

Vasconcelos, became naturalized through several intersecting projects of nation building, from Catholic education (Lester 2005), to state-sponsored art and archaeology (Alonso 2004; Lomnitz 2008), to programs of economic development (Kearney 1986; Walsh 2004). Vasconcelos himself, in addition to being a public intellectual, was a policy maker and state official. In these capacities, he worked his mestizo imaginary into the material and ideological infrastructure of state institutions. He created and led the Secretariat of Public Education, which he saw as a stepping stone for the production of a state apparatus that would promote and manage the country's moral development (Alonso 2004: 464, 468—see also Faudree 2013: chapter 1). During his tenure at the Secretariat of Public Education, Vasconcelos commissioned Mexico's great muralists—David Alfaro Siqueiros, José Clemente Orozco, and Diego Rivera—to paint depictions of Mexico's mestizo past and future on state buildings, from public libraries to the Palacio Nacional, which houses the offices of Mexico's president (Alonso 2004; Joseph and Henderson 2002: 15; Stepan 1991: 146ff.). In developing the Mexican public education system, he ensured that the mestizo imaginary was not only painted on the walls of the state but written into the national school curriculum. Vasconcelos also promoted the mestizo imaginary of moral mobility internationally through Mexico's exhibits at the 1922 World's Fair, where he presided as the lead diplomat representing the country (Tenorio-Trillo 1996: chapter 12).

Despite the revolutionary ambitions of this period, mestizo imaginaries did not generate egalitarian national belonging. Rather, they merely reversed the terms of Porfirian racialization, creating a new racial hierarchy. If racial purity had been superior and normalized before, considered the natural state of being, now it was the mixed-blood person who was treated as normative and racial purity as suspect. *Mestizaje* thus generated a conflation between being Mexican and being mestizo, which endures into the present. Recent studies have shown that Mexicans who speak Spanish as their first language (as opposed to one of Mexico's Indigenous languages) treat the terms "Mexican" and "mestizo" as synonymous and interchangeable (Dowling 2014). This perspective was vigorously affirmed by the Uriangatenses with whom I worked. The conflation of *lo mexicano* with *lo mestizo* positions anyone who is not mestizo as not fully Mexican, thus reproducing the variegation of national belonging. Consider the stance of postrevolutionary nation builders toward Indigenous peoples.

Since this period indigeneity has been available to Mexican state institutions as a "mythical cultural heritage" that helps define Mexico's uniqueness (Napolitano 2016: 138). Indigeneity is quickly elided, however, when it may highlight inequality or foment political resistance. For all their glorification of Mexico's "Indigenous past" as the source of Mexican authenticity, postrevolutionary politicians largely ignored the needs of the country's Indigenous peoples and instead focused on co-opting them to the apparatus of the state, developing policies that would hasten their transformation from Indigenous to mestizo (Castellanos 2010; Faudree 2013; Rus 1994; Stepan 1991: 146, 150). As a result, mestizo imaginaries positioned any effort to fight for the rights of Indigenous peoples as unpatriotic and un-Mexican (Alonso 2004; Faudree 2013). They also erased the Afro-Mexican community from the country's history, public awareness, and policy, as this community put into question the Spanish-Indigenous narrative of *mestizaje* (Lewis 2000). Although Indigenous groups and Afro-Mexican communities have achieved greater political recognition in recent decades, they are still marginalized from the centers of political economic power (Alonso 2004; Castellanos 2010; Faudree 2013; Lewis 2000; Napolitano 2016: chapter 5).

At the same time that mestizo imaginaries marginalized Indigenous and Afro-Mexican people, they generated an ambiguous form of "whiteness" for mixed-raced people, especially for those who are poor and working-class. Because *lo mestizo* is naturalized as *lo mexicano*, mestizos have a certain race privilege not dissimilar to the privilege enjoyed by whites in the United States. Yet their whiteness is unstable, context-specific, and precarious (Moreno Figueroa 2010). In stark contrast to US racial ideologies that envision firm lines between "black" and "white," *mestizaje* produces a fluidity of race in which who counts as mestizo is dynamic, as a matter of both ideology and embodiment (cf. Roth-Gordon 2017; Wirtz 2014).

Mexicans who have features associated with the histories of migration into the Americas from Europe—such as light skin color, blond hair, and blue eyes—and therefore have a more indisputable whiteness are in the minority. Most Mexicans have features that can be read as more "Indigenous" and therefore less mestizo relative to others. As Mónica Moreno Figueroa (2010, 2013) has shown in her studies of the experience of race in Mexico, many mestizos will claim that "we aren't racist because we are all mestizo" (Moreno Figueroa and Saldívar Tanaka 2015: 515). At the same time, however, they are acutely aware of their potential to be read as nonmestizo and sensitive to the forms of discrimination that can be prompted by such readings.

To be sure, mestizo imaginaries carry on the racial projects of the

Spanish colonial and post-Independence periods, positioning indigeneity and Afro-Mexicanidad as inferior (Alonso 2004; Lewis 2000; Moreno
Figueroa 2010). They also continued to favor the western European.
For example, postrevolutionary policy makers forwarded efforts to create a race-based immigration system that would discourage the migration of Asians, Middle Easterners, and eastern Europeans, arguing that
they would delay the realization of mestizo moral mobility (Fitzgerald
2009: 39; Stepan 1991: 152–153). As this suggests, mestizo racial "improvement"—like other projects of racial engineering found across the
region in the early twentieth century (Stepan 1991)—involved a light-
ening of the national body, a movement from Indigenous to Spanish
(Alonso 2004; Lewis 2000; Moreno Figueroa 2013—cf. Roth-Gordon
2017; Wirtz 2014). The idea that it is a national imperative *mejorar la
raza* (to improve the race and nation) by making it whiter endures into
the present (Dowling 2014; Moreno Figueroa 2010). I heard this idea repeated frequently by my research participants. True to the mestizo vision of moral mobility, my interlocutors often asserted that the goal was
not to produce children with US white people—who are suspect as morally depraved—but to partner with lighter-skinned people of Mexican
descent.

Uriangatenses' valuing of racial "improvement" is an expression of
their awareness of the ambiguity and instability of their mestizo whiteness. Although residents of Uriangato are overwhelmingly monolingual
Spanish-speaking mestizos who claim that they do not have a race, they
nevertheless elaborate distinctions between mestizos/as who are more
güeros/as (lighter skinned) and those who are more *prietos/as* (darker
skinned). And they generally place a greater value on lighter skin and
fair features, associating these with beauty, refinement, and morality (cf.
Irvine and Gal 2000; Moreno Figueroa and Saldívar Tanaka 2015).

For working-class mestizo/as, the ambiguity of their mestizo whiteness is a feature of a general positioning that defines the experience
of being working-class. Their political economic marginalization is
erased by national narratives that posit them as already within the fold
of the mestizo nation (see chapter 3). As a result, working-class people are placed outside the groups who receive state affirmation: middle-
and upper-class mestizos who enjoy fuller access to the fruits of Mexican modernity. But they also do not belong to the groups who receive
state patronage, such as the poor, rural, and Indigenous people who frequently become the objects of poverty alleviations programs, which entail their own processes of marginalization. Therefore the Othering of

mestizo working-class people is distinct from the marginalization experienced by members of marked racial groups in Mexico. As long as they can "pass" as mestizo, they enjoy a certain race privilege. But at the same time they are rendered invisible when they seek recognition because their needs betray the failures of progress in Mexico. Such needs grate against the linear narratives of progress, in which the nation is to move from the rural/poor/Indigenous to the urban/prosperous/mestizo.

Thus, like Porfirian imaginaries, mestizo visions posited Mexicanidad as a moral work-in-progress. As Vasconcelos put it, Mexico needed more time "to ripen its fruit" (1926: 8). Thus mestizo imaginaries continued the notion that Mexico was in a condition of becoming. As during the Porfiriato, it was state institutions that would make possible the ripening of Mexico's moral fruit (Lomnitz 2001b; Walsh 2004: 122). Mestizo imaginaries also relied on the same modernist contrasts that defined Porfirian Mexicanidad—between the modern, progressive, scientific, rational and the traditional, backward, religious/spiritual, irrational (Alonso 2004: 467; cf. Roth-Gordon 2017; Wirtz 2014). As before, these contrasts became iconic of types of persons: progress and its associated features aligned with the European, the lighter-skinned, the wealthy, the urban, and the masculine and tradition with the Indigenous, the darker-skinned, the poor, the rural, and the feminine (Alonso 2004: 468; Castellanos 2010; Faudree 2013; Lewis 2000; Moreno Figueroa 2010, 2013; Moreno Figueroa and Saldívar Tanaka 2015).

Because mestizo imaginaries continued the Eurocentrism that had characterized Porfirian imaginaries, they involved an unequal embrace of tradition and the people who putatively represented it. The cultivation of tradition was never to get in the way of progress: when development faltered, traditionality and its water-bearers were assumed to be responsible. The unequal embrace of tradition and progress helped justify the repression and/or occlusion of the needs of people identified as members of Mexico's traditional groups. This occurred even as these groups were "celebrated" as the essence of Mexicanidad. As noted above, the production of this paradoxical form of belonging was part of a project to co-opt potential political opposition to the apparatus of the state, a process exemplified in the postrevolutionary treatment of Catholicism.

Celebrating and Co-opting Mexican Catholicism

During the postrevolutionary period, Mexico's folk Catholic practices, such as the cult of the saints (see chapter 5), were held up as prime ex-

amples of *mestizaje*. As these practices combined European and Indigenous traditions, they iconized the country's history as a postcolonial
nation, wounded by the exploitations of Spanish colonialism but nevertheless able to persevere (Faudree 2013: chapter 1; Lomnitz 2008: 35–
36; 48–50; Napolitano 2016: chapter 5). Religious nationalism is a familiar strategy that many postcolonial nation-states have employed against
Western hegemony (Asad 2003; Bonfil Batalla 1990; Lester 2005; Mahmood 2005). This strategy belies theories of nationalism, like Anderson's, which posit that the nation-state emerges only after the abandonment of religious affiliation as the centerpiece of political life (Eisenlohr
2004, 2006; Lomnitz 2001b; Woolard 2004). To be sure, Mexico's religious nationalism dates back to the early nineteenth century Mexican
independence movement (Lester 2005: chapter 12; Lomnitz 2008). Contemporary manifestations of religious nationalism, however, have their
roots in the postrevolutionary period, when religion became elevated
as a signal feature of the potential superiority of Mexico, grounding its
moral development in Catholicism (Lomnitz 2008; Vaughan and Lewis
2006). Like the elevation of *mestizaje* more generally, the promotion of
an association between Catholicism and Mexicanidad was part of a rejection of Porfirian policies, which in the name of reforming "Mexican
inferiority" had actively encouraged Protestantism, which Díaz associated with a superior work ethic that would hasten industrialization (Sánchez 1993: chapter 7).

But for all their elevation of Mexican Catholicism, postrevolutionary
elites were expressly anticlerical and antagonistic not only toward the
church, long associated with the politics of foreign intervention, but
also toward practicing Catholics. Mexico's 1917 Constitution, a water-
shed document that helped bring the Revolution to an end, stripped the
Catholic church of its landholdings and much of its political power.[4] The
implementation of these antichurch provisions led to a resistance movement, known as the Cristero Rebellion or La Cristiada (1926–1929). The
postrevolutionary government violently repressed La Cristiada, seeking
not only to keep the institution of the church in check but also to contain the public celebration of many of the same rituals that its new national narratives were upholding as the essence of Mexico (Butler 2004;
Farr 2006: 51–54; González Navarro 2001; Napolitano 2016: 133–134).
Thus, rather than being an actual promotion of either Mexico's Catholic church or its citizens' popular piety, postrevolutionary nation builders' lauding of syncretic Catholicism was part of a broad-based effort
to consolidate state power by taking over the symbolic and material re-

sources of potential opposition (Alonso 2004; Lomnitz 2008; Napoli-tano 2016: 129–130).

Although the 1917 Constitution suggests an egalitarian vision in which Mexico's people have uniform access to rights and resources (Gil-breth and Otero 2001), the postrevolutionary government's primary fo-cus was on consolidating state power, as it had been under Díaz. But this consolidation was executed in a different way, as the government sought to "harness corporate groups and sectors" to state institutions by making workers' unions part of the state, for instance (Lomnitz 2001b: 319). The lead architect of this corporatist style government—the still-popular progressive President Lázaro Cárdenas (who held office from 1934 to 1940)—believed corporatism would lead to the realization of the rights established in the 1917 Constitution (Rus 1994). However, it ended up enabling a "more intimate form of domination" (Rus 1994: 267), as less progressive presidents used it to incorporate potential polit-ical opposition into the state, limiting, for example, the extent to which labor unions could advocate for workers' rights.

Corporatist governance played a key role in solidifying the control of the Partido Institucional Revolucionario (PRI: Institutional Revolu-tionary Party), which was formed in 1929 and held control of most of Mexico's political offices, including the presidency, until the late twen-tieth century (Gilbreth and Otero 2001). The PRI style of governance called people to national belonging by becoming "massified citizens," connected to the nation-state through exchanges with the state institu-tions that putatively represented their sector of society (Lomnitz 2001b: 321–322). The forms of interpellation rendered by corporatist gover-nance make someone a subject of the state not by virtue of inalienable, individual personhood—as per the classical liberal concept of citizen-ship—but by virtue of having a role in a preexisting corporate organism of interdependent but unequal parts (Lomnitz 2001b; cf. Dick 2010b; Rouse 1995). Therefore people are called to be Mexican through a pro-cess of learning to realize membership in corporate groups determined by state institutions. These institutions seek to reign in political oppo-sition in ways that tend to reproduce the questionable character of mar-ginalized people and, as a result, their exclusion from full membership in the polity. The PRI style of co-opting political opposition through massified belonging is traceable in a new role that working-class peo-ple were to play in Mexico's political economic advancement during the postrevolutionary period, as illustrated in discourse about a common working-class figure: *el pelado.*

El Pelado: The Working-Class in
Postrevolutionary Imaginaries of Moral Mobility

As discussed above, Porfirian imaginaries of moral mobility placed *las clases populares* (the nonelite masses) along a continuum from good to bad, where the greatest virtue was a willingness to accept the moral tutelage of elites. Within this continuum, the figure of *el pelado* was one of the most lambasted incarnations of the masses, "beyond the pale of citizenship" (Lomnitz 2001b: 318). But after the Revolution public intellectuals made *el pelado*, and the broader "urban rabble" that he represented, into the quintessential Mexican (Lomnitz 2001b: 318). This transformation was an expression of the same spirit that inspired Vasconcelos to elevate the once-derided mestizo as an icon of *lo mexicano*. To be sure, the two are interrelated, as *el pelado* is generally envisioned as mestizo.

The inclusion of this once-reviled working-class persona at the heart of discussions of national belonging was consonant with the postrevolutionary state's expansive nation-building project, one key feature of which was the codification of workers' rights in the 1917 Constitution (Lomnitz 2001b: 318–319). *El pelado* is an image of Mexicanidad popular in working-class Uriangato. I saw more than one vehicle adorned with a widespread depiction of *el pelado* as a man of beefcake proportions, standing in an aggressive posture on top of the words: *¿Qué me vez?* (What are you looking at?). But this figure also reincarnates the double-bind of belonging for working-class people. This point is made clear through a consideration of the work of the central postrevolutionary champion of *el pelado*, Samuel Ramos: another thinker whose discourse continues to influence imaginaries of moral mobility.

In his 1934 work *El perfil del hombre y la cultura en México* (The Profile of Man and Culture in Mexico), Ramos crystallized elite understandings of *el pelado* as an emblem of the Mexican national character (Schmidt 1976: 179). He argues that this character is marked by a collective "inferiority complex" exemplified, as adumbrated above, in the attitude of *el pelado*, who is "so wounded by the other's gaze that he replies [to it] aggressively with the challenge of *¿Qué me vez?/*"What are you looking at?" (Lomnitz 2001b: 318). Ramos celebrated this figure because it embodied a desired quality that nation builders also found in Mexican Catholic practices: an unflappability and playfulness in the face of struggle (cf. Lomnitz 2008; Mendoza-Denton 2008: chapter 4). But he also rendered *el pelado* as an icon of Mexico's struggle (and failure) to modernize, depicting him as having moved from a past spent in

Mexico's countryside to work in its industrial centers. *El pelado*'s aggression was interpreted as a manifestation of Mexico's enduring insecurity and "backwardness," despite efforts to progress (Bartra 1992; Lester 2005: 288). So Ramos held up *el pelado* as yet another sign of the country's need to endure a period of development before it could fully extend national belonging to all its members.

In creating this portrait of the so-called Mexican national character, Ramos engaged in the production of what Michael Herzfeld's ethnography of nationalism in Greece (1997) describes as *cultural intimacy*. Herzfeld uses this term to refer to co-citizens' recognition of aspects of a national imaginary "considered a source of embarrassment but that nevertheless provide insiders with their assurance of a common sociality" (1997:3). As he shows, the embodiment of these forms of cultural intimacy enables disenfranchised groups to think they are rebelling, while simultaneously assuring the effectiveness of their marginalization (cf. Willis 1981). *El pelado* is just such a figure—working-class people take him up as an irreverent emblem, even as performances of this brand of Mexicanidad ensure that they will be placed outside full belonging. This point is underscored by the fact that Mexican elites cultivated the figure of *el pelado* in dialogue with images of Mexican life in the United States (Bartra 1992). The persona of the volatile Mexican "macho man"—a regular feature of US popular culture by the early twentieth century (Gutmann 2007)—has much in common with the image of the easily offended *pelado*. They are two equally denigrating personae that help justify the Othering of working-class people, particularly men. Indeed, as is suggested by my use of the masculine pronoun throughout this discussion, the celebration of *el pelado* promoted an expressly masculine image of national belonging in Mexico, which further marginalized women even as it only partially included working-class men (Lester 2005: 290).

As noted above in the discussion of *mestizaje*, interdiscursivity with US imaginaries is a regular feature of state-endorsed discourses of national belonging in Mexico, which endeavor to resist US imperialism while also placing a once-marginalized cultural persona in the pantheon of national icons. But, as revealed in the discussion of Mexican religious nationalism, this process is not about granting full recognition of the rights of marginalized people. Ramos did not consider *el pelado* the ideal citizen—to him, the model citizen was exemplified by elites, as it had been during the Porfiriato. Rather, the life of *el pelado* was indicative of the position of Mexico vis-à-vis other countries, especially the United

States. So the "typical Mexican working-class person" was construed as both the essence of Mexico's struggle and off-center from Mexico's ideal future as a fully modernized country (Lomnitz 2001b: 319). The strategy of producing such images of personhood supported state co-optation over "problematic" populations, a method of governing that coalesced during the late 1930s and early 1940s, when Ramos was at the height of his influence (Bartra 1992). This strategy is observable, as well, in the migration discourse of the postrevolutionary period, as I show through an examination of the new mandate that migrants to the United States were given in fostering Mexico's development after the Revolution.

Migrant Repatriation and Postrevolutionary Moral Mobility

For much of the twentieth century state-endorsed imaginaries of moral mobility posited US-bound migrants as threatening to the Mexican state and specifically to the PRI political order. Migration to the United States limited the Mexican government's ability to manage its labor markets and thus its economic growth (Fitzgerald 2009: 39, 50–53). Moreover, migration exposed the limits of Mexican nation-state building and sovereignty (Schmidt Camacho 2008: 72; Walsh 2004: 122–123). For example, after the Revolution, it was Mexican federal policy to restrict emigration to the United States. Yet between 1917 and the 1940s both Mexican municipal officials and US employers and lawmakers routinely ignored Mexico's federal emigration laws, creating a material and political economic infrastructure that encouraged migration (Fitzgerald 2009: 39–46). Moreover, the transnational networks migrants subsequently built were a potential source of egalitarian imaginaries that could challenge the variegation of Mexican national belonging (Lomnitz 2009; Schmidt Camacho 2008). Writers and activists who lived in the Mexico-US cross-border region have long spotlighted the exploitation of laborers on both sides of the border, criticizing the United States and Mexican governments' complicity in creating socioeconomic inequality within Mexico and between Mexico and the United States (Schmidt Camacho 2008: 96). Such transnational imaginaries, however, were not adopted by state institutions in Mexico, which continued to forward a politics of dependency, positing an absolute divide between Mexico and the United States and placing Mexico in a subordinate position (Lomnitz 2009).

Federal officials sought to co-opt migrants to the cause of state consolidation and economic growth by crafting an imaginary of moral mobility that blamed migration on migrants. Rather than turning attention to the needs of migrants or to the political economic forces that encourage migration, federal officials posited migration as a manifestation of the inferiority of the Mexican national character. They represented the humiliations of emigrants (low wages, abysmal working conditions, and racial discrimination) as "humiliations not only of individuals, but of Mexico herself" (Fitzgerald 2009: 40). Thus elites construed emigration as a moral failing, signified by the migrants' weakness for "the siren call of the dollar" (Schmidt Camacho 2008: 74; see also Fitzgerald 2009: 47; Ngai 2004). This depiction of the immorality of migrants persisted into the mid to late twentieth century (Yeh 2012). Consider debates over the Bracero Accord, a bi-national agreement that allowed US employers to recruit Mexican labor to work at US farms and factories between 1942 and 1964 (Ngai 2004: chapter 4). Many Mexican senators argued against the accord because they saw migration as an expression of the Mexican people's character as *un pueblo andariego* (a wandering nation), who disregarded the authority of the state with their sojourns in "distant lands" (Schmidt Camacho 2008: 72). So migration should be curbed, not kindled.

Although opponents of the Bracero Accord lost the policy debate, such discourse nevertheless helped reproduce a national imaginary that construed the United States as utterly foreign. While this depiction was born from the anti-imperialist spirit of the Revolution, it also erased the long histories of migration and political economic relations between Mexico and the United States, converting migration into a matter of individual character. As part of this, elites depicted migration as anathema to Mexican national belonging—as a process that leads, in the words of Mexican president Plutarco Elías Calles (1924–1928), to *desmexicanización* (de-Mexicanization) (Fitzgerald 2009: 190, n. 5; González Navarro 1994: 253). Framings of migration as de-Mexicanizing built on the state-endorsed imaginaries of moral mobility, which articulated *lo mexicano* through contrasts with images of the United States and its people as irreligious and immoral. Therefore the northward movements of Mexicans were posited as potentially morally threatening, a viewpoint that was furthered by the Catholic church's discourse on Mexico-US migration in the first half of the twentieth century (Fitzgerald 2009: chapter 3) and is robustly reproduced by working-class Uriangatenses, as I discuss in later chapters.

At the same time, the federal government endeavored to mitigate against the supposed threat that migrants presented to the state by integrating returnees into economic development projects. Such integration would allow migrants to be co-opted as citizen laborers (Dick 2010a; Walsh 2004). This policy approach and its associated imaginary of moral mobility took on its clearest form during the "repatriation" of hundreds of thousands of Mexican nationals, and Mexican Americans, who had been deported by the US government during the Great Depression (Balderrama and Rodríguez 1995; Dick 2011b; Ngai 2004: chapter 4; Walsh 2008: chapter 7). Mexican policy makers and institutions were overwhelmed by the influx of nearly a half a million people and perceived their sudden arrival as a threat to social and political order (Fitzgerald 2009: 47).

Discussions among political elites over how the Mexican government should manage *los repatriados* (the repatriated) often involved assertions that the nation's progress depended on turning returnees into "property-owning, politically stable, middle-class small farmers and that it was the state's responsibility to oversee this process" (Walsh 2004: 124). Consequently, political elites focused on the problem of creating programs that would ensure this goal of simultaneously capitalizing on the economic potential of returnees while restricting their political engagements in Mexico. Indeed, in 1932 the National Repatriation Committee distributed posters to municipal governments urging the public to help support the process of migrant reincorporation into "the bosom of the motherland" in order to stave off potential resistance to the political status quo (Fitzgerald 2009: 47).

The central scholar and policy maker who shaped debates about *los repatriados* was Manuel Gamio (1883–1960). A student of Franz Boas, Gamio is widely recognized as the father of Mexican anthropology (e.g., Gamio 1924; see also León-Portilla 1962: 356). His scholarship addressed not only Mexico-US migration (e.g., Gamio 1930, 1931), but the dynamics of Mexico's development more generally (Gamio 1922, 1987). Gamio, like his contemporary and co-author José Vasconcelos (e.g., Vasconcelos and Gamio 1926), was a complex figure who sought to empower Mexico in the face of US racism and imperialism while also helping institutionalize an imaginary of moral mobility that variegated national belonging in Mexico (Walsh 2004: 127). Gamio authored key works of mestizo nationalism on a par with *The Cosmic Race*, most notably his 1916 work *Forjando patria* (Forging the Nation) (Gamio 1964).[5] But in contrast to the views of many postrevolutionary elites, Gamio advocated for migrants, raising awareness about the abuses they suffered in the United States (Schmidt Camacho 2008: 22-23, 73). He asserted that Mexican policy makers should envision a place for returnees (Walsh 2004: 134),[6] arguing that *los repatriados* could act as a progressive influence that would modernize the country by importing modernist ideals from the United States (innovation, individuality, discipline, and rational industrial production), thus eroding Mexico's backward traditionalism (Gamio 1931; see also Dick 2010a; Gonzalez 2004; Kearney 1986; Walsh 2004).

This is another idea that persisted through the Bracero Accord era, which further institutionalized the federal government's positioning of returnees as potential agents of modernization. The offices that managed *los braceros* called on them to prove allegiance to the motherland by using their knowledge of US industry to facilitate the moral development of poor and working-class Mexicans (Schmidt Camacho 2008: 63). To be sure, Gamio's argument that *los repatriados* make superior workers influenced mid-twentieth century economic policy. Returnees were recruited by the Mexican government to work on key development projects in the 1930s and 1940s, such as the federally funded Valle Bajo Río Bravo agricultural project, which created industrial cotton farming in the northern part of the country (Walsh 2008: chapters 7–8).

Gamio's work on migration and development coincided with President Cárdenas's creation of a corporatist style of government, discussed above. Cárdenas supported Gamio's vision, creating programs that he hope would realize this vision in practice. He crafted a six-year relocation plan for *los repatriados* that would have established returnee communities in sparsely populated northern Mexican states (Fitzgerald 2009: 46). In theory, the incorporation of returnees into both farming and industry would bring them into the fold of the state apparatus, as they would become members of the official "corporate" sectors of the agricultural and workers' unions. In reality, however, neither the federal nor municipal governments had the capacity to manage the returnee population overall (Fitzgerald 2009: 48).

By the beginning of World War II Mexico's elites were still faced with a large number of unemployed working-age males, whom they saw as a threat to sociopolitical stability. As a result, while state-endorsed imaginaries continued to posit migration as morally corrupting, traitorous, and de-Mexicanizing through much of the twentieth century, the federal government increasingly used migration as a release valve to manage people who might otherwise be unemployed and stir political unrest at home (Fitzgerald 2009: 48ff.; Ngai 2004: chapter 4). As such, state-endorsed migration discourse in Mexico produced a politics of contradiction, in which it encouraged US migration while rendering it a sign of moral corruption and individual responsibility—a pattern found in US immigration policy as well (Chávez 2015, 2017b; Coutin 2005; De Genova 2005; Dick 2011b; Durand and Massey 2003; Ngai 2004).

As these examples of postrevolutionary discourse (about *mestizaje, el pelado,* and migration) make clear, the types of Mexicans that working-class people and migrants were called to be during this period of Mexican nation building took shape through a genealogical interdiscursivity with Porfirian imaginaries of moral mobility—and with US discourse about Mexicans. Postrevolutionary imaginaries overtly rejected some of the main tenets of Porfirian imaginaries. The elevation of *lo mexicano* during the postrevolutionary period was resonant because it repudiated the influence of the United States and critiqued the Porfirian idea that foreign intervention could facilitate Mexico's development. Yet these imaginaries also created strong points of ideological resemblance with Porfirian imaginaries.

The "celebration" of *lo mexicano* took shape in express contrast with images of life in the United States, so that "being Mexican" is about what the United States is or is not. The creation of this absolute difference between Mexico and the United States helped negate egalitarian, transnational imaginaries and legitimate the variegation of belonging in Mexico by construing migrants as morally flawed. Even as Mexican citizenship expanded during the twentieth century, interpellation into national belonging continued to be shaped by the idea—central to Porfirian imaginaries—that members of marginalized groups must develop socioeconomically and ethico-morally before they can fully belong and enjoy the fruits of progress. This replicates the temporal framing of Porfirian imaginaries, placing the moment when Mexico can actualize unmitigated national belonging and full sovereignty in the distant future. Moreover, the terms of moral and economic development continued to be construed through distinctions between tradition and modernity—except that now the goal was to integrate the two, not replace one with the other. This framing racialized Mexicanidad as the property of mestizos/as and worked to put them in opposition to Mexicans of Indigenous or Afro-Mexican descent.

The cumulative effect of these genealogical links was to generate a double-bind of interpellation into national belonging wherein marginalized groups had to demonstrate that they were endeavoring to progress while at the same time ensuring that they acted as the main preservers of Mexican traditions. This double-bind enabled a regime of belonging in which people's inability to progress or maintain their traditionalism was a sign not of the failures of nation-building but of people's individual failings—and hence yet more evidence that they were not ready for full belonging. Therefore the elite discourse that crafted state-endorsed imaginaries of moral mobility during the postrevolutionary period, such as the writings, murals, and archeological exhibits created by Mexico's great intellectuals of the era, served a dual interpellative purpose.

On the one hand, these forms themselves probably did not directly reach their objects of representation in any immediate way; most migrants, for example, probably had not read Gamio's influential works in Mexico–US migration. So it is unlikely that they directly called marginalized groups to recognize themselves in these representations. Rather, they hailed middle- and upper-class urbanites as certain kinds of Mexicans who could recognize the importance of Mexico's "traditions" and "traditional people" and "celebrate" them in ways that carefully controlled the access that those people had to state resources. On the other hand, postrevolutionary imaginaries were also codified in state policy toward the church, working-class people, migrants, and other "massified citizens," whose implementation called these groups to belong to the nation in certain ways. These policies—and their interdiscursive connections with earlier national imaginings—created a national milieu in which the questionable morality of marginalized groups became naturalized, a hegemonic starting point for Mexicanidad. As the rest of this book shows, even as Uriangatenses seek to critique and transform the ways they are interpellated by state-endorsed imaginaries, they end up replicating many of their terms.

At the same time, however, across the period explored thus far, the possibilities of national belonging have changed. The codification of workers' rights in the 1917 Constitution, for example, creates a basis for laying claim to rights and resources (cf. Gilbreth and Otero 2001; Lomnitz 2009) and therefore opens up the possibility of change, though in ways that always rely on establishing genealogical linkages with the past. I explore this point below through a consideration of the late twentieth century neoliberal period in Mexico, which most immediately informs the lives and imaginings of the working-class Uriangatenses with whom I conducted my fieldwork. During this period, there were important changes in Mexico's political establishment, in its economic policies, and in its relationship with migrants in the United States. Yet neoliberal imaginaries of moral mobility also have robust genealogical resemblances to both the Porfirian and postrevolutionary imaginaries. These interdiscursive links combine earlier terms of national belonging in ways that expand participation in the state, while further restricting access to belonging and its resources.

Migrant Heroes, State-Led Transnationalism, and the Moral Mobility of Co-responsibility

In 1993 second-time Mexican presidential candidate Cuauhtémoc Cárdenas, son of former president Lázaro Cárdenas and leader of the leftist opposition Partido de la Revolución Democrática (PRD: Party of the Democratic Revolution), visited Mexican workers in Chester County, Pennsylvania. He was there to support the workers' recent strike protesting low pay and poor living and working conditions in the local mushroom industry (Franklin 1993). The strike and the workers' potential unionization signaled the beginning of a period of change for Mexicans in southern Pennsylvania. Coinciding with the regularization of many migrants' legal status in the United States, largely due to the 1986 Immigration Reform and Control Act, in the last decade of the twentieth century migrants actively sought ways to be more fully incorporated as legitimate participants in local civil and political life (Garcia 2008; Lattanzi Shutika 2011: chapter 5). This period also witnessed the increased migration of families into the region and an uptick of settlement-oriented migration, which helped make Mexican migrants seem more sympathetic to non-Mexican residents and spurred an increase in services for migrants and their children. But this period of transformation was not only about life in southern Pennsylvania. It was also a time when the image of migrants and their place in the Mexican national polity was changing, signaled by Cárdenas's visit to his compatriots, as they fought for their rights in this sleepy agricultural region.

Cárdenas's 1993 visit was part of a campaign strategy that he initiated during his 1988 bid for the Mexican presidency. In order to distinguish himself from the PRI's long-term positioning of migrants in the North as traitorous, he embraced Mexican communities in the United States, developing a distinctly transnational vision of Mexican belonging that welcomed people living in the United States into the national fold (Fitzgerald 2009: 56–57; Goldring 2002: 56). On posters printed in the PRD's Los Angeles offices for Cárdenas's 2000 presidential bid, for example, his visage appears before an image of the United States and Mexico without a border separating them. The words emblazoned above the image demand: *"Amnistía para la gente; voto de los Mexicanos en el extranjero; Diputados y Senadores mexicanos electos en el exterior*/[US] Amnesty for unauthorized migrants; absentee voting rights and congressional representation for Mexicans abroad" (Fitzgerald 2009: 57).

Although Cárdenas's bids for the Mexican presidency were never successful, his campaigning in the United States helped legitimize migrant influence over Mexican politics. During the late twentieth century, migrants in the United States formed transnational organizations that raised funds for candidates who opposed the PRI, such as Cárdenas, empowering opposition candidates to gain traction in their fight against the establishment (Goldring 2002). Non-PRI candidates made unprecedented electoral gains, first winning municipal and state races, followed by victories in races for positions in the federal government. This trend reached its denouement in 2000, when Vicente Fox of the Partido Acción Nacional (PAN: National Action Party) became the first non-PRI president in seventy-one years. Along with these electoral changes came a transformation in Mexican state-endorsed migration discourse. In sharp contrast to earlier rhetoric, President Fox famously called migrants the country's national "heroes," heralding a new era of relations between the Mexican government and its citizens abroad (Durand 2004). Embracing Mexicans in the United States into the national fold—what Luin Goldring (2002: 56–57) calls "state-led transnationalism," which she contrasts with the preexisting "migrant-led transnationalism"—became de rigueur for all politicians in the late twentieth century.[7]

In response to the opposition parties' embrace of migrants as sources of political power, the PRI began to adopt a more inclusive approach to migrants (Goldring 2002; Smith 2006: chapter 4). Prior to Fox's victory, PRI politicians created programs to protect the rights of Mexicans in the United States and to ensure their safe passage home, such as the Programa Paisano (Compatriot Program), which seeks to curb abuses against returnees by Mexican officials (Fitzgerald 2009: 58; Goldring 2002: 66). There was also an increase in the citizen rights of migrants, who now have access to the absentee ballot and dual nationality. Moreover, Fox and his successors—including subsequent PRI presidents—have engaged in efforts to protect undocumented Mexican migrants, arguing before the US Congress and in meetings with US presidents that the United States should create ways for Mexican citizens to migrate legally (Fitzgerald 2009: 60–63). At home, presidential administrations have commissioned public service campaigns that seek to educate the public about the dangers of crossing the Mexico-US border illegally. Yet, not unlike the postrevolutionary "celebration" of *lo mexicano*, the reframing of migrants as heroes has continued to constrain the national belonging of migrants in ways that replicate imaginaries of moral mobility from previous eras.

There was, for instance, substantial decades-long resistance on the part of many federal politicians to establishing the absentee ballot, which was not implemented until 2005, as they continued to see migrants as a political threat. Moreover, policies produced under the auspices of state-led transnationalism continued to advance the idea that migrants represent a political threat that needs to be co-opted to the state through incorporation into national development schemes (Lopez 2015: 71-96). Consider that dual nationality—the other major political gain of the era of state-led transnationalism, along with the absentee ballot—grants the right to own property in Mexico but not full political rights (Goldring 2002: 69). As in policies toward *los repatriados*, the focus on giving those with dual nationality property rights but not political rights aims to harness migrants' potential to foster economic development in Mexico while controlling their political influence. Moreover, state-led transnationalism carries on the "asymmetric interdependency" in Mexico-US relations when it comes to immigration issues (Keohane and Nye 1987).

Since the Fox administration (2000–2006), Mexican presidents have been unsuccessful in convincing the United States to reform its immigration policy so that it better protects Mexicans working in the United States. Moreover, since the 1990s Mexico has supported the US approach of "cracking down" on unauthorized migration, developing its own border patrol and adopting militaristic policies toward migration (Abrego 2014; Delgado-Wise 2004). But state-led transnationalism did not merely repeat the variegation of belonging and international asymmetry from previous eras. It was part of a wider effort to use already established ideas about Mexicanidad to justify another major transformation in Mexico's relations with the United States: the implementation of neoliberal political and economic reforms. This transformation (re)created the variegation of national belonging in ways that affected all marginalized groups in Mexico.

Neoliberalism is a philosophy of political and economic life, which posits that "human well-being" can be expanded through (among other things) the decrease of state regulation of economic production, the opening up of national markets to international trade, and the increased role of private industry in all sectors of society (Harvey 2006: 145). Neoliberal policies first entered Mexico by imposition after the 1982 sovereign debt crisis that led Mexico to default on its loans from the International Monetary Fund (IMF). This crisis threatened to spread across the entire region, potentially damaging a global economy that had only recently pulled out of a prolonged recession (Ffrench-Davis 2005; Pastor 1989). In response, head economists at the IMF, World Bank, and US Treasury posited that the Latin American debt crisis had been brought on by the protectionist economic policies of the mid-twentieth century and thus made the bail-out loans it gave Mexico and other countries in the region contingent on the adoption of neoliberal policies (Harvey 2006).

Shortly thereafter, Latin American politicians and policymakers actively embraced neoliberal principles, as evinced in Mexico's aggressive pursuit of inclusion in the North American Free Trade Agreement (NAFTA) (Phillips 1997).[8] In taking up neoliberalism, state actors had to persuade citizens that this policy regime would be fruitful for Mexico. Because neoliberalism was first imposed on Mexico by the authors of the Washington Consensus—which in Mexico is largely understood to be a product of US political economic interests—and because it undid the previous era of development that had been expressly anti-US, people were concerned that this new policy approach was just another form of US economic imperialism (O'Toole 2003). In making the case for neoliberalism, Mexican government officials crafted an imaginary of moral mobility that involved the creative combination of Porfirian liberalism with the new nationalism of the postrevolutionary period, producing genealogical links that both replicated and transformed the terms of national belonging in Mexico.

The adoption of neoliberalism in Mexico involved the transformation of state-citizen relations and, specifically, the promotion of a form of participatory citizenship, which entailed moralizing imaginaries of citizen responsibility that promoted the reduction of state welfare programs (O'Toole 2003). This process has unfolded as part of neoliberal reforms across the globe, though its expression is distinct in each locale (cf. Muehlebach 2012; Paley 2001; Phillips 1997; Wacquant 2009). In the United States, for example, the dramatic reduction of welfare programs in the mid-1990s relied both on the circulation of images of welfare recipients as immoral and semicriminal and on the marketing of neoliberalism's core ideals of individuality and choice. These fed elegantly into US national imaginaries of "American freedom"—so that in the United States "participatory citizenship" came to mean being free of government assistance in order to be empowered to take care of yourself (cf. Carr 2011: chapter 1; Harvey 2006; Muehlebach 2012; Wacquant 2009).

Participatory citizenship came to mean something quite different in Mexican neoliberalism, however. This was in part because its US version could not work in an imaginative context where the individualism of life in the United States had long been lambasted as itself immoral. Indeed, images of the United States as immoral persisted into this period, especially in media coverage of migration (see chapter 2). Rather than taking up the terms of co-responsibility as they developed in the United States, Mexican political discourse argued that free-market capitalism allowed Mexicans to be more fully Mexican by facilitating increases in their social obligations to the state (O'Toole 2003: 271). In public discourse, such as policy statements circulated to newspapers and speeches to voters, state actors argued that the citizen participation enacted through neoliberal programs animated "ancient cultural" forms of Mexican sociality and collectivity (Rojas Gutiérrez 1992: 9), which value the delay of personal reward in favor of the fulfillment of a commitment to others (Goldring 2002: 69; O'Toole 2003: 279, 284). This promotion of distinctly Mexican forms of national belonging, now coded as neoliberal co-responsibility, harkened back to the new nationalism of the postrevolutionary period, with its search for *lo mexicano*. But it also interdiscursively pointed back to Porfirian discourses, which had argued that Mexico needed a period of patronage from the outside to right its political economic development. The integration of the Mexican and US economies as part of NAFTA was represented in presidential rhetoric as a form of interdependence, during which the brief incursion of the United States' greater economic strength would bolster the competitiveness of Mexican markets (O'Toole 2003: 282–284).

Visions of Mexican co-responsibility have been articulated through a new, often state-funded, infrastructure of public intellectualism (debate programs on television, political magazines, etc.) that emerged in the late twentieth century (Escalante 2006: 268) and, like the public intellectualism of the postrevolutionary era, helped promote imaginaries of moral mobility. While working-class Uriangatenses have access to the products of this infrastructure, neoliberal imaginaries of moral mobility have been conveyed and enacted most potently—again as in previous eras—through development programs, both those that have sought to incorporate migrants as massified citizens and those aimed at poverty reduction, which are often interrelated. Take, for example, the development initiative "Tres por Uno" (Three for One), a government matching program that encourages migrants to invest remittances (the money they have earned abroad) in Mexican businesses and public works projects, from repairing churches to improving infrastructure: paving roads, installing better water systems, and so forth (Lopez 2015: 71-96; Smith 2006: 55–58). This program, expanded by President Fox from the original "Dos por Uno" established in the early 1990s, matches every dollar raised by a migrant organization with three dollars, one dollar from Mexico's federal government and one dollar each from the organization's home state and municipal government (Fitzgerald 2009: 59; Goldring 2002: 66–68).

By the late twentieth century the remittances sent to Mexico from migrants working in the United States totaled billions of US dollars per year. By 2005 they reached 20 billion dollars, becoming the second largest source of foreign income in Mexico after oil sales (Fitzgerald 2009: 63). Politicians hoped to harness remittances to development not only to improve the economy but also to "construct transmigrants . . . as one more in a series of corporate groups that the Mexican state could co-opt" (Goldring 2002: 68; see also Guarnizo 1998)—that is, to incorporate migrants into the massified citizenship of the neoliberal era. Indeed "Dos por Uno" was part of President Carlos Salinas de Gortari's effort to promote citizen co-responsibility by encouraging their financial investment in the country's improvement (Goldring 2002: 66)—a stance that is replicated in Mexico's poverty alleviation programs, which were created in close dialogue with remittance-based development policies. To be sure, "Dos por Uno" was a sister program to Salinas's central antipoverty initiative.

Co-responsibility and Poverty Alleviation Programs

El desarrollo social es el proceso permanente mediante el cual se amplían las capacidades y las opciones de las personas y comunidades para que puedan ejercer plenamente sus libertades y derechos.
[Social development is the permanent process through which the capacities and opportunities of people and communities are expanded, so that they can fully exercise their freedoms and rights.][9]

This quotation is from a 2002 World Bank report by Josefina Vázquez Mota, then secretary of the Secretariat of Health, which oversees Mexico's key poverty alleviation efforts. Vázquez Mota underscores a central way economic development informs the variegation of national belonging for poor and working-class people: progress is an elusive and endless process of moving toward greater "capacities." That is, those who are not already wealthy, educated, propertied, and so forth will never be finished developing, and therefore will always be outside the bounds of belonging (see also chapter 3). As with remittance-based development in the neoliberal era, poverty alleviation programs inculcated this notion by interpellating citizens to forms of co-responsibility with the state.

Consider Mexico's contemporary flagship development program PROGRESA-Opportunidades. The acronym combines the first five letters of the word *programa* (program) with the letters "e.s.a.," which stand for *educación, salud y alimentación* (education, health, and nutrition), producing the abbreviation PROGRESA. PROGRESA is a double entendre: it means "*México progresa* (Mexico progresses)," while also serving as the informal command form of the verb *progresar* (to progress), thus ordering that fellow citizens (addressed in the familiar second person) progress. This program is advertised throughout Mexico via billboards, commercials, and other promotional materials, helping create a habitus that favors citizens' enactment of "progress" over all other forms of engagement with the nation (cf. Dick 2010a; Messing 2002, 2007). But it not only reiterates the enduring idea that Mexico is behind and in need of catching up; it articulates this notion with the moral imperatives of neoliberal co-responsibility (Teichman 2009). This point is evinced in President Fox's addition of the word "opportunities" to the end of the program's name; this addition underscores the idea that Mexican progress depends on citizens recognizing and taking advantage of co-responsibility (cf. Paley 2001).

Moreover, such neoliberal imaginaries of moral mobility continued to portray development programs as enabling Mexico's poor and working-class people to improve morally as well as economically, leading to the moment when full belonging is put off again to the future. For example, the eligibility requirements for PROGRESA-Oportunidades position participants as morally unstable characters who need guidance from the state, by requiring them to complete regular visits to health clinics, where they must also partake in workshops that teach them "proper nutrition and sanitation" (Molyneux 2006: 428–429). Such frameworks are part of a history of national belonging in Mexico in which the state has never been able to extend the rights of citizenship to the entire polity. Therefore ability to lay claim to those rights is competitive—shaped by the ability successfully to enact morality to the state bureaucrats who distribute the resources associated with those rights (Lomnitz 2001a: 299, 321; Stack 2012a). To be sure, the ideals and practices of a certain kind of Mexican Catholic womanhood have been central in delineating co-participation, helping create gendered forms of citizenship that associate women with the moral failures of poverty while also making women's desires subordinate to those of their families and the country (see chapter 5).

This chapter delineates the central features of state-endorsed imaginaries of moral mobility as they have been reformulated during key moments of political economic transformation in Mexico. In detailing the genealogical links between state-endorsed imaginaries produced at these moments, this chapter shows that imaginaries take on form and consequence in dialogue with one other. Those who produce state-endorsed imaginaries have had to reckon with the ideological and symbolic features of prior imaginaries. The putative elevation of Mexican "traditions" in the postrevolutionary period took hold because it was a critical comment on the denigration of these traditions during the Porfiriato, just as the return to nineteenth-century liberalism in the late twentieth century had to take this postrevolutionary history into account to seem "authentically Mexican" and not just an imperialist imposition from the North. A core element of the imaginaries discussed has been the ways they repeatedly variegated the national belonging of working-class people, migrants, and other marginal groups in Mexico. This variegation calls people to be and see themselves as certain members of the polity, not as a direct process of call and response, in which people are hailed to be Mexican along a linear chain of speech. Rather, the production of imaginaries weaves an interdiscursive web: over time similar framings of belonging—and exclusion—are replicated across diverse contexts, from museum walls to poverty alleviation protocols. This creates a social milieu in which some ways of being Mexican are normalized and others are not. It would be difficult, for example, after over 100 years of Mexico and the United States being rendered as foils, to pry Mexicanidad away from "not being gringo" and successfully argue for the cross-border similarity that activists in the late nineteenth and early twentieth centuries argued could be a basis of national imaginaries.

A thorough unpacking of the interdiscursive web that connects the imaginaries explored in this chapter to those that take up the remainder of this book is outside the scope of this project. However, the robust similarities in propositional content and chronotopic framing between state-endorsed imaginaries and Uriangatense imaginaries that I explore in later chapters suggest their interconnection. I also point to some direct links, such as working-class Uriangatenses' interaction with Mexico's welfare state, in which the enduring propositions of state-endorsed imaginaries of moral mobility help order interactions between state actors and citizens. These propositions—that Mexico is behind and in need of catching up; that Mexico deserves its asymmetrical interdependence with the United States; that Mexico will not progress until after a period of moral development by its "underdeveloped" members—create a series of double-binds for migrants and working-class people. These double-binds generate a labyrinth of national belonging (with a nod to Octavio Paz 1994), in which marginalized people are damned if they do and damned if they don't. As I show in chapters 3–5, migration discourse is a central way working-class Uriangatenses seek to find an exit from this labyrinth (Lomnitz-Adler 1992), a way to assert their rightful belonging in Mexico by critiquing the failures of progress and envisioning a new form of national collectivity.

As noted above, the late twentieth century witnessed an expansion of democratic processes and citizen rights in Mexico. This coincided with increased numbers of people organizing to critique the PRI establishment and its forms of massified citizenship, urging Mexico to realize the promise of the 1910 Revolution and extend the rights of full belonging to all citizens (Gilbreth and Otero 2001). At the same time, however, the rise of neoliberalism has been accompanied by an increasing number of people, including working-class Uriangatenses, who are unprotected by the Mexican state and who occupy unstable positions in the labor and housing markets (see chapter 3). This suggests that the variegation of national belonging has been intensified by late capitalism (Lomnitz 2001a: 324–326). This point is indicated by Mexico's inability to protect the rights of its citizens in the United States while at the same time increasingly adopting the US approach of securitizing the flow of people across national borders (Abrego 2014). This approach exposes not only Mexican migrants but also migrants from Central America to atrocious human rights violations as they travel from home to their migration destinations (Delgado-Wise 2004; Durand and Massey 2003). As later chapters show, in endeavoring to navigate the variegation of national belonging in the contemporary period, working-class Uriangatenses respond to the lineage of state-endorsed imaginaries outlined in this chapter. Before turning attention to this process, however, I consider how I navigated a sociopolitical landscape in which being from the United States is a politically and ethico-morally loaded social positioning.

CHAPTER 2

Private Eyes, Good Girls: Authoritative Accounts and the Social Life of Interviewing

Tentative, I step out of the house where I will live for the next year onto Calle Emiliano Zapata (Emiliano Zapata Street).[1] Here there are no yards or porches: leaving a house puts you immediately onto the street and into the bright lights of neighbors' observations. My heart races on my short walk to the small convenience store run by Doña Susan where I plan to buy a jug of water. Each time I leave the house, private eyes are watching, peering from behind curtains and partially opened doors. I never catch this watching myself. I learn of it through after-the-fact reports of my comings and goings: you were out early this morning; my niece told me you were walking to the town center yesterday; I saw you buying fruit at the market just now. At first these reports seem peculiar to me—why would someone see me and not say "hello," only to tell me later that she had seen me? In time I come to understand that such reports are meant to communicate both interest and warning—our eyes are on you and we are wondering: are you a "good girl"? Having already spent a year doing ethnographic research with relations of many of the residents here, I know gringas do not have the best reputations in Mexico. We are known to be sexually promiscuous and unconcerned about the cultivation of family life. Images of US female immorality are widely distributed in Mexico. They even make it onto the news during the annual spring-break migration of US college students, when the nightly news reports on the activities of gringas "gone wild" in Cancún and other tourist destinations.

Knowing about these images, I am anxious not to misstep. I endeavor to steer people's readings of me into positive territory by being my own kind of private eye—using the knowledge I have of my neighbors, gathered from friends and research participants in Pennsylvania. I first learned of Doña Susan when a relative of one of her neighbors returned to Pennsylvania after a visit to Uriangato: she is a green-eyed, redheaded flirt who wears heavy makeup and heart-shaped sunglasses. She adores the Golden Age of 1940s Mexican cinema and can often be heard loudly singing the popular music of that era. In time I start calling her simply "La Doña," the nickname of the great Golden Age actress María Félix. I also know Doña Susan's neighbors decry her as *muy chismosa* (an incorrigible gossip)—so much so that a sister-in-law of the family I lived with in Uriangato tells her children that Doña Susan runs a kidnapping ring so they won't go to her shop and inadvertently share family secrets. Before I leave the house that first morning, I am exhorted by my host family not to let La Doña pull any information out of me. I choose to buy water from her, instead of the three other merchants on my block, because I know these things. This was more than an errand: it was my audition for entrance into Uriangatense society. My hope is this interaction will go well: Doña Susan will determine, at least for now, that I am a good girl. And the whole block will know about it by sundown.

When I enter the store, Doña Susan moves swiftly into my personal space, appraising me closely; she wants to know all about my incongruous presence: a tall white woman from the United States, unmarried—no relation to anyone here but living with a family. Instead of just buying the water and leaving, I make sure also to pay my respects: she is an elderly woman, deserving of my time. She shows me the merchandise in her store. She tells me about her son and his family who own the house where she lives and has her store. She tells me that she likes my earrings, and I get the feeling that she wants them (indeed she asks for them a month later; a year later, when I'm about to move back to Pennsylvania, I give them to her). But all this is prologue. Her real interest is to interview *la güera* (the light-skinned woman—me): why are you here, where are you from, do you have pots and pans in the house where you're staying? Remembering my host family's admonition not to say too much, I try to honor her curiosity without exposing them to the circulation of talk about their household. I explain my research project but dodge the question about pots and pans. Doña Susan excitedly informs me that her son-in-law has been migrating to Pennsylvania for years. I should meet her daughter, who is about to join him in the North. "She is an expert on the subject!" La Doña declares. As for the pots and pans, I learn later that my reserve on that front was unwittingly wise. One of my host sisters tells me that Doña Susan's culinary query was an effort to gauge the economic status of my host family: revealing my hosts' private affairs to bond with the neighbor would have been a sure marker of my untrustworthiness.

Such are the shoals of social life on Emiliano Zapata.

In this chapter I consider the closely interrelated processes of how my research activities in La Libertad became positioned within the ongoing circulation of discourse—about migration, about Mexicanidad, about the differences between life here and life there—and how I and those around me made my presence legible. Central to these processes is the constitution of authoritative migration discourse in Uriangato: talk and writing positioned as verifiable and ratified by some kind of institution. The creation of authoritative migration discourse depends both on contrasts between "expert" accounts of migration and forms of nonauthoritative speech, such as gossip (Paz 2009), and on speakers' interpellation into politically loaded ideas about ethico-moral personhood, which organize who can and cannot speak authoritatively.

As the opening vignette suggests, being a good person who can speak with authority is rooted in the successful performance of proper womanhood or manhood, so that women and men lay claim to authority in different ways. Working-class Uriangatenses see not only the production of authority, but their social world more generally as fundamentally gendered. They frequently articulate concepts of gender difference, enacting them through an array of practices discussed in this chapter, from forms of talk to spatial and interactional sex segregation. The process through which I became legible centrally involved my interpellation into norms of respectable womanhood in Uriangato. These norms draw on but also elaborate aspects of the imaginaries of moral mobility discussed in chapter 1, especially the positing of US personhood as fundamentally immoral and anathema to mestizo Mexicanidad. This framework made my presence loaded from the outset and organized how I could be positioned as someone of decent ethico-moral character who could be welcomed into people's lives (see also Dick 2017).

As this suggests, gendering in Uriangato exists in dialogue with racial difference. Most working-class Uriangatenses see themselves as (and are recognized as) mestizo: the privileged, "neutral" racial category in Mexico (see chapter 1). The working-class Uriangatenses I know do not see race as an organizing feature of social life, as they do gender. At the same time, however, they express an awareness of the ambiguity of their racial privilege. They know that as working-class people, they are vulnerable to racial discrimination unless they are read as "white" and non-

Indigenous. Enactments of proper manhood and womanhood are a way working-class mestizos resist this ambiguity and reassert themselves as ethico-morally right and deserving of race privilege.

Moreover, proper manhood and womanhood in Uriangato—and in Mexico more broadly—exist in contrast to images of US people. Such contrasts are also racialized, as the United States is envisioned as a primarily white county (see chapter 1). Therefore ideas about the immorality of US people are figured as aspects of US whiteness, and white womanhood in particular (Dick 2017). Images of wanton, degraded white women, such as the "gringas gone wild" broadcast on Mexico's nightly news during the spring break season, are known to working-class Uriangatenses. These images profoundly informed my efforts to be a good girl: someone who, though forever identified as a person from the United States, was decent enough to resist the corrupting forces of US whiteness and at least attempt to observe the norms of proper Mexican womanhood. Therefore, while this chapter focuses on the gendering of Uriangatense social life, the dynamics between gendering and racialization are an undercurrent that also informs the analysis of my interpellation.

This interpellation unfurled in close dialogue not only with images of US whiteness but also with people's coming to identify me as a student learning how to produce authoritative accounts of migration. Such identification simultaneously gave me a respectable social role that pushed against images of gringas gone wild and helped enact the activities seen as part of my research as sites where my interlocutors could produce their own expert accounts of migration. As discussed in chapter 1, there is a long history of accounts of migration produced by nation builders and public intellectuals in Mexico. These state-endorsed accounts exist in conversation with other authoritative accounts generated by Mexican and US academics, who sometimes work with politicians to produce policy that not only constrains how migrants can move and what happens to them when they do but also informs who can and cannot be properly Mexican.

Working-class Uriangatenses are aware of these accounts and their consequences, which enter their lives via the media, encounters with immigration policy regimes, and other pathways of circulation. Although these accounts shape their lives, working-class Uriangatenses have little access to the sites where they are produced; they are marginalized from these sites of production, as is their migration discourse. Awareness of this marginalization is observable in the fact that a number of my friends and neighbors sought to participate in my research work, as Doña Susan did on her daughter's behalf the day I met her. This was especially the case with my interviews in La Libertad. Not only were people willing to participate in them when asked. People I knew complained when I interviewed their neighbors but not them, asserting, as Doña Susan did, that they or their loved ones are experts on migration. Recording a neighbor's migration discourse and not theirs was tantamount to saying that their accounts were not as consequential or trustworthy as those produced by their neighbors.

Interviews are familiar forms of interaction for working-class Uriangatenses, who know they can be used to produce authoritative accounts that impact lives. They have witnessed this in encounters with social workers, immigration officials, and other officers of the state. As a result, my interviews stood in contrast to various forms of nonauthoritative speech, against which authoritative accounts emerge as reliable. Indeed, as I discuss below, people were quite willing to be recorded in the context of the interview frame. But they were critical of—and shut down—my efforts to record them outside this frame, when they were more likely to engage in forms of discourse considered nonauthoritative, such as gossip. Discourse labeled gossip is deemed untrustworthy, as are the people who produce it—a point illustrated by my host family's concern about what I might say to Doña Susan.

In seeking inclusion in my interviews, then, people sought to counteract the marginalization of their discourse and position it as authoritative. In doing so, they also commented on and pushed against the ways the migration discourse of working-class people in general is positioned as untrustworthy, like the discourse of an incorrigible gossip (cf. Paz 2009). Their positive reception of my interviews thus offers a window into their confrontation with the variegation of national belonging—that they are called to be Mexican in ways that (re)create their exclusion from full membership in the polity, a process that includes the marginalization of their discourse. As such, my interviews became part of ongoing interpellative processes.

Consequently, interviews are more than occasions where people say things about a given object of analysis, such as migration. They are events of interaction that emerge interdiscursively with past interviews and talk about interviews before and after the interview itself (Briggs 1986, 2007; De Fina and Perrino 2011; Koven 2014). The central aim of this chapter is to show that people's uptake of my interviews relied fundamentally on a process of discourse circulation, through which I became identified as a student researcher with access to sites that produce authoritative accounts (e.g., the university) who was herself learning to make authoritative accounts and become an "expert."

Of particular importance in this regard was my participation in the Mexican Migration Project, a decades-long research initiative run out of the Universidad de Guadalajara and Princeton University. My involvement with this project gave me an institutional base in Mexico and involved several activities, most notably training by a Mexican PhD student who visited me in Uriangato, and a series of survey interviews. These activities gave me respectable social role as a diligent student sent to do work by her *jefe* (boss: i.e., dissertation advisor). As illustrated in the opening vignette, my being positioned in this way involved the imbrication of my research activities, including talk about that research, with my efforts to steer clear of pejorative images of gringas gone wild—to perform myself as a good girl. People's willingness to see my interviews as sites where they could counteract their marginalization required, first, that I become interpellated as someone with a sound ethico-moral character according to Uriangatense concepts of personhood.

This chapter builds on a point made by Judith Butler (1993, 1997) in her theory of interpellation. She argues that the forms of call and response that make people into distinct kinds hinge on culturally specific understandings of personhood, which define not only what "a person" is as an entity but also what kinds of collectivities people can belong to and what kinds of agency they are imagined, and allowed, to have.[2] Concepts of personhood are pivotal to the ways working-class Uriangatenses point to, re-create, and critique the politics of belonging in Mexico and between Mexico and the United States (Dick 2010b, 2017). Specifically, my ability to be received as a good girl depended on my enacting what I call *gracious personhood*, defined below. Uriangatenses pit this concept of personhood against the greedy and selfish forms of life they imagine unfolding in the United States. As such, the valuation and enactment of gracious personhood is a form of commentary on the United States, its relationship to Mexico, and the dangers that migration presents for Uriangatenses. At the same time, in trying to enact themselves as experts on migration, working-class Uriangatenses critically engage their positioning within Mexico as marginal to the processes, such as the creation of policy, that nevertheless shape their lives. As they engage these broader processes, they also position each other in ways that create them as authoritative or nonauthoritative, as trustworthy or untrustworthy—and as men or women.

Being positioned as a woman with a sound ethico-moral character who could observe gracious personhood despite being from the United States required that I engage in an activity that Summerson Carr (2009, 2011: 16 and chapter 5) describes as *anticipatory interpellation*. Such interpellation involves a process of foreseeing how we are likely to be positioned and preemptively responding to that positioning. Carr shows that her research participants (women enrolled in a US drug rehabilitation program) use anticipatory interpellation to lay claim to subject positions into which they were frequently called by social workers to signal their preparedness to speak in settings where their discourse is often dismissed, such as board meetings. In this chapter I show how I anticipated the ways people were likely to read me (as a gringa gone wild, an immigration official, or some related figure) and redirected these potential readings into more socially and ethico-morally acceptable forms of personhood.

This process meant not only cultivating my graciousness but also emulating a form of womanhood that constrains mobility. Such emulation became especially important, and especially difficult, in my research work. This work threatened my respectability by, for instance, putting me out in the street, talking with unfamiliar men—clear violations of proper womanhood, as discussed below. But it also gave me the opportunity to display that I was a good girl by realizing this work in ways signaling that I could observe the tenets of proper womanhood. Therefore I begin this chapter with a discussion of the salient forms of personhood in Uriangato and their associated cultural concepts; especially *voluntad* (will), *confianza* (trust), and *respeto* (respect).

The Flowers Are Your Will: Mexicanidad and Ethico-moral Personhood in Uriangato

On December 12 I went to the house of my friend Doña Marisol to celebrate the feast day of the Virgin of Guadalupe. This is a national holiday that runs the full twenty-four hours of the feast day, during which people show their devotion to the Virgin Guadalupe by holding masses at the many shrines to her that populate the country in churches, in homes, and on the street. Doña Marisol, a leader in her parish, arranged with the municipality to have the road in front of her house closed on this particular day so that a mass could be held in front of the mural of the Virgin painted on the storefront opposite her home. As part of such masses, people make offerings to the Virgin. The most common offering is flowers, especially the red roses featured in the Virgin's iconography. Starting a few days before the feast day, florists stay open late into the night to meet the demand for flowers. I had enough cultural competence to know that I should buy some rose offerings before the mass at Doña Marisol's. But I waited too long. Except for a few trampled remnants tossed to the floor, the red roses were gone by the time I went to purchase flowers. I opted instead for a multicolored collection of a dozen pert bulbs I thought would nevertheless please the Virgin. Satisfied I would not play the stupid gringa—who would have shown up empty handed—I trotted off to Doña Marisol's house.

When I arrived to our makeshift church, my self-satisfaction was promptly interrupted by the rushing heat of embarrassment as I caught view of the other flower arrangements. All around me were enormous displays of flora suitable for Guadalupe, Reina del Cielo (the Virgin of Guadalupe, Queen of Heaven). I faltered as realization came in waves: Other people's flowers must have cost more than the weekly wages of most of the people here—and only a fraction of the stipend that I received on my research fellowship. My flowers were worth a pittance. What an insult to lay these flowers down in offering.

Suddenly feeling extraordinarily tall and out of place, I moved to the back of our congregation and stood against Doña Marisol's house, tucking my flowers behind my back. When we reached the part of the mass dedicated to the offerings, I hesitated, too mortified to come forward with my bargain-basement bouquet. Doña Marisol, who always took an attitude of caring but challenging instruction toward me, placed her warm, strong hand on my shoulder, firmly guiding me to the altar. Unable to protest without interrupting the ritual, I conceded. Shoulders slumped, head down, I placed my roses on the altar, only to watch them be speedily squashed under the parade of glorious arrangements that followed. After mass Doña Marisol and I cleaned up, leaving the offerings below the mural, enshrining my shame for the night. We retired to her house for dinner with the priest, who left after a few of Doña Marisol's signature tamales: a neighborhood favorite.

Once we were alone, I told Doña Marisol how ashamed I was for bringing such a pitiful nosegay. I have never been to a feast day mass before, I explained. Now I know to—

Doña Marisol interrupted my justification: "¡No, no, no! Jili, no hay que tener vergüenza; las flores: ellas son tu voluntad [Hily, there is no need to be ashamed; the flowers: they are your will]."

On the day I attended mass at Doña Marisol's, my flowers were part of an effort to project myself as someone who could realize the ideals of ethico-moral life in Uriangato (and forestall readings of me as an immoral gringa). Doña Marisol's admonition that I not explain myself because the flowers were my *voluntad* is revealing of these ideals, as it points to the Uriangatense concept of gracious personhood. I use the descriptor "gracious" because it is related to the Iberian-Catholic concept of *gracia*. Not unlike the English "grace," *gracia* is a state of being defined by moral and aesthetic beauty, virtuous selflessness, godly favor, and gratitude achieved through the fulfillment of obligations to the divine realm of heaven and a person's earthly community (Pitt-Rivers 2011: 432–434).

Because this concept was brought to the Americas as part of Spanish conquest and religious conversion, it powerfully indexes Mexico's history as a postcolonial nation-state endeavoring to achieve autonomy (see chapters 1 and 5; cf. Napolitano 2016). As I discuss below, it also points to the ways Uriangatenses envision Mexicanidad in contrast to life in the United States. Gracious personhood locates what it means to be human in the successful occupation of social roles that exist outside and endure beyond any one individual.[3] At the mass honoring Guadalupe, I fulfilled the role of religious supplicant with only partial success. Uriangatenses contrast gracious personhood with what I call "autonomous personhood," which posits humans as individuals who possess intrinsic characteristics: inalienable rights, a personality, an ethno-racial background, a culture (Dick 2010b; Keane 2007; Rosaldo 1980; Rouse 1995). In gracious personhood humanity is rooted in the ability to realize preexisting roles, while in autonomous personhood humanity is located in the ability to act independently of preexisting roles, standing apart from the world (Carr 2011; Keane 2007: 6, 12, 52–53; Mahmood 2005). Scholars often treat autonomous personhood as synonymous with the ability to effect change, equating forms of gracious personhood with passivity and seeing it as nonagentive (Keane 2007; Mahmood 2005; Rosaldo 1980). Yet both forms of personhood entail agency (Mahmood 2005): culturally and historically specific views on how to "interpret actions and assign responsibility for events" (Ahearn 1999: 13; see also Agha 2007a; Kockelman 2007).

Uriangatense views of agency are encapsulated in the concept of *voluntad*. In the first instance, this term refers to the power to make decisions in moments of choice, such as when I decided how to honor the Virgin Mary. In this way it is similar to the English term "volition." It is also used as a mass noun, a quantity. Some people have more of it than others, which is to say they inherently possess a stronger ability to resist immoral desires and also have a greater capacity to improve themselves. Each person has a unique combination of these valences of *voluntad*: the power to choose and the ability to make choices, typically referred to with the possessive (e.g., *tu voluntad*, as Doña Marisol said to me). Therefore *voluntad* helps constitute a person's ethico-moral character. But that is not all. When used in the possessive, *voluntad* is understood not just as an inherent feature of someone's character but also as an index of relationships. Thus, enacting gracious personhood places the center of a person's humanity in relations with others, including divine figures. The central relationships at stake in the event depicted in the above vignette were mine with the Virgin Guadalupe—and by extension with Doña Marisol. When Doña Marisol said, "The flowers are your will," she did not mean that the offering was perfect because, as is often said in the United States, "it's the thought that counts." The flowers were perfect because the humility that the inadequate offering made me feel pointed out where I was in my relationship with the Virgin, revealing that I needed to move closer to a state of grace by improving how I fulfilled my social roles.

As I learned to enact gracious personhood, I had to grasp where it centers the appraisal of ethico-moral character. Notice that Doña Marisol's assessment of my actions at the offering was not rooted in discussion of my intentions. To be sure, people often use the term *voluntad* to shut down acts of self-justification that explain intentionality, as did Doña Marisol. *Voluntad* and gracious personhood do not draw on the "intentional theory of language" that often informs ideas about agency in the United States, where discerning people's motives is a crucial feature of ethico-moral evaluations (Briggs 2007; Duranti 1993; Hill 2008). By contrast, Uriangatense concepts of agency are more dialogic, as people are more interested in the consequences of actions than in prior aims (cf. Hill 1998). It is not that people do not think about intentions. If Doña Marisol thought I had disrespected the Virgin on purpose, she certainly would not have been as kind—as gracious—to me (cf. Keane 2014). Similarly, autonomous personhood is familiar to working-class Uriangatenses. Differences between autonomous and gracious personhood are not absolute; they emerge in dynamic relationship with one another (see also Dick 2010b; Keane 2007). This point is evinced in the conceptualization of *voluntad* as both an inherent quality and a result of interaction. But Uriangatenses are unlikely to make first appeal to autonomous personhood as a warrant for action or an axis of ethico-moral evaluation; gracious personhood plays that role. Autonomy and intentionality are not the driving engines of ethico-moral life; the gracious—careful and considerate—management of the impact of actions is.

Therefore, in that conversation with Doña Marisol, what mattered was not what I had hoped to achieve but what I had actually done. She was forgiving of my sad offering because I was, after all, just a *gringuita* trying to figure out life in Mexico and time would tell if I managed to improve and next time bring a bouquet befitting a queen. As this suggests, the successful enactment of anticipatory interpellation—and of ethico-moral personhood more generally—requires not only the virtuosic assertion of such personhood but its intersubjective and interactional uptake by others (a point to which I return in chapters 4 and 5).

Voluntad and gracious personhood are part of what could be described, drawing on Didier Fassin's (2012a, 2012b) theory of the political dimensions of ethics and morality, as a *consequentialist* view of ethico-moral life. This view asserts that conforming to moral norms or successfully achieving an ethical self (see the introductory chapter) does not encompass the actions that produce the good life. Consequentialist ethics combines a concern with norms and self-enactment with assessments of the outcomes and effects of actions. Similarly, assessments of ethico-moral practice and character in Uriangato are based on whether or not someone has harnessed the normative dimensions of social roles to virtuous performances of personhood in order to have positive effects on others. This last part is essential; without it, "the thought" does not count for much at all. As such, it is the visible evidence of good behavior or wrongdoing that marks someone as ethico-morally sound or not (cf. Hirsch 2003: 97). That is, enactments of gracious personhood are only successful if they are socially shared.

Although autonomous and gracious personhood are not mutually exclusive in practice, their differential valuation is part of Uriangatense understandings of moral mobility. Recall that moral mobility is the idea that to be properly Mexican people must integrate tradition and modernity in ways that allow Mexico to advance socioeconomically, while distinguishing Mexican progress from the greedy, immoral progress that putatively typifies the United States (see chapter 1). As part of this, autonomous and gracious personhood has come to represent differences between the United States and Mexico. Therefore the elevation of gracious personhood is a form of political commentary on the United States and the US treatment of Mexican migrants, which is aligned with the greedy individualism of autonomous personhood (cf. Chávez 2015; Dick 2010b, 2017; Dick and Arnold 2017a). Moreover, its realization plays a fundamental role in working-class Uriangatenses' efforts to respond to the interpellative call of state-endorsed imaginaries. The casting of autonomous and gracious personhood as national emblems grounds Mexicanidad in *communitarianism*, a vision of the social world considered moral because it values community over the individual. Therefore, in the next section, I explore the beliefs and practices that order the realization of gracious personhood and its associated communitarianism.

Confianza, Respeto, and Verbal Sociality

If *voluntad* orders how people conceptualize the agency of gracious personhood, it is the cultural concepts of *respeto* (respect) and *confianza* (trust) that organize its realization. The relevance of *respeto* and *confianza* to ethico-moral life has been documented across Mexico (Alonso 1994; Farr 2006; Hirsch 2003; Napolitano 2002), and in Uriangato it is especially salient to the way people construct Mexicanidad in contrast to forms of life in the United States. *Respeto* is generated from the observance of hierarchies, especially those of age and gender (young respect old; women respect men) (Farr 2006; Rouse 1995). *Confianza* is produced from relationships of shared obligation, such as that between parents and *padres de gracia* (godparents), most commonly referred to as *compadres* (co-parents). *Respeto* is the essential basis of proper social relations. It is impossible to have *confianza* without *respeto*, though some relationships—such as those between a store clerk and a customer—may entail *respeto* but not *confianza* (Hirsch 2003). Being a "person of respect" or a "person of trust" is simultaneously a standardized role (being a priest, a mother, etc.) and an achieved interactional effect, realized through the observation of hierarchy and obligation in a range of interactions from sacred rituals (such as December 12 masses) to everyday interactions (such as buying a bottle of water at a convenience store) (Dick 2010b). Although *confianza* and *respeto* are important to the realization of gracious personhood for everyone, their enactment is highly gendered (cf. Pitt-Rivers 2011): being properly Mexican is a markedly different proposition for men and for women.

Respectable Uriangatense womanhood is organized by a culturally specific understanding of the public/private contrast that is a recurrent feature of modernity across many contexts (cf. Cody 2013; Gal 2002, 2005; Gal and Woolard 2001; Hill 2008; Paz 2009, 2015; Yeh 2012). In

Uriangato this contrast is anchored in a distinction between *casa* (home) and *calle* (street). In some ways, *la casa* is imagined similarly to the classical "private sphere" of the bourgeois home described by Jürgen Habermas (1989). Its interior, idealized as a space of modesty, order, and safety, is the essence of the private realm (Gal 2005; Hirsch 2003: 100; Hyams 2003: 537; Wright 2006). *La casa*, however, has historically not been associated with personal privacy as it is in the United States. Indeed, my host family found my habits of privacy such as remaining alone in my room for long periods worrisome and would often send child-emissaries to invite me back into their communion. Rather the home is conceptualized as a place of family sociality and freedom from the dangers of the street (cf. Hirsch 2003; Hyams 2003; Mendoza-Denton 2008).

In contrast to the safety and order of *la casa*, Uriangatenses envision *la calle* as a public space of potential promiscuity, immodesty, and disorder—and it is, definitively, the realm of men. Therefore "good girls" are to be *recogida* (tucked in) at home, which is the physical and symbolic locus of their respectability (Hirsch 2003). Of course, Uriangatense women have social and work lives outside the home. But they are not free to engage in these lives in the unfettered way men are. Women who are perceived to move freely in public "like men" are the subject of intense gossip; such freedom is readily interpreted as a sign of failed morality. They are often called *callejeras* (streetwalkers) a term that (as it does in English) suggests the woman is prostituting herself.

Because proper womanhood is realized in the home and through kin relations, I had a special challenge before me as I endeavored to anticipate people's negative readings of me and redirect them to respectable social roles. When people saw me with members of my host family, they were often asked how I was related to them. The uncomfortable response (at least for me) was quite simply: we are not kin. My lack of family in Uriangato was a potential sign of my lack of ethico-moral personhood—a mark of my immaturity at best and of my sinfulness at worst. Though I was in my late twenties at the time, I was frequently assumed to be a teenager—for what would a grown woman be doing in a foreign country detached from family obligations?

Such questions were made all the more pointed by the fact that Uriangatenses also use the gendering of sociality and mobility to make sense of the differences between Mexico and the United States. When Uriangatenses explain what makes people from Mexico different from people from the United States, they assert their talent for creating relationships of *respeto* and *confianza*. By contrast, people from the United

States are constructed as not grasping the importance of these aspects of social relations. Echoing Vasconcelos (see chapter 1), Uriangatenses see US people as too focused on themselves, creating accomplished but morally bankrupt lives. This is presumed of US people in general but especially of US women. Uriangatenses imagine US women to have greater mobility in ways that destabilize the conditions of respectability (cf. Hirsch 2003; Rouse 1995; Smith 2006). As the United States is envisioned as a white country, it is white women in particular who embody the worst of womanhood: not only sexually loose, but too autonomous socially and financially—they earn their own income, do not defer to their men, and do not concern themselves with the cultivation of family.

While this racio-gendered imaginary did not automatically position me as Other in any straightforward way, it was always a haunting presence I had to anticipate and redirect (see also Dick 2017). There I was, a white gringa with no family present and with no purpose other than a research project—work that required me to frequent *la calle* alone. My independence was striking to those around me. As I got closer to people, I was frequently asked: Why you are here by yourself, doesn't your father love you? No loving father would leave his unmarried daughter to navigate the temptations and dangers of life without his protection. I was taken aback the first time someone asked me this—of course my father loves me! Allowing me to build a life independently is part of how my father expresses love. Given working-class Uriangatenses' experience with life in the United States, many of the people I knew were familiar with the idea that cultivating child independence is part of US ideals of parental care, and they even sometimes extol the virtues of this parenting style. Yet, even though they understand this practice intellectually, it always seems wrong affectively: it is just too much a violation of gracious family life.

To perform respectability as I pursued a life in Uriangato that was far from *recogida*, I built an approximate family life. I was sure to live with a family, rather than rent my own house—and I rooted my life in the social world of my host family, sharing their daily routines and participating in the quotidian and extraordinary events of their lives. The connection to my host family made me plausible as a respectable woman, enabling me to deflect my potential interpellation as a US bad girl. With several of my hosts and members of their extended family, I became a person of *confianza*, even becoming a godmother to one of the boys of the family for his primary school graduation. In time, people in the neighborhood came to identify me with this family, even though they knew we were not related. They said how *bonito* (beautiful) it was that I could be there as a companion to Doña Lupe's two unmarried daughters after her death. In addition to my association with my host family, I engaged in a range of activities that helped signal my respectable womanhood. I was always "tucked in" at home by 10 P.M.—the informal curfew for all good girls in Uriangato—and carefully observed practices of sex segregation, spending most of my time with women and children and only socializing with men in the presence of their female relations (Dick 2017; cf. Hirsch 2003).

Within this range of respectable activities, verbal interaction was paramount. My research participants understand *echando plática* (making small talk) to be essential to the cultivation of *confianza* and *respeto*. It is a foundation of gracious personhood (cf. Farr 2006: 12; Guerra 1998). In business transactions, for example, people respectfully acknowledge one another through small talk, as I did my first morning in Uriangato, when I chatted with Doña Susan after I purchased water. If time does not allow for such exchanges, people ask for permission to leave the interaction after the business transaction is complete, usually by explaining some other social obligation they must meet. Urban Uriangatenses associate loquaciousness with civility, graciousness, and cosmopolitanism and contrast it with what they assume to be the more laconic discursive life of rural people. Many of the urban-dwelling Uriangatenses with whom I worked regard the perceived terseness of rural people as iconic of the negative qualities of county life—uncouth, "backward," ignorant (a stereotype that is of course not born out in practice: cf. Chávez 2015; Farr 2006). Urbanites who are retiring verbally are suspected of being *mal criado* (poorly raised) and/or immoral, up to no good: their quietness is interpreted as secretiveness. Small talk is thus a way to signal not only being respectful of others but also being respectable. As such, it is an important ritual of interpellation: a way for people to call each other to be and to see themselves as proper Mexicans (cf. Irvine 1989). Consider a practice that I refer to as *sidewalk sociality*.

Every night my host family and I pulled out chairs in front of the house, as did nearly everyone else on the block. Those who did not were considered suspect, and we endlessly gossiped about them. During sidewalk sociality, we interpellated self and other through actual calls, respectfully acknowledging neighbors and passersby with a nod of the head and the greeting *adiós* (literally "to God," a salutation that means both hello and good-bye). We would exchange small talk with people we knew, which largely involved asking about people's comings and goings and describing our own. I learned quickly from such exchanges—and our dissection of them after people left—that it was essential to answer questions about my comings and goings openly: thus showed not only that I was sociable and other-oriented but that I was living a life about which I could be transparent. As this suggests, respectability is directly linked to the reports about movements in public space. Far from being just something to talk about, like the weather (and there was plenty of that too), queries about mobility are an indirect interpellative call—a way of asking: have you been up to no good? In other words, such queries realize a somewhat literal interpretation of moral mobility, probing whether or not a person's physical movements are related to obligations and therefore are expressions of graciousness and communitarianism.

Talk of mobility is also a strategy for anticipatory interpellation—a way to "get ahead of the story" in talk about oneself. The women I lived with would often respond to a neighbor's mobility query by saying some version of "not much, just been at home." I never stopped finding this strange, considering that these women all worked outside the home and lived extraordinarily busy lives. As someone raised in a social milieu shaped by the Protestant work ethic, my instinct was that they should assert their respectability by proclaiming their intense business. But in saying they had "just been at home" the women of my host family deflected speculation, asserting that the women of the house are *recogidas*, morally if not physically. Indeed, the very act of sidewalk sociality is such an assertion—for there they are, with family, in front of their house quite evidently doing nothing immoral.

Sidewalk sociality therefore was an especially important practice for my performances of respectability and trustworthiness as I endeavored to stave off people's readings of me as a typical gringa, who is unmoored socially and therefore immoral. Admittedly, I was often on the edges of my host family's nightly conversations. Not knowing enough about local happenings to offer any especially juicy speculations or having enough linguistic sophistication to play verbally as my companions did, I took up a social role as respectful listener, interjecting affirmative utterances as seemed relevant. But being included in these conversations at all was significant. Sidewalk sociality is a public display of relationships of *confianza*—only family or very close friends are invited to sit in front of a particular house, to be observed by others on the street as members of the microgrouping of that home. By inviting me to sit with them watching passersby and witnessing their family-internal talk, members of my host family signaled to the neighborhood they had taken me in; I was a respectable member of their household who did not need to be hidden away.

But if my life with my host family was the fundamental grounding of my respectability in Uriangato, my research work—and in particular my interviews—also paradoxically became the central practice that allowed me to be legible as a respectable young woman. It forced me to exist on the edge of respectability: living far from home, walking around on the street alone, sometimes talking to strangers, including strange men. But its agitation of gendered norms created an ethico-moral gauntlet through which I could pass to display my *voluntad* and show I was a woman worthy of *respeto* and, for some, of *confianza*. At the same time, this work, and especially my training into the Mexican Migration Project (MMP) survey protocol, allowed me to be recognized as an expert-in-training who was learning to produce authoritative accounts and could therefore help render working-class migration discourse as authoritative. In the next section I consider the discursive universe out of which the MMP emerges: authoritative scholarly accounts of Mexican migration, which play a central role in defining who "the Mexican migrant" is as a figure in migration discourse. This analysis shows that the circulation of discourse was crucial to my own and my research participants' ability to render authoritative accounts, in ways that reveal the gendering of authoritative discourse.

Casos de la Vida Real (Real Life Cases): Authoritative Accounts of the Mexican Migrant

In Mexico state discourse about US-bound migration often unfolds in conversation with social science research on this subject. Mexican scholars, such as Manuel Gamio in the early twentieth century and many since then, have sometimes directly informed Mexican immigration policy and/or have served in high political office (see chapter 1). Understanding the whys and wherefores of migration to the North and envisioning the life of Mexicans in the United States and their impact on Mexico has long been a preoccupation for these scholar-politicians. Their theoretical and empirical work on these questions has informed the state-endorsed imaginaries of moral mobility that enable and are (re) produced through policy making (see chapter 1). Many of these scholars have also had close ties with US scholars and the US granting agencies that have funded research on migration. Gamio, for example, was recruited to lead the Social Science Research Council's first major research program on Mexico-US migration and had close ties with lead US social scientists working on the relationship between migration, development, and culture (Kearney 1986; Walsh 2004). The Mexican Migration Project (MMP), which formed the most visible part of my research life in Uriangato, is part of this intellectual tradition.

The MMP is a collaboration between a prominent US sociologist, Douglas S. Massey, and a leading Mexican anthropologist, Jorge Durand. It supports collaborations between US and Mexican graduate students, who work together implementing the MMP survey protocol across Mexico and in migrant communities in the United States. The MMP has helped launch the successful careers of a number of migration scholars on both sides of the border, whose works, including Massey et al.'s seminal 1987 book *Return to Aztlán*, have played a central role in shaping studies of the causes of migration.[4] A review of the vast literature on the causes of migration is outside the scope of this chapter (see Durand and Schiavon 2010; Massey et al. 2005). Here I instead highlight an important unifying feature that this literature shares: it is centrally occupied with understanding how, when, and why people migrate and thus it is programmatic in orientation (De Genova 2002). To be sure, Massey and other leading migration scholars serve as expert witnesses for the US Congress during periods of policy reform—they also have lives as public intellectuals shaping policy discussions by, for example, writing high-profile op-eds and incisive scholarly critiques of the contradictions of US immigration policy (e.g., Durand and Massey 2003).

While the relationship between policy makers and scholars is often contentious, this work has nevertheless played a key role in institutionalizing figures of migration that animate discussion of immigration restrictions. Debates over immigration policy depend on the production of images of who migrants are (Chavez 2001, 2008; Coutin and Pease Chock 1995; Mehan 1997; Santa Ana 2002). The discussion of how the United States should manage undocumented migration, for example, hinges on the production of contrasting images of migrants, circulated across the country through media coverage, activism, and the speeches of politicians: are these migrants dangerous law-breaking criminals "flooding" our shores or taxpaying, contributing members of our society who are victims of an unjust immigration system? Which of these images is taken up in policy has a dramatic impact on the lives of migrants.

Over the last several decades negative images of Mexican migrants have helped legitimate a policy regime that treats migrants' violations of immigration law as signifiers of an inherently corrupt personhood, which it then uses to justify the removal of migrants at all costs (Coutin 2005, 2007; Dick 2011b, 2012). This policy regime and its political economic infrastructure, including a militarized border, have helped criminalize undocumented migrants, especially those from Mexico and other parts of Latin America (Abrego 2014; Berg 2015; De Genova 2005; Dick 2011b; Durand and Massey 2003). Just as working-class Uriangatenses are aware of and respond to the ways they are interpellated by state-endorsed imaginaries of national belonging in Mexico, so too are they aware of these politics of representation and their consequences. Indeed, migration scholars and migrants alike vigorously critique the criminalization of migrants (cf. Dick and Arnold 2017a; Chávez 2015, 2017a, 2017b; Gálvez 2007; Mendoza-Denton 2008; Yeh 2017). This is not to say that Uriangatenses have read migration scholarship or are expert in the content of policy debates. They are, however, routinely exposed to and interact with these authoritative accounts through several pathways of circulation.

Circulation of Authoritative Accounts from "Beyond Here"

One key pathway that brings state-endorsed and/or scholarly accounts of migration into Uriangato is interaction with immigration lawyers. During my fieldwork, lawyers on both sides of the border sought to inform potential clients of immigration policies and procedures through Spanish-language media, church newsletters, or social service activities. During the year of my research in Pennsylvania, several free legal clinics were offered, coordinated by the Mexican Consulate in Philadelphia. In Uriangato immigration lawyers bought regular radio spots explaining relevant aspects of US immigration law and advertising their services to help clients navigate them. Through interactions with lawyers, as well as with friends and family who have migration experience, aspirant migrants learn how they are interpellated by Mexican and US immigration policy and develop critical commentaries on it.

For example, people routinely regaled me with stories of the harrowing experiences they or their loved ones had trying to get a visa to enter the United States. Getting a US visa involves an expensive process of gathering documentation to prove their intent to return to Mexico and traveling to US embassies in faraway cities to be interviewed by the officials who distribute visas. "And what do people from the United States have to do obtain a Mexican visa?" they would ask me pointedly. "Walk through an immigration checkpoint with a US passport, no more." Discussions of such asymmetries, which are endemic to US-Mexico relations (see chapter 1), reveal not only people's awareness of authoritative accounts of their migration but also their stake in wanting to contribute to such accounts.

Spanish-language news coverage is another important pathway of circulation for authoritative accounts of migration produced beyond Uriangatense migrant enclaves. This coverage also focuses on migrants' positioning inside immigration policy regimes. Working-class Uriangatenses are active news consumers—they watch the national news nearly every evening and read the national and local newspapers several times a week. They generally see the news, especially the national news, as reliable and authoritative (a belief found across Mexico: see Consulta 2014; Pew Research Center 2014). While living in Uriangato, I collected the city's three local newspapers each morning and watched the national news each evening, in order to track representations of migration. I found that coverage of Mexican migration to the United States in the national news is almost always negative, reporting, for example, on the abuses Mexican migrants suffer at the hands of human traffickers or immigration officials. There were roughly one to two migration-focused stories a week on the national news, and not once did I see coverage that represented migration in a positive light.

This coverage was rife with critiques of US immigration policy and the treatment of Mexicans in the United States. Reporting almost never spotlighted the abuses migrants suffer at the hands of Mexican authorities, thus positioning the Mexican government itself as being at the mercy of the United States, like migrants. This coverage thus reinforces the idea that sojourns in the North are harmful, a familiar theme of state-endorsed imaginaries of moral mobility (see chapter 1). This idea is also promoted in the coverage of migration in Uriangato's local newspapers. These papers usually did not have stories expressly about migration; instead, like much local news, they focused on crime and other woes. Yet US migration was nevertheless lambasted in this coverage, consistently appearing as an explanation for a person's disruptive or dangerous behavior. One story, for instance, told of a husband who stabbed his wife nearly to death because, as the reporter explained, his mind had been demented by his migration experience in the North.

Overall, Mexican news coverage generates an imaginary of migrant vulnerability, highlighting the dangers of undocumented migration and criticizing US immigration policy that exposes migrants to exploitation by officials and human traffickers. The depiction of migrant vulnerability is also widely distributed in popular media accounts of migration—from movies to soap operas to songs (e.g., Herrera-Sobek 1993). Popular depictions of migration are not necessarily tied to the effort to reproduce events exactly as they happened as news accounts are—and hence are not authoritative in the same way. But they do rely on the public authorship of experts, in this case those versed in storytelling. Moreover, the wide distribution of these accounts and tacit support by the media outlets that distribute them help authorize and legitimate them. In addition, they often cite more traditionally authoritative accounts, weaving reference to the news or to policy into their descriptions and explanations.

An especially interesting example of authoritative accounts of migration in the popular media is a now-defunct show that blurred the line between storytelling and news-telling: *Mujer, Casos de la vida real* (Woman, Real-Life Cases), which was hosted and produced by Silvia Pinal, a grand dame of Mexican cinema. *Casos* first aired after the earthquake of 1985: an 8.1 magnitude macroseism that devastated Mexico City. The show's initial aim was to recruit assistance for victims by circulating "real-life cases" of the earthquake's impact. Televisa, the network that aired the show, continued the program after it garnered an outpouring of support, expanding the stories it depicted beyond the quake. Its final episodes aired in 2007. *Casos* featured the reenactment of stories sent in by audience members. The show's target audience was women, as is suggested by its name, which addresses an individual woman as friends do while talking intimately, as if to say: I'm about to share with you some profound truths. But I often saw my friends' male relations watching the show too.

Doña Silvia began each episode introducing the featured story from a softly lighted living room. Seated on a cozy couch and dressed beautifully with impeccable makeup and coifed hair, she would discuss the audience member's letter that formed the basis of the episode. She would then play the prerecorded reenactment, animated by *telenovela* (soap opera) actors. She concluded each episode by explaining the moral of the tale that had just been recreated. The format and setting of *Casos* modeled the ideal of feminine authoritative discourse in Mexico. As I explore in chapters 4 and 5, for women to be authoritative and persuasive they ground their claims in the personal—in family and intimate relationships. The realization of such womanly authority also requires displays of femininity in dress and other aspects of self-presentation, such as makeup, and *cariño* (care) or nurturing affect, a rhetorical tactic of which Doña Silvia is an absolute master. Inside its softly lighted femininity, however, *Casos* was hard-hitting, as it carried on the original activist design of the show. It would often be the first public forum in which taboo topics such as LGBT discrimination and domestic violence were critically engaged. It became a platform for social reform in large measure because of Doña Silvia's artful performance of female authority.

During my fieldwork, the show regularly featured migration stories, usually depicting the experiences of women. The show told stories of women abandoned by their husbands after the men moved north; stories about women raped and sold into sex trafficking while migrating; and stories of the loneliness and poverty encountered by migrant women in the United States. Collectively, these stories further elaborated the morbid imaginary of migrant vulnerability found in mainstream news coverage, in which the real story of migration was a diasporic one of loss, violation, and isolation (cf. Schmidt Camacho 2006). Many of the women I knew watched *Casos* every afternoon, often with their children, to whom they underscored the moral of the story, as authorized by Doña Silvia. As this suggests, Uriangatenses integrate media accounts into their migration discourse. This practice allows people to position their accounts of migration as authoritative, especially within the frame of my interviews as I discuss below.

La Güera Callejera (The White Streetwalker): Interviews, Respectability, and Authoritative Accounts

During my fieldwork in Uriangato, I did two kinds of interviews (see the Technical Note at the beginning of the book). The first was the Mexican Migration Project (MMP) survey, which involved interviewing the heads-of-household of 170 randomly selected homes. The second was open-ended ethnographic interviews, mostly conducted with people I knew well. Collectively, these interviews created links between the here-and-now of life in Uriangato and the "beyond here" of authoritative accounts of migration—not only for me but also for the people I interviewed. Although my fieldwork overall could be said to have created this effect, the interviews became emblematic of these links because they stood apart from the regular flow of life. The interviews involved setting up an infrastructure of interaction (digital recorder, notebook, list of questions) that broke from usual interaction and signaled a shift into an authoritative frame. Moreover, they had been authorized by official institutions, not only universities but also the municipality of Uriangato.

On the recommendation of the MMP, I began the survey work by first visiting the city hall to notify municipal officials of my research activities and to acquire a letter of permission to conduct them. I had previously met the mayor through a journalist friend during a preliminary field trip. He had told me to come visit him if I returned; when I did, he penned my letter of permission. The letter explained that I was a student from the Universidad de Guadalajara, in town to learn about migration. It stated in bold that my work was not contracted by the mayor or any government office and would not be used to develop municipal programs. I carried this letter with me while conducting all phases of the survey, along with my letter of affiliation from the Universidad de Guanajuato, which I had as part of my Fulbright fellowship.

As I discuss above, this research work abraded the expectations of proper Mexican womanhood, as it highlighted my independence and forced me out into the street to interact with strangers. Yet my interviews became a key practice that allowed me to be legible as a respectable young woman by forming an ethico-moral gauntlet through which I could prove and display respectability. Through the interviews, I worked to project myself as a gringa who had at least a basic competence in gracious personhood and the norms of proper womanhood. I did this by integrating routine performances of femininity with the process through which I became recognized as an expert-in-training—a form of recognition facilitated primarily by my work with the MMP survey.

My ability to pass successfully through the ethico-moral gauntlet that my research presented relied in part on people's preexisting experience with interviews, which made them legible as a kind of authoritative interaction. The working-class migrant enclaves where I did my fieldwork are what Charles Briggs (2007) and others (see Koven 2014: 500 for a review) have called "interview societies," in which people regularly participate in and witness interviews and become familiar with their effects. For one thing, working-class Uriangatenses routinely observe interviewing on television. One popular interview-based program during my fieldwork was *Cristina*, hosted by Cuban-born Cristina Sara-legui, often called the Latin American Oprah. Her eponymous show, which last aired in 2010, featured her interviewing prominent Latino/a and Latin American entertainers and political figures. Many of the children I knew would imitate the Cristina-style interview as a form of play, through which it became intertwined with other genres of interaction, from teasing to gossip.

Beyond observing television interviews, working-class Uriangatenses routinely participate in interviews themselves in interactions with government officials. They do so to prove their eligibility for welfare programs (see chapter 5). They do so when the municipality surveys households to assess the city's infrastructural needs: a common activity that my MMP survey interviewees sometimes thought I was part of, until I showed them my letter from the mayor. They become interviewees as aspirant and actual migrants when they apply for visas or deal with border patrol officers. Moreover, the long history of research on Mexico–US migration is largely based on interviews (Walsh 2004: 128). Guana-juato is one of Mexico's traditional migrant-sending states; I was not the first researcher to show up in this part of Mexico asking to interview people about migration (cf. Lattanzi Shutika 2011). Journalists from the United States and Mexico have also interviewed people in Urian-gato's migrant enclaves for exposés on migration between the municipality and various parts of the United States. Because of these varied experiences with interviews, working-class Uriangatenses widely recognized them as sites for the production of "authoritative and consequential knowledge" (Koven 2014: 499) that directly affects their lives.

My research interviews became linked to Uriangatenses' preexisting experience with the genre through my interpellation as a student and expert-in-training, illustrated by my participation in the MMP survey protocol. The first stage of the survey required me to count all 2,987 houses in La Libertad (recall that this a pseudonym used to protect the enclave, as per MMP guidelines). Working off a map of the municipality, I sketched every street and block into a notebook, one block per page, on which I drew a square for each house, which I then numbered. Creating the house map meant that I was out every day for several hours, walking the neighborhood and drawing in the streets. It took me just over six weeks to complete the map, so I became a familiar presence.

My public documenting of the neighborhood aroused curiosity, if not suspicion, in this context, where people are generally vigilant of comings and goings. My physical appearance and the activity in which I was engaged stood out. Most people would just watch me with close-tracking stares, but some would ask me what I was doing, thus facilitating talk about my research and the survey in particular. I would oblige with responses about my interviews and their content and show them my letters of permission and affiliation when requested, which identified me as someone with links to official institutions who was nevertheless just a student and not working for the government. At the same time, being in the street day after day required that I learn to discern respectable from shameless encounters. For example, I studiously keep conversations with men to the tersest possible minimum, lest I be seen as *una sinvergüenza* (a shameless, sexually loose woman) (Dick 2017; Hirsch 2003). By contrast, I talked at length with several of the women who asked about my activities, and a few of these interactions led to lasting friendships (such as my relationship with Elena, discussed in chapter 5).

Before beginning the survey, I received training from MMP members in the United States and Mexico. My trainers, who were both Mexican nationals, fellow female graduate students and native Spanish speakers who had implemented the survey multiple times in different parts of Mexico, helped me learn its "language of expertise" (cf. Carr 2011; Cody 2013), necessary for me to project competence as a researcher. During this training, we ran several mock interviews, during which my trainers taught me relevant idioms and other vernacularisms and helped me practice the most effective ways to run the interviews. They explained, for instance, that I should introduce the project as being run out of the Universidad de Guadalajara—and sideline mention of the United States, to stave off concern that I was there on behalf the US government. To be sure, I intentionally left my affiliations with the University of Pennsylvania and Princeton University off my permission letter from the municipality, anticipating and seeking to avoid interpellation as a US immigration official (something that had happened to other researchers I knew).

Zoraya, my trainer in Mexico, came to Uriangato, where we worked together for several weeks. In order to protect her respectability—and by extension mine—Zoraya's fiancé Pablo (who also worked on the MMP) accompanied her to Uriangato and got her settled at the house where I had arranged for her to stay with the elderly mother of one of my friends. His presence helped position Zoraya and me as respectable women, occupying a place in a hierarchy under the charge of male authority. Indeed several people described Pablo as our supervisor. He embraced his role as male protector. After Zoraya said she adored the screensaver on my computer—a scrolling crawler of the phrase *grandota fuerte* (strong tall woman)—Pablo urged us to remember that men in Uriangato might not appreciate our "modern, independent" womanhood. He instructed us to signal our respectability by dressing modestly and never conducting interviews after dark.

Zoraya's work with me played an especially important role in helping me enact myself as a student and member of a Mexican university project, in which I was an underling. Zoraya met and spent time with my host family, explaining the MMP project with an ease and depth of linguistic competence I could never have managed. Moreover, she accompanied me on my first weeks of interviews, conducting the first several of them while I listened, positioned as her trainee. Indeed, she would often introduce me this way if people questioned my presence at the interview. After a few days of shadowing her, I ran several interviews with her observing and advising. Then she and I worked separately for a few more days, after which she returned to Guadalajara. While we were conducting the interviews together, several people asked if Zoraya and I were sisters. She has light brown hair, fair skin, and blue eyes, not unlike my coloring. And her name, like mine, is unusual in this part of Mexico (I have used a pseudonym for her here that is similarly unfamiliar in Uriangato). Our mutual strangeness in concert with Zoraya's obvious native skill in Mexican Spanish and its associated interactional norms encouraged people to place us as Mexican but "not from here." People often presumed we were from Los Altos, a region just outside Guadalajara city famous for its large population of tall people with fair features. Once I started speaking at any length, however, it was clear I was from the United States. My speech is tinged with a readily identifiable *voz de gringa* (gringa accent) (Carris 2011). But even then some people would persist—you must be related! Perhaps they thought I had grown up in the United States and become one of those *norteñas*: Mexicans in el Norte who do not learn proper Spanish (see chapter 3). Such inquiries were part of people's trying to make sense of us. My being placed not only as a trainee but also as someone with relatives from a place not so remote as Pennsylvania was a sign that at least some people were trying to interpellate me as a good Mexican girl of family.

The survey interviews required us to follow the house map that I had made and "cold call" those households selected by an Excel random sort program. I was apprehensive because this was not a method I was comfortable with as an anthropologist inculcated into the value of ethnographic methods that rely on the cultivation of long-term relationships with research participants. I could not imagine that people would want to talk to me—a stranger and a gringa—about their family's migration histories. I anticipated hostility, doors slamming in my face. But I was successful: out of 171 cold calls, I got only one rejection. This was in part because of Zoraya's role in introducing me to the neighborhood. But I facilitated positive readings of my personhood in other ways, which also pivoted on my being interpellated as a student and on the circulation of talk about the interviews.

Before we began the survey interviews I called into a popular radio talk show on the local station Radio Alegría to explain that I would be interviewing in La Libertad; this program airs every morning and has a wide listenership in the city. In an act of anticipatory interpellation, I explained in my accented Spanish that I was a student there to learn about migration and that the information I was collecting was not solicited by the US or Mexican government. Taking up my self-presentation, the kind radio host exhorted his audience to "help out the student," thus further authorizing my interpellation into this social role. After that, people on the street would frequently stop me and ask if I was the "girl from the radio." One of my acquaintances told me that her mother, who lives in Pennsylvania, heard me when I called in—listening to Radio Alegría is a way to access the sounds of home while in the United States. She called her daughter afterward to see if she knew me and ask if she would be interviewed. Moreover, the survey interviews themselves were public, held *en la calle*. Rarely did my survey interviewees invite me inside. So I would administer the survey in doorways, under the strong sun, clipboard in hand, in full view of curious neighbors.

After Zoraya left, I proceeded to conduct the remaining 140 survey interviews alone. I dutifully got up every morning, shared breakfast with my host family, and headed out for a long day of cold calls and interviews. Increasingly my friends and neighbors would comment on how sociable I must be to get (as they put it) notoriously suspicious Uriangatenses to talk to me. This was a compliment, I knew, having figured out by then that verbal sociality was a lynchpin of ethico-moral life in Uriangato. My host family used my daily interview efforts and my success at engaging in verbal sociality as evidence that I was a serious, diligent person—a person of *respeto*. I might not be related to them, but I had a decent purpose: I was not here to rob women of their husbands or otherwise "go wild." I heard my host family say to people that I was completing a project my boss at school, always assumed to be male, had given me to do, again positioning me inside a hierarchy of relationships in which I was subservient to male authority. I learned from such overhearing, as well as from conversations in which I was a participant, that people had begun to describe me as respectful and respectable—as a good girl. People highlighted the content of my interviews: I know not to ask anything "disrespectful" but largely talked about family, as any good girl should.

My success at performing respectability was augmented by other semiotic displays beyond the denotational content of the survey interviews. Taking my cue from Doña Silvia's performance of female authority on *Casos*, I always wore makeup (including elaborately decorating my lash lines with liquid eyeliner: a skill it took months to acquire); styled my hair (no easy feat, as I have thin, fine hair that does not easily accommodate the glorious hairdos of working-class Uriangatense women); and donned heels and feminine but modest clothing, even as I trudged over the rocky streets of La Libertad. Following Pablo's admonition, I never interviewed after dusk. I knew I had at last convinced at least some people I was trustworthy and respectable woman when my female friends started teasing me about my interview work, calling me *la güera callejera* (the white streetwalker). Such teasing is something they would never have done if they thought I was actually prostituting myself, so it was a sign of my growing *confianza* with them.

While doing the survey, I made note of people who were willing to go "off script" and discuss migration in more detail with me. I asked these people if they would mind my returning another time to talk more about their experiences, and most welcomed me back. I compiled a list of about a dozen households that I then visited each week, bringing soda and snacks and enjoying long afternoons exchanging small talk. This process, along with living with my host family, allowed me to ground my life in Uriangato in family. These visits were always with women and children (and men only in that context). They also enabled me to further develop and display my verbal sociality and communitarianism, as I took time to build networks of relationship and not just be on my own. Some of these visits blossomed into genuine friendships: people with whom I would join on daytrips to neighboring towns, spending time taking care of their children, and sharing intimacies.

After a couple of months of visiting I asked people if I could interview them again. When I shifted into the open-ended/ethnographic interviews—both with these families and with other friends—I decided to go through the motions of reviewing the survey questionnaire at the beginning of each interview, while not observing its protocol. The questionnaire neatly hooked onto my clipboard had become iconic of being interviewed by *la güera callejera*, and leaving it out might make some people feel they were not getting the real interview experience. At the same time, these ethnographic interviews signaled my moving into a position of not only *respeto* but *confianza*, represented by the shifting geography of their enactment. No longer was I forced to stand in doorways; now I was invited into *la casa* (the home).

As this history of the social life of my interviews shows, both how I learned to conduct the interviews and the way I conducted them (being somewhat publicly trained and observing local norms of proper womanhood) allowed me to assert ethico-moral personhood as a respectable young woman—and for people to ratify that positioning in how they treated me. It also helped interpellate me as someone who was learning how to make an authoritative account and who had access to the sites from which at least some of those accounts are produced. As talk about the MMP survey spread, people in the neighborhood became interested in participating in the interviews. My friends and host family chided me for ignoring their stories and asked me when I was going to interview them. Not at all convinced by my explanation of needing to collect a random sample, people told me their migration stories were just as interesting and important—no, more so!—than those of the people I had been interviewing. Over the course of my year in La Libertad, the interviews became, as one of my friends put it, a moment of gratifying diversion in which routine talk about migration became elevated to the level of recognition by a respectful outsider. I wrote their perspectives down on an official document, situating their talk of migration within the universe of authoritative accounts through the material artifacts of their production: survey protocol, recorder, and so on. Thus, the interviews became a site that, unlike sidewalk sociality, could enable people's discourse about migration to became institutionally recognized and circulated, finding its way ultimately to this pages of this book.

Not surprisingly, then, people identified my effort to record discourse as my work. While this allowed me to be positioned as respectable, it also constrained what kinds of talk I could record. A key principle for the realization of gracious personhood is that activities deemed to be "work" should not intrude on non-work-related sociality (Dick 2010a). Given the alignments between US personhood and economic productivity (see chapters 1 and 3), work can index the corrupting force of life in the United States, where careers become too important, especially for women (see also Dick 2017). In order to deflect my interpellation as one of those bad gringas, I had to be mindful not to make work too much a part of my life. When it was time to be sociable, I was expected to put the recorder away. To turn it on during sidewalk sociality or other everyday discursive interactions would have risked my being read as selfish, greedy, and immoral. Thus, I was confined to the recording of "interview talk" and was only able to capture talk outside of my interviews in after-the-fact field notes. But more than just being a force that disciplined me into conducting my research in particular ways, people's association of my interviews with work—and their desire not to be recorded when we were relaxing—bespeaks working-class Uriangatenses' sensitivity to the marginalization of their migration discourse.

The Bragging Migrant and *Cosas Verídicas* (Truthful and Real-to-Life Things)

As suggested throughout the discussion above, the production of authoritative accounts requires contrasts with forms of discourse that are considered nonauthoritative (Paz 2009; Gal and Woolard 2001). In Uriangatense talk, authoritative accounts are brought into relief through contrasts that juxtapose them with accounts of migration rendered by a common figure of working-class migration discourse: the "bragging migrant" who tells tall tales of migration (see also Dick 2010a; Dick and Arnold 2017a). This image of personhood is usually introduced into migration discourse with some version of the stock phrase *solo cuentan lo bueno* (they only tell the good).

Consider the following excerpt from an interaction analyzed in detail elsewhere (Dick 2010a). These words were uttered by Jesús, a young man who eschewed migration to study industrial engineering at Uriangato's technical institute, even as most of his friends, cousins, and siblings moved north:

Todos de allá solo platican lo bueno. Todos platican que, "ay, que esto que ganas y este que—" ¡Pero nunca te das cuenta que vas a trabajar de *obrero*! Todos cuentan que "bien bonito," pero no te cuentan que "me levantaba a las 2, 3 de la mañana a trabajar, que no me podía acostar porque le espalda me dolía." No que "ganaba mil dólares."
[All the people {who come home} from there only talk about the good parts {of migration}. All of them say, "Oh, that this that you earn and this that—" But you never realize that you go {to the United States} to

work as a *laborer*! They all say, "{It's} very beautiful," but they don't tell you, "I was getting up at 2, 3 in the morning to work, I could not lie down because my back was hurting me." No {they say}, "I was earning a thousand dollars."]

In this excerpt, Jesús juxtaposes the erroneous world of the bragging migrant, who returns to tell those who have not migrated of his financial success, with the actual life of a migrant who cannot lie down because his back hurts from hard labor. The bragging migrant is a trickster figure who lures aspirant migrants to the North with his pretty lies of life on the other side. This figure operates as a straw man for speakers. Never have I heard someone take up the bragging migrant as representative of himself or herself—nor have I ever spoken with a migrant who was not more than willing to recount the "not good" of migration. Rather, speakers use this migrant persona to distinguish themselves as knowing the facts, thus asserting that they are capable of making an authoritative account of migration.

Jesús displays his migration savvy by sketching a generic image of the bragging migrant; he is not describing any actual person. While I often heard speakers represent the bragging migrant this way, people also use the figure to characterize the migration discourse of actual people. The women of my host family, for example, readily situated the things that friends and neighbors said they accomplished in the North in the realm of the bragging migrant. Consider this reconstructed segment from a conversation with my host family, which I captured in field notes:

Oooooh, Jimena quien vive aquí por el otro lado de la calle—ella me dijo que en Pennsylvania aprendió manejar en un solo mes. ¡Pero después cuando regresó pa'ca, chocó la camioneta de su tío en como cinco minutos! Ay no, solo cuentan lo bueno.
[Ooooooh, Jimena from down the street—she told me that in Pennsylvania she learned to drive in just one month. But then she came back here and crashed her uncle's truck in like five minutes! Oh no, they only recount the good.]

The narration of other people's false migration discourse is both routine—I heard this sort of thing frequently—and gratifying. It almost always elicits raucous laughter among those who see how ridiculous the migration discourse, and by extension the person who uttered it, is. In the case of the preceding conversation, it is the idea of a woman learning to drive in a month that is absurd. In general, women in Uriangato do not drive cars and see it as a nearly impossible skill to acquire. Although many Uriangatense women drive scooters, most of them see driving a car as a violation of respectable womanhood, as it facilitates their physical mobility in too masculine a way: it is too fast and empowers you to go too far. Even the scooter driving is seen as somewhat exceptional; few women over thirty drive them. Nevertheless, in the immediate region Uriangatense women are identified with scootering: it is forwarded as a sign of their modern independence and cosmopolitanism, fostered by the textile industry (see chapter 3). But because of the associations between driving, mobility, and masculinity, most working-class women, even those who own scooters, prefer to have their male relations to drive them. It is a way to signal publicly that they are respectable: they may be modern, but they are still connected to family and taken care of by their men.

Whatever the subject of the bragging migrant's tall tale (about making easy money, learning to drive a car in a month, or some equally implausible feat), associating the talk of actual people with the talk of this figure of migration serves to discredit the subject of the depiction. At the same time, it positions the person who is depicting the bragging migrant as credible. That is, it produces a *double indexicality*, which characterizes both speakers and those spoken about (see chapter 5). In this example the women of my host family sought not only to expose the falsehood of Jimena's claim to driving prowess but to portray her as someone whose claims in general are not believable. Indeed, Jimena was already seen by the women on the block where I lived as having a questionable character, as a *mujer abandonada* (abandoned woman). Her husband left her and their son to fend for themselves, and—in response— she experienced merciless shunning by her neighbors. As I discuss in chapter 5, a wife's abandonment is often assumed to be the result of a moral failing on the part of the woman. Jimena was one of two abandoned women who lived on the street, and the other people I knew would avoid socializing with her.

Talk of the bragging migrant serves similar functions as gossip and indeed is often part of gossip sessions. It points to scandalous topics that are of interest because they go to the core of ethico-moral personhood in Uriangato—and can therefore only be understood by those familiar with this social milieu. Therefore, like gossip, such talk helps create and maintain social group boundaries (Paz 2009: 118, and citations therein), both between those who understand the absurdity of certain behaviors and those who do not and between those who tell tall tales about migration and those who tell its truths. Therefore the act of designating discourse as authoritative or nonauthoritative has social indexical functions, helping construe people as certain types. Moreover, some people are more readily able to lay claim to the ability to speak authoritatively—and make designations about types of speech than others (Carr 2011; Gal and Woolard 2001; Paz 2009, 2016). Within the social milieu of La Libertad, for example, it was much harder for abandoned women like Jimena to have their discourse taken seriously by others (see also chapter 5).

As this suggests, authoritative and nonauthoritative discourse are *shifters* (Jakobson 1971; Paz 2009; Silverstein 1992): their points of reference change across contexts and according to who is making the designation (see also Gal 2002; Gal and Woolard 2001). What might seem like authoritative speech in one context or to one group of speakers may not seem so to another (Hill 2008). While my friends who were not *mujeres abandonadas* would discredit these women and their discourse, Jimena and her fellow abandoned women, who understandably formed a tight-knit group, questioned the veracity of those who shunned them. But people do not only invoke the bragging migrant to bring into question the credibility of particular people. Working-class Uriangatenses also associate this figure with the discourse of Mexican migrants in general. And it is especially this association that expresses working-class people's awareness of the position of their migration discourse vis-à-vis the authoritative accounts produced by policy makers, scholars, and so on. In the excerpt above, for example, Jesús posits that the accounts of all migrants—"those who come back here from there"—are collectively untrustworthy and therefore not authoritative. Far from being isolated to this one speaker, the association of migrant accounts with untrustworthy discourse is widespread in Uriangato: people routinely suggest that the talk of migrants is dubious.

When I asked people if it was possible to distinguish those who had migrated from those who had not, they would most readily assert that it was not possible except to say that migrants as a group *solo cuentan lo bueno* (only recount the good). In other words, the main thing that distinguished them from nonmigrants was their migration discourse's lack of veracity. And it is not only nonmigrants who advance this position—migrants do as well, sometimes directing to the population of aspirant migrants. For example, in Philadelphia I knew a group of Mexican migrants who (with the assistance of a nonprofit that supports community building among Latin American migrants) developed an education initiative they called "Mitos y realidades" (Myths and Realities). Not unlike the US program "Scared Straight," which attempts to keep young people from becoming criminals by telling them terrifying tales of life in prison, "Mitos y realidades" aims to curb migration by exposing aspirant migrants the painful realities of life in the United States. In stark contrast to the bragging migrant, these migrants returned to their hometowns once a year, usually just before the summer when migration tends to spike, to recount the hardships of migration and try to encourage youths to stay home. In so doing, they perpetuated the idea that most migrants do not tell the truth about migration to aspirants.

Talk of the bragging migrant, then, is also a form of anticipatory interpellation, as it allows speakers to stave off interpretations of their speech as untrustworthy or unknowledgeable. Such interpellation is accomplished in concert with another discursive practice: citing media stories. In describing their own experience of migration people often refer to media accounts—typically news stories but sometimes also accounts on popular shows such as *Casos*. They detailed these accounts as if telling me about something that had happened in the neighborhood. Initially I found this media-citation strange—why tell me about a story they saw on television when there was so much migration news happening in the immediate social world? In the beginning I assumed this practice was a way to protect themselves: to stave off the circulation of their personal information or to avoid reliving it through the telling of it. While it may sometimes have served those purposes, that was not all it did. People frequently recounted their personal experiences of migration to me—they were not generally secretive about them, though I am sure they kept events to themselves. Moreover, most speakers would follow descriptions of media accounts with descriptions of their own or their loved ones' migration experiences.

Media citation principally functions to distinguish their migration discourse from the tall tales of the bragging migrant asserting that their migration discourse is trustworthy, truthful, and authoritative, like the news. When citing the media, Uriangatenses often conclude with the phrase *esas son cosas verídicas* (these are truthful and real-to-life things). Consider the following discussion, drawn from an interview I conducted with Don Octavio and Doña Isabel: an elderly couple I met doing the MMP survey and subsequently came to know well. I spent many an afternoon discussing migration and family life with them before recording an ethnographic interview. Perhaps not surprisingly, given the widespread association between interviews and authoritative discourse, this couple did not engage in media citation until I interviewed them, a pattern I found with many people.

At the beginning of my interview with Don Octavio and Doña Isabel, I asked them to tell me how they feel now that their three adult sons are living in the United States. Don Octavio had migrated for many years before the strain became too much on his family life. He and Doña Isabel had then built a life together in Uriangato and had hoped their sons would do the same. To their disappointment, however, their sons had all chosen to migrate and raise their families in Pennsylvania. Don Octavio began his response to my question about their son's migration by recounting news coverage of the Minutemen Project, the self-declared title of the Arizona vigilantes who were, to use his word, *cazando* (hunting) undocumented migrants crossing the Mexico-US border.[5] He then asked me to imagine how I would feel if I heard that coverage after a family member had migrated north. He concluded his media citation by saying:

> Ese caso [of the Arizona vigilantes] es como una historia en las relaciones entre México y los Estados Unidos. Son historias que realmente son vivas—son cosas verídicas, cosas reales.
> [That case is part of the history of relations between Mexico and the United States. They are real, live histories—they are true things, real things.]

Don Octavio, a songwriter and member of a popular local band, then contrasted these "real histories" from the news with the act of making an account of things by writing a song. He explained that, like the words of a bragging migrant, song lyrics may or may not refer to real things. But the accounts of migration from the news are verifiable, authoritative. After making the comparison between songs and the news, he explained his experience of his sons' migration, asserting it is part of the demonstrable history between Mexico and the United States and thus asserting an authoritative voice that reports on the truths of migration and exposes their harsh realities.

As Don Octavio's words suggest, Uriangatenses' association of the accounts of migrants with the tall tales of braggarts does not reflect an absolute disregard for their own perspectives or those of their fellow Uriangatenses (particular subjects of derision, like Jimena, aside). For people to describe the migration discourse of "those who come here from there" as like the discourse of the bragging migrant, as Jesús does, is to say that it is has the evidentiary status of storytelling, a form of discourse that conveys the world by taking artistic license. This is not to say that storytelling is maligned as untruthful. Working-class Uriangatenses value storytelling, songs, and other forms of verbal artistry as a type of truth telling, and skilled verbal artists garner interactional influence and authority within their immediate social world (see the discussion of the voicing of the *mujer sufrida* in chapter 5)—a pattern found in many Mexican communities on both sides of the border (Chávez 2017b; Farr 2006; Faudree 2013; Mendoza-Denton 2008).

Rather than being a repudiation of verbal artistry, Uriangatenses' alignment of the bragging migrant with storytelling is an expression of their marginality outside of their immediate world (cf. Chávez 2015; Dick and Arnold 2017a; Paz 2009). Not unlike Alejandro Paz's (2009) argument that Latino/a migrants in Israel embrace a self-designation as *chismosos* (gossips) because it communicates their exclusion from the centers of Israeli political power, working-class Uriangatenses' association of the talk of migrants with the tall tales of braggarts is a form of recognition that their migration discourse is peripheral to the production of authoritative accounts.[6] And it is therefore also a form of political critique (Dick and Arnold 2017a). Media citation counteracts the positioning of their discourse as nonauthoritative, as when Don Octavio places his family's experience in league with news accounts, making it clear that his migration discourse is not part of the world of storytelling. By framing their migration discourse with these media accounts, Uriangatenses acknowledge and also push back against the migrant vulnerability constructed in such accounts (cf. Chávez 2015).

Depicting the world of the bragging migrant is therefore an activity in which people engage to distinguish between truthful, legitimate, authoritative accounts of migration and suspect accounts. Through such distinctions, people establish themselves as able to discern truth from fiction, as people who can speak with authority, in contrast with people who only tell tall tales and thus cannot be trusted. This, in turn, shapes the judgment about whose discourse does and does not deserve to circulate beyond the confines of the immediate social context of the migrant enclave (cf. Briggs 2007: 556; Shoaps 2009: 465). Nonauthoritative discourse is circumscribed, not fit for wide circulation. But people also invoke the bragging migrant as a form of critical commentary on migrant vulnerability and marginality—to highlight it and resist it, as they do when they cite media coverage of migration and link it to their own migration accounts. Moreover, that people would engage in media citation in the context of my interviews, in particular, suggests that the interviews became a site for producing their discourse as authoritative and legitimate. In chapters 4 and 5 I return to this point by examining the specific discursive strategies through which speakers try to assert legitimacy, focusing on the gendered, ethico-moral dimensions of these practices in actual interactions.

This chapter explores the mutually constitutive process through which my interview work enabled me and my interlocutors to interpellate ourselves as people of respect and authority—a process that depends at every turn on language beliefs and practices. Uriangatenses are aware of how they are positioned in the world of migration discourse that is produced in institutional sites of authority. Although the discourse generated at these sites affects their lives—through policy and through how they shape and contain what it means to be properly Mexican—they generally have little access to or control over interactions that produce authoritative accounts. Their discursive marginalization is part of the variegation of their belonging—in Mexico and in the United States. Their acknowledgment of this marginalization as they endeavor to elevate their discourse from the realm of the bragging migrant is a form of critical commentary on that variegation. Migrants are represented in many (though certainly not all) authoritative accounts of migration as immoral, suspect, and criminal, so the stakes for wanting to contribute to the politics of their representation are high. In the next chapter I use the analysis of homebuilding practices to explore working-class Uriangatenses' engagements with the ways they are depicted in the state-endorsed imaginaries of moral mobility in Mexico that interpellate them as beyond the pale of full belonging.

CHAPTER 3

Diaspora at Home: Homebuilding and the Failures of Progress

Snapshot One

Rosario and Fernando González want their own home. Renting is too unstable and living with relatives too invasive. When their youngest was a baby, Fernando left for Utah, where his brother could help him find work in construction, thinking—as do many working-class people in Uriangato—that the most expedient path to a family home is for the father to work in the United States and send money back to Mexico. Fernando departed with the faith of many a first-time migrant—that realization of his family's dream of home ownership required only some hard work in the North, the United States. A carpenter by trade, Fernando was no stranger to hard work. While he was away, Rosario, like many women whose husbands go north, moved in with her parents, who live in a home built by remittances sent by Rosario's brothers in Pennsylvania. This would allow the couple to save money, while giving Rosario support as she raised her three small children in the absence of her husband. Rosario's sister Ana, an unmarried middle-aged woman living, as per custom, with her parents, took a motherly stance toward Rosario and her children, helping her much younger sister buy clothes, food, and school supplies when Fernando's monthly remittances dwindled to a trickle and eventually stopped. But this financial aid came with a price: Ana never let Rosario forget Fernando had failed his wife financially. Fernando had found, as many do, that work is not so plentiful on the other side as he had imagined. Finally he returned home, having to admit that *al final de las cuentas, no realizé mis sueños* (at the end of the day, I did not achieve my dreams).

Unwilling to live under Ana's critical gaze, Rosario and Ferr have spent the better part of their marriage since his return mc from one side of town to another. They are like gypsies, they say, paying rent while struggling to save money to build a home of their own. When I lived in Uriangato, they had recently started renting the home of a relative of Fernando's. This place, located on an edge of town that borders one of the municipality's ranchos (rural communities), is in a state of partial construction, with a few completed rooms and a dirt floor. The incompleteness of the home never escaped mention by Ana. Ana was a neighbor of mine, and we had become friends as her family and my host family shared positive neighborly relations, including frequent sessions of sidewalk sociality (see chapter 2). She routinely fosters Rosario and Fernando's daughter Serena, in order, as Ana put it, to keep the filth of the dirt floor off the girl. She feels a sense of duty to provide Serena access to life in the urban center to counteract the influence of the country ways that the child was exposed to at the rental house. Conscious of these judgments and aware the rental home's owner could ask for the house back at any moment, Rosario and Fernando know the development of their family unfolds across a razor's edge between stability and displacement.

Snapshot Two

Verónica and Héctor Torres did it the right way, Verónica's mother Doña Susan would frequently say to me with no small measure of pride. They bought the land for their house before they had their children. They then built the house bit by bit, thanks both to Verónica's dutiful management of the home construction over many years in Uriangato and to the income that Héctor earned in Pennsylvania's mushroom industry, as he worked his way up from picker to truck driver to supervisor. This house on the other side of the street where I lived in Uriangato represents the zenith of standards of living for homes in La Libertad. Its exterior is finished with bright paint, tinted windows, and a slanted roof; it has two stories; and its interior floors are finished with tile—not dirt. The average house in the neighborhood, by contrast, even if it is no longer under construction, shows signs of at least marginal roughness, such as a coarse brick exterior. So Héctor's migration has been successful. He went north *para ver si Dios me socorre hacer una casa* (to see if God will help me build a house). And it seems, in the end, God was willing to fulfill that dream.

But in the summer of 2002—more than twenty years after the Torres family began to build their home in Uriangato—the house stood empty except for the solitary presence of their eldest son. One by one, the Torreses have moved to Pennsylvania, including—finally—Verónica herself. She left her finely appointed residence in one of the best parts of La Libertad to live in a two-bedroom trailer in a muddy Pennsylvania field with her husband, daughter, middle son, and daughter-in-law. The family's aspiration then became to bring their eldest son to the United States and buy a home in Pennsylvania. At that point, the house in Uriangato will be closed to stand *abandonada* (abandoned) except on the Torres family's visits home—no renters will be allowed to occupy it. When Verónica departed, I was still living in Uriangato. After she left, her move was a popular topic of discussion during sidewalk sociality. Talk would start with concern for her unmarried son, as we watched his lonely bachelor comings and goings: who makes him dinner, who cleans his clothes? But invariably the conversation would come around to the topic of housing. The women on my block were perplexed that Verónica would leave her beautiful home for a trailer. Most of these women have family in the United States. They know about trailers—these are small, uncomfortable, and expensive dwellings; indeed, the Torres family paid $900 a month for theirs. Why migrate after all those years of sacrifice for a house they had finally completed in their homeland, to live in a crowded, overpriced trailer in the middle of a northern field?

These stories are characteristic of working-class Uriangatenses' efforts to build home and find belonging within a social milieu informed by the imperatives of moral mobility—the idea that Mexicans should achieve socioeconomic advancement in a moral way that distinguishes Mexican progress from the crassly individualistic and greedy forms of progress believed to typify life in the United States. As I show in chapter 1, state discourses of development in Mexico have long produced imaginaries of moral mobility, which create distinctions between right and wrong kinds of Mexicans based on how well they integrate modernity and tradition, ensuring that tradition will never impede progress. Therefore state-endorsed imaginaries elevate progress over tradition. Such imaginaries involve a paradoxical pragmatics of interpellation for working-class people and other marginalized groups. They are construed simultaneously as the beating heart of authentic Mexicanidad—as the most traditional, the essence of what distinguishes Mexico as its own sovereign nation—and also as the central cause of the country's failure to progress. They are the reason why Mexico is still "behind" other industrialized nations, especially the United States. This paradox produces a double-bind of belonging that is especially pressing for migrants and their loved ones, because life in the United States and therefore US migration are figured in state-endorsed imaginaries as morally corrupting and therefore potentially de-Mexicanizing (see chapter 1). In this chapter I turn to the important question of how working-class people respond to the paradoxical interpellation entailed in state-endorsed imaginaries: do they adopt its terms—and, if so, in what ways and to what ends?

The opening snapshots provide the outline of an answer to these questions. They reveal that working-class Uriangatenses embrace the central values of progress and mobility, manifested in their efforts to own and enhance their homes. At the same time, homeownership in Uriangato forms the foundation of proper family life (Dick 2010b). The cultivation of family via home acquisition is the central practice through which working-class Uriangatenses envision and enact what they see as "traditional" ethico-moral life (Dick 2013). Having a home of their own is a key way working-class people respond positively to the interpellative call of state-endorsed imaginaries of moral mobility. Through their homes, they signal that they are advancing socioeconomically while remaining rooted in family and thus moral. That is, in homebuilding, they take up the mandate to integrate tradition and modernity that is at the heart of state-endorsed imaginaries of moral mobility. But these stories also suggest that working-class Uriangatenses revise their interpellation into state-endorsed imaginaries by spotlighting that moral mobility is difficult for working-class people to achieve for reasons beyond their control. Despite (as it is often described) *todo su empeño* (all their persistent determination), homebuilding seems invariably to result in displacement, whether to another rental home or to the United States.

This chapter argues that as working-class Uriangatenses endeavor to realize moral mobility through homebuilding they encounter, push against, but also reproduce *diaspora at home*: a fractured process of belonging, in which people's attempts to achieve moral mobility are characterized by an impassable divide between the lives state-endorsed imaginaries mandate them to lead and the lives to which they can actually lay claim. For working-class people, their paradoxical interpellation into Mexicanidad produces lives of perpetual alienation and longing: a diaspora lived not only by migrants but also by people who never leave home. Rosario and Fernando's ever-incomplete efforts to acquire a home are an example of such diaspora. But so too is Verónica and Héctor's homebuilding success, which has only led to further dislocation.

Scholars generally use the term "diaspora" to describe the loss of a homeland located in a distant past or remote future. It is typically associated with forced removal from a homeland (Clifford 1994; Daswani 2013a; Eisenlohr 2006; Quayson and Daswani 2013), which is not the case here. I use this term because it more accurately describes Uriangatenses' experiences of Mexicanidad than its sister term "transnationalism," which tends to connote a sense of connection across borders (Basch et al. 1994; Rouse 1992). As others have noted, migrants always endure forms of loss better captured by the concept of diaspora (Hallett and Baker Christales 2010; Werbner 2013). But this concept also helps illuminate the politics of national belonging "at home" (cf. Brah 1996).[1] Because national belonging is variegated (see chapter 1), interpellation into the nation-state will necessarily be fractured for some. Therefore built into the project of the nation-state is a diaspora of sorts, an estrangement from the forms of inclusion and access that would enable marginalized groups to be fully at home, better described as national longing than belonging. Such estrangement is exacerbated by imaginaries of moral mobility because—as the opening snapshots show—"progress" is a moving target, the completion of which is elusive by design (see also the discussion of "co-responsibility" in chapter 1). Thus, I use "diaspora" to refer not primarily to physical displacement but to a process of estrangement from national belonging and its associated resources.

I explore the production and resistance of diaspora at home through the analysis of working-class Uriangatense homebuilding practices. By this I mean the closely interconnected activities of physical home construction and the migration discourse through which people fashion the significance of home. "Home" is both a metonym for belonging in the national "family" of Mexico and also the material site of dwelling through which people seek membership in the here-and-now of family, street, neighborhood, and city. The multivalence of "home"—that it can refer to the nation and to more immediate social formations—has long been remarked upon by scholars of nation-building (e.g., Alonso 1994, 2004; Herzfeld 1997). And while migration scholars have attended to the centrality of home acquisition in processes of migration (Hirsch 2003; Lattanzi Shutika 2011; Lopez 2015; Pader 1993), little attention has been paid to how people in contexts of migration, including nonmigrants, use homebuilding to respond to their interpellation into the nation-state. To understand how homebuilding is a form of interpellation requires consideration of its *language materiality*: the way descriptions of homes, as well as the rendition of the nation through talk of migration, interact with the materiality of the homes themselves (cf. Keane 2007; Shankar 2015: 13; Shankar and Cavanaugh 2012; Wirtz 2014). Examining language materiality means developing a multimodal analysis that considers how the semiotics of home construction are intertwined with the talk about home, through which people locate houses and those living within them with respect to each other, to Uriangato, Mexico, and to the United States (cf. Duranti 1997; Keane 1995, 2007: chapter 9).

In the following discussion I describe the key semiotic processes that produce diaspora at home for working-class Uriangatenses, through which I elaborate the contours of what it means to be working-class in Mexico. Specifically, I detail the recursive frameworks that order how state-endorsed imaginaries of moral mobility interact with homebuilding in La Libertad. In homebuilding Uriangatenses both take up and push against state-endorsed visions of Mexicanidad. While they agree that the hallmark of Mexicanidad is the achievement of moral mobility through the integration of tradition and modernity, they elevate the traditional so that it is an equal partner with and not an impediment to progress. Through this elevation working-class people criticize and resist the diaspora at home that characterizes the variegation of their belonging. But they also re-create national longing and its associated estrangements from full membership in the polity.

Golden Donkeys: Working-Class Liminality and the Erasure of Urban Need

State-endorsed imaginaries of moral mobility help produce Uriangatense diaspora at home through a semiotic process called *fractal recursivity*—the projection of an opposition salient in one context into other contexts (Irvine and Gal 2000: 38). Evidence of such projection is identifiable in the similarities between state-endorsed and Uriangatense visions of moral mobility. These similarities are grounded in a shared set of fundamental contrasts, which makes it possible for homebuilding to function both as a positive interpellative response to state-endorsed calls to Mexicanidad and also as a form of resistance to those calls. Later in this chapter I show how working-class people take up and revise state-endorsed Mexicanidad. But first I use the concept of fractal recursivity to illuminate the paradoxical positioning of working-class people within state-endorsed national imaginaries, situating this process in the political economic context of Uriangato. The diaspora at home of working-class people is defined by two key processes of marginalization, which fundamentally rely on fractal recursion. One is their social positioning between "morality" and "mobility," such that they can never fully embody the requisite qualities of Mexicanidad. The other factor is that the recursive frameworks of moral mobility erase their socioeconomic need. These processes distinguish being working-class from other forms of marginalization in Mexico, such as those experienced by racialized groups (see chapter 1). As such, they help illuminate the contours of working-class life in Mexico.

As I explore in chapter 1, state-endorsed imaginaries are ordered around a modernist chronotope that contrasts the future-oriented, ever-changing "modern realm" of industrialization and progress with the now-oriented, stable-through-time "traditional realm" of religion and morality. These imaginaries rely on an *anchoring* contrast between modernity and tradition, each of which is aligned with complementary qualities—progress/futurity and religion/morality, respectively—that are framed as similar and contrasted with the qualities associated with the opposite term (Gal 2016: 96–98). Such contrasts are often mapped onto spaces, in this case the United States and Mexico, and the people who inhabit them. They are fractal and recursive because they repeat the same related contrasts across settings (Dick and Arnold 2017a; Gal 2016). For example, as discussed earlier, the US/Mexico contrast is aligned with a correlated urban/rural contrast, so that all of the United States and its people are understood to possess qualities associated with urbanity and modernity and all of Mexico's qualities associated with ruralness and tradition.

These alignments have been foundational to scholarly, governmental, and Uriangatense discourse about migration, wherein movements to the North are often represented as a passage from the rural/traditional to the urbane/modern (Dick 2010a; Walsh 2004). Such contrasts also recur within the confines of Mexico, so that "rural Mexico" is understood as inherently distinct from "urban Mexico" and urban Mexico as more like the United States, less Mexican. Indeed rural-urban contrasts are a key feature of many modernist frameworks in a wide array of settings (Comaroff and Comaroff 1992: 155–178; Hannerz 1980; Messing 2002, 2007; Williams 1973). Not unlike these other frameworks, state-endorsed imaginaries of moral mobility in Mexico treat the rural as both "backward" and more moral—and therefore more "authentically Mexican"—than the urban (see chapter 1). Indeed, *lo ranchero* (the essential country) and its markers (rebozos, cowboy hats) are signal emblems of Mexicanidad (cf. Farr 2006; Nájera-Ramírez 2002). The rural/urban contrast also repeats within smaller units in Mexico: the municipality of Uriangato is divided into an urban center and rural towns: a structure of differentiation found in most Mexican municipalities.

These distinctions are not a way to describe a fixed taxonomy of differentiation (Gal 2016). Rather, the analysis of recursive frameworks helps illuminate the pragmatics of how politically loaded social difference gets taken up and reformulated from different perspectives (Dick and Arnold 2017a; Gal 2016). Consider a recursion particularly relevant to working-class Uriangatenses' liminal position between modernity/tradition: the mapping of urban/rural onto types of cities, so that some are understood to be more "urban" and others more "rural." This contrast makes possible the idea of a provincial city, like Uriangato, whose residents are neither rural nor urbane but live between the two. They can never be truly moral like those rancheros who make up the heart of the nation (cf. Farr 2006). At the same time, they cannot be truly urban, like people from Mexico's major cities. Uriangatenses readily remark on this liminal positioning, explaining that their town is much more "advanced" than the ranchos, with its textile industry and internet cafes. But in the same breath they note that they have no movie theater or megastores, like the newly arrived Walmart in nearby Morelia, Michoacán—a store that, like Morelia itself, epitomized modernity for Uriangatenses (cf. Dávila 2016).

The provinciality of Uriangato is also highlighted by Uriangatenses in the United States, for whom distinctions between rancho and urban center fade. The granddaughter of a man I knew in Uriangato, for example, dreads visiting Uriangato because there *¡Comen puros frijoles y chiles!* (All they eat is beans and peppers!). For this US-reared child, the diet an urban Uriangatense would associate with the ranchos becomes a metonym for all of Uriangato. This girl's grandfather, a lifelong urban dweller, finds the blurring of the rural-urban distinction absurd. I once heard him say to her over the phone: *¡No te creas, hija, acá también hay hamburguesas!* (Don't believe [it], my dear, there are hamburgers here too!)—hamburgers being iconic of development and its luxuries for grandfather and granddaughter alike.

The liminal positioning of working-class Uriangatenses is captured in a biting moniker commonly used to describe people from this city: Burros de Oro (Golden Donkeys). Uriangatenses are "golden" because the textile industry affords them more economic opportunity than people from comparable Mexican cities have, so they are more mobile. Yet many Uriangatenses have a low average educational level. Most city residents—and the vast majority of working-class people—enter the textile workforce after the completion of primary school at age twelve. Therefore they are "donkeys" because they are uneducated. As a well-established symbol of rural Mexico, "burro" also suggests that, despite living in a city and having money, they are "backward" like a rural person: ignorant and stubborn like a donkey. Although "Golden Donkey" can be used to describe anyone from Uriangato, it is an especially harsh form of hailing for working-class people. Being interpellated as *un burro de oro* implies failing to be mobile in the right way: a recursion of their marginalization by state institutions within the social landscape of their immediate world.

The marginalizing liminality produced in talk of urban Uriangato transforms nondiscursive signs into potent emblems that inscribe this liminality into every facet of life—from the food people consume to the way they run the textile industry (cf. Cavanaugh 2007, 2009; Riley and Cavanaugh 2017). For example, while I was teaching English as a second language at Uriangato's Instituto Tecnológico Superior del Sur de Guanajuato (ITSUR: Greater Southern Technological Institute of Guanajuato), one of the state's institutions of higher learning, people would often use the descriptor Golden Donkeys to critique Uriangatense manufacturing. In such critiques students and faculty, many of whom were from Uriangato, blamed people's unwillingness to adopt modern production techniques on their irrational, ignorant attachment to "traditional" methods, which typically meant they were being criticized for eschewing the use of robots and computer-based inventory tracking systems. Members of ITSUR would argue—in a fashion resonant with state-endorsed imaginaries of moral mobility (see chapter 1)—that attachment to traditionality was the principal factor holding back the progress of Uriangato's textile industry. Consequently, even the most "modern" aspect of life in Uriangato indexes the city's provinciality, as handwritten ledgers and the use of human labor iconize Uriangatense backwardsness. Such alignments of people, objects, and practices in talk of Uriangato and its people produce a language materiality in which recursions of modernist contrasts conceal working-class people's lack of access to the resources that could facilitate their mobility. At the same time, they fuse these alignments with the very ingredients and fabrics of life, making them seem natural.

The concealment of working-class need is made possible through a semiotic process called *erasure*: the obscuring or dismissal of any information, process, or event that does not match the ideological assumptions of a recursive framework (Irvine and Gal 2000: 38). The erasure of working-class need in Uriangato is observable in the local implementation of development policy, especially poverty alleviation and welfare programs, which further extend the naturalizing effects of language materiality. As shown in chapter 1, such programs are prime sites for the production of state-endorsed imaginaries of moral mobility; they are also a central way these imaginaries arrive in Uriangato. Mexico does not have a comprehensive welfare system with universal entitlements but a collection of poverty alleviation programs run out of different offices (Molyneux 2006: 426). The assistance offered by these programs is targeted—and the leading criterion in the majority of these programs is living in a rural area (Kurtz 2002) These kinds of requirements write codify the idea that poverty is a feature of rural life. Although this marginalizes rural people from full national belonging (as their poverty is a sign of "backwardness"), it does grant them a basis upon which to make claims on resources. At the same time, it denies the needs of urban people. Recall the story of the Christmas gift drive run by Desarrollo Integral de Familias, which restricted access to the gifts to people from Uriangato's ranchos so that no urbanites, even poor single mothers, could benefit from it (see introductory chapter).

State-endorsed imaginaries of moral mobility erase the economic need of working-class people not only by envisioning poverty as a feature of rural life but also by construing progress as linear, as a movement from past to future, from country to city (see the discussion of *el pelado* in chapter 1). People in the city are progressing; they are integrated into the city's booming economy, which provides more work and a better standard of living than not only the ranchos but their sister cities as well—or so the story goes. To acknowledge urban need would be to recognize the failures of mobility that are actually endemic to the textile industry. Consider that textile employees should be able to collect social security, which is meant to grant people health care and other benefits (Dion 2009: 67), including funds to finance home ownership (UN-Habitat 2011). But these benefits are only provided to people who work in the formal economy—and Uriangato's *informal* economy encompasses the majority of the city's factories. Many owners do not register their companies as required by law to avoid paying taxes. According to Uriangato's Office of Economic Development, the municipality had roughly forty registered factories in the early 2000s. But there were easily over two hundred factories in operation. Consequently, a majority of textile workers cannot access the social security benefits to which they are entitled as citizens.

This is an open secret—municipal officials readily admit that they know about the unregistered factories. Although these factories are located in the heart of the city and would not be difficult to find, the municipal, state, and federal governments rarely take action against employers' violations of the law. I did not hear of a single workplace raid during over five years of fieldwork.[2] This tacit sanctioning of illegal business practices obscures the failures of the city's textile industry to provide working-class people full membership in the polity, while legitimating worker exploitation. Consequently, government inaction helps produce state-endorsed imaginaries of belonging just as much as the proactive delineation of belonging in poverty alleviation programs does.

A parallel process of erasure is evident in ideas about who migrates to the United States. It is widely assumed in Mexico that migration is the practice of rural people.[3] Many state-run programs like "Tres por Uno" (discussed in chapter 1) use migrant remittances to develop rural areas, ignoring the fact that urban migration is also about attempts to overcome barriers to socioeconomic mobility. Consider, for example, that Mexican mortgage markets are essentially closed to people who do not already have collateral in the form of a pension or an existing property (UN-Habitat 2011). Because most Uriangatense workers are members of the informal economy, they are excluded from pensions and generally too poor to own property. Consequently, in order to acquire a home working-class people must either purchase an existing house with cash, which few of them can afford, or buy a plot of land and then slowly build their home over many years.[4] To circumvent their exclusion from Mexico's credit markets, many working-class families turn to migration. Acquiring capital to build a home in Mexico is a leading motivator for migration country-wide (cf. Hirsch 2003; Lattanzi Shutika 2011: chapter 3; Lopez 2015). But state and municipal officials erase these processes.

I was struck by the power of such erasure in my interactions with the mayor of Uriangato, Carlos Guzmán. A former migrant who lived most of his forty-some years in Chicago (always migrating from Uriangato's urban center), Mayor Guzmán promoted concern for migrants as a signal feature of his administration. Even though he was himself an urban migrant, he continually construed Uriangatense migration as a rural phenomenon. When Guzmán issued me a letter of permission for the MMP survey (see chapter 2), he expressed surprise at my decision to focus on migration out of the city, despite the fact that he knew a majority of households in La Libertad have migration experience. Every time I visited his offices, he drove me to one of Uriangato's ranchos to see *la verdadera migración* (the real, authentic migration). Moreover, his migration-related programs—from a Tres por Uno project supporting the development of a tomato farm to a monthly lecture series on how families can manage the stress of transnational separation, developed with help from a federal government initiative called "Atención a migrantes" (Attention for Migrants)—were exclusively targeted at the ranchos. This targeting influenced how urban-born Uriangatenses responded to government efforts to support migrants and their families. The people I knew did not participate in "Atención a migrantes" projects because they understood them to be, as one friend put it, for *los rancheritos* (the little country people): a group with whom working-class urbanites did not want to be associated.

The third key arena that produces the liminality of working-class people and the erasure of their need is land tenure in La Libertad. As in many working-class neighborhoods in Latin America (cf. Paley 2001), the establishment of La Libertad was unlawful. The area that today makes up this area was originally an *ejido*, a communally owned property reserved for farming. Before 1994 it was illegal to subdivide *ejido* land.[5] However, as commercial agriculture made small-scale *ejido* farming untenable in the early 1970s, Uriangatense municipal officials informally granted *ejidatarios* permission to sell *ejido* property (Aranda Ríos 2000: 52). As the municipal historian informed me, *ejidatarios* divided up the area between them over the next decade and sold it off as housing plots of less than a tenth of an acre each.

The municipality demonstrated approval of the development of La Libertad by permitting the extension of electricity, plumbing, and paved roadways into the neighborhood. Yet it did not provide the new landholders with documentation that they own their plots, which would have been tantamount to admitting they had enabled violation of federal *ejido* law. Therefore people who bought a plot before 1994, when it became permissible to sell *ejido* land (which is most of the neighborhood), legally do not own the land on which their houses are built. This land tenure ambiguity constrains homeowners from making demands on the municipality. For example, during Uriangato's weekly utility shortages, La Libertad is the first area to lose electricity and running water. Residents are charged a daily fee for utilities by the government-run companies that manage them, whether or not they receive these resources. While no one in La Libertad thinks this is fair, most residents I knew were reticent to take it up with officials because they do not want to risk contestation of land ownership.

Collectively these erasures—of their economic vulnerability, the migration, their land tenure—help create diaspora at home for working-class people by normalizing and making invisible the barriers that they experience between the life they are meant to lead to be properly Mexican and the lives to which they can actually lay claim. As government institutions deny their needs and sanction the violation of rights to which they are entitled as citizens, they constrain working-class people's basis for making claims on the state in ways that keep them outside full membership in the polity (cf. Lomnitz 2001b: 319–321). This is in part because denials of their needs force them to participate in practices that reinforce the idea that there is something wrong with their ethico-moral character, such as ambiguous land tenure or migration, while ignoring the ways these practices point to the failures of development in Uriangato. Yet these failures of progress are a central force encouraging working-class reliance on such practices. In denying those failures, the state leaves working-class people open to accusations that their migration, land tenure, and other practices are senseless and morally questionable—why don't they just buy property the right way; why don't they just get ahead in Uriangato, where work is plentiful; don't they know the harm they do to their families by migrating? These questions are frequently raised by many middle- and upper-class Uriangatenses (see the introductory chapter; cf. Yeh 2012).

As shown in chapter 1, accusations of moral failure have been mobilized repeatedly in state discourse to justify the variegation of citizenship. Underscored in each practice discussed above is the point that recursion and erasure rely on the symbolic loading of forms of non-discursive materiality—from hamburgers to housing plots—and their elaboration in talk that differentiates Uriangatenses from other Mexicans and working-class people from both the rich and the poor. The remainder of this chapter spotlights such language materiality, focusing on the complex ways working-class people respond to their liminal positioning through homebuilding, asserting their Mexicanidad and critiquing their marginality while also reproducing it.

The Beautiful Life: Homebuilding, Traditional Morality, and Being Mexican in Uriangato

Working-class Uriangatense homebuilding practices—both the building of homes and the construal of "home" in migration discourse—recursively take up the modernist contrasts found in state-endorsed visions of Mexicanidad. They reflect robust agreement with the idea that being properly Mexican is about integrating tradition and modernity, morality and progress. This point is illustrated in the core themes of working-class Uriangatense migration discourse, in which talk of housing is a centerpiece: *siguiendo adelante* (getting ahead) and creating *una vida bonita* (a beautiful, moral life) (also discussed in Dick 2010a, 2013). *Seguir adelante* is to gain access to the employment, consumer goods, education, and other material and ideological resources that facilitate socioeconomic advancement (cf. Berg 2015).

In talk of migration, Uriangatenses regularly assert that a central goal of their lives and leading motivator of their migration is the effort to get ahead. At the same time, people also assert that an equally important goal is creating *una vida bonita*. In Mexican Spanish *bonito/a* conveys not only the idea of beauty but also that such people, objects, and activities are morally good (cf. Stack 2012b). While "getting ahead" comes with its own ethico-moral imperatives (discussed below), the conceptualization of the good that Uriangatenses associate with *la vida bonita* is about cultivating the traditional practices they see as uniquely Mexican. For working-class Uriangatenses—as in state-endorsed discourse—Mexicanidad is about getting ahead, but in the context of a beautiful life; that is, it involves realizing moral mobility.

Homebuilding is a signal practice of a moral mobility because, through it, people integrate *siguiendo adelante* with *la vida bonita* (see also Dick 2013). For many working-class Uriangatenses, homebuilding is the prime symbol of and arena for the enactment of traditionality, even as it also is at the heart of their efforts to be socioeconomically mobile and "modernize." Creating *la vida bonita* means mitigating the self-focused individualism encouraged by the imperatives of progress—and epitomized by life in the United States—by prioritizing the needs of the collective over those of the individual. Such communitarianism is integral to the gracious personhood that working-class Uriangatenses see as central to their Mexicanidad (see chapter 2).

The primary idiom through which people realize and express communitarianism is in the development and maintenance of family, emblematized in the model of the "traditional Catholic family," wherein the father is the supreme authority, the children are the flock, and the mother is an intermediary between the two (Dick 2010b; Hirsch 2003; Rouse 1995). Therefore this model of family is distinctly patriarchal and heteronormative (cf. Chávez 2017a). Although ideals of Mexican family life are changing as people adopt family nucleation and a more egalitarian ethos in marriage, the image of the traditional family nevertheless continues to be a key signifier of communitarianism. Uriangatenses' positive valuation of communitarianism is legitimated by the Catholic church, which promotes such visions of family life as the primary way laypeople can serve God. Indeed, relationships among laypeople, the church, and God are envisioned within a Catholic vision of humanity as being organized like the traditional family—God, the father; Mary, the maternal intercessor; and people, the children of God: a recursive framework of holy communion that draws family life to the divine (Napolitano 2016). So for working-class Uriangatenses family life is a practice of both religious faith and national affiliation—it involves an interweaving of Mexicanidad and Catholicism that resonates strongly with state-endorsed imaginaries of moral mobility (see chapters 1 and 5). As part of this, it entails a commentary not only on their positioning within Mexican imaginaries but also in US discourse, which often uses Catholic family life as the basis for claims about the unassimilatability of Mexican migrants (Chávez 2017a; Dick 2010b). As such, the "traditional" view of family life (and gender) does not preclude forms of political protest and resistance (see chapter 5).

If the creation and maintenance of family is the central practice through which people realize Mexicanidad, then the home is the site in which this practice is rooted and made possible. Homeownership and the cultivation of family are strongly associated, as illustrated in the dominant residential values and patterns. Owning a home is seen as a goal *only* for people building their own family. Adults without children generally do not concern themselves with owning—or renting—a home of their own but live with their parents and/or siblings in their natal home. In migration discourse, speakers routinely (re)create the association of home and family life by situating the home as the bedrock of family development.

Consider the following example, taken from a conversation I had with Verónica Torres, the woman from the second opening vignette, on the eve of her departure for Pennsylvania (also discussed in Dick 2010b). Here is her response to my question as to why her husband decided to migrate:

> Porque, mire, nosotros no teníamos casa, no teníamos nada. Y luego compramos, pues con trabajo, un terrenito. Y es de, me dijo, me voy para ver si Dios me socorre hacer una casa. Y por eso se fue allí. Bueno,

primero fue la casa, enseguida ya crecieron los niños: los gastos de la escuela, los gastos de ir, componiendo poquito la casa. Que ya crecieron, pues que no salgan ellos de escuela. . . . Ya después de que crecieron, de que anduvieron en escuela, pues tenía que, es de, se me casó el muchacho.

[Because, look, we didn't have a house, we didn't have anything. And then we bought, well with work, a little piece of land. And so he told me: I am going {to the United States} because I want to see if God will help me build a house. That's why he went there. Well, first it was the house, then the kids got bigger: school expenses, {and} the expenses to build the house bit by bit. And when the kids were older, well {we didn't want them} to leave school. . . . And then after they grew up, after they were in school, well he had to, um, my son got married.]

Verónica reveals the foundational importance of having a home of one's own as this motivator for migration with respect to the others that follow. In the beginning of her nuclear family life, they had "nothing" because they did not own a home. The purchase of a plot of land on which they were to build their home then motivated her husband's migration and the growth of their family. Homebuilding is the fundamental aspirational rationale that later leads to other reasons for migrating, which in turn sketch the proper unfolding of family life: after the home, they have children, who grow, go to school, get married, and so forth. Such implicit associations between home and family are a routine feature of Uriangatense migration discourse.

The association of homebuilding and family is part of a widespread cultural construct (discussed in chapter 2) that contrasts *la casa* and *la calle*, positioning home as the source of ethico-moral stability (Hirsch 2003; Hyams 2003; Mendoza-Denton 2008). As exemplified in the story of Rosario and Fernando, if parents do not have their own home, they risk being seen as not fulfilling their obligations and thus risk ethico-moral failure. Indeed, the importance of having *donde llegar* (a place to arrive)—which means having your own home to return to—is underscored by the fact that families that move to the United States typically keep their home in Mexico as a placeholder for a future when they may return (cf. Lattanzi Shutika 2011: chapter 3; Lopez 2015). Return migrants who do not have *donde llegar* are seen as childlike, immature, and certainly having failed to do migration the right way—something Rosario's sister Ana would somewhat relentlessly say about Fernando.

The association between home and stability is also produced through a related iconicity—or relationship of resemblance—between moral and residential *instability*. This iconicity is revealed in Uriangatense beliefs and practices about renters. Renters are seen as shifty transients and potential squatters; either way, they are not to be trusted. Indeed most families who move to the North would rather leave their homes *abandonadas* (empty) than rent them out (cf. Lattanzi Shutika 2011: chapter 3). Similarly, people who rent out their homes do not provide renters a lease for fear it would encourage squatting. Because of the putative untrustworthiness of renters, they are subject to close scrutiny. Two of my neighbors—a quiet middle-aged couple who were renting while their own house was being renovated—were not only endlessly gossiped about. The niece of the owners inspected the rental home weekly to ensure that they were not doing anything untoward. Rather than being bothered by this monitoring (as I was), the couple tolerated it patiently, explaining they had nothing to hide and would do the same if the roles were reversed.

The relationship of home, family, and stability is also expressed through the semiotic loading of different kinds of building materials. Concrete, for example, is the preferred construction material for walls, exteriors, and floors because it is taken as a sign of stability. This signification is illustrated by many Uriangatenses' reactions to the wooden homes that for them epitomize homebuilding in the United States. Wooden homes, they frequently point out, may be more aesthetically pleasing than concrete homes but are far too fragile to serve as the foundation of a family. Contrasts between concrete and wooden homes are recursively aligned with working-class understandings of the differences between Mexican and US family life.

My research participants routinely describe the United States as *puro reloj—puro trabajar y encerramiento* (all [by the] clock—all work and isolation). They argue that this state of being damages the unity and stability of the family and therefore threatens people's ethico-moral character (Dick 2010a, 2013; Dick and Arnold 2017a). Uriangatenses depict the United States as a place where children drift away from parents and have too much freedom, where siblings no longer look out for each other. Such disunity is symbolized not only by the perceived fragility of US wooden homes but also by US patterns of residence. Many US children move out of their parents' home long before marriage and often when they are still teenagers. This is indicative of a style of parenting that Uriangatenses find anathema to proper Mexicanidad (see chapter 2). The valuation of US homes also reveals a critique of the vulnerability and instability of migrant lives, reproduced in talk of housing. Verónica and Héctor's daughter complained to me right before Hurricane Isabel hit in 2003 that the trailer she shares with her parents, brother, and sister-in-law is made of "wood," saying: *aquí se lo va a llevar el huracán* (the hurricane is going to carry this place away). This comment was followed by a chorus of affirming but nervous laughter by her family. Their anxious good humor also pointed to the danger they faced as we watched the tempest's dark clouds roll in. For, to be sure, trailers are often the first dwellings to become flooded, uninhabitable, or even dislodged during storms.

Homebuilding practices are also a form of political commentary on the variegation of belonging in Mexico, as they elevate tradition from the place it has in state-endorsed imaginaries of moral mobility. Because state-endorsed imaginaries position tradition as the central impediment to progress, even as they posit it as the essence of authentic Mexicanidad, any practice or group of people considered traditional should be tightly controlled, co-opted, and "scheduled" by state institutions into discrete times and places (Alonso 2004; Lomnitz 2008; cf. Urciuoli 1996). But for Uriangatenses, their traditionality is not something to be corralled into museums or paraded around on holidays. It is built into the physical environment of their homes and neighborhood, which express their effort to craft a stable and loving milieu for the development of family life.

Thus, in homebuilding working-class Uriangatenses not only respond to calls to moral mobility. They use the recursive framework of modernity/tradition to create their own imaginaries of moral mobility that are more inclusive of working-class lives, saying in effect: our traditionality is not an impediment to progress, it is the cornerstone of progress, its beginning and its end. If a person is not building a family, there is no need for progress in the first place. The examples above illustrate the production of a language materiality in which types of building materials, patterns of residence, and the socio-emotional meaning of "home" come together to create a habitus in which familialism and communitarianism serve as a measuring stick against which working-class Uriangatenses evaluate themselves. They thereby establish their own boundaries around national belonging that seek to dignify tradition further and, in turn, make a place for themselves in Mexico.

Norteño/as Desobligado/as: Communitarianism and Boundaries of Mexicanidad

Working-class renderings of Mexicanidad are evinced in nonmigrant talk about migrants, which is shot through with evaluations of whether

their relations abroad have become *desobligados* (disobliged): do they ne-
glect the obligations associated with gracious personhood and communitarianism? To accuse someone of being *desobligado* is not only to say,
"You are not taking care of your obligations to me." It is also a way to
assert that the subject of your accusation has become a *norteño/a* (northerner). Working-class Uriangatenses use this designation as shorthand
for a process of alienation, in which the person becomes un-Mexican
(cf. Mendoza-Denton 2008).[6] Accusations of disobligation are not unlike
discourse about the bragging migrant (see chapter 2), which exposes the
degradation and alienation of migrants.

Assessments of *desobligación* center on how migrant family members
manage the distribution of resources, from money and consumer goods
to time spent talking with them on the phone (cf. Abrego 2014; Arnold
2016; Castellanos 2010; Dick 2017; Dick and Arnold 2017a; Hirsch 2003;
Hondagneu-Sotelo 1994).[7] As in the examples discussed above, such assessments rely and reproduce the language materiality of homebuilding,
interweaving talk of family with the symbolic loading of possessions.
For example, Magdalena, a nonmigrant woman whose life is the focus
of chapter 5, stopped taking care of her aunt's house in Uriangato after she received a letter from her mother (who was living with this aunt),
explaining that this woman labeled her food and wouldn't share it. *¡Ni
la pinche leche!* (Not even the damned milk!), Magdalena told me, hor-
rified. This was one of many stories I heard about family in the United
States managing food in shameful ways. As suggested above, food is often a focal point of talk about Mexicanidad. It represents not only distinctions between urban and rural, the United States and Mexico, but
also the dissolution of the Mexican family in migration. More than one
return migrant told me s/he returned to Mexico because relations in the
United States no longer shared meals but would eat alone at different
times—a perversion of family life beyond the pale.

True to the workings of fractal recursivity, assessments of *desobligación* and their politics of personhood carry over to the United States
(Dick and Arnold 2017a; Mendoza-Denton 2008). They invert the assumptions of discourses of family disunification by arguing—contra
older models of migration—that family separation is just as dangerous
morally as the perversions of the United States (Dick 2006a). These parents assert that children should be raised by their mother and father in
physical proximity, that such proximity is essential to the realization of
proper family life that lies at the heart of Mexicanidad—and moral mobility. At the same time, Uriangatense parents raising children in the
North actively worry that their children will drift away from them, be-

coming so *norteño/a* that they cannot even understand Spanish. Migrant parents counter this possibility by performing extensive affective and financial labor to maintain connection with family in Mexico and to ensure the Mexicanidad of their children (cf. Abrego 2014; Arnold 2016; Dick and Arnold 2017a; Smith 2006).

For example, many Uriangatense parents in Pennsylvania do not allow their children to participate in Halloween, which they see as immoral, coming as it does at the same time as Los Días de los Muertos (The Days of the Dead, the Mexican celebration of All Souls Day) (cf. Brandes 1998). In Uriangato this is a holy time of communion with deceased loved ones. From the perspective of Mexican migrant parents, Halloween is a prototypical gringo perversion: it transforms a religious celebration that enables people to enact their gracious personhood (by realizing the obligation to honor the dead) into a commercialized excuse to engage in avarice and gluttony. The prohibition against Halloween is not an isolated example. Migrant parents incorporate communitarianism into the context of a putatively self-centered US culture: expecting teenagers to contribute to the household economy, requiring that children attending college continue to live at home in order to help with the care of their younger siblings, and so forth. They also integrate the skills children acquire in the United States, especially their abilities in English, into familial obligations. Attending the parent-teacher conference of a younger sibling as a translator for your parents, for instance, becomes part of being a good child and sibling (Orellana 2009; Reynolds and Orellana 2009).

In assessments of *desobligación* on both sides of the border tradition is elevated as the central force that keeps progress from going off the rails and undoing all that makes the social world function properly—robbing people of love, of connection, even of the damned milk! But Uriangatenses also replicate the marginalization of working-class people in Mexico—their diaspora at home. This is revealed in the ways they talk about the children of migrants, whose behavior comes up frequently in Uriangato, as people remember loved ones abroad or anticipate visits with family or just sort through the rights and wrongs of social life.

Migrant children's command of Mexican Spanish is often at the center of these conversations. Migrant children must have the right materiality of language: speak with a "Mexican" accent and intonational patterns; know the local slang; and be able to engage in distinctly Mexican genres of interaction, such as *relajo* (joking rituals) (cf. Chávez 2015; Farr 2006; Mendoza-Denton 2008). If the children fall short in any of these respects, people question not only their Mexicanidad but their basic intelligence. The nonmigrant Uriangatenses I know regularly claim that these children cannot speak either Spanish or English properly, putting their abilities to communicate at all into doubt. Questioning the allegiances and intelligence of people not competent in dialects of a "national language" is a well-documented feature of life for migrants in the United States and other migrant-receiving countries (see Dick 2011a for review; Koven 2007); it is also typical to the politics of migrants' reception when they "go home" (cf. Hernández-León and Zúñiga 2016; Koven 2013b; Zentella 1990). In Uriangato such assessments strongly parallel the history of state-endorsed discourse, in which US migration has repeatedly been posited as morally corrupting because it is de-Mexicanizing (see chapter 1). When working-class people police the boundaries around Mexicanidad, they reproduce the idea that the character of working-class people is inherently flawed: they migrate for the wrong reasons and are further corrupted by migration, which is fundamental to the production of their diaspora at home, their exclusion from the polity.

From Adobe House to Adorned House: "Getting Ahead" and the Landscapes of Progress

The relationship between Uriangatense traditionality and homebuilding practices reveals that working-class Uriangatenses revise but also reproduce the marginalizing ways they are positioned inside state-endorsed visions of Mexicanidad. A similar process is observable in their efforts to embrace modernity, especially as evinced in their understanding of the concept of *siguiendo adelante* (getting ahead). This is a central theme in migration discourse, especially when people discuss the relationship between home acquisition and migration. The idea that the central goal in life is to get ahead is a hegemonic point of departure for the evaluation of a wide range of sociocultural and political economic activities in La Libertad, organizing talk about family life and education, among many other topics (Dick 2010a, 2010b, 2013).

Working-class Uriangatenses are fully interpellated into the imperatives of progress that undergird state-endorsed imaginaries of moral mobility. In their homebuilding practices, they robustly reproduce and elaborate these imperatives. Just as homebuilding is the key idiom for the conceptualization and realization of the beautiful life in Uriangato, it is a prime modality through which people endeavor to get ahead. The relationship between homebuilding and *siguiendo adelante* is evinced in the built environment of La Libertad, which has developed in concert with a language materiality that saturates this environment with the imperatives of progress. As in state-endorsed discourse, such social landscaping is organized around the projection of a contrast between modernity and traditionality onto a divide between rural and urban.

Consider the following conversation I had with Lupe, a woman who spent the first twelve years of her life on a rancho before moving to urban Uriangato and then later migrating to Pennsylvania. Her response to a question about why she moved away from the rancho is representative of talk about the country produced by many working-class Uriangatenses:

> Pues, mucha gente se ha venido de los ranchos porque aquí es más fácil hacerse la vida que en un rancho. Me imagino yo, que por eso mucha gente se ha venido de los ranchos a Uriangato porque aquí hay mucho comercio. Y la gente lo que busca es donde mantenerse y es imposible hacer eso en los ranchos. Allá solo tienen su tierra.
> [Well, a lot of people have come from the ranchos because here it is much easier to make a life than on the rancho. I imagine that because of that a lot of people have come from the ranchos to Uriangato because there is a lot of commerce here. And what the people look for is a place where they can maintain themselves, and it is impossible to do that in the ranchos. There they only have their land.]

Lupe uses the here/there contrast typical of talk about migration to the United States (discussed in the introductory chapter) to depict the ranchos as places of destitution where "all they have is their land," so even basic survival is impracticable. By contrast, urban Uriangato is a locale of relative opportunity where people can live off of more than just the land. Such contrasts do not necessarily represent real rural and urban lives. There are many urbanites for whom basic survival is impracticable—and many people in rural communities who have more material resources than people in the city.

By occluding these realities, such discourse—like that of Mexico's poverty alleviation programs—positions rural life as poverty-ridden, thus erasing urban needs. Therefore Uriangatense talk of the country helps reproduce working-class marginality, a point to which I return below. Rather than describing actual differences between rural and urban, "country talk" is an act of social distancing. Urbanites both objectify and Other *lo ranchero*, as they dress up as rural people on special occasions like rodeos, for example. But anyone who appears ranchero in day-to-day life is seen as old-fashioned and backward. Urban Uriangatenses studiously avoid this positioning or any routine association with rancheros, as intimated above in the discussion of Uriangato's "Atención a migrantes" programs. Working-class social networks also reflect and enact this distancing. While many Uriangatenses maintain transnational relations with family in the United States, they are largely disconnected from their relatives in the ranchos, seeing them only at the occasional wedding or funeral. They treat the country as part of their past, remaining aloof from their contemporary connections to it.

This rural/urban distinction is reproduced in the semiotics of home construction in the neighborhood, which produces a language materiality that writes into La Libertad's landscape a tale of transition from a rural past to a modernized future. The rural past is emblematized by adobe homes. These single-story arrangements are topped with crumbling tile roofs and encased by stone walls, encompassing a few multipurpose, dirt-floored rooms. For urbanites, adobe homes point to the dusty, impossible country life depicted in the excerpt above, which many residents of La Libertad left behind in the 1970s. The rurality of these homes is intensified by their placement on the outskirts of the neighborhood, where paved roads find an unceremonious terminus in farmland: another form of distancing the pastoral from the metropolitan.

In opposition to the adobe homes are homes made with brick and concrete. A few blocks from the edges of town, these concrete structures overtake the adobe homes. Concrete homes represent modernity (and stability, as discussed in the preceding section) and embody the neighborhood's effort *seguir adelante*, to engineer the infrastructure of their daily lives with urbanity and "progress." Such engineering is evinced by the distinctions they craft among types of concrete homes, which are made based on degrees of completeness in construction. These degrees are on a continuum from the most basic homes (single-story spaces composed of a kitchen, a bathroom, and one multiuse room) to fully completed homes like the Torres family home.

In their scale and simplicity, basic concrete homes are similar to adobe residences but have a future that adobe homes do not. These are "for now" dwellings that occupants hope to transform into multistory structures. Most concrete homes have unfinished rooftops, where the skeletal framing stands bare except for a Mexican flag hung from the rafters as if to signal: this household is expanding in the name of our nation. Such houses imbue the neighborhood with sense of striving and continual improvement, as partially fulfilled aspirations reach skyward through the rebar that will hold the home's next level. At the end of the continuum of completeness are *las casas arregladas* (adorned houses). The verb *arreglar* is a multivalent word that can mean to arrange, as in to get one's affairs in order, or to fix up, as in to renovate. It also means to adorn or "to doll up," as when a woman gets dressed up for a date. When Uriangatenses use this term to refer to houses, all of these valences are connoted.

Adorned houses are painted and decorated, usually with ornamental tiling, tinted windows, and elaborate iron gates. Within the category of *casas arregladas* are finer distinctions that index the degree of socioeconomic advancement achieved by the household. The more decorations and stories a home has, the further its household members have progressed. A pinnacle of domicile adornment is represented in features associated with US styles of home construction, such as slanted rooftops and front yards (cf. Pader 1993). Therefore *casas arregladas* represent not only urbanity but also the US-bound migration that funds most construction in La Libertad and inspires changes in home design (cf. Hirsch 2003: 67–80; Lopez 2015). If adobe homes point to the rural past, adorned homes point to a future when everyone has achieved modernity and at last gotten ahead.

Distinctions between past/future, rural/urban, and traditional/modern are also replicated in home interiors. These distinctions not only organize processes of "dolling up" the inside of the home but inform residence patterns and the internal organization of homes. Before the 1970s most Uriangatenses lived in family compounds in which parents shared a residence with their unmarried children and their sons' nuclear families. Over the last several decades, however, families have nucleated, and couples have adopted egalitarian models of marriage. Working-class Uriangatenses associate these ideals with modernity: a pattern found across Mexico (cf. Hirsch 2003) and in other parts of the world (see Miller 1994). Concordantly, family residence patterns have changed. While extended families still seek to live near one another—ideally in homes lining the same city block—each nuclear family prefers to live in its own home, arguing that this helps support communitarianism by preventing conflict over household management and resource distribution.

Nucleation is also rendered inside homes. As discussed in chapter 2, home interiors in Uriangato have historically been conceptualized as places of communion with family not as places in which to assert personal privacy. But, increasingly, home interiors enable individualization and personal privacy, also coded as modern. Most younger parents I know aspire to build houses large enough for the bedrooms to be separate from the spaces for socializing, versus the less modern homes, where the parents' bedroom doubles as a living room during the day (cf. Hirsch 2003: 67–80). They also want the parents and each child to have their own bedrooms. Just as communion between nuclear families is better supported by independent homeownership, the communion of parents, children, and siblings is supported by personal space, so the argument goes.

As in talk of *norteños/as desobligado/as*, the semiotics of home construction help animate and organize processes of differentiation—and inequality—in Uriangato in ways that both push against and replicate diaspora at home. Crucial to this process is the ethico-moral loading of mobility, which produces its own vectors of evaluation. Consider the following statement by Fernando, the man from the first vignette in this chapter, from a conversation I had with him and Rosario (also discussed in Dick 2013):

Pues, como digo, antes no—la gente no pensaba en el futuro. No pensaban en el futuro, y en sobresalir, tratar de sobresalir. Y ahora sí. La gente de antes—yo sí lo veía: casitas de piedra y con cartones y todo eso. Sí. Y ahora, ya no. Ya tratan de superarse un poquito más, y piensan más. Quieren vivir ya mejor.
[Well, as I say, before, no—people didn't think about the future. They didn't think about the future, and in advancing, in trying to advance. And now, yes. People from before—I myself used to see: stone houses with cardboard and all of that. Yes. And now, not anymore. Now people try to improve themselves a little bit, and they think more. Now they want to live better.]

In this statement Fernando constructs a temporal framework contrasting the life of Uriangatenses "then and now," commonly replicated in working-class migration discourse (Dick 2010a: 280–281, 2013) and resonant with the social landscaping of the neighborhood. It did not matter before if people were satisfied with houses of stone and cardboard because they did not know better; they were satisfied with *estándola pasando* (getting by), earning just enough to have basic food and a simple roof over their heads. In much migration discourse, this past is represented as a time of innocence and ignorance, when *amarraron los perros con longaniza* (they tied up dogs with sausage): when people were as naive as a dog who does not know he can eat his way through a leash of sausage. By contrast, people in the present day are described as having *mucha viveza* (a lot of cleverness and awareness). Now people know better than to be satisfied with a house of stone and cardboard; now they think about the future, about "improving," about getting ahead (Dick 2010a; cf. Miller 1994).

As this implies, working-class people understand *siguiendo adelante* as a process not only of economic change but also of awakening and improvement, coded as an ethico-moral good (Dick 2010a; cf. Keane 2007; Napolitano 2002). Because people know better now, only the lazy dwell in such homes: their unwillingness to "live better" is a moral failing. In their efforts to realize moral mobility through their homebuilding practices, working-class Uriangatenses endeavor to integrate the ethico-moral imperatives of tradition and modernity—to have a beautiful life in which they also continually improve.

Such efforts are in the physical foundations of Uriangatense homes: concrete represents the stability of the communitarian Mexican family in contrast to the fragile US family/home made of wood. Similarly, ideals of family nucleation evince the integration of tradition and modernity—families build their own home near those of their parents and siblings, an extension of the family compound across entire blocks. Through such practices they seek to distance themselves not only from the rural but from the underbelly of urban immorality. La Libertad has a bad reputation as a den of sin, where crime and loose sexuality abound—indeed, many residents of other parts of the city told me I should not be living there. Acutely aware of this reputation, many residents of the neighborhood claim that they do not reside in *La mera* Libertad (the real core of La Libertad). *La mera* Libertad is always somewhere farther up the hill, near the "backward" rural realm.

The figuring of progress as a process of ethico-moral improvement has an affinity with modernist frameworks across a range of historical and contemporary settings (cf. Carr 2011; Keane 2007; Miller 1994; Napolitano 2002). More immediately, the landscaping of La Libertad resonates with the chronotopia of state-endorsed imaginaries of moral mobility: the adobe home is on the outskirts, read as part of the rural past and backwardness, while the adorned home is placed centrally, signaling urbanity and adumbrating a modern future, but positioning the full realization of moral mobility at a distance. The ethico-moral loading of getting ahead in Uriangato resonates in particular with the state-endorsed figuring of the working-class person as *el pelado*—the once-urban scoundrel who became an icon of the nation's process of industrialization and its awakenings during the postrevolutionary period (see chapter 1). This resonance not only links *siguiendo adelante* with state-endorsed imaginaries; it reproduces working-class diaspora at home. *El pelado* is a problematic emblem for working-class people. Not unlike the Golden Donkey, he represents the ways Mexico's economic development is stunted and ineffective: the mascot of what we might call the country's *underindustrialization*. Such resonances help further legitimate the idea that there is something flawed about working-class people, which legitimates their exclusion from full belonging.

Overall, the ethico-moral loading of the semiotics of home construction reveals a patterning, typical of processes of fractal recursion, of ever-finer replications of the same contrasts across domains, from home interiors to dynamics between Mexico and the United States. Despite pointing to working-class people's efforts to get ahead these processes generate a social landscape that nevertheless reproduces the idea—typical of state-endorsed imaginaries of moral mobility—that their full belonging in Mexico awaits in *algún futuro*, when the whole neighborhood is *arreglado* inside and out. As working-class people imbricate their lives with modernity, they also reproduce their diaspora at home—a process poignantly exemplified in homebuilding. Since the 1970s the proper development of family life—creating a nurturing and stable environment in which children can be raised to be properly Mexican—has become contingent on being able to own a single family home, in other words. Uriangatenses link the aspiration to build the ever-more luxurious and atomized living environments with communitarianism and the process of creating a beautiful life.

Yet, as home construction becomes ever more important as a display of *la vida bonita* and *siguiendo adelante*, homeownership becomes ever more difficult to achieve for working-class people. This is not only because of the failures of Mexico's labor and credit markets but also because migration facilitates a perpetual increase in living standards that makes it more and more unlikely that working-class people will be able to get ahead in Mexico. At the same time, as Fernando and Rosario learned, migration often does not result in socioeconomic advancement; indeed migration frequently only impoverishes families further (Dick 2013; cf. Massey and Sánchez 2010). Even those who do succeed in their migratory goals, like Verónica and Héctor, still experience displacement. Consequently, in endeavoring to get ahead, working-class people experience a seemingly never-ending diaspora at home, a labyrinth of ruptures between the life they are meant to lead to be properly Mexican and the life to which they can actually lay claim.

The language materiality that interweaves discourse about homes and migration with the physicality of home construction helps produce diaspora at home. Objects—concrete blocks, exposed rebar, Mexican flags, tinted windows, tiled floors—and talk about them together recreate a political economy that constrains working-class Uriangatenses' ability to fully claim Mexicanidad. Yet they also resist their marginalization by highlighting what they see as its causes. I close the chapter with a consideration of this resistance.

Exits from the Labyrinth: Homebuilding as Critical Commentary

La gente que viene de allá, de Uriangato, de donde nosotros somos,
es por tratar de seguir adelante. Para comer, a lo mejor sí se consigue.
¿Pero ya para querer tener una casa? No. Es bien difícil para hacer una
casita allí.
[The people that come from there, from Uriangato, where we are from,
they do so to get ahead. To eat, yes, you can most likely earn enough.
But for wanting to have a house already? No. It is very difficult to build
even a little house there.]

Cuando está uno allá en México le dicen, "¡Vamanos pa'l Norte!"—allá
dicen, "¡Vamanos pa'l Norte!" Ay, uno se imagina el Norte diferente: Al
llegar aquí, dice uno, "¿¡Esto es el Norte!?"
[When they are there in Mexico, they say, "Let's go to El Norte!"—
there they say, "Let's go to El Norte!" Oh, you imagine El Norte differently: Upon arriving here, you say, "This is El Norte?!"]

In 1950 renowned Mexican poet and diplomat Octavio Paz published a book-length essay called *El laberinto de la soledad* (*The Labyrinth of Solitude*), which captures on a grander regional and historical scale what I call diaspora at home. Paz and many other theorists of Mexican nationalism locate the perpetual dislocations from belonging like those described here in the country's postcolonial history as a mestizo nation: neither Spanish nor Indigenous but always in between—a liminality that produces a melancholy solitude of isolation and alienation. As noted in chapter 1, this "in between" has long vexed Mexican elites. Indeed the production of imaginaries of moral mobility is an effort to find, as Claudio Lomnitz-Adler (1992) described it, *Exits from the Labyrinth*, though (as illustrated in this chapter) the struggle to achieve moral mobility does not provide egress for working-class people; it (re)creates diaspora at home.

As is suggested in the excerpts above, taken from a conversation I recorded with Lupe, mentioned earlier in this chapter, working-class people also engage in critiques of diaspora at home. They turn a critical eye not only on the ways state-endorsed discourses view tradition as an impediment to progress but also on the failures of progress in Mexico and their vulnerability in the United States (cf. Chávez 2015, 2017a, 2017b; Dick 2017; Dick and Arnold 2017a). Certainly, the fact that US migration is the main route for working-class people to finance their homes is a commentary on the failures of Mexico's labor and credit markets. But Uriangatenses also articulate their own imaginaries that revise the terms of state-endorsed moral mobility, exposing a political economy that erases their needs and positions their inability to get ahead as a moral failing.

In the first quotation above, Lupe expresses a common proposition of much Uriangatense migration discourse—the idea that working-class people must go to the United States to get ahead: a hegemonic idea in Uriangatense migration discourse I call the "*seguir adelante* proposition" (Dick 2010a). While most working-class people positively value getting ahead, many believe that the barriers to doing so in Mexico are insurmountable for them because of their liminal positioning in Uriangato's political economy. They do not have access to the resources that facilitate mobility—advanced education, business loans and mortgages, stable income, and government assistance. Thus the *seguir adelante* proposition is a way of simultaneously saying: we are trying to get ahead and it is not our fault we cannot do it in Mexico.

Homebuilding practices therefore revise the terms of state-endorsed imaginaries in ways that accommodate and validate working-class methods for getting ahead. It is not tradition or their individual failings to progress that impede working-class people from realizing moral mobility. It is their government's failure to provide them access to the resources and opportunities that would make socioeconomic progress possible for them in Mexico. As part of this, they amend the positioning of the United States in processes of Mexicanidad. State-endorsed imaginaries overtly disassociate Mexicanidad from the United States and its prevailing forms of progress (see chapter 1), making migration anathema to proper Mexicanness. By contrast, working-class Uriangatense homebuilding practices entail a less absolutist here-there relationship, positing the necessity of links with the United States in order to fulfill the imperatives of moral mobility, exemplified in practice of homebuilding in Uriangato. In this way migration to the United States is posited as making Mexicanidad possible for working-class people, though only when carefully managed, as I show in chapters 4 and 5.

But such visions of the North are not about pledging allegiance to the United States. Uriangatenses also articulate critiques of the condition of migrant lives in the United States. Lupe expresses this point artfully in the second quotation above, which describes the disappointment many feel when they arrive in the North and experience the humiliations of migration (poignantly described by Don Arturo and Doña Cecilia, who are at the center of the next chapter). Rather, talk of the United States is (as argued in chapter 5) a way of reimagining Mexico. In their migration discourse working-class Uriangatenses shine a spotlight on their marginalization from full national belonging and their longing to be fully incorporated into the polity so that they may access the resources that would allow them to be morally mobile at home.

As the following two chapters show, through the interactional dynamics of actual instances of migration discourse working-class speakers produce imaginaries of moral mobility that link their immediate lives to broader political economic and sociohistorical processes. These links allow them to assert their ethico-moral fortitude—their proper Mexicanidad—and undo the erasures endemic to their diaspora at home, re-creating Mexico in ways that grant them full belonging not in some distant future but now. My analysis turns from a consideration of language materiality to a more central focus on discourse analysis, though I keep an eye on multimodality throughout (see especially chapter 5).

CHAPTER 4

Possibility and Perdition:
Discursive Interaction and Ethico-moral
Practice in Traditionalist Talk of Migration

The story of our lives becomes the story of the lives we were prevented from living.

(PHILLIPS 2013: XIII–XIV)

Fracasa la familia para allá {en los Estados Unidos}—porque para allá, hay mucha posibilidad, pero también hay mucha perdición de esto: de la droga, y está difícil la vida para allá. Mucha tentación. Muchas . . . hay muchas cosas allá, muchas diversiones, mucha . . . em, mucha perversión allá. Hay mucho. Y la gente que no ha ido ve todas esas cosas, y ve todo eso, y pues no—se les hace fácil, y caen en todas esas cosas. Espero que no, que no se dejen llevar por tantas cosas . . . tanta tentación, pobres; no se detienen.

[The family falls apart there—because there, there is a lot of possibility, but there is also a lot of perdition: of drugs, and life is hard there. A lot of temptation. A lot . . . there are a lot of things there, a lot of diversions, a lot, um, a lot of perversion *there. There is a lot. And people that haven't gone see all those things, and see all that, and well, no—it seems like no problem to them, and they fall prey to all those things. I wish that, no, that they didn't let themselves get carried away by so many things . . . so much temptation, poor things; they don't hold themselves back.]*

DON ARTURO, FORMER MIGRANT TURNED NONMIGRANT

In the mid-1970s Don Arturo, the man who uttered the above words, was just barely in his twenties, recently married to Doña Cecilia, his wife of many decades now. They were quickly blessed with their first child, a boy, who filled them with an expansive but weighty joy, as they wondered how to cultivate a fertile ground for their family to grow. They did not see a lot of options in urban Uriangato, where they have been lifelong residents. Uriangato's textile industry was then itself a newborn;

the jobs available mostly went to women and did not pay enough to support a family. More and more people in urban Uriangato were adopting a practice in which people from the rural towns surrounding the city had been engaging for decades: migration to the United States. So Don Arturo and Doña Cecilia struck a difficult bargain that was becoming common in working-class Uriangatense families at the time. Don Arturo headed to the North for work, to send money home to Doña Cecilia to build their home and support their growing family. For eight years they developed their family in the style of the *bracero* workers described in chapter 1, though like most migrants of the post-*bracero* era, Don Arturo moved north without legal authorization to do so. He worked in agriculture in Texas and Pennsylvania for several months per year, returning home whenever he could. During this time, he and Doña Cecilia brought three more lives into this world—another boy and two girls. Doña Cecilia nurtured them while Don Arturo was *en el otro lado* (on the other side). His migration was brought to an abrupt halt by an attack of *los nervios* (the nerves)—an ailment that Uriangatenses commonly associate with the stresses of migration: long work hours, separation from family, fear of deportation, the siren call of "perversions." When things got so bad Don Arturo could not work, he went back to Mexico. He never returned to the United States.

Over thirty years have passed since that final northern sojourn, their final separation. Since then Don Arturo and Doña Cecilia have built *una vida bonita* (a beautiful life) in Uriangato (see chapter 3). Don Arturo works as *un ambulante* (an independent street vendor), selling roasted peanuts from a cart. Between his food sales and the money Doña Cecilia earns as a seamstress, they have been able to complete construction of their home and support their household, which at the time of my meeting them consisted of Don Arturo and Doña Cecilia, their two unmarried daughters, and one of their grandchildren. We might think migration was something settled for this family, a thing of the past. Yet migration is still alive in their present. In some ways this is true of everyone in migrant enclaves in Uriangato. Migration and discourse about it are regular practices that affect people every day, so the lives imagined in migration become measuring sticks against which people evaluate their present lives (Dick 2010a). But each person, each family, has a unique point of intersection with the broader practice of imbricating present life with the imagined lives of Mexican migrants, a particular link to such imaginings. This process is centrally shaped by their interpellation into state-endorsed Mexicanidad and their positioning within and critical perspective on the political economic processes that shape their physical and social mobility.

Don Arturo did once want to return north. In 1986 La Amnistía (The Amnesty, the Immigration Reform and Control Act: IRCA) passed, granting legal permanent residency ("green cards") to 3 million undocumented migrants (Durand and Massey 2003).[1] But *los nervios* made him too sick to move. Try as he might, he could not migrate. Don Arturo's regret that ultimately he was incapable of returning to the United States, even as the reward of a green card hung before him, stretches beyond himself. When I met this couple, their eldest son Juan Carlos was contemplating his own northern departure, not in the *bracero* style practiced by his parents but in the more common form of contemporary border-crossing: whole family migration. Had Don Arturo gotten a green card during the amnesty, he would have had legal status to pass on to his children.[2] Don Arturo's inability to do so has created a sense of failure as a father. If Juan Carlos and his family migrate, it will be as unauthorized migrants, crossing a border that is even more dangerous than it was in Don Arturo's day. He and Doña Cecilia would never have envisioned that prospect for themselves, let alone for their children and grandchildren.

The history of migration in Don Arturo and Doña Cecilia's family straddles dramatic demographic, political economic, and sociocultural shifts that happened in Mexico and between Mexico and the United States at the end of the twentieth century. During this period, Mexican migration went from being a largely seasonal flow of men to a more settlement-oriented movement of entire families (Hondagneu-Sotelo 1994; Lattanzi Shutika 2011; Smith 2006). IRCA helped spark this shift by creating entitlements for legal permanent residency for 9.2 million spouses and children who were related to the 2.3 million IRCA green card recipients from Mexico: a total of 11.5 million visas (Durand and Massey 2003). Dividing this total by the average size of a Mexican family in the late twentieth century—two parents and three children (Chavez 2008; Hirsch 2003)—shows that roughly 2.3 million Mexican families gained US legal status after the implementation of IRCA, catalyzing family migration. The children of IRCA recipients who received green cards could then sponsor legal permanent residency applications for their future spouses if they were not already US citizens or green card holders and/or for any children born outside of the country.

IRCA also created regional and community-internal divides between families who participated in the program and thereby got cross-generational access to US legal permanent residency and those who did not, like Don Arturo's family (cf. Gálvez 2009; Hirsch 2003; Hondagneu-Sotelo 1994). These families migrate without authorization, under an immigration policy regime that has responded with ever-increasingly draconian measures since IRCA, as discussed in the introductory chapter (see also Abrego 2014; Chávez 2017a, 2017b; Coutin 2005; De Genova 2005; Dick 2011b, 2012; Durand and Massey 2003; Stephen 2004, 2007). Moreover, IRCA recipients were overwhelmingly from the traditional migrant-sending states of western-central Mexico, including Guanajuato, where Uriangato is located. US migration has spread across Mexico since the 1990s, but few of these migrants have access to US legal status (Varsanyi 2010; Wortham et al. 2002).

These changes coincided with shifts in the status of women and ideals of marriage and family in Mexico. As couples came to adopt the ideals of companionate marriage and nuclear family life over more patriarchal visions of these institutions (see chapter 3), *bracero*-style migration became undesirable. As women increasingly entered the paid workforce and had more earning power, they came to have more influence over household decision making (cf. Hirsch 2003; Hondagneu-Sotelo 1994; Smith 2006; Wright 2006). I heard many Uriangatense women in their twenties and thirties say things along these lines: "I did not get married to become a single parent who has to be both mother and father to my children; we can build a family here [Mexico] or there [the United States], but we will do it together." Many older women I knew found such statements confounding, because to them they violated the masculinity and autonomy of their daughters' husbands (cf. Hirsch 2003). Despite the consternation of some of the elder generation, many younger couples began prioritizing nuclear family integrity—keeping parents and children together. And IRCA gave them a way to migrate as a unit without facing the dangers of unauthorized migration. Once family migration became a widespread practice, spearheaded by the millions of families who got US legal status as result of IRCA, however, more and more families began to migrate regardless of legal status. Consequently, IRCA inadvertently encouraged an increase in unauthorized family migration as well (Passel and Cohn 2009; Smith 2006), even as it helped make undocumented migration increasingly dangerous.

The articulation of migration discourse is a central site where Uriangatenses confront and contribute to these changes. For people like Don Arturo who were unable to avail themselves of IRCA, migration discourse becomes a lament for the lives that they were prevented from leading. Such lamentation is highlighted in the discursive construction of migration histories, which foreground people's relationships to migration and the possibilities and displacements they entail—literal and imaginative. I understand migration history as an assemblage not only of the articulated facts of migration's unfolding (if, when, and how someone migrated) but also of dynamically generated stances on those happenings. That is, a migration history is produced through how people mobilize the past to understand their present in interaction with others. It may seem strange to talk about migration history in a book focused on nonmigrants. But in migrant enclaves everyone has a relationship to the possible lives they could lead if they migrated, as well as positions on the impact of migration. So everyone has a history of relating to migration, regardless of actual movements abroad. The elicitation of migration histories has long been a core practice of migrant researchers, though it is generally used to ascertain empirical facts of migration and not to access the interpretive and interactional practices of people affected by migration (e.g., Hondagneu-Sotelo 1994; Massey et al. 1987; Walsh 2004; see De Fina and King 2011 and Dick 2006b for discussion). Yet these histories are rich resources for understanding how people connect themselves and their immediate world to broader patterns of migration and the enduring influence that the imagination of migration has had on the variegation of national belonging in Mexico (as discussed in chapters 1 and 3).

The construction of "history"—the ways discursive and other semiotic practices enable people to make virtual contact with times and places in the past—has become a core interest in linguistic anthropology (Blommaert 2015; Cavanaugh 2009; Das 2011; Dick 2010a; Divita 2014; Eisenlohr 2006; Inoue 2004; Lempert and Perrino 2007; Silverstein and Urban 1996; Wirtz 2014, 2016).[3] In rendering nonpresent spaces and times through language, people do more than just represent sociohistorical processes, such as transnational migration; they contribute to the unfolding of those processes. Consider the state-endorsed imaginaries of moral mobility that the shape the variegation of national belonging—and interpellation—in Mexico (see chapter 1). These imaginaries are produced through the selective uptake of features of Mexico's past as the essence of the nation, valorizing some groups, while occluding and denigrating others. This political use of history has repeatedly played a central role in ordering nation-building practices in Mexico and is a common feature of nation-building across contexts (cf. Castellanos

2010; Das 2016; Eisenlohr 2006; Faudree 2013; Lomnitz 2008; Trouillot 1997; Wirtz 2014; Woolard 2004). In responding to such variegation, working-class Uriangatenses generate their own imaginaries of moral mobility, which spotlight the failures of Mexican progress. These imaginaries invert the terms of state-endorsed imaginaries, so that departures to the immoral United States become migrants' best option for remaining properly Mexican. At the same time, both state-endorsed and working-class imaginaries generate interpellative practices that turn in on themselves, always drawing into question the ethico-moral character of working-class people. Imaginaries of moral mobility, then, produce a diaspora at home for Uriangatenses—a fractured interpellation that unfolds in the divide between the lives working-class people are meant to lead and the lives they can actually realize (see chapter 3).

The central claim of this chapter is that the construction of migration history is a site where Uriangatenses endeavor to resolve diaspora at home by articulating imaginaries populated with differentially valued figures of migration, in which they emplace and enact themselves as people of sound ethico-moral character. This process relies fundamentally on acts of *stancetaking* through which speakers not only evaluate what ways of orienting to the world are right and wrong; they evaluate self and others according to those terms (cf. Du Bois 2007; Jaffe 2009). As such, the ethico-moral dimensions of migration histories are found not only in their evaluative impulse as they posit some migrants as "good" and some as "bad." They are also found in the "inherently intersubjective nature" of their production, as interlocutors foment agreement, compatibility, or contest (Keane 2011: 170). Consequently, understanding how migration histories enable resolutions of diaspora at home requires examining discourse interactionally, exploring the practices through which people position themselves and others in talk. In this chapter I analyze a recorded conversation with Don Arturo and Doña Cecilia. As this analysis reveals, the key stancetaking practice through which actors create imaginaries into which they plot themselves is *calibration* (Dick 2010a; Eisenlohr 2006; Silverstein 1993).

The concept of calibration was developed by Michael Silverstein (1993) to describe how speakers link an interaction to places, people, and times beyond the present. Calibration is an important part of how people generate social imaginaries—visions of the social world populated by differentially valued figures of personhood. It involves two interrelated processes: creating a world "beyond here" and latching oneself and others to that world.[4] These processes centrally involve stancetaking:

asserting positions on an object of evaluation and thereby on oneself and others. The vision of a world beyond that Don Arturo, Doña Cecilia, and I create as we construct their family's migration history is one in which the proper practice of migration is posited as the movements of men, in contrast to the settlement-oriented migration of families. I call this a *traditionalist* imaginary of moral mobility, as it values the form of migration practiced by earlier generations (solitary male migration), rooted in patriarchal visions of family life, over the form engaged in by many people today (whole family migration), rooted in the egalitarian ethos of companionate marriage. We create this imaginary by differentially valuing various figures of migration, from virtuous fathers to wanton single mothers, placing them in relationship to one another and to us (cf. Agha 2007a; Hill 1995; Keane 2011).[5] In crafting these images of personhood or *social personae* (Agha 2007a; Dick 2010a), we create a rendition of diaspora at home that speaks to the circumstances of Don Arturo and Doña Cecilia's family, in which even the achievement of a beautiful life in Mexico leads to further dislocations—in particular, the potential departure of their son and his nuclear family. In rendering our imaginary, we employ aspects of what Patrick Eisenlohr (2006: 263) calls "diasporic calibration": linking the present interaction to an imagined homeland from which one has been displaced (see also Dick 2010a: 281). Though true to the experience of diaspora at home, the forms of displacement are about separation from the life someone is compelled to lead to be properly Mexican and not necessarily about literal separation from a homeland (see chapter 3). So analysis of the first process of calibration—what kind of "world beyond" we create—reveals that we create a traditionalist world that replicates diaspora at home.

At the same time, however, attention to the second process of calibration—how we latch ourselves to that world—shows that Don Arturo and Doña Cecilia also seek to resolve this diaspora and its displacements. The principal way they accomplish such resolution is through their patterns of pronominal usage and the associated images of personhood that they create with these patterns. An important lineage in language studies examines the semiotics of pronoun use, exploring their fundamental role in shaping not only interactional contexts, but also relationships between individuals and the world beyond the present (e.g., Benveniste 1971; Urban 1989). In this chapter I show that the pronominal patterns of Don Arturo and Doña Cecilia are part of their interpellation into Mexicanidad, as they are distinct in ways typical of the migration discourse of working-class Uriangatense men and women.

Through how they connect themselves to the world beyond via pronominal patterns, Don Arturo and Doña Cecilia construct themselves as a proper man and woman, respectively. In so doing, they resist their positioning as outside proper Mexicanidad. As this suggests, the production of migration histories allows people to imbricate the complexities of interpellation into imaginaries of moral mobility—the ways they are called to be and see themselves as particular kinds of Mexicans—with the effort to envision and find a place within more immediate forms of group membership, such as the family. To be sure, in our conversation Don Arturo and Doña Cecilia's efforts to assert Mexicanidad are filtered through their efforts to establish proper familyhood—"being Mexican" is a secondary indexical effect.[6] At the same time, the entanglements between family life and the imaginaries of moral mobility, which render family an icon of proper Mexicanness, are what make it important to be good family people (cf. Keane 2010: 75; Lempert 2013).

I begin by unpacking how the production of this family's migration history presents a particular kind of challenge for Don Arturo, focusing on the conflict it presents to his ethico-moral personhood as a strong and caring Mexican man. I develop the chapter's discussion of calibration by analyzing how we construct the world beyond here in our conversation, considering the gendered differences in personae creation in Don Arturo and Doña Cecilia's migration discourse. Though Don Arturo and Doña Cecilia both create a traditionalist—and diasporic—world in constructing their migration history, they link themselves to that world through different techniques of calibration, which I call *universalizing* and *domestic*. The processes of intersubjective agreement that emerge during the conversation allow us successfully to enact ourselves as being of sound ethico-moral character. Within this process Doña Cecilia plays an important role as an instigator of ethico-moral work. She introduces points of potential tension that inspire Don Arturo's assertions of morality. In so doing, she allows Don Arturo to project himself as authoritative, while she is able to perform being a good wife who cultivates the morality of her husband.

Manhood and Migration History

I first met Don Arturo and Doña Cecilia when their house was selected at random as part of the Mexican Migration Project (MMP) survey I conducted in La Libertad (see chapter 2). When I asked if I could return to talk with them further, they agreed, becoming part of a group of households I visited routinely. We arranged the visit that is the focus of this chapter for me to audio-record their migration history, which we had discussed casually several times in the months since I had met them. The entire 55-minute recording is summarized in the conversational outline in the appendix to this chapter. As the outline shows, this interaction begins—as did the other open-ended, ethnographic interviews I recorded—with a series of questions that combined features of the MMP survey protocol (asking Don Arturo and Doña Cecilia if they had ever migrated, when they had migrated, what jobs they had held, and so on) with evaluative questions about migration and the United States, which I had developed inductively from people's talk of migration outside of interview interactions (see the Technical Note).

Although I had already conducted the MMP survey with Don Arturo and Doña Cecilia, I still began the interaction with this instrument. It had become iconic of my interviews and their links to the realm of authoritative discourse about migration, which were central to people's uptake of the interviews as sites where their own migration discourse could be rendered authoritative (see chapter 2). Unlike the survey interviews, however, in the ethnographic interviews my interlocutors and I were not beholden to the MMP protocol questions. Instead their principal purpose was to signal the shift into the "work frame" in which people would allow me to record them, and we would frequently abandon the questions once talk began to flow. This happened with Don Arturo and Doña Cecilia: around minute 13 we begin to transition into a more relaxed conversational interaction (segments 2 and 3 in the outline). At this point we more evenly share the labor of introducing topics and asking questions, all of which nevertheless remain grounded in this family's migration history and a comparison of life "here in Mexico" and "there in the United States."

The migration history of Don Arturo and Doña Cecilia's family represents that many other families in which the male head of household migrated long in the past and the wife and children have never migrated. Speaking of "nonmigrants" in the context of such families is not strictly speaking about an absence of migration. Don Arturo is not a nonmigrant in the same way that Doña Cecilia (who has never left Uriangato) is. But if nonmigration is conceptualized as a stance—as involving not just people's actual movements or lack thereof but also their relationships to the possibility of migration—then Don Arturo can be thought of as a nonmigrant. His migration history is deep in the past. Thirty years have gone by since he last went to the United States. As someone entering late middle age with a successful life in Uriangato, he is unlikely to migrate again. Given the short-lived and long-past character of his migration, it seems inaccurate to call him a "return migrant" or "former migrant," as if migration was the distinguishing feature of his life. Demographically, most working-class men of Don Arturo's generation have migrated at least once. The ones I knew who had not migrated were largely estranged from their families—their lack of migration was a feature of a general lack of obligation to their relations. In order to maintain my respectable womanhood I only cultivated relationships with men through their families (see chapter 2), so I did not have access to the discourse of the estranged family men who had never migrated. What differentiated the men of Don Arturo's generation who were not estranged from their families was that some, like Don Arturo, had tried migration for relative brief periods and stopped, while others had continued to migrate for decades until moving their families north or retiring in Uriangato. I consider all the men in the former group nonmigrants because of their relatively limited experience with migration and their subsequent rejection of the practice for themselves and their families.

This chapter is centered around Don Arturo and Doña Cecilia because their relationship to migration is somewhat unique. On the one hand, it is representative of the struggle of many families of their generation, as they make sense of changes in migration practice and the related political economic shifts that happened in the late twentieth century. On the other hand, it reveals an interesting break from broader patterns of Uriangatense migration discourse, especially for Don Arturo. Like other nonmigrant men of his generation, Don Arturo rhetorically positions his rejection of migration as an indicator of the strength of his ethico-moral character and of his identity as a devoted father. Such rejection is a form of critical commentary on the ways working-class Mexican men are represented not only within state-endorsed visions of Mexicanidad in Mexico, but also in US migration discourse. On both sides of the border, working-class Mexican men have long been posited as hot-headed, domineering, and dogmatic, as evinced in discourses about *el pelado* and the "Mexican macho" (see chapter 1). In sharp contrast to these images, most of the men I knew deeply value their roles not just as providers (the classical patriarchal view of the father) but also as gentle, affectionate caregivers (cf. Gutmann 2007). The embrace of this form of fatherhood is an expression of the value working-class Uriangatenses place on gracious personhood and communitarianism. And, as such, it is a way to resist and revise the imaginaries that marginalize and degrade them (cf. Alim 2006; Alim and Smitherman 2012; Chávez 2017a; Dick 2010b).

Unlike other working-class men with similar migration pasts, however, Don Arturo continues to hold onto migration. This creates a tension around migration in his family—it continues to haunt them in ways that are not evinced in other families with similar profiles. This tension is particularly evident for Don Arturo because his inability to migrate during IRCA grates against the performance of a Mexican masculinity rooted in freedom of mobility, in contrast to the ideals of *recogida* femininity (discussed in chapter 2). Potentially at least, this makes him seem lazy, selfish, weak: a bad provider for his family. In constructing his migration history, then, Don Arturo grapples with his manhood. This point can be illustrated through a consideration of the gendered ways working-class Uriangatenses are hailed to migration discourse. Don Arturo struggles to affiliate with this practice, pointing to the conflict his migration history presents for him.

Across instances of working-class Uriangatense migration discourse I found a gendered iconicity between men's and women's migration experience and the stances they take on the *seguir adelante* (SA) proposition: the idea that working-class people must migrate to get ahead (see chapter 3). Overall, men are able to realize migration in accordance with their stances much more easily than are women. Don Arturo both breaks from this pattern and seeks to realign himself with it as we discuss his migration past. In an analysis of over thirty recordings of working-class Uriangatenses, I found that men are much more likely to disagree with the SA proposition; they are more likely to argue that working-class people can get ahead in Mexico. Such claims posit a tidy resolution of the double-bind of diaspora at home, as they propose that people find progress in the morally superior land of Mexico. This is a privileged position that is much harder for women to claim successfully (Dick 2010a). As in other parts of Mexico, working-class women have restricted access to the resources that allow for mobility: migrant networks, postprimary school education, and so forth (cf. Hondagneu-Sotelo 1994; Molyneux 2006; Wright 2006). Their most expedient way to get ahead is to marry upwardly mobile men, who are usually migrants: for them, *siguiendo adelante* often means *siguiendo al esposo* (following the husband). Therefore their robust acceptance of the SA proposition is an enactment of their positioning as women and a critique of the glass ceiling in Mexico.

The gendering of stancetaking toward the SA proposition is reinforced by a parallel iconicity between migration discourse and migration practice. Among the people I knew in Uriangato and Pennsylvania, the men were much more able to enact their migration as they proposed it in their stancetaking: those who agree with the SA proposition migrate; those who reject it do not. This uninterrupted alignment between discourse and migration is less attainable for women. Their stance toward the SA proposition aligns with their migration desires but often not with their migration behavior. Some women agree with the SA proposition, want to migrate, but are forbidden to do so by relatives. Others disagree with the SA proposition, do not want to migrate, yet are compelled to do so by family. In nearly every case I documented across the two dozen households I knew well on both sides of the border, women's migration behavior was restricted by male relations who controlled access to the resources that facilitate migration, such as migrant networks and US legal status (cf. Hirsch 2003; Hondagneu-Sotelo 1994). So women's migration practices, including their migration discourse, are refracted through the wills and deeds of others, while men are generally able to be more self-determining. This pattern is replicated in the interactional features of conversations, as I discuss below.

As Don Arturo takes up his discursive mantle as a man, he encounters a conflict: he was not able to enact his migration in accordance with the propositional stance that he would have liked to have remigrated during the IRCA period. In failing to migrate during the amnesty because his *nervios* made him too weak, he became, like a woman, unable to align migration desire and practice. Interestingly, however, in response to this conflict Don Arturo does not reject the SA proposition, as most other men who have either ceased to migrate or never have migrated do (see Dick 2010a). Don Arturo keeps migration alive: he credits it for the good of his present life in ways other men who rejected migration typically do not. He maintains the necessity of migration, persisting in agreeing with the SA proposition. He says several times in our recorded conversation that "the little they have" (their home; their elder son's advanced education, which enabled him to become a manager in a textile factory; and so on) is due to Don Arturo's trips to the United States, even though these trips ended in the early 1980s and the couple did not finish building their house or raising their children until many years later. In continuing to embrace the SA proposition, Don Arturo forges an ongoing attachment to the life that he was prevented from living. This produces a contradiction of manhood he must resolve over and over: a poignant enactment of diaspora at home as he is unable to make his words and his will align, as a good man should. But he and Doña Cecilia also seek to rectify this diaspora by (re)asserting their proper Mexican manhood and womanhood through the imaginary of moral mobility we create.

Migrating for a Little Season:
A Traditionalist Imaginary of Moral Mobility

In constructing their migration histories Uriangatenses endeavor to resolve diaspora at home by articulating imaginaries populated with differentially valued figures of migration. In so doing, they emplace themselves as people of sound ethico-moral character—a process rooted fundamentally in acts of stancetaking, particularly calibration. As discussed above, calibration involves speakers creating a "world beyond" to which they then attach themselves. The world beyond that emerges through my conversation with Don Arturo and Doña Cecilia is a traditionalist one that valorizes the solitary and seasonal migration of men. This imaginary of moral mobility harkens back to a time before the demographic, political economic, and sociocultural changes that prompted the shift toward family migration, when most migrants went north periodically or, as Don Arturo puts it, for *una temporadita* (a little season). Throughout our conversation this vision of moral mobility unfolds in contrast with an alternative vision grounded in the family migration of the post-IRCA period. Over the course of our conversation the seasonal migration of men emerges as the only acceptable form of migration. This positioning takes form through the patterned ways the images of personhood that populate our migration discourse are situated with respect to one another and us.

This patterning of personae can be illustrated through an analysis of the stances Don Arturo takes toward the migratory figures who populate our conversation, considering which ones he holds up as "right" and "wrong." Don Arturo was the principal author of our traditionalist imaginary. As the conversational outline shows, Doña Cecilia and I consistently relate our discourse to Don Arturo's, deferring to it as the starting point for a range of topics, from the dangers of undocumented migration to the beauty of their family home. Although we assert some disagreement with his portrayal of women's migration (as discussed below), we do not offer an alternative imaginary. Rather, we affirm Don Arturo's fundamental framework—the images of migration he produces and his stances on them. Therefore Don Arturo's vision of migration serves as the orientation for our mutual ethico-moral work—it is our compass.

Like other Uriangatense imaginaries of moral mobility, our traditionalist vision relies on a structure of contrast between in the distinct life possibilities in Mexico and the United States, produced through the use of *aquí* (here) and *allá* (there) as stable shifters (see the introductory chapter; cf. Dick and Arnold 2017a). In the following excerpt from segment 1, part 1, in the conversational outline Don Arturo responds to a question I put to him about why he migrated. I spoke the boldfaced line; the use of "here" and "there" is flagged with underlining:

{Uno migra} para buscar una ayuda para uno—
Una ayuda para . . . pues, económica—ayudarse económicamente.
Aha—y es de . . . ¿Entonces, no tenía trabajo <u>aquí</u>, o qué estaba pasando <u>aquí</u>?
Sí, yo tenía trabajo, pero pues, <u>aquí</u> se gana más poco que ni estando <u>allá</u>.
Estando <u>allá</u> y llegando y trabajando, pues . . . pues sí se ayuda a uno <u>aquí</u>, ah?
<u>Allá</u>, pues, ya sé que estando <u>allá</u> se gasta igual que <u>aquí</u>. Pero <u>aquí</u> es donde rinde lo poquito que uno ahorre <u>allá</u>, rinde un poquito más. Es lo que le ayuda a uno: que ahorrando un poco, y más lo poquito acá es donde rinde, pa'uno, para la familia.

[{One migrates} in order to help oneself—
Help for . . . well, economically—to help oneself economically.
Aha—um . . . So you didn't have work <u>here</u>, or what was going on <u>here</u>?
Yes, I had work, but well, <u>here</u> you earn less than even being <u>there</u>.
Being <u>there</u> and arriving and working, well . . . well yes, it helps one <u>here</u>, right?
<u>There</u>, well, I know that being <u>there</u> one can spend the same as <u>here</u>. But <u>here</u> is where the little that one may save <u>there</u> lasts longer, it lasts

a little longer. That's what can help one: saving a little, and more than a little <u>here</u> is where it lasts, for oneself, for the family.]

As this excerpt illustrates, like many Uriangatenses, Don Arturo depicts <u>there</u>/the United States as a place where life is full of economic possibility but also potential ruin, and <u>here</u>/Mexico as the place of family, the ballast of proper life. This contrast is maintained throughout our conversation, forming a sociopolitical geography in which Mexico is the source of the good life and the United States presents a threat to proper Mexicanidad (cf. chapter 3; see also Hill 1995). As in other migration discourse, this framing takes up some of the terms of state-endorsed imaginaries of moral mobility, which similarly portray the United States as anathema to being properly Mexican. Yet such North/South contrasts (Dick and Arnold 2017a) help produce the double-bind of belonging that is part and parcel of the variegation of Mexicanidad for working-class people. In their migration discourse working-class speakers confront this double-bind in a manner specific to the unique unfolding of their lives and particular instances of interaction. In my conversation with Don Arturo and Doña Cecilia we recreate the here/there framework but position figures of migration in ways that resolve the double-bind of belonging by uplifting the traditionalist imaginary of moral mobility.

We Who Have More Will: The Ethico-moral Spectrum of Don Arturo's Migratory Figures

Shortly after Don Arturo made the statement about families fracturing in the United States that opens this chapter, I asked him what are the qualities of those who do not fall prey to perdition. He responded: *Tenemos más voluntad—tenemos voluntad de vivir sin tantas cosas esas* (We have more will—will to live without so many of those things) (segment 1, part 4, of the conversational outline). *Voluntad* refers to a cultural concept of ethico-moral personhood that interrelates desire, the ability to choose, and self-control with a sense of process toward a more moral life (see chapter 2). It is also used, as Don Arturo does, as a mass noun—a quantity: some people have more of it than others, which is to say some are better able to resist immoral desires and also have a greater capacity to improve morally. *Voluntad* is a signal feature of proper Mexican personhood, the very embodiment of moral mobility, in contrast to the immorality of the United States. Don Arturo's statement about *voluntad* is the central contrastive moment that demarcates the social boundaries of the traditionalist imaginary, a point exemplified by a change in pronominal usage that happens in this statement. As the preceding excerpt in which Don Arturo explains why he migrated shows, he tends overwhelmingly to favor the use of general pronouns, such as "one," a point to which I return below. By contrast, in the statement about *voluntad*, he uses "we" for the first—and one of the only—times in the conversation. Through this shift, Don Arturo creates and lays claim to membership in an ethico-moral community whose fortitude is not just greater than that of other migrants; it brings him, and others like him, closer to proper Mexicanidad because it allows them to stay moral, even in the United States.

Don Arturo's break into groupness signals the entrance of a new cast of characters: they who fall prey to the temptations of life in the United States, to whom Don Arturo takes consistently negative stances. Thus, against the backdrop of people who migrate the right way is a population of "theys" who do not. This positioning is illustrated, for example, in the two excerpts of Don Arturo's discourse presented above—one pertaining to families who become fractured in the United States and the other to why he migrated. Such "us"-"them" contrasts are a well-documented feature of the creation of national and transnational group affiliation (cf. Appadurai 2006; Benhabib 2002; Dick 2011a, 2011b; Mehan 1997; Santa Ana 2002; Sidorkina 2015; Urban 2001). They underscore a common aspect of ethico-moral personhood and group formation: these processes rely on a "clash of voices" (distinct social personae), as the wrong unavoidably troubles articulation of the right (Hill 1995—see also Gumperz 1982; Keane 2011). Linking all Don Arturo's migrant personae is a mediating figure of the migrant who suffers in the United States. This figure represents every migrant—we and they. Don Arturo asserts repeatedly that a migrant's life is one of suffering, at one point even likening migrants to veterans who return from war with posttraumatic stress disorder (segment 2, part 9).

Yet despite the general suffering of migrants, not all migrant personae receive Don Arturo's compassion. He distributes his sympathy according to the persona's gender, age, and reason for migrating, internally distinguishing the "theys of migration" according to who is most in violation of our traditionalist imaginary of moral mobility. I depict this distribution in the following diagram, which portrays the stances Don Arturo takes toward the figures of migration in our conversation. The circle on the left, labeled "Morally Right Figures," represents Don Arturo and other people who migrate in the correct way.

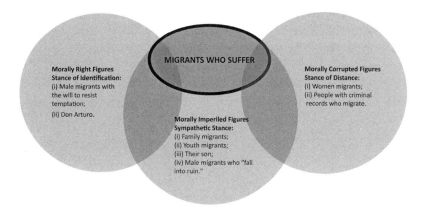

As the diagram shows, the most sympathetic "they" figures are seasonal male migrants who travel alone and cannot resist the allurements of the United States, indicated in the circle labeled "Morally Imperiled Figures." Don Arturo takes a stance of compassionate paternalism toward these personae: they are the *pobres* (poor things) that he wishes did not fall into perdition, but they can't help themselves. Their immorality is understandable, even forgivable. Within this category, he speaks most kindly of male youth; their immaturity makes them that much more vulnerable, as they have had less time to cultivate their fortitude. This is the "they" grouping closest to Don Arturo's migratory past—he could have belonged to this group, if not for his greater natural proportion of *voluntad*. Not too much farther from his sympathy are the sad families who migrate, only to fall prey to ruinous temptation. This is the group to which Juan Carlos and his family may potentially belong, should they move north. Considering that Juan Carlos was still a young man at the time I recorded this conversation, he may also be likened to those sympathetic poor young men who don't know any better.

Beyond these morally imperiled but sympathetic characters are the most immoral figures, who inhabit a territory outside Don Arturo's understanding: women who migrate alone without the accompaniment of their natal or nuclear families (represented in the righthand circle labeled "Morally Corrupted Figures"). Don Arturo portrays these women in the most general and vague—and thus distancing and impersonal—terms. Perhaps not surprisingly, it is in regard to this feature of the traditionalist imaginary that Don Arturo encounters resistance from Doña Cecilia and me. Consider the following (segment 2, part 8, outline) of the conversation:

Women Migrants

#		Spanish	English
1	A	La mujer se va solamente, la mujer que se va . . . pues, solamente está casada que deja su marido y se vaya para allá.	Women only go, women that go . . . well, {the only women who migrate are} married ones who leave their husbands and go there.
2	H	**No—pues no, normalmente se van a seguir a los esposos.**	**No—well, no, they usually go to follow their husbands.**
3	A	No, pues hay muchas que sí, hay muchas que sí se van solitas. Dejan a sus esposos—	No, well there are many that do, there are many that do go alone. They leave their husbands—
4	H	**¿Dejan a sus esposos aquí y se van?**	**They leave their husbands here and go?**
5	A	Sí, aquí—	Yes, here—
6	H	**¿Quién? Nunca he encontrado a una mujer así.**	**Who? I've never met a woman like that.**
7	A	Sí, sí hay—	Yes, there are—
8	C	*¡¿Con hijos?!*	*With children?!*
9	A	Sí hay casos aquí; dejan la familia y se van—	Yes there are cases here; they abandon their families and go—
10	H	**¿Para qué?**	**What for?**
11	A	Pues, a perderse . . . a perderse. Sí hay aquí.	Well, to lose themselves . . . to lose themselves. There are {cases like that} here.

Don Arturo asserts that women migrate to "leave their husbands" (line 3) and "lose themselves" (line 11, a euphemism for engaging in promiscuous sex), both dramatic violations of the terms of proper Mexican womanhood (see chapters 2 and 5). Shortly afterward Don Arturo also likens women to criminals who move to the North to evade arrest in Mexico—quite a damning commentary on the mobility of women. Doña Cecilia and I clearly find these claims incredible, as we repeatedly interrupt him with questions (lines 4, 6, 8, 10): something neither of us does in other parts of the conversation. Nevertheless, Don Arturo maintains his stance that the migration of women is the greatest abomination, while the migration of male youths and families (like his son's) is gravely concerning, though more understandable.

Don Arturo's patterns of stance-toward-personae forward a traditionalist imaginary based on three key propositions, highlighted with underlining in the conversational outline. Doña Cecilia and I overwhelmingly affirm these not only in our response to Don Arturo but in our own discourse, as discussed below. First, as already intimated above, in this imaginary migration is posited a form of suffering for Mexican migrants of every kind. Second, because of this suffering, migration should be avoided by families, children, and women. Only men should migrate. Third, even for men, migration should be conducted in a limited way. Don Arturo frequently asserts, as he does in the excerpt above, that migration is only beneficial when done seasonally to support a family in Mexico, where income from the United States *rinde más* (goes further). "Real life" should be rooted in Mexico. By contrast, migrants who settle in the United States are "poor like here"—a status that renders nonsensical not only settlement-oriented migration but also the seasonal migration of anyone who is already financially stable in Mexico. Don Arturo and Doña Cecilia struggle in particular with this point because their son has a job as a manager in a textile factory and so, in their view, does not need to migrate. In sum, Don Arturo's stances toward these personae posit the kind of migration that he practiced as the only one that allows for moral mobility.

In crafting this traditionalist imaginary, Don Arturo, with support from Doña Cecilia and me, employs diasporic calibration: linking the present interaction to an imagined homeland from which someone has been displaced (Dick 2010a: 281; Eisenlohr 2006: 263). This sense of drawing a distant land near is at play in the ways Don Arturo and Doña Cecilia link their present life to imagination of life in the past and in the United States. But their imaginary is not animated by a desire for a distant homeland in any literal sense, often associated with classical diaspora (see chapter 3). Rather, they imbue the here-and-now of Uriangato with a diasporic rupture—a longing for the Mexico of their youth and for continued family unity and proximity in the future, threatened by the possible migration of Juan Carlos. Yet the construction of a diasporic world in our conversation is not just a form of lament. It is a way for Don Arturo and Doña Cecilia to work through the longing and displacement endemic to diaspora at home by reestablishing the moral universe of the past, recuperating a world in which patriarchal patterns of migration and family life prevailed.

By placing the best of Mexico's migration in the past, this imaginary excuses Don Arturo's inability to remigrate, effectively saying: they don't do it as we used to, and the way they do it now is no way to do it at all. This is both an effort to reclaim his manhood and a critique of the conditions that have encouraged family migration. This view opens a space of understanding for his son: after all, Juan Carlos's potential migration does not represent the very worst of mobility—that is reserved for women. It is not Juan Carlos's fault he cannot migrate as his father did. As such, the production of Don Arturo's migration history allows him to draw his son near—to create connection in the face of separation. At the same time, in elevating a patriarchal past that predates the world of migration his son confronts, Don Arturo asserts an ethico-moral self to which only an increasingly select group of men can lay claim, a mark of generational privilege that separates him from his son (cf. Goodson-Lawes 1993). And so the interpersonal ruptures endemic to diaspora persist.

Therefore, though the traditionalist imaginary reaffirms life as Don Arturo has lived it, it does not erase the tension migration still represents for his family. The "world beyond" we create as part of the process of calibration in our conversation maintains the labyrinthine quality of diaspora: it never seems to end, despite people's efforts to exit it. To ascertain how Don Arturo and Doña Cecilia resolve this diaspora the other aspect of processes of calibration must be considered: the discursive practices that actors use to connect themselves to the world beyond. In our conversation Don Arturo attaches himself to the traditionalist imaginary through distancing and disassociation, as can be observed in his patterns of pronominal use. Don Arturo's pronominal patterns rely overwhelmingly on the use of general pronouns that enable him to assert broad truths of migration. Therefore, building on Silverstein (1993),[7] I call this *universalizing calibration*: the linking an event of interaction to a realm, such as the abstract generalization common to economic models, posited as ontologically distinct from the present. Universalizing calibration is gendered: a majority of men use it in their migration discourse. And it contrasts sharply with the migration discourse of Doña Cecilia and other working-class Uriangatense women, who tend to create what I call *domestic calibration*, because it links speakers to the migratory beyond by rooting them in the realm of home.

Generalization and Gender: Proper Manhood and Universalizing Calibration

Like the migration discourse of other men—at least when they are addressing female audiences—Don Arturo's migration discourse is dominated by the general second person "you" and third person "one" when referring to himself (cf. De Fina 2003: chapter 3). This pattern is part of a tendency toward generalization in men's talk (cf. Farr 2006). Men's migration discourse is characterized more by hypothetical personae (versions of migrants they have heard of and/or imagined) than by biographical ones that depict actual people. In contrast, women, including Doña Cecilia, favor speaking in particulars; they relate their experience to events that have unfolded with their own relations, neighbors, or friends, crafting portraits of migration populated by biographical figures. Don Arturo's pronominal patterns link him to his diasporic and traditionalist imaginary through acts of fact making, a technique of universalizing calibration. In using universalizing calibration, Don Arturo places his migration history at a remove, reinforcing the sense of diasporic rupture, but also protecting himself from it.

Consider the following conversation, which is a fleshed-out version of the excerpt in which Don Arturo explains why he migrated:

Don Arturo's Migration

1	H	¿Y por qué se fue {al Norte}?	And why did you go {to the United States}?
2	A	Por necesidad.	Out of necessity.
3	H	¿Por necesidad?	Out of necessity?
4	A	Para buscar una ayuda [para] . . .	One needed help [for] . . .
5	H	[Aha.]	[Aha.]
6	A	una ayuda para . . . pues, económica—ayudarse económicamente.	help in order to . . . well, economically—to help oneself economically.
7	H	Aha . . . y es de . . . ¿Entonces, no tenía trabajo aquí, o que estaba pasando aquí?	Aha . . . So you didn't have work here, or what was going on here?
8	A	Sí yo tenía trabajo, pero pues, aquí se gana más poco que ni estando allá.	Yes, I had work here, but, well, here you earn less than even being there.
9	H	Sí.	Yes.
10	A	Estando allá y llegando y trabajando, pues . . . pues sí se ayuda a uno aquí, ah? Allá,	Being there and arriving and working, well . . . well yes, it helps one here, right? There,

		pues, ya sé que estando allá se gasta igual que aquí.	well, I know that being there one can spend the same as here.
11	H	**Sí.**	**Yes.**
12	A	Pero aquí es donde rinde lo poquito que uno ahorre [allá]	But here is where it lasts a little longer, the little one may save [there]
13	H	**[Sí].**	**[Yes.]**
14	A	rinde un poquito más. Es lo que le ayuda a uno: que ahorrando un poco, y más lo poquito acá es donde rinde, pa'uno, para la familia.	lasts a little longer. That's what can help one: saving a little, and more than a little here is where it lasts, for one, for the family.
15	H	**Sí . . . y es de . . . Entonces usted se sentía como que: ah sí, puedo sobrevivir aquí en México, pero para seguir [adelante].**	**Yes . . . well . . . So you felt like: oh yeah, I can survive here in Mexico, but to get [ahead].**
16	A	[¡Sí!]	[Yes!]
17	H	**Tengo que irme allá.**	**I have to go there.**
18	A	Sí, pues si yo no me hubiera ido por allá, si no hubiera ido, no hubiera podido tener aquí la casita en que vivo a lo mejor—	Yes, well if I had never gone there, if I had never gone, I would probably not have the little house that I live in here—
19	H	**Aha.**	**Aha.**
20	A	Hubiera pagado renta también.	I would have paid rent as well.
21	H	**Aha.**	**Aha.**
22	A	Gracias a las idas que yo he dado, pues tenemos aquí una casita donde vivir todos, y no pagar renta.	Thanks to my trips {north}, well, we have a little house here where all {of us} live, and not pay rent.
23	H	**Sí, está muy bonita su casa.**	**Yes, the house is very beautiful.**

Throughout this interaction, I prompt Don Arturo to speak of his own migration (lines 1, 7, 15, and 17) and not of the generalities of migration. However, Don Arturo interweaves reference to his personal experience with reference to the realm of a theoretical "everyman migrant" with his use of the general "you" or "one." His switching between the specific and the general is exemplified elegantly in line 8, where he says, "Yes, I had work here, but, well, here you earn less than even being there."

The pattern of interleaving reference to himself with reference to a general persona becomes easier to distill when correlated with Don Arturo's shifts between verb tenses. For example, in the underlined lines below Don Arturo refers to himself and/or to a "we" consisting of him and his family.

Patterns of Pronominal Usage—Verb Tense and Persona

Line 1: H   **Specific "you" (Don A, past): why did you migrate?**

Line 2: A   Ø

Line 3: H   Ø

Line 4: A   General "one" (past): one needed help economically.

Line 5: H   Ø

Line 6: A   General "one": to help oneself economically.

Line 7: H   **Specific "you" (Don A, past): you didn't have work in Mexico?**

Line 8: A   I (Don A, past) ⟶ General "you" (present): I did have work, but there you earn more.

Line 9: H   Ø

Line 10: A   General "one" (present) ⟶ I (present—Don A: animator) ⟶ General "one" (in present)

Line 11: H   Ø

Line 12: A   General "one" (present): here is where the money lasts longer for one.

Line 13: H   Ø

Line 14: A   G: "one" and "the family" (present): here money lasts longer, for one and the family

Line 15: H   **S: "you" (past) ⟶ I (Don A represented speech—past): "I have to go to get ahead"**

Line 16: A   Ø (YES!)

Line 17: H   **I (Don A in represented speech—past)**

Line 18: A   I (in past) ⟶ I (present): my migration gave me my house here.

Line 19: H Ø

Line 20: A   I (past—hypothetical Don A): I would have had to pay rent without migration.

Line 21: H Ø

Line 22: A   Specific "we" (Don A's family): we have our house.

Line 23: H Ø

With the exception of line 4, every other generic persona in this excerpt is placed in the present tense, which is used in Spanish, as in English, to make statements about general truths—as in line 12: "But here is where it lasts a little longer, the little one may save there lasts little longer." By placing the statement in line 4 in the past, Don Arturo links himself to the generic persona represented therein (someone who needed economic help). The past tense in line 4 establishes the initial positive footing between Don Arturo and the generic personae constructed in the second- and third-person singular "you" and "one," hereafter referred to in concert as *general singulars*. The positive alignment between Don Arturo and the general singulars is maintained through line 14. When prompted by my representation of Don Arturo's hypothetical speech in line 15, he then speaks of himself directly until the end of the exchange.

Both the pattern of presenting self through interrelating personal personae and generic personae and the pattern of positive alignment between Don Arturo and the general singulars are maintained throughout the entire conversation. Indeed he follows these patterns whenever he speaks about his experience of migration. All eight exchanges where we directly address his migration history in this conversation replicate these patterns. The use of generalizing speech has a strong gravitational pull on Don Arturo's migration discourse more generally. Well over half of the statements he utters during our conversation make claims on the general truths of migration (see analysis in Dick 2006a: 94–97), whether these be realities he draws close to his own life, as above, or unhappy facts of migration's perversions, as depicted in the excerpt about families falling apart in the United States. When Don Arturo uses generic personae to make totalizing generalizations about migration, he is accomplishing something more than merely recounting his personal experience with migration—although by implication he is also doing that. He is producing an icon of the total experience of migration from Mexico to the United States and thus constructing a point of interconversion between the sensible world of the immediate context and the intelligible world of this totality (cf. Urban 1996), in which he places himself as a good migrant.

By interrelating his personal experience with the realm of general truth, Don Arturo also construes himself as an expert eyewitness who can explain the driving forces of migration. At the same time, his universalizing calibration allows him to create distance between his present self and his failure to take advantage of IRCA and to raise a son who would not engage in family migration: these things belong to a world of abstraction, not to the immediately sensible world of now. Such calibration insulates him from the parts of his migration past that put question marks around his masculinity, representing Don Arturo both as in control (of the situation, of himself) and as an independent, self-determining actor, free to assess migration and make his own decisions about it. Even though he only migrated after he got married and became a father, he largely describes his migration and the migration of the general singulars as events that unfold independently. In linking himself to the traditionalist imaginary of moral mobility, then, Don Arturo is able to assert himself as a proper masculine subject, thus potentially rectifying the challenges to his masculinity presented by his ongoing attachment to migration.

But the enactment of personhood requires more than a person's assertion of a particular version of himself or herself. An actor can claim to be a certain kind of "right person," but that personhood is not fully realized without its ratification by other people (cf. Irvine 1989, 2009). Just as people can experience diasporic connections with lives they have been unable to live (such as the IRCA migrant Don Arturo could have been), the lives to which people lay claim can be also fractured, denied, prevented. Tracking the ratification of Don Arturo's ethico-moral personhood means understanding how it unfurls in relationship with the forms of personhood Doña Cecilia and I assert, for which we seek ratification in turn. Creating an ethico-moral self, then, is a fundamentally interactional and intersubjective process.

The next section considers this process from two perspectives. First, I examine the type of ethico-moral personhood to which Doña Cecilia lays claim through an analysis of the personae she sketches in her pronominal use and other features of migration discourse. This analysis shows that Doña Cecilia links herself to our traditionalist imaginary of moral mobility via domestic calibration, which latches the here-and-now to the beyond through the particular and personal—through hearth and home. This domestic calibration works in tandem with Don Arturo's universalizing calibration, creating a gendered-pair part that legitimates the rightness of their manhood and womanhood, respectively. Second, I discuss the vital role Doña Cecilia plays as facilitator of the ethico-moral labors of our interaction, which enables her to ratify the ethico-moral personhood of all three of us.

Then I Would Have Gone for Him: Domestic Calibration and the Production of Proper Womanhood

Recall from chapter 2 that working-class Uriangatense imaginaries of moral mobility figure the physical and socioeconomic mobility of women as problematic. Good women are meant to be *en casa, recogida*: at home and cloistered by family. Their mobility is to happen only in service to family relations (see also chapter 5). This view of female mobility is exemplified in Don Arturo's positioning of women migrants: any woman who initiates her own migration is anathema; only women who migrate with family deserve any measure of understanding. But it is not only men who (re)produce the constraint of women's mobility. It is manifested as well in the recurring features of women's migration discourse. This constraint is observable, for instance, in the patterns of alignment to the SA proposition. As discussed above, working-class Uriangatense women are much less able than men to do migration in the ways they propose it because their desires are cambered through the demands of family more extensively than are men's (cf. Dick 2010b, 2013; Farr 2006; Hondagneu-Sotelo 1994).

But even for women who are satisfied with their relationship to migration, which is the case for Doña Cecilia, their migration discourse enacts the *mujer recogida* whose life is rooted in home and family (see chapter 2). Although such enactments index (and reproduce) the constraint of women's mobility, they are not some uncritical replication of "tradition." They are a strategy women use to express and legitimate their perspectives as they face the political economic changes that have encouraged their mobility, even as their morality continues to be rooted at home (a point to which I return in the next chapter). Women employ "traditional Mexican womanhood" to establish their ethico-moral soundness, which in turn allows them to speak with authority (see also chapter 5). Consider the following excerpt from segment 1, part 5, in the conversational outline:

Doña Cecilia's Migration

1	H	Y señora, usted nunca ha ido allá, ¿verdad?	And ma'am, you never went there, right?
2	C	*No.*	*No.*
3	H	¿Y nunca ha tenido ganas, o . . . ?	Have you ever wanted to, or . . . ?
4	C	*Pues yo creo que no. No. Como él iba y venía, iba y venía, pues no. Solo que si hubiera estado ahí sin venida entonces si hubiera ido, sí habría ido por él—*	*Well, I don't think so. No. Since he was coming and going, coming and going, well no. Only if he would have settled there, then I would have gone, I would have gone for him—*
5	A	Yo le decía, déjame ver si arreglo papeles y si te arreglo para que te puedas echar la vuelta y venida. Como te digo, nada más me gustaría ir pa'una temporadita, unos meses, y venirme.	I would tell her, let me see if I can arrange my papers and if I can make arrangements so you can come and go. As I told you, I only liked going for a little season, a few months, and {then} return.
6	H	**Sí.**	**Yes**.
7	A	El interés nada más es que si vas allá y trabajas. Aquí te rinde más el dinero un poquito más.	The idea is only to go there and work. Here is where the money lasts a little longer.

In this excerpt Doña Cecilia establishes her ability to speak about migration by asserting a stance on how she knows the experience of migration. This stance is established via a form of self-presentation I call *rhetorical refraction*, which is integral to Doña Cecilia's domestic calibration.

Notice that when Doña Cecilia describes why she never migrated (line 4), she does not use her personal experience as an occasion to generalize—as Don Arturo does (again) in lines 5 and 7, where he reiterates the ideal of migrating for a little season. Doña Cecilia has extensive exposure to migration's impact on life in Uriangato; she could have articulated the facts of migration from this perspective. Instead she speaks of migration through reference to biographical personae (representations of actual people), especially her family. Thus she implies that it is through cultivating relationships with family that she comes to know migration. In realizing this epistemological stance, Doña Cecilia refracts her individual experience through familial relations. In contrast to Don Arturo, who represents his migration as a solitary act—even though he migrated to support his wife and children—Doña Cecilia presents her migration as subsumed to her husband's choices, saying that because he did not settle in the United States she never had any reason to move.

Such rhetorical refraction is further enacted in this excerpt with the aid of Don Arturo, when he cuts off Doña Cecilia just as she is about to articulate the conditions under which she would have migrated (line 5). Even though I have invited Doña Cecilia to the discursive stage by asking about her migration past, she is not able to articulate a complete response before Don Arturo wrests the conversational focus back to his positions on migration. Rather than seeing his interruption as an inappropriate interactional rupture, however, Doña Cecilia is deferential to Don Arturo's interventions into our exchange. It is her husband's role to link the experience of migration in their family to the general realities of migration, as he does in line 5 when he begins with particular reference in the form of the first-person pronouns and then finishes with a statement about the general truths of migration in line 7. Doña Cecilia authorizes Don Arturo's role as fact-maker by allowing him to interrupt her, thus performing her respect for him.

Here and throughout our conversation, Doña Cecilia thus affirms our traditionalist imaginary of moral mobility, linking herself to it through a domestic calibration that cloisters her inside family. All of her discourse strategies—speaking personally, construing the world of migration within the confines of her particular experience and the biographical personae of her family, permitting Don Arturo to interrupt her—allow her to assert herself as the epitome of proper Mexican womanhood: a caring and respectful woman of family. Don Arturo and I accept this positioning, which, in turn, ratifies Don Arturo's proper manhood.

Such calibration and its interactional effects are not idiosyncratic to Doña Cecilia. Working-class Uriangatense women on both sides of the border favor the production of specific portraits of migration that use the crafting of biographical (and not abstract or hypothetical) personae to establish their knowledge (see Dick 2010b, 2013; Dick and Arnold 2017a—see also chapter 5). In addition, women overall are more likely to be interrupted while speaking—by themselves, by participants in the conversation, and by bystanders—than are men (see Dick 2010b, 2013). Consequently, working-class women hold court discursively in a more dialogic way than do men (cf. Farr 2006).

As these broader patterns of domestic calibration in women's speech suggest, cloistered (*recogida*) femininity (and the related sociospatial divide between house and street discussed in chapter 2) is a widespread semiotic ideology that helps order how women manage the production of their ethico-moral personhood even as they realize mobile lives (cf. Dick 2010b; Gal 2005; Hyams 2003; Keane 2003; Mendoza-Denton 2008). Although such cloistering is a reflection of women's oppression, it is not just that. Rhetorical refraction and the other techniques of domestic calibration produce a different style of speaking migration that can be just a persuasive as men's, though in distinct ways (cf. the discussion of *Mujer, Casos de la vida real* in chapter 2). And women often employ these techniques to highlight and resist their marginalization (see chapter 5).

Indeed Doña Cecilia, though deferential, is far from docile. Her domestic calibration allows her to complicate Don Arturo's traditionalist imaginary of migration. Take, for instance, her portrayal of women migrants. Doña Cecilia—without prompting—makes a point of talking about her two best friends, both single mothers living in the United States. She explains that they are better able to provide for their children and therefore to be better mothers and more morally mobile in the United States than in Mexico (segment 3, part 12). This is the only part of the conversation where Doña Cecilia switches into generalizing speech, as she touts the superior care that the US government gives its residents compared to the care that poor and working-class people receive from the Mexican government. "Over there, they give them help; here no," she says, echoing the words of many working-class women (see chapter 5). As this suggests, Doña Cecilia's migration discourse personalizes and intensifies our conversation, drawing us into the experience of her family and other close relations. In so doing, she plays a provocative and pivotal role in enabling the ethico-moral work of our exchange that illuminates the intersubjective nature of ethical work, as the next section shows.

Doña Cecilia as Ethico-moral Agitator

Throughout it is Doña Cecilia who links our conversation to the conflicts that motivate both her own and Don Arturo's enactments of ethico-moral personhood: the impending migration of their son and Don Arturo's failure to return to the United States because he was ill. This role as an agitator, if a gentle one, is evident in the conversational dynamics in our interaction, detailed in the conversational outline. In segment 1 (which involves a fairly standard interview question-and-answer exchange, as noted above) we speak mostly in general terms, as Don Arturo establishes the fundamental features of the traditionalist imaginary of moral mobility. At this point, Doña Cecilia's input is minimal. The interview phase is followed by a transition in segment 2, in which the interaction becomes conversational, largely thanks to Doña Cecilia, who at this point begins to interject more. Not surprisingly, given Doña Cecilia's use of domestic calibration, we start to talk in increasingly personal terms about migration. This prompts us to break into a fully conversational mode, sparked by discussion of Don Arturo's border-crossing experiences (segment 2, part 9). Doña Cecilia is the one who crafts two key features that make this exchange more informal and conversational. First, she routinely introduces new topics, pushing away the interview frame in which I was the topic-initiator. Second, she consistently pulls Don Arturo's discussion of the general back to a consideration of their domestic world.

Consider the following excerpt, where Doña Cecilia helps Don Arturo respond to a question that I pose in line 1:

Juan Carlos's Migration

1	H	¿Y mucha gente que no ha ido allá piensa, verdad, que sí es puro gozar?	And a lot of people that have not gone there think that yes, it is all enjoyment, right?
2	A	Sí, va y mete la juventud, los jóvenes que se van de 16, 17, 18 [años].	Yes, the young people that go at 16, 17, 18 years [old].
3	H	[Aha.]	[Aha.]
4	A	Que se van con el fin de gozar la vida. No ganan mucho, no van con el fin de ahorrar algo, sino con el fin de gozar.	They go with the goal of enjoying life. They don't earn much—they don't go with the goal of saving but of enjoying themselves.
5	H	Sí.	Yes.
6	C	*Nosotros tenemos un hijo que no tiene la necesidad de, bueno, sí tiene, pero {también} no. Aquí tiene su trabajo, y el está con la idea de conocer, que no le cuenten.*	*We have a son that doesn't have the need to, well, yes, he has, but {also} no. But he has his work here, and he has the notion of discovering, that they don't tell him.*
7	H	Aha.	Aha.

8	C	*Y dice que ahora para diciembre . . . para diciembre {planea irse}. Pero no, {aún} no se ha ido.*	And he says that now for December . . . for December {he's planning to go}. But no, he hasn't gone {yet}.
9	**H**	**No**.	**No.**
10	C	*Nosotros le decimos que le va a sufrir, pero él: "Pa'que no me cuenten." Quiere ir.*	We tell him he is going to suffer, but he {says}: "So that they don't tell me." He wants to go.
11	A	Quiere ir para que no le cuenten. Y yo le dicho, "Mira, aquí estás ganando más o menos."	He wants to go so that they don't tell him. And I told him, "Look, here you are earning more or less."
12	**H**	**¿En qué trabaja aquí?**	**What does he do here?**
13	A	Trabaja en un taller [cuidando máquinas]	He works in a factory [maintaining machines]
14	C	[*Cuidando las máquinas.*]	[*Maintaining the machines.*]
15	A	de hacer ropa y gana más o menos—no mucho, ¿verdad?, pero va bien.	that makes clothes and he earns more or less—not a lot, right?, but he's doing well.
16	C	*Y como no tiene ningún vicio, gracias a Dios, por eso está más bien.*	And since he doesn't have any vices, thanks be to God, that's why he is better off.
17	**H**	**Aha, aha . . .**	**Aha, aha . . .**
18	A	Pero muchas {personas}, aunque tengan aquí, muchos aunque tengan aquí a un buen trabajo se van con el fin de conocer {los Estados Unidos}, a ver que es andar por allá—se van, y se acaban allá.	But a lot {of people}, even though they have a good job here go with the aim of discovering {the United States}, to see what it is to be there—they go, and they finish themselves there.

This part of the conversation comes on the heels of Don Arturo's statements that life in the North is suffering for migrants, which prompts my question in the first line. This exchange (from segment 3, part 11) happens several minutes after Don Arturo and I speak at length about the migration of young men in general (in segment 1, part 3). During that exchange, Don Arturo never mentions Juan Carlos's plans to migrate, although it is clear that he and Doña Cecilia categorize their son's migration as part of the unnecessary migration of young people.

Rather, it is Doña Cecilia who shifts our focus from the life of hypothetical youth to their son's potential migration (line 6—a topic she reasserts several times in part 11, even as Don Arturo attempts to change the subject).

Here, as throughout, Doña Cecilia's migration discourse moves us away from universalizing into the intimate, drawing our attention to a proximal future without their son and his family. As in the excerpt analyzed in the prior section, Doña Cecilia recruits herself to our discussion via knowledge of her son's life, thus presenting herself as an attentive mother, a positioning Don Arturo and I ratify through our uptake of her personalizing discursive moves. At the same time, her discussions of Juan Carlos's migration raise the specter of Don Arturo's failure as a father: he fell short of remigrating in 1986 and getting US legal status for his family; he fell short of convincing his son that he need not migrate. But rather than trying to humiliate Don Arturo, Doña Cecilia uses these putative failures to bolster and reaffirm Don Arturo's positions on migration and therefore his authority and legitimacy. Each time Doña Cecilia brings up her son's migration, as she does here, it is to say that it is unnecessary—he has work in Mexico; he should not migrate with his family. Each time, then, she supports Don Arturo's traditionalist imaginary. Consequently, her personalizing discourse allows Don Arturo to pull the focus back out to the masculine realm of the general, as he does in line 18. He does this every time Doña Cecilia brings in the personal. Her discourse creates the conditions for him to extrapolate out to statements of fact.

Similarly, it is Doña Cecilia who elaborates how ill Don Arturo was when he mentions it the first time. Indeed it is this reference to his illness that first motivates her to speak when Don Arturo and I are engaged in the interview exchange (segment 1, parts 1–5). Doña Cecilia brings his illness back into our conversation several times, in segment 2, parts 6 and 9, and segment 3, part 10. She is persistent in conveying the pivotal importance of this part of their migration history. For example, in part 6 I ask Don Arturo: what was the hardest thing you had to deal with in the United States? When Don Arturo falters, Doña Cecilia answers for him, saying that the worst thing was his wanting to work and not being able to because he was sick. Her discussions of his illness emphasize how much his failure to remigrate was out of his hands; he was innocent of any wrongdoing. Over and over, she reanimates Don Arturo's inability to remigrate to humanize him and root him in his family, another characteristic of a good wife.

She also takes pains to represent the success of her marriage and her motherhood. In line 10 above she offers a portrait of herself and Don Arturo speaking in unity to their son, thereby projecting their partnership as parents and endorsing Don Arturo's stance on migration: we tell him he is only going to suffer. Notice as well her claim in line 16 that her son "doesn't have any vices." As I discuss in the next chapter, women often stress this point about their children, a form of ethico-moral guidance (you had better not have any vices, young man!) and as a way to broadcast to others their success as mothers.

Finally, then, Doña Cecilia asserts her ethico-moral personhood as a woman of family: she knows her son's desires, is close enough to give him advice even in adulthood, and collaborates lovingly with her husband. But, as with Don Arturo, her assertions do not constitute enactment of personhood unless ratified interactionally and dialogically. She needs Don Arturo's and my uptake of her domestic calibration to become that woman. Her affirmation of the proper manhood Don Arturo asserts (allowing him to display his knowledge, authority, and compassion) establishes her proper womanhood. Thus, the enactment of personhood rests in the successful cultivation of intersubjectivity in acts of calibration: the production of agreement about the terms of the world and who we are inside that world. This process is traceable in the enactment of my ethico-moral personhood as a "good gringa" (see chapter 2), in which Doña Cecilia again plays a central role.

Intersubjectivity and Becoming a Good Gringa

One way Doña Cecilia enables me to be a good gringa is by simply being there. Working-class Uriangatense women realize proper Mexican womanhood through practices of sex segregation: not socializing alone with men other than their husbands and blood relations (cf. Dick 2017; Hirsch 2003). As I had no husband or blood relation in Uriangato, in order to perform myself as a woman of virtuous character, I spent the majority of my time interacting both personally and professionally with other women (see chapter 2). When I interacted with men in any extended way (beyond, say, purchasing goods at the market), I did so in the presence of their wives and/or other female relations, as was the case with Don Arturo and Doña Cecilia. As this suggests, sometimes the very fact of a particular arrangement of interaction is evidence of "underlying moral commitments" (Keane 2011: 170). Consider that when I first arrived the day I recorded the conversation analyzed here, Don Arturo was in his and Doña Cecilia's bedroom watching television, while Doña Cecilia was preparing lunch. She promptly invited Don Arturo and me to the kitchen table. I gladly accepted the invitation, feeling uneasy at the prospect of interviewing Don Arturo alone. Doña Cecilia and I thus tacitly maintained my feminine virtue and the sanctity of her marriage through our co-presence. Beyond this tacit ethico-moral work, Doña Cecilia's highlighting of the ethico-moral tensions in her family also draw me increasingly into the interaction in ways that contribute to the enactment of my ethico-moral personhood as a good gringa (beginning in segment 2, part 9, and taking hold fully in segment 3, parts 10–12).

In part 9, after Doña Cecilia states how young Don Arturo was when he first migrated to the United States, I tell a crossing story of another migrant family I knew. This leads me to expound on the familial dynamics that often unfold when a migrant father has been away for a long period and then returns. I describe the difficult process of family reunification that my mother and her parents went through after my grandfather returned from World War II. This story prompts Don Arturo to compare the lives of migrants to war veterans who suffer from posttraumatic stress disorder. He explains that when he was in El Norte in the early 1970s he saw many veterans returning from Vietnam. It always seemed to him that some migrants (himself?) ended up the same way as those veterans did when they returned to Mexico—so exhausted, so traumatized, as if they had been to war. Doña Cecilia's domestic calibration therefore generates a dynamic of closeness among the three of us, which encourages the intersubjective agreement on the ethico-moral personhood that we each claim.

But, as with her footing in regard to Don Arturo, Doña Cecilia's interactional moves toward me are not just peaceable. She also plays a provocative role here, creating a key moment of ethico-moral enactment for me and—ultimately—of intersubjective recognition between us. Consider segment 3, parts 11 and 12. In part 11 Doña Cecilia speaks about her son's migration, describing her own and Don Arturo's parenting style, which inspires Don Arturo to ask me about my life in the United States. He begins with questions about the size of my family, which prompts us to compare US and Mexican families. This raises the specter of improper US womanhood (see chapter 2). Many Uriangatenses will assert that US people, especially white women, do not invest sufficiently in family life—it is assumed that we are too focused on our careers and have small families as a result. Moreover, people are struck by the increased amount of freedom women have in the United States, which, as Don Arturo and Doña Cecilia note in part 12, is reinforced by legal institutions, especially laws protecting women against domestic violence. The potential for the state to intervene in relations between husband and wife is the very opposite of the paradigmatic "traditional" Mexican family, in which the husband's say and actions take precedent—socially and legally—over those of the wife and the state is unlikely to curb him (cf. Hirsch 2003; Smith 2006). Even as both Don and Doña assert that it is a good thing that women in the United States have more legal protections against violence, the affirmation of women's independence across social realms, from the bedroom to the courtroom, is still striking to them. It is not, as Doña Cecilia points out, like that *aquí en México* (here in Mexico).

The discussion of the size of US families and women's independence indirectly presents an ethico-moral conflict for my personhood. My presence in Uriangato alone, unmarried, and childless always presented this tension (see chapter 2). In bringing up discussion of the size of US families, Don Arturo and Doña Cecilia were effectively asking: what kind of gringa are you? Largely because of the conversational moves realized by Doña Cecilia, I am given an opportunity to present myself as a good gringa who appreciates the gendered imperatives of Mexicanidad. While I did not always navigate these moments of ethico-moral conflict well, I did so that day.

In perhaps the culminating moment of our intersubjective agreement, Doña Cecilia follows up on Don Arturo's (of course, general) points about women's independence in the United States by telling a story about a couple that visited from Pennsylvania during Christmas (segment 3, part 12). This story exemplifies a common discourse of migration not only in Uriangato but in other Mexican migrant enclaves as well: *en el Norte la mujer manda* (in the North the woman is in charge) (cf. Hirsch 2003; Smith 2006). The protagonists in Doña Cecilia's story were a husband (the son of one of their neighbors) and his wife (a white woman from the United States). Doña Cecilia explained that one day she heard them walking by the house, having a fight. The woman was crying, tired of her husband being domineering with her. Finally, the woman said, "Fine, go ahead and boss me around, but just wait until we get home [to the North]—where I can boss you around. Then you'll be sorry!" This tickled us, prompting giggles all around. In the voice of the woman in Doña Cecilia's story, I said: *Vas a ver* (You will see), a common admonishment used when scolding someone lovingly.

After this story I express my disappointment with my fellow gringas when they would visit Uriangato with their husbands during various Catholic holidays. Unimpressed by their manner of self-presentation, I described the embarrassment I felt seeing them on the street in baggy T-shirts and sweatpants, wearing sneakers, without their hair done or any makeup on: all signs of improper public femininity. Indeed, I kept my distance from these women, never engaging them in small talk as I did many other strangers during my time in Uriangato, because I perceived their violations of proper Mexican womanhood and did not want to be associated with their typical gringa behaviors (see chapter 2). "*Ay mi paisanas* [Oh my fellow countrywomen], what a disgrace they are to my country," I said to Don Arturo and Doña Cecilia. "It shames me that these are the US women your compatriots marry!" At this they laughed uproariously, saying dismissively that those men only marry *esas gringas feas* (those ugly gringas) to get papers (that is, to get legal status in the United States). The mutual recognition made possible by this exchange, affirmed through their warm laughter (at least it was warm toward me), not only allowed me to enact my ethico-moral personhood by laying claim to being a person who knows how to comport herself in Mexico (and who is thus a decent person and not a "bad gringa," even if I am from the United States). It was also a moment of us-them collusion that creates an ethico-moral kinship, which confirms the proper personhood to which each of us lays claim and the traditionalist imaginary of moral mobility we construct. The cozy communion we co-create through crafting their migration history is further established by what happens after our discussion of gringas. Don Arturo and I briefly recap the main points of our conversation, as Doña Cecilia receives Juan Carlos's wife and son, who stop by toward the end of the recording. After the recap, I turn off the recorder and Don Arturo and Doña Cecilia—along with their daughter-in-law and grandson—take me on a tour of parts of their house I had not seen on previous visits. This house tour is not insignificant.

As discussed in chapter 3, the home is the bedrock of ethico-moral life in working-class Uriangato. Moreover, the organization of the home is associated with degrees of closeness between the people who live in the home and those who visit it. If the sidewalk and garage are the most impersonal and the kitchen is an intermediary space, the bedrooms are the spaces in which the most trusting and interconnected relationships unfold. This final point may seem obvious, but as noted previously bedrooms are not exclusively private spaces in Uriangato. They are centers of socializing for family members and close friends (cf. Hirsch 2003). Houses, in other words, are crucibles that relationships pass through, as interior spaces demarcate—and thus help create—relative degrees of closeness between people. Inviting me into the entirety of the house at the end of this conversation is itself a signal of the interactional and intersubjective success of our conversation. We found points of ethico-moral agreement that created an ethico-moral community between us, at least for that one day.

Expressed in and through the migration history of Don Arturo and Doña Cecilia are potent acts of care, in which they not only seek to establish themselves as right and good in the face of ethico-moral conflict but also tend to the character and safety of their offspring—and to some extent my own personhood and well-being. Such caring is not only about creating and maintaining the bonds of family. It is also a way of manifesting a critical stance on ethico-moral life: acts of care comment on the historical and political economic conditions that motivate and constrain such life (cf. Arnold 2016; Garcia 2014: 56). In this case Don Arturo and Doña Cecilia confront, in particular, a period of dramatic change in the practice and imagination of migration, which has encouraged family migration and which may pull their son and his young family away from them.

As such, the analysis in this chapter shows that families prepare for and navigate the diasporic separations rendered by migration long before, and sometimes regardless of, actual movements across borders. It also suggests the ways that even the most seemingly simple acts of ethico-moral work, such as telling a story about the fight of a couple passing by your house, are political (a point that forms the centerpiece of analysis in the next chapter). The production of migrant histories is a uniquely efficacious ethico-moral practice because it enables people to move between confronting the complexities of interpellation into state-endorsed imaginaries of moral mobility and the effort to find a place in more immediate forms of group membership between family and neighbors. As we create their migration history through acts of calibration, we position ourselves as right kinds of people within the social landscapes produced by state-endorsed imaginaries and by other working-class Uriangatenses. This facilitates Don Arturo and Doña Cecilia's ability simultaneously to lay claim to national belonging—to respond to calls to be Mexican in a certain way—while also situating us in the ethico-moral geography of Uriangato. This process makes possible the resolution of the particular conflicts of our lives: Don Arturo's migration failure, my potential to be a bad gringa. So interpellation involves the negotiation of multiple calls across different spheres of interaction, from nation-state to family—a process that depends fundamentally on the production of intersubjectivity in interaction.

This chapter, therefore, suggests several interrelated points relative to the study of ethics and morality more generally. First, ethico-moral life is not an objectified totality but a fluid process (cf. Keane 2011; Zigon 2011). It is always potentially alterable, even when formalized. Therefore migration discourse can serve as a site of ethico-moral transformation. Second, ethico-moral work is not immanent in any social milieu or kind of interaction (Garcia 2014; Keane 2010, 2011, 2014; Lempert 2013). While the terms of imaginaries of moral mobility (which always draw into question the ethico-moral character of working-class people) create some conditions of possibility for ethico-moral work, those conditions are not sufficient for the kindling of assertions of ethico-moral personhood in any given context. Rather, ethico-moral work is sparked by the particular and emergent assemblage of a range of factors in a given exchange (Dick 2017): people's ongoing conflicts and desires; the dynamics of particular genres of communication, such as interview exchanges (which tend to prompt justifications) (cf. Keane 2014); and other contingent features of ongoing relationships and moments of interaction.

In illuminating these points, I complicate how ethico-moral work has been described in some anthropology (e.g., Zigon 2011), which asserts that such work happens in moments of conscious choice between conflicting moral options. While ethico-moral practices become more easily observable in such moments, reducing them to conscious choice is too limiting (cf. Lempert 2013). Patterns of discursive interaction that are often below the conscious awareness of speakers, such as pronominal patterns, are integral to ethico-moral work. Moreover, the successful enactment of ethico-moral personhood involves collusion between interlocutors about the substance of the right and the wrong. This informs the production of relationships between actors and therefore not just ethico-moral selves but social formations. This chapter can be thought of as a microcosm of how such formations emerge across many domains, including that of the nation-state (cf. Anderson 2011). Here I document a successful moment of ethical community building, as Don Arturo, Doña Cecilia, and I come to recognize each other as being of like mind on family and migration. The next chapter shows that such felicitous outcomes are not a given; intersubjective recognition is an interactional accomplishment that interlocutors sometimes fail to realize.

Appendix: Conversational Outline

Key
- A = Don Arturo
- C = Doña Cecilia
- H = Hilary
- Except where noted otherwise, Hilary introduces questions/topics
- <u>Single underline</u>: key features of the traditionalist imaginary of migration/mobility.
- Roman: Don Arturo and Hilary
- *Italic*: Doña Cecilia

Segment 1: Interview Phase (Minute Markers—0:00–13:00)

1. Don Arturo's migration north (1:00–3:27)
- H to A: Why did you migrate?
- A: Out of necessity
  - <u>Migrating for a little season (Excerpt 1)</u>

2. Don Arturo's return migration to Uriangato (3:37-5:38)
- H to A: Why did you stop migrating?
- A: I got sick with "los nervios"
  - Mentions how hard life is in the US for migrants
  - Talks about the 1986 Amnesty
  - *Doña Cecilia talks for the first time—affirming how sick A was*

3. Family migration (5:28–9:04)
- H to A: If life is so hard in the United States and it's better to migrate only for a little season, why do whole families migrate there?
- A: <u>They think it will be easy, and then they fall apart there</u> <u>(Excerpt 2)</u>
  - H and A: Discuss the role of loneliness and depression in leading to perdition, especially among youth migrants

4. *Voluntad* (will) and migration (9:40–10:17)
- H to A: What qualities do migrants who don't fall into ruin have?
- A: We have more will.
  - They offered me drugs; I never took them

5. Life in the United States (10:17–12:56)
- H to A: You didn't like life in the United States, it seems?
- A: Reiterates points from above:
  - <u>Life is too hard there for migrants, too fast—too much pressure</u>
  - <u>You should only migrate "for a little season" to support the family in Mexico</u>

- H to Doña Cecilia: Did you ever migrate?
- *C: No, I had no reason to (Excerpt 3)*
- A: Interrupts her—you should only migrate "for a little season"

Segment 2: Transitional Phase (Minute Markers—13:00–32:00)

6. Life in the United States, Part 2 (12:56–15:00)
- H to A: What was the hardest thing that happened to you in the United States?
- A: Can't think of what to say . . .
- *C: Interjects that the hardest thing was getting sick, elaborates on his illness*

7. Youth Migration (15:00–16:30)
- H to A: Many people migrate because they think it will be easy/fun, right?
- A: Talks in general terms about why young men migrate
- *C: Redirects conversation to potential migration of their son (Excerpt 4)*
- A: Moves the conversation back out to the general

8. Men's vs. Women's Migration (16:30–20:00)
- H to A and C: Does your son want to migrate because his relatives and friends have?
- A responds: Talks in general about how it is the man's job to migrate (for a little season)—and women only migrate for suspect reasons, like criminals
  - H: Disagrees with his view of women migrants

9. Don Arturo's Crossing Story (20:00–32:00): **Transition to More Fully Conversational**
- H to A: So you crossed to the US over the Río Bravo?
- A: Tells a crossing narrative of one-time crossing
- *C: Talks about how young A looked when first migrated, before he got sick*
- H: Tells another crossing story she heard recently
- H: Says she's always thought of migrants as being like men who come home from war
  - A and C: Strongly agree
  - A: Says he thinks it is as though some migrants have PTSD

Segment 3: Conversation (Minute Markers—32:00–52:00)

10. *C Introduces* Why Don Arturo returned to Mexico (32:00–40:00)
- *C: The work there is all agricultural, too hard—that's why A got sick*
- A: Most migrants are rancheros and can do that work. They get used to it and to the money they earn and then they never come back.

- *C: I have a female friend in the US who gets a lot of assistance from the government*
  - *There the government helps you more than here*

11. *C Introduces* Son's Impending Migration (40:00–47:00)
- *C: Explains why her son wants to migrate*
- *C: Her son's friends' migration—some have "gotten lost there"/fallen into perdition*
- *C: I didn't like it when Don Arturo would migrate—I felt alone*
  - *Life in Mexico is hard for a woman when you are alone*
- *C: We have a good relationship—DA is a good man*
- *C: Her vision of their parenting style/their family*
- A question to H: How many siblings do you have?
- H: Only one brother
- A: US families are small
- A: Tells a story of a white family he knew in Texas that had a lot of children; he liked that; but most US families aren't like that
- *C: Points out the number of failed pregnancies she had—they would have had a larger family; they wanted a larger family*

12. A Introduces Women's Lives in the United States (47:00–52:00)
- A questions H: Women have more legal protections in the US, right?
- All three of us compare women's freedom and protections from domestic violence in the United States versus Mexico
  - A: In Mexico a woman's world "closes"—there women have more possibilities
  - *C: Tells the story of the neighbors, a couple visiting from the United States—the man is Mexican and the woman a white gringa who says: just wait until we get home!*
  - H: Talks about how ashamed she is of the other white women who come to Uriangato from the United States.

Segment 4: Recap (Minute Markers—52:00–55:00, end)
[Doña Cecilia leaves to talk to her daughter-in-law, who arrived shortly before the previous exchange]

13. Life without migration (52:00–55:00)
- H to A: What would your life had been like without migration?
- A: I wouldn't have a house here—migrating for a little season is good

CHAPTER 5

Saints and Suffering: Critical Appeal in Relationships with the Divine Beyond

Scenes from Semana Santa, Part One

It is the Thursday of Semana Santa (Easter Week), and Mexico is on the move.[1] This is a day of pilgrimage to the shrines that link the country's landscape to heaven, a day to give thanks for prayers answered. After so many months blessed with others' generosity, it is time to take a pilgrimage myself. A friend (a devout Christian who attended the same Episcopal Church that I did in Pennsylvania) is visiting from the United States and is excited to join me. Although large saint sanctuaries that draw enormous crowds are only a few hours away, we decide to stay local. I've heard there is a shrine to a particularly *milagrosa* (miracle-working) incarnation of the Virgin Mary in La Soledad, a rancho that belongs to the neighboring municipality. In accordance with the Catholic custom of displaying faith through bodily practice, we walk to La Soledad, about a three-hour trip by foot. By 7 A.M. when we reach the dirt path to La Soledad, there is already a steady flow of pilgrims. Once we arrive in the town, we find the streets flanking the shrine alive with small amusement rides, music, and a buoyant conviviality reminiscent of a country fair. It seems as if all the people in town have put tables in front of their houses, selling tacos, tamales, and fresh juices. Traveling merchants are hawking balloons, key chains, and CDs.

In the radiant morning light the shrine, housed in a small chapel, is glowing with pride, dressed up for the occasion with fresh paper garlands hung by loving supplicants. The chapel is surrounded by a pocket of solemnity. Its interior is framed by plain wooden benches that lead up to the altar where a doll-like image of the Virgin stands, a cascade of flowers at her feet. To the Virgin's left and right are offerings people have made to her—not just today but throughout the years: photos of loved ones she has helped, small paintings, handicrafts, and other precious items. Among the offerings are bright green US dollars in a range of denominations—a sign that La Virgen de La Soledad has overseen the safe passage of migrants to El Norte. The streets of La Soledad are lined with evidence of migration: cars with the US license plates of returnees stand in front of three-story homes unlikely to have been financed by employment in this otherwise economically depressed town. We enter the shrine, joining the stream of people. To one side is a small room where people are lighting candles in thanksgiving. I kindle one in memory of Doña Lupe, the mother of my host family, who died in December. After a few moments of prayer, we leave the shrine's solemnity and enter anew the country-fair atmosphere of the street. We buy lemonade and a few souvenirs and then make our way home. When we reach the pathway back to the city, people are still heading toward La Soledad, even though it is after noon and the sun blazes dangerously. We pass a family. One of the women is barefoot. This must have been part of her pilgrimage promise: to walk those many miles of the rocky, thorn-filled path to the shrine with no shoes. Moved, I watch her pick her way carefully toward the Virgin.

Scenes from Semana Santa, Part Two

The afternoon of the next day—Viernes de Dolor, Viernes Santo (Sorrowful Friday, Holy Friday)—is split in two by a violent thunderstorm, which my friend Carmen's mother called the "tears of God." After all, today is the day when Christians memorialize the Crucifixion. I wait until the torrent passes and Carmen can safely take me home on her scooter. While we are waiting, her mother takes the opportunity to exhort me to attend this evening's reenactment of the Passion of Christ. The Passion is the period from the night before the Crucifixion to Jesus's death. It includes his multiple agonies during this time: his betrayal by Judas Iscariot; his abandonment by the disciples; his arrest, trial, beatings; and his suffering on the cross. As in many Mexican municipalities on Good Friday all of urban Uriangato becomes a stage for the Passion, called Las Tres Caídas (The Three Falls). Later that day, bolstered by the moral urgings of Carmen's mother, I walk down to the center of town to join the audience. It feels like the whole town has come to witness Christ's final days.

The reenactment starts in front of the city's principal church, Templo San Miguel, where Jesus's mortifications begin. As a throng we move over several blocks through multiple outdoor staging areas between the church and the city's recreation center, where the Passion culminates. Here, on the hill above the municipal basketball courts, we crucify Christ. The now far-off lightning from the afternoon's storm illuminates the distant mountains, forming the backdrop for the story's climax. Our congregation spreads across the landscape to watch the Roman guards mount Jesus and the thieves who die beside him onto crosses that stand tall before us. Uriangato is not one of the places where participants drive nails into people's hands, though Carmen told me one such town is not too far from here. The guards encourage us to shout damnations on Jesus as he dies for our sins, making us complicit in the Crucifixion.

After the Passion ends, I find my host family at home. We eat a small dinner and then head to the center of town for La Procesión del Silencio (The Procession of Silence), which reenacts Jesus's removal from the cross and interment. Participants follow a route from the hill of Crucifixion to the municipal graveyard. Through the streets of Uriangato walk Christ's mourners, including the Virgin Mary dressed in black, head bent in humble sorrow, behind the lifeless body of her son. Witnesses to the procession fill the sidewalks along the route from hill to grave. Everyone is silent: an entire city quiet on a usually cacophonous Friday night. The occasional tapping of funeral drums and sounding of a lone trumpet are the only noises. The silence in proximity with so many people is arresting. I am flooded with memories of my host mother's death and the somber walk that her family and I took behind her coffin from house to grave. When the procession ends, the regular city soundscape rushes back in like water released from a dam. My friend and host sister Angélica turns to me and asks if I want to get some cake in the plaza. Sure: some cake after our lamentations sounds good. And into the noise of usual life we go.

These archetypal images of Catholicism—Christ's Passion, Mary's silent sorrow, the humble pilgrim walking barefoot through scraggly brush—point to the practices through which Uriangatenses cultivate relationships with figures of the Catholic narrative. While such practices are common in Catholic communities worldwide, they also have a unique valence particular to the history of religious conversion in a given place. In Mexico people's relationships with these figures are embroiled with the country's struggle to realize sovereignty and citizenship. This struggle has generated imaginaries of moral mobility: the idea that being properly Mexican is a project of integrating tradition and modernity so that people "get ahead" in a moral way distinct from the greedy forms of progress in the United States. Such imaginaries draw on Catholicism as a source of the essence of Mexicanidad, the core of the morality that distinguishes Mexico from the United States. Calls to be morally mobile always index Catholicism to some degree. Engagement with Catholic practices is therefore bound up with people's interpellation into variegated national belonging: hailing people to be Mexican in ways that (re)create the marginalization of some groups, a process that has affected not only working-class people and migrants, but practicing Catholics as well (see chapter 1).

As this chapter reveals, the Catholicism of working-class Uriangatenses is not only an expression of religious devotion and national identity—though it is that: most Uriangatenses I know strongly identify being Mexican with being Catholic, even if they are not especially devout. But it is also an arena in which they confront and seek to transform their exclusion from full belonging. As such, it is a key site for the effort to undo diaspora at home described in chapter 3, which characterizes working-class people's interpellation into Mexicanidad: the perpetual reproduction of the seemingly impassible divide between the lives people are meant to realize to be morally mobile and the ones to which they can actually lay claim.

The development of relationships of devotion and mutual obligation with the saints and other divine figures offers an especially illuminating perspective on the role Catholicism plays in processes of interpellation in Mexico. As discussed in chapter 1, religious nationalism has long been a feature of state-endorsed efforts to co-opt Catholic practices—and practitioners—into the project of creating the Mexican state. Relationships with the saints are a central practice through which working-class Uriangatenses both take up and resist such efforts. Saintly relationships are a routine part of life, even for people who may only attend mass a few times a year. Nearly everyone I know in the migrant enclaves of Uriangato and Pennsylvania maintains active relationships with the saints. Indeed people are much more likely to go on a pilgrimage to a saint's shrine than on a vacation to a tourist destination.

The central claim of this chapter is that the practices through which people cultivate relationships with divine figures allow working-class Uriangatenses to generate an alternate imaginary of moral mobility that both forgives them for the conditions of their lives and demands their political recognition, their inclusion in the fullness of national belonging—not in some distant future, but now. I consider this process through an exploration of two key practices that cultivate divine relationships: *promesas* (commitments) to saints; and the voicing of a common figure of Mexican womanhood—*la mujer sufrida* (the suffering woman). This figure is part of the gendering of national belonging in Mexico, as women are meant to be like the Virgin Mary (cf. Napolitano 2002). Through these practices, people do more than spotlight the failures of nation building. They make appeals for the resources denied to them by local, national, and transnational political economies, from the repudiation of their ethico-moral personhood to their lack of access to material goods. Therefore divine (or saintly) relationships are a way to both elegize and seek to resolve the pain and alienation of diaspora at home (see chapter 3; cf. Garcia 2010).

The cultivation of saintly relationships is particularly important for working-class women. As discussed in earlier chapters, the double-bind of belonging that working-class people experience in Mexico is harder to escape for women. Women are much more readily positioned as deviating from proper Mexicanidad, so it is easier for them to be excluded from the benefits of membership not only in the polity, but in their family and immediate community as well. A central way women navigate this double-bind—this diaspora at home—is by establishing relationships with the Virgin Mary. They do so not only through practices that overtly call her into their lives—as we see with *promesas*—but also through emulating her virtuous character, iconized by her humble suffering and sacrifice. Therefore for women the accomplishment of Mexicanidad is closely linked to successful enactments of Marian virtue. I explore this point below in my analysis of the voicing of *la mujer sufrida* in an interaction I had with Magdalena, a woman I met during the Mexican Migration Project survey (see chapter 2); her friend Belén; Magdalena's son Rigoberto; and Belén's daughter Sofía.

Understanding how saintly relationships function as forms of forgiveness for the imperfections of working-class lives and political recognition for the needs of working-class people requires paying attention to the interactional features of *promesas* and voicing the *mujer sufrida*, through which saintly relationships come to shape and comment on social life. An important body of literature examines the connections among Mexican nationalism, Catholicism, and Marian womanhood as a form of political protest (e.g., Bejarano 2002; Gálvez 2006, 2007, 2009;

Martín 2013; Napolitano 2016; Peña 2011; Stephen 1995, 2013; Wright 2006). I build on this literature by highlighting the central role that interaction plays in enabling and shaping these processes, paying particular attention to the multifunctionality of language. Over the last several decades sociocultural studies of language have emphasized the indexical or expressive function of language: how language and other signs come to serve as markers of social difference and therefore can be used to create group membership and also social exclusion and inequality (Duchêne and Heller 2011; Hastings and Manning 2004; Jakobson 1995: chapter 4). *Words of Passage* carries on this tradition in showing that people use migration discourse to render and contest national belonging. In this chapter, however, I draw attention to how the expressive function interacts with what Roman Jakobson (1995: chapter 4) calls the *conative* function: the effort to change a situation by making an appeal or trying to convince. Consideration of this function is especially important in understanding how working-class Uriangatenses in general, and working-class women in particular, seek to reform state-endorsed Mexicanidad.

As discussed in chapters 1 and 3, working-class people are figured in state-endorsed imaginaries of moral mobility as ethico-morally questionable and therefore not deserving of access to full belonging in the nation-state and its associated resources. This positioning is doubled for women, whose mobility is construed as problematic by the beliefs and practices that produce gender difference in Uriangato (see chapters 2 and 4). Hence responding to calls to be Mexican necessarily involves making appeals to your interlocutors—convincing them first that you are properly Mexican and then that you deserve access to the rights and resources of belonging. Such acts of appeal spotlight the practice of anticipatory interpellation (Carr 2009, 2011): foreseeing how you are likely to be interpellated, and preemptively responding to it, redirecting readings of your personhood (see chapter 2). In examining *promesas* and voicings of the *mujer sufrida* as forms of appeal, this chapter illuminates two interrelated processes. First, how Uriangatenses use saintly relationships to assert their proper Mexicanidad, even as they face threats to their ethico-moral standing, such as migration to the United States. Second, how these relationships function as requests for the resources that facilitate socioeconomic and geopolitical mobility.

The everyday interactional genres through which people cultivate saintly relationships—making *promesas* and voicing the *mujer sufrida*—also suggest ways people use language and other semiotic practices to

revise imaginaries of moral mobility and thereby reform the sociopolitical landscape. Although none of my research participants are political
activists per se, their religious nationalism critically comments on and
endeavors to correct social inequality: another facet of acts of appeal,
one that highlights how people call on the government to change their
relationship to working-class people and migrants. In considering this
process, I show that the dynamic between speaker and hearer is central to the efficacy of saintly relationships as a technique for transforming sociopolitical life. The interactional elements of acts of appeal—the
ways people are positioned to one another and may or may not be convinced by their interlocutors—are essential to understanding how the
here-and-now of routine life becomes imbricated with long-term and
more formal reform efforts. It is through the success or failure of such
interactions that sociopolitical transformations do or do not become
plausible and possible in the first place. So acts of everyday appeal help
provide the ground for political movements.

Divine Relations as Transformative Interpellative Practice

On a Friday afternoon during Lent I was at my friend Elena's house for
a seafood lunch—meat being off the menu on Fridays during this period of sacrifice leading up to Easter. Elena and I met while I was conducting my survey interviews. One afternoon I entered the convenience
store that she and her husband owned to buy a soda and some peanuts.
Elena—an extrovert by nature—struck up a conversation with me. She
was curious to know more about what I was doing there and offered in
return to let me use her bathroom during my long afternoons trudg-
ing over the hills of La Libertad as I completed the survey. Because using the bathroom meant entering the inner sanctum of the home, a
space reserved for family or close friends, I was never offered a bathroom break while doing the survey—so this was a rare and precious gift
I gratefully accepted. In time we were sharing sidewalk society, meals,
and trips to the rodeo. Elena's store was on a corner in front of a bus
stop. Sometimes it seemed she knew the whole world, as she would greet
the bus drivers and their passengers, sharing gossip and jokes as they
paused from their daily grind to buy snacks. She graciously welcomed
me into that world, introducing me to people and telling them I was a
"good gringa" (see chapter 2).

That particular Friday before Lent we had the divine on our minds.

I asked if she and her children wanted to join me on my impending pilgrimage to La Soledad. She declined. She had to keep the store open. You don't want to promise to visit one of these saints and not show up, Elena told me. Then she began recounting a story to illustrate the power of divine figures: the tale of El Señor del Zapotito:

> H: ¿¡El Señor del Zapatito?! [Our Lord of the Little Shoe?!]
> Elena: No, Jili: ¡zaPOtito! [No, Hily: zapote fruit!]
> H: Ah, OK . . .

An incarcerated man—falsely accused, he claimed—prayed every night for intercession: that Mary or Jesus would plead with God the Father to release him from his wrongful imprisonment. One night a visitor came, a man—just like you and me. He offered to free the prisoner, but only if the jailed man visited him, once he was free. The visitor said he was from Lagunilla del Rico, a rancho that belongs to Uriangato, where Elena grew up. He was known there as El Señor del Zapotito (the man of the little zapote, a fruit found in the region). The prisoner wondered: did he perhaps sell zapote? Lagunilla del Rico is a community of less than three hundred souls, the man of the little zapote explained—it won't be hard to find me. Unsure and confused, the incarcerated man nevertheless agreed. Just as quickly as the visitor had appeared, he departed, leaving the doors open behind him. The prisoner seized the chance to escape. A few days later he made his way to Lagunilla del Rico. When he arrived, he described the man of the little zapote to the people he encountered. They told him: there is only one by that name, and he is in the shrine at the town church. No, the visitor protested: the man was flesh and blood before me; there must be someone of this height and build who lives here. We don't know what to say; why don't you just go to the church and see for yourself? There he found an image of Christ—El Señor del Zapotito—who looked just like the man who had visited the jail. The freed man realized he was a supplicant and fell to his knees in thanks for the mercy he had received.

When Elena began this story, her elder daughter, then a girl of twelve, and some of their neighbors lent only half an ear to the tale. They carried on discussing some new clothes Elena had gotten the girl for her graduation from primary school. But as Elena continued the audience listened with increasing attention—and also skepticism, interjecting: that's not really true, is it? Man, you don't really believe that, do you?

When Elena finished the story, she was practical in her response to the queries: it might not be true, but I choose to believe it. I don't want to make anyone mad and get myself in trouble. If that Señor is powerful enough to get someone out of jail, who knows what else he can do?

Picking up this thread of the agency of divine figures, Elena and her neighbors then compared notes about the incarnations of Jesus and Mary that populate the Bajío, the region of central Mexico where Uriangato is located. As Elena's daughter and I listened, they parsed which divine figure is kind and forgiving; who is the most effective at advocating before God that your prayers be answered; and, above all, what are the consequences if you do not complete your promises to them. El Señor del Zapotito, Elena informed us, is an especially effective and vengeful divine actor. She personally knew people maliciously haunted by El Señor when they did not complete their commitments to him—in one case, he set a kitchen on fire after answering a woman's prayer for a new stove when she gave him no public thanks or tribute in return.

Elena's story and the subsequent discussion are part of what is called the Catholic cult of the saints: the cultivation of relationships of devotion and mutual obligation with divine figures. The cult of the saints was originally a practice of European Christians. It became associated with Catholicism after the Protestant Reformation (Brown 1981). Brought to the Americas by Spanish missionaries as a tool of conversion and conquest, the Mexican cult of the saints is overwhelmingly focused on Mary Immaculate, depicted as a young woman with the moon at her feet. This image highlights Mary's Immaculate Conception (God's act of preserving Mary from the taint of original sin at the moment of her conception), her virgin fertility, and her giving birth to Christ (Napolitano 2016; Taylor 1987). The most prominent of these Marys is La Virgen de Guadalupe, but there are many others. Some are recognized across wide swaths of the country, such as La Virgen de San Juan de los Lagos, a favorite among migrants (Durand and Massey 1995; Hagan 2008), while recognition of others is more spatially delimited, such as La Virgen de La Soledad.

Incarnations of the Virgin Mary are only one grouping in a community of divine actors who make up the cult of the saints. The divine actor in Elena's story, El Señor de Zapotito, is one of numerous images of Christ found across Mexico. Such images usually take the form of doll-like statues a few feet high, as is also the case with a range of figures from the Catholic pantheon, from saints like Mary to other divine entities such as the Archangel Michael.[2] In Catholic doctrine saints, angels, and Jesus are different types of beings: saints were once humans, angels were not, and Jesus is an incarnation of God. Contrary to doctrine, however, most Uriangatenses treat these beings in similar ways: people pray to them all; view them all as intercessors before God; and tell stories of their images taking human form and interacting with people.

The cult of the saints is relevant to people's interpellation into Mexicanidad because it helps make Mexico legible as a nation-state—as a place with specific life trajectories, histories, and futures into which people can be hailed. It also creates fissures in imaginaries of national belonging, inside of which people can resist and revise who they are called to be by state institutions (cf. Napolitano 2016: chapter 5). In Mexico—as in other countries in Latin America and Europe where the cult of the saints is robust (e.g., Christian 1989; Wirtz 2007)—every level of secular government also has a divine patron (Lattanzi Shutika 2011; Stack 2012b). The most well known of these is La Virgen de Guadalupe, patron of Mexico. Her image is found all over the country and in Mexican migrant communities abroad (Gálvez 2009; Napolitano 2016; Peña 2011). But nearly every rancho and municipality has its patron. Divine patrons represent a place before God—acting like lawyers on behalf of their people; indeed Guadalupe is often called *nuestra abogada* (our lawyer). But they also represent that location symbolically within the imaginary of greater Mexico, becoming emblematic of its historical and political economic life (Lattanzi Shutika 2011; Napolitano 2016; Stack 2012b; Taylor 1987).

For instance, El Señor de Zapotito, patron of Lagunilla del Rico, indexes the agricultural labor that characterizes the rancho, which once involved producing zapote. The initial arrival of a divine patron is typically regarded as the baptismal moment when a place becomes a location "on the map," with a government, town square, marketplace, and so forth (Stack 2012b). Divine patrons also emblematize the people of that place, becoming iconic of it (cf. Irvine and Gal 2000). When Elena said El Señor de Zapotito is an especially effective and vengeful intercessor, she was also saying something about people from Lagunilla del Rico, including herself. She often described her rancho as producing a people who are unpretentious, kind, and helpful—but who also will not tolerate any disrespect. In this way she resisted the common framing of rural people as uncivil, backward, and docile (cf. Farr 2006; see also chapter 2).

As this suggests, relationships with divine patrons allow people to express attachments to the places those patrons represent, calling them to see themselves as part of that place. They can also literally summon people to those places, an activity poignantly illustrated in contexts of migration. Although Mexican migrants in the United States have developed an infrastructure for saintly veneration in the North, many still believe the most genuine pilgrimages are to particular shrines in Mexico, and they will return to them to fulfill their devotions (cf. Durand and Massey 1995; Gálvez 2009; Lattanzi Shutika 2011; Peña 2011). As this suggests, the links between divine patrons and specific towns are not disassociated from the production of national identity or Catholicism. Every Señor or Virgen is an incarnation of Christ or Mary, so they are related not only to their principal beings in heaven but also to their signal national icons, such as Guadalupe. As Benedict Anderson (1991: 56–57) illuminates in his classical work on nation building, pilgrimage—whether the movement of religious devotees or of bureaucrats taking censuses—is a central practice that connects places that would otherwise be unrelated, thus making imagined communities possible (see also Lomnitz 2001c).

Consequently, religious nationalism not only helps distinguish Mexico as a nation-state distinct from, say, the United States. It also helps make Mexico into an integrated whole into which actors can be interpellated. Therefore pilgrimage to sacred sites, along with other religious practices, is not supplanted by bureaucratic practices, as Anderson theorized: they work in tandem to render the nation (cf. Daswani 2010; Eisenlohr 2006; Woolard 2004). In cultivating relationships with local patrons, people (re)generate associations among their town, their nation, and their faith, affirming their commitments to all three. This is elegantly exemplified in Uriangato, where the annual celebration of the municipality's founding on September 16 coincides not only with the celebration of its divine patron (San Miguel, the Archangel) but also with Mexico's independence day.

At the same time, the relationships people cultivate with divine figures belie the mythology of uniform national belonging. The cult of the saints engenders a popular religiosity that pushes against the boundaries of proper practice as set by either Mexican state institutions or the Catholic church (Gálvez 2009; Ingham 1986; Napolitano 2016). In Mexico there are thriving cults of devotion to figures outside the official pantheon of saints such as Mexican revolutionary Pancho Villa, who are very unlikely ever to be recognized as saints by the church (Martín 2013). Moreover, dedication to town patrons is part of a history of regionalism in Mexico, in which local governments have often come into conflict with the federal government over questions of both policy and national identity (Farr 2006; Fitzgerald 2009; Stack 2012b: chapter 7). In part because of the rebellious possibilities of Mexican Catholicism, state-endorsed projects of religious nationalism have often had a contentious relationship with people's actual religious observance. As discussed in chapter 1, religious practices like the cult of the saints were used by elites after the 1910 Revolution as part of the project of creating a mestizo nation that co-opted potential opposition to the institutions of the Mexican state (Lomnitz 2008; Napolitano 2016). The history of religious co-optation is especially significant for municipalities in the Bajío, including Uriangato, because this region is associated with strong religiosity (cf. Lattanzi Shutika 2011; Stack 2012b).

The Bajío—not unlike the US Midwest—is posited in state-endorsed imaginaries of national belonging as the heartland of the country: populated by a straight-shooting and humble people of faith who are largely mestizo and thus represent "real Mexico" (Farr 2006). But, as with other features of Mexicanidad in imaginaries of moral mobility, the religiosity of the Bajío is also central to the production of the double-binds that generate diaspora at home. This religiosity is constructed at once as a symbol of that which is authentically Mexican and also as a prime barrier to the country's economic progress and full sovereignty. Therefore, in building relationships with divine figures, Uriangatenses encounter the central tensions of Mexican nation-state building: between secularism and religiosity, progress and tradition, sovereignty and transcendence (Napolitano 2016: 129; Peña 2011).

Consider the careful way Elena and her neighbors managed talk about divine intercessors. In both questioning and affirming the ontological status of these figures—saying they may not be real, but why take any chances?—they walked the fine line between the enduring tensions of nation-state building in Mexico. They showed themselves to be religious and therefore moral and Mexican but not so religious that they are ignorant and backward. Likewise, Elena usually couched her touting of the people of Lagunilla del Rico within discussions of the cosmopolitanism and class mobility that she and her husband had achieved by moving to urban Uriangato: they were from "real Mexico" but not so rural they were going to impede progress. Similarly, urbanites more generally see the practices that signal piety, like regular attendance at mass, as social indexes of rural backwardness and old-fashionedness (cf. Koven 2013a, 2013b). When I first moved to Uriangato, I attended weekly mass, thinking this was a surefire way to broadcast that I was not a gringa gone wild (see chapter 2). But I dialed back my frequency of attendance to roughly once every six weeks after my host family began teasing me for acting like *una viejita* (a little old lady). For most of my young and middle-aged urbanite friends, the ideal is to have just enough religion seem morally right, but not so much religion that you seem unsophisticated.

In their religiosity, then, working-class Uriangatenses manage the tensions of Mexicanidad by reproducing classically modernist contrasts (between rural and urban, backwardness and cosmopolitanism, and so forth), which are characteristic of imaginaries of moral mobility (see chapters 1 and 3). In so doing, they express the diaspora at home that such framings engender for working-class people, while at the same time differentiating them from other marginalized groups in Mexico (like people from the ranchos). But working-class Uriangatenses use religiosity to do more than elegize that diaspora. They seek to transform it, by enabling themselves to claim the resources and ethico-moral recognition they need to be morally mobile. These processes are most evident in the act of making a *promesa*.

A *promesa* is a type of instrumental prayer in which supplicants ask a divine figure to intercede on their behalf to petition God that the supplicant be granted aid (Christian 1989; Pitt-Rivers 2011; Wirtz 2007). In making a *promesa*, the supplicant commits to fulfilling a public display of gratitude if the prayer is granted. Such displays usually involve a pilgrimage, during which the supplicant gives thanks not only by worshipping at the shrine of the divine figure but also by performing an act of mortification, such as walking barefoot, and/or by presenting a gift, as illustrated in the opening vignette (cf. Brown 1981; Christian 1989; Hagan 2008; Wirtz 2007). Typically, *promesas* are rendered at times of crisis, when people's ethico-moral status is under threat, so they illuminate the kinds of events that can trigger ethico-moral work, such as the impending migration of your child (see chapter 4).

Not One Single Vice: The Interactional Effects of *Promesas*

Making appeal to divine figures (not unlike the citation of news stories discussed in chapter 2) is a way migrants and their loved ones associate their needs, desires, longing, and struggles with forms of authority. By forging such authorizing associations, they legitimate their experience and assert their ethico-moral personhood—their worthiness for protection and for access to the resources that facilitate socioeconomic and geopolitical mobility. Imbricating saintly relationships with people's migration and other forms of suffering amplifies and extends the legitimating effects of such authorizing. This produces a multilayered indexicality that allows people to reaffirm but also potentially rework their connections across several social domains: the individual and familial, the municipal and national, the transnational, and the divine (cf. Dick and Arnold 2017a). I illustrate this point below through attention to the interactional aspects of *promesas*—how they position self and other with respect to a topic. *Promesas* are complex, multistage events, which involve private moments of prayer; the semiotically dense rites of pilgrimage and ceremonies of offering; and sometimes long lapses of time from the initial prayer to the completion of the promised public display of gratitude. It is challenging to provide a close analysis of the interactional effects of all stages of promesas within the constraints of a single chapter. However, it is not only the *promesas* themselves that can illuminate how Uriangatenses use relationships with the divine to transform their interpellation into Mexicanidad. Talk about *promesas* is also revealing of these processes.

Such *promesa* talk, like that I observed between Elena and her neighbors that Friday during Lent, is common in Uriangato. The production and circulation of *promesa* talk has been noted in other contexts where the cult of the saints is practiced (e.g., Christian 1989). But little attention has been paid to its effects: how it does not simply reflect the social world but helps make it. These effects offer a productive perspective on the ways *promesas* can transform interpellation into Mexicanidad. As intimated above, *promesa* talk often focuses on the consequences suffered by people who did not fulfill *promesas*, from the more gentle humiliations of guilt to the terrors of vengeful hauntings. Such talk plays a central role in determining the efficacy of a *promesa* and the relative power of divine beings (cf. Wirtz 2007). Therefore *promesa* talk helps establish the authorizing powers of the cult of the saints, through this simultaneously creating links between God and nation and rendering "Mexico" as an entity that can interpellate. At the same time, *promesa* talk works upon people's relationships with each other, as people use such talk to shape the ethico-moral character of their interlocutors (cf. Shoaps 2007).

In the interaction between Elena and her neighbors that day during Lent we see an example of overt discussion of the divine. But *promesa* talk can also be elliptical. Consider the following excerpt from my recorded encounter with Magdalena, Belén, and their children. This excerpt highlights the importance of *promesas* as people confront the dangers of migration. Magdalena and her seventeen-year-old son Rigoberto answer a question I put to them about what it takes for a person to go north and not become immoral.

Not a Single Vice: Magdalena and Rigoberto

1	H	Y, es de . . . ¿qué?— ¿Qué necesita uno para . . . para seguir adelante allá? ¿Si se va allá? Porque hay gente que se mete en muchos vicios, ¿verdad?, cuando se van allá.	And, um . . . what?— What does one need in order . . . in order to get ahead there? If one goes there? Because there are people who get involved with a lot of vices when they go there, right?
2	R	[Ey, pues, eso sí {es verdad}.]	[Yeah, well, that {is true} yes.]
3	M	[¡Ay no—mi muchacho no! Yo primero le llevo a la iglesia.]	[Oh, no—not my boy! I'll first take him to the church.]
4	R	[Allá no más se encierra.]	[There you just stay inside.]
5	M	[Yo primero le llevo a la iglesia pa'que me lo jure.]	[I'll first take him to church so that he swears it to me.]
6	R	[Pos, es igual que aquí: hallar trabajo, ir al trabajo, y a dormir—echar un baño, y ¡a dormir!]	[Well, it's the same as here: find a job, go to the job, and go to sleep]—take a bath and go to bed!
7	H	{to R} Ey.	{to R} Yeah.
8	M	Ya se lo dije, "Te voy a llevar al Templo que me lo jures que {no vayas a coger} ni un vicio—ni tomar, ni ningún vicio de nada."	I already told him, "I will take you to the Temple so you swear to me that {you will pick up} not one single vice—not even drinking, not any vices at all."

The *promesa* talk in this excerpt is entailed in lines 3, 5, and 8, where Magdalena repeats that she will take Rigoberto to church before he migrates. In English the phrase "take to church" is sometimes used metaphorically to say that you will engage in an act of revelatory truth-telling. In this exchange Magdalena is endeavoring to set Rigoberto straight, as when taking someone to church in the metaphorical sense. But she also means that she is actually going to take Rigoberto to church, and not just any church: *el Templo* (line 8). Uriangatenses use "el Templo" to refer to the municipality's main church, El Templo de

San Miguel, which houses the image of Uriangato's patron saint, the Archangel Michael, along with several images of Mary Immaculate. While any church is a sacred space, *templos* are places where divine entities are understood to dwell and therefore can be encountered. In saying she will take Rigoberto to this church to swear he will not fall into vice, Magdalena is implying that she is going to require him to make a *promesa* in front of Michael and Mary that he will not adopt one single vice. Otherwise she would not need to mention the Temple at all; she could just say that she will make him promise her to stay vice-free. By implying that she will ensure her child's morality by requiring him to make a *promesa*, she is also saying that—should he migrate—she will enlist Mary and Michael as proxy guardians. They will watch over Rigoberto when his mother cannot, helping him stay properly Mexican as he ventures into the moral morass of the North.

In this exchange we see a multilayered process of interpellation in which Magdalena positions herself, Rigoberto, and me within a framework of relations overseen by a divine that is imbricated with extant ideas about proper Mexican personhood. Consider the multifunctionality of Magdalena and Rigoberto's statements. First, they are responses to a question I posed. In answering, they replicate broader patterns of male and female migration discourse (discussed in chapter 4). Rigoberto utters responses that I heard from many men on the topic of how to stay moral in the United States: you just go to work and go home to bed, on repeat each day. As in Don Arturo's discourse (see chapter 4), Rigoberto asserts himself as able to speak knowledgeably by using a voice of generalizing authority, which both positions him as an expert on the subject and keeps me at arm's length about his personal experience. Magdalena redirects this generalizing talk to talk of her family in line 3, when she says: Oh, no—not my boy (he will not fall into vice)! Linking general talk to the specific experience of migration, as Magdalena does here, is a familiar strategy used by women to establish the "rightness" of themselves and their family members and, through that, to assert their authority (see chapter 4). To be sure, line 3 is one of many statements Magdalena makes asserting her son's good character.

Therefore Rigoberto's and Magdalena's responses to my questions interpellate them as gendered subjects who uphold the proper roles of mother and son according to the norms of proper Mexicanidad in Uriangato, a pattern similar to that documented in my conversation with Don Arturo and Doña Cecilia. In so doing, they are not just responding to a query about migration; they are speaking about who they are and what their relationship is—and should continue to be. As such, the purpose and meaning of what they are saying is multiply indexical.[3] Magdalena's statements are both assertions to me that "my son is a good boy; he is not like those migrants who fall into vice" and commands to her son: "Boy, you'd better be good!" This point is especially evident in the reported speech in line 8, where Magdalena says *ya se lo dije* (I already told it to him). People often use the phrase *ya decirse* to assert something that is firm and clear. Here Magdalena augments this sense of fixity by adding the direct object pronoun "lo" (it), which changes the indirect object pronoun "le" (him) to "se." Thus, she represents the impending *promesa* as a settled commitment between Rigoberto and her: you are not going anywhere until I take you to church and you swear before our intercessors that you will be good.

Similarly, in explaining to me how to migrate and avoid vice, Rigoberto is both performing himself as an authority to me and saying to Magdalena: I know how to avoid vice, Mom. This point was especially important for him to convey because Belén's daughter, who had just recently become Rigoberto's fiancé, was also present and listening intently as we spoke. By interweaving these elements of the interaction—which could have happened regardless of *promesa* talk—with reference to the divine, Magdalena shifts the overall dynamic of the conversation. In the rest of the recording, Magdalena is deferential to Rigoberto when they both want to talk, allowing him to assume the interactional mantle of male adulthood. Yet in this exchange Magdalena is insistent, speaking over Rigoberto (lines 3 and 5) until she commands the interaction (line 8).

Magdalena's uncharacteristic insistence with Rigoberto in this exchange suggests the significance of this subject for her, an effect amplified by the sonic quality of her utterances. In each statement, she speaks with greater forcefulness, depth of tone, and volume. The weight of this subject is most dramatically underscored by Magdalena's pointing to the role of the divine in the management of her son's migration, saying in effect: Rigoberto's ethico-moral standing as a son is so important it mandates divine attention. Indeed the vices of migration were a central topic for us that day. Immediately before this exchange Magdalena recounted the shock she experienced when her mother migrated to the United States and found that Magdalena's aunt labeled the food and would not share it with her mother: *¡Ni la pinche leche!* (Not even the damned milk!). Magdalena told me this several times, each time more aghast. Talk of the *desobligación* of family in the North (see chapter 3) is particularly loaded for Magdalena and Rigoberto. When Rigoberto was a toddler, Magdalena's husband left her after migrating to the United States, after which she raised Rigoberto without financial support from her husband. Thus, for Magdalena a common concern that migration will corrupt their children is made yet more pressing by her fear that her son will repeat his father's abandonment.

In imbricating their interpellation as a proper Mexican mother and son with their religiosity, Magdalena takes up the terms of state-endorsed moral mobility (see chapter 1), but she also resists and revises them. Relationships with divine actors create the sense of a permeable border between the here-and-now of human life and the divine realm of heaven. As portals into a heavenly realm that is not only alternate to the here-and-now but morally superior to any earthly institution, relationships with divine figures potentially allow Uriangatenses to transform their diaspora at home. Enlisting the aid of divine figures helps make the practice of migration ethico-morally sound. So it pushes against visions of Mexicanidad that posit migration as a corrupting force on Mexicanidad: a common feature of state-endorsed imaginaries of moral mobility. There is a widespread practice of using *promesas* to receive the protection needed to manage the existential and ethico-moral dangers of migration to the United States and the vulnerabilities they have as migrants (Durand and Massey 1995: 67–84; Hagan 2008: 21, 53–55, 133–153). Many such *promesas* involve parents enlisting divine figures as proxy mothers and fathers who will manage their children's morality and safety when the parents are separated from them, something that Magdalena proposes to do in soliciting Rigoberto to make his *promesa* to Mary and Michael.

In this context where being moral is figured as the essence of Mexicanidad, in contrast to the forms of life in the United States, calling on the saints to help oversee migration means also interpellating the divine, rendering saintly guardians as both uniquely Mexican and universal: able to travel freely across national borders, as migrants cannot. Therefore *promesas* generate a radiating "moral here" that extends proper Mexicanness as far as relationships to divine figures will stretch (cf. Sidorkina 2015). That is, it makes moral mobility both transportable—a process that can also be realized in the United States—and transcendent: something that points to a heavenly beyond that supersedes the nation-state.

Rather than merely replicating extant links between Mexicanidad and moral mobility, relationships with divine figures also offer an alternative imaginary of the nation. For many working-class Uriangatenses, the *promesa* represents the most elevated form of communitarianism understood as a consequential ethics wherein collectivities are envisioned as a series of relationships of mutual obligation: people effectively and publicly fulfill their obligations or penalties are paid (see chapter 2). Indeed, as a form of promise, *promesas* highlight the relational and consequentialist aspects of ethico-moral practice—the idea that proper personhood is formulated with attention to the effects of actions on others, regardless of intentions (cf. Garcia 2014). As William Christian (1989: chapter 3) shows in his work on popular religiosity in Spain, Catholic laypeople use *promesas* in ways that reflect their earthly relationships and forms of material exchange. This pattern is evident in how Uriangatenses relate *promesas* to their relationships with their government. However skeptical Uriangatenses are about the ontological status of divine figures, they nevertheless understand *promesas* as non-negotiable covenants. If a prayer is granted you must fulfill the promise to give thanks or face the consequences (cf. Christian 1989; Wirtz 2007). The *promesa* therefore offers a model of resource management that serves as a foil for the ways Mexican state institutions interact with working-class people. In this model, service to others and the respectful observation of hierarchies lead to the fulfillment of obligations—as such, *promesas* highlight what their relationships with state institutions in Mexico lack (see chapter 3).

Consequently, making *promesas*—and saintly relations more generally—is an ethico-moral practice that accomplishes several effects. It allows people to lay claim to proper Mexicanidad and thus national belonging, wherever they or their family reside in geopolitical space. In so doing, Uriangatenses not only respond to state-endorsed interpellation into moral mobility but harken back to and reenvision Mexico as a place where they can make appeal for protection and resource and actually receive it. In this case we see a woman extend her maternal authority to ground her son in his proper Mexicanidad, even as he ventures to the North. There he hopes to earn income both to establish himself as a man and to support his mother, in his father's stead. Thus relationships with divine figures offer an escape route from diaspora at home that allows working-class Uriangatenses to feel at home anywhere and provides what they need to be morally mobile.

As the above shows, the transformative potential of saintly relationships is made evident in the interactional analysis of talk about the practices through which people cultivate those relationships. Such analysis reveals the multiple messaging of this talk—a process that makes possible the forms of critical commentary on existing dynamics—not only between family members but with the nation and God as well (cf. Mittermaier 2011). In addition to *promesas*, working-class Uriangatenses cultivate relationships with the saints by emulating them. This practice is especially apparent in acts of voicing the *mujer sufrida*—a particularly potent form of interpellative response and transformative appeal for working-class women. The act of voicing the *mujer sufrida* unfolds in a complex dynamic with the ideals of Mexican womanhood, which make it difficult for women to be moral and mobile at the same time. Such voicing is a way women resist this double-bind, as I show below in my analysis of Magdalena's and Belén's speech.

Suffering Mexicanidad: Marianism, Mobility, and Marginalization

In both working-class Uriangatense and state-endorsed imaginaries, proper Mexican womanhood is bound up in emulating the virtuous character of the Virgin Mary. The cultivation of Marian womanhood is a widespread gender ideal in Mexico, referred to as Marianismo (Gutmann 2007; Hirsch 2003; Wright 2006). It urges women to model themselves after the Virgin Mary by sacrificing personal desire to the needs of others; nobly enduring suffering; and remaining *recogida* (tucked away) (see chapter 2). The persistence of Marianismo as a modality of Mexican womanhood exists in concert with the dramatic shifts in the political economic position of women in Uriangato, which have afforded them greater income and more say in the unfolding of their lives (cf. Hirsch 2003). These shifts have coincided with changing ideals of family life, which have moved toward family nucleation and egalitarian models of marriage, discussed elsewhere in the book.

In this shifting sociohistorical, demographic, and political economic context, preexisting concepts of virtuous womanhood grate against newly emergent regimes of family and migration that challenge respectable womanhood because they potentially increase the physical and socioeconomic mobility of women. Moreover, many working-class women continue to embrace the values they associate with traditional models of family life and womanhood as they face the possibility of their own increased mobility (Dick 2010b). Because Marianism is a signal of feature Mexicanidad, and because "liberated womanhood" is figured as characteristic of gringas, who are envisioned in the most unflattering terms in imaginaries of moral mobility (Dick 2017), they are wary of abandoning Marian womanhood altogether (cf. Hirsch 2003; Lester 2005).

Marianismo is an intimate form of saintly relation that shapes how women present themselves, interact with others, and move through social and geopolitical space (cf. Lester 2005). It positions women's independent movements away from a *recogida*, cloistered here-and-now—say to a future in the United States—as anathema to proper womanhood (see chapter 2). Yet in the face of national imperatives to progress and the routine possibility of migration, women are also asked to be mobile so they do not inhibit the progress of the nation. The contradictory pull between cloistering and mobility potentially places all Mexican women in a state of ethico-moral hazard in which they can be blamed for their suffering. Melissa Wright (2006: chapter 4) has explored this point in her work on the mass killings of women in Ciudad Juárez. She shows that concepts of proper womanhood enable Mexican authorities to blame women for their own murders and thus erase these murders as an issue of public concern.

The tension between cloistering and mobility is especially acute—and therefore highlighted—in the lives of *mujeres abandonadas* (abandoned women) like Magdalena and Belén. It is usually assumed that a husband's abandonment of his wife is the result of the woman's failure to achieve Marian womanhood (by sleeping around; putting herself before others; and so forth). Consequently, abandoned women often lose access to family networks and their associated resources, for their relations do not want to become associated with the woman's moral taint. Thus the immorality of women's abandonment is a self-fulfilling prophecy: social isolation requires the abandoned woman to engage in blatant expressions of need and suffering, which violate the Marian imperatives of silent, dignified suffering and therefore can serve as verification of immorality.

The lives of abandoned women bring into sharp relief the double-binds of moral mobility that produce diaspora at home for working-class women more generally. These are played out in people's relationships not only with neighbors, friends, and family, but with Mexican state institutions as well. Marianismo shapes women's access to state resources, especially its welfare system, as evidenced in Mexico's poverty alleviation programs. Such programs are generally available only to mothers, rendering this role the key that unlocks the benefits of citizenship for women of limited means (González de la Rocha 1994, 2001; Molyneux 2006). Moreover, they offer few forms of assistance that would enable the socioeconomic mobility of the women themselves, such as job training (Molyneux 2006). Rather, any benefit derived by mothers from such programs is in true Marian fashion a by-product of the sublimation of their mobility in service to their children. At the same time, poverty alleviation programs require mothers to engage in practices that perform their suffering and position them as vulnerable figures who need guidance from the state, rendered as the father-patriarch. Take Mexico's flagship antipoverty program PROGRESA-Oportunidades. As discussed in chapter 1 PROGRESA-Oportunidades makes the receipt of benefits contingent on women's visits to health clinics, where—in addition to having their health monitored—they are required to participate in workshops that teach them proper nutrition and sanitation (Molyneux 2006: 428–429). This regulation presumes and performs the putative ignorance of participants. Therefore Marianismo is central to the interpellative processes through which women can be recognized as properly Mexican and, in turn, lay claim to citizen resources—processes that marginalize women even as they place them in relationship with the state (see chapter 2) (cf. Carr 2011; Wacquant 2009).

Yet enactments of Marian womanhood are also a skill that women harness to protest their ethico-moral and political marginalization. This practice is well documented in the feminist literature on the role of women in political protest in Mexico and other parts of Latin America (e.g., Bejarano 2002; Bouvard 1994; Friedman 1998; Stephen 1995; Wright 2006: chapter 7). As this work shows, women employ Marian womanhood to spotlight and potentially transform their subordination and victimization by state actors. This point was hauntingly exemplified in the protests of the Madres de la Plaza de Mayo in Argentina (mothers of people who were disappeared during the country's dirty war). These women enacted their Marian suffering by wearing mourning dress and engaging in genres of lament, demanding that the government tell them what happened to their children (Bouvard 1994). This protest received international attention and has been replicated in other countries (Stephen 1995), including in Mexico by the mothers of the victims of the mass murders in Ciudad Juárez (Bejarano 2002; Wright 2006).

Within this history of protest, scholars have emphasized the pivotal role that discursive enactments of suffering can play in igniting political transformation, as we can see in work on the practice of oral testimony. A testimony is an elegizing account aimed at enabling the public witnessing of suffering toward the end of terminating that suffering (Stephen 2013; Warren 2001). The tradition of oral testimony is robust throughout Latin America as a form of political protest (Warren 2001). In Mexico it has been used to revise dominant national imaginaries so that they are more inclusive of marginalized groups, a point illustrated in work on the country's Indigenous movements (Stephen 2013).

I examine a related but distinct form of discursive witnessing: voicing the *mujer sufrida*. The linguistic anthropological concept of "voice" does not necessarily refer to the patterned sounds that represent a particular person's way of speaking (or singing), though it can (e.g., Harkness 2014). Rather, drawing on Bakhtin (1996: 259-422), this concept refers to the array of semiotic features associated with social personae: cultural images of persons, like the suffering woman (Agha 2007a: 165, 177, 181–182; Harkness 2014; Paz 2016; Shankar 2008; Wirtz 2013, 2014). Voicing the *mujer sufrida* involves creating portraits of suffering that position the speaker as an innocent victim of circumstances beyond her control. As in the case of testimonies, people engage in such voicing to highlight wrongdoing, recuperate ethico-moral standing, and assert their right to resources and other forms of support. But, unlike testimonies, voicing the *mujer sufrida* is not necessarily part of a formal, organized protest—it is a quotidian form of witnessing in which even women who are not especially politically active routinely participate. Indeed, it is a crucial tool for working-class women as they navigate the double-binds of diaspora at home. Thus, it is not unreasonable to suggest, as I do in the conclusion, that such voicing, along with other forms of everyday appeal, helps make testimony plausible and legible as a form of political protest.

The following interactional analysis reveals that the dynamic between speaker and hearer is central to the efficacy of political witnessing as a form of appeal that can transform sociopolitical life. Such dynamics are underexamined in the broader literature on Marianism and political protest. Yet for any enactment of suffering to be transformative it must work successfully upon the listener. Therefore it is imperative to consider not only the role of the person who enacts her suffering but the role of the listener, who variably takes up what is offered for witnessing. Not all who hear such enactments are convinced. Sometimes hearers reject, ignore, or cannot process the suffering enacted (as we see in the discussion of my responses to Magdalena and Belén below). These dynamics speak meaningfully to the politics of whose suffering is and is not legible (cf. Carr 2011; Das 2006; Garcia 2010).

I Left the Clothes White, White!: The Interactional Accomplishment of the Suffering Woman

I first met Magdalena while conducting survey interviews in La Libertad (see chapter 2). I found her life intriguing. In this neighborhood where

85 percent of households have family in the United States, she claimed hers had none. I was curious to document the migration discourse of a woman who, though surrounded by migration, purportedly did not have access to it. When I asked if I could return at a later date to talk with her more informally, she agreed. Other people that I met during the survey became part of a weekly rotation of socializing. But months intervened before I returned to Magdalena's house. Shortly before leaving Uriangato, I sheepishly returned, asking if she remembered me. She did. We made a plan for me to return the next day. I came back with a bag of mini-mangos deliciously in season and a bottle of soda, expecting to have Magdalena to myself. But I found her gathered in the small dimly lit front room with Belén, Rigoberto, and Belén's sixteen-year-old daughter, Sofía, who was recently engaged to Rigoberto. It seemed Magdalena planned our interaction as a witnessing event, or at least her friends and family wanted to partake in our conversation. In the typical aspirant style of homes in La Libertad, the front door faced steps heading to a second floor that did not yet exist, where Belén sat with Sofía. To my right was a long table where Magdalena took a seat and invited me to join her and set up my recorder. In front of us was the kitchen, separated from the dining area by a flowery curtain, behind which a friend of Rigoberto's was fixing Magdalena's stove, a task in which he remained singularly focused, never leaving the kitchen or joining our conversation. Sofía promptly washed the mangos and put them out for us to share with glasses of soda. After some pleasantries and an affirmation of consent, we began.

For roughly the first twenty minutes of the hour-long recording, Rigoberto dominated. Contrary to Magdalena's prior claim that no one in her family was a migrant, he told me that both he and his grandmother had been the United States and that his father currently resided there. Disparities between accounts given in my survey and ethnographic interviews were familiar to me. In survey interviews people would deny migration experience for a variety of reasons. Family members were no longer migrants or were estranged from the interviewee, so it did not seem relevant to them; or they were concerned with protecting people living in the United States; or they did not want to reveal their access to migrant remittances; and so forth (see Dick 2006b). So I was not surprised to discover the disparity, but I wanted to know more about migration in this family. Throughout this part of the conversation—with the exception of the excerpt about "not a single vice" discussed above, Magdalena is deferential to Rigoberto, allowing him to be the focus of our interaction. Belén takes Magdalena's lead, only occasionally interjecting. Sofía is silent throughout the entire recording, except for the occasional giggle. About twenty minutes in, however, a dramatic interactional shift happens as Magdalena and Belén take over the conversation.

At this point Magdalena launches into her voicing of the *mujer sufrida* (transcribed below). Immediately sensing the shift to a markedly female form of interaction, Rigoberto not only stops talking but excuses himself to the kitchen to help his friend with the stove.

Magdalena's Suffering at Work

1	M	Antes iba hasta el borde de la orilla {por mi trabajo}. No más que ahora ya no. Queda muy lejos.	I used to go all the way to the edge of town {for work}. But not anymore. It's too far.
2	H	**Aha . . .**	**Aha . . .**
3	M	Pero esa señora era pero difícil con {inaudible} la ropa!	But that woman was nothing but difficult {inaudible} her clothes!
4	B	*Ohhhhh . . .*	*Ohhhhh . . .*
5	M	En tres días tenía que lavar y con un puro [jabón de teja].	In three days I had to wash {all her clothes} and with just one [bar of soap].
6	H	**[¡Ha!]**	**[Ha!]**
7	M	{Me dijo} que ningún jabón más le agarraba. Y con eso tenía que acabar y dejar [la ropa blanca].	{She told me} I couldn't use any other kind of detergent. And I had to finish with that {one bar} and leave [the clothes white].
8	B	*[Ay, {inaudible} dos días.]*	*[Ay, {inaudible} two days.]*
9	M	¡Oh, bien blanca la dejaba!	Oh, I would leave the clothes really white!
10	B	*Oh, no.*	*Oh, no.*
11	H	**Ay, no.**	**Ay, no.**
12	M	Y planchaditas—¡bien planchaditas!	And ironed: well-ironed!
13	H	**Sí. ¿Y todo el día así? {I bend over}**	**Yes. And the entire day like this? {I bend over}**
14	B	*¡Lave, lave!*	*Washing and washing!*

15	M	Y puro lavadero {para hacer el lavado}, en la lavadora: no—pero, sí, tenía lavadora.	And only in the sink {was I allowed to do the wash}, not in the washing machine: no—but she did have a washing machine.
16	B	*Hm.*	*Hm.*
17	M	Pero todo quería a mano.	But she wanted it all done by hand.
18	B	*Hm.*	*Hm.*
19	M	Mantel—	Tablecloth—
20	H	**¿¡Estaba [loca!?]**	**Was she [crazy!?]**
21	M	[¡Manteles!] ¡Manteles de {taps the table} de mesas esas pa'salón! ¡Las quería: blancas, blancas!—{las quería} que no tuvieran ni una manchita: ¡nada! Y tres tinas grandototas con pura ropa blanca.	[Tablecloths!] Tablecloths {taps the table} for those dining room tables! She wanted them: white, white!—{she wanted} them to have not one little stain: nothing! And three enormous tubs with nothing but white clothes.
22	H	**Ohhhh.**	**Ohhhh.**
23	M	Y así las dejaba y así salía la ropa blanca, como me la pedía.	And that's how I would leave them and that is how the white clothes would come out, as she requested of me.

Based on the denotational content alone, this exchange appears to be about explaining the job of a domestic worker, but this is not the primary objective of the interaction. In the minutes just before this conversation, Magdalena explained in some detail her duties in this woman's employ. In fact in line 2 I was about to change the subject because I thought we had sufficiently covered the topic. But Magdalena had other aims—to spotlight her suffering, voicing the *mujer sufrida*. Although such voicing can involve the performance of particular genres of interaction (see Dick 2010b), it can also be achieved, as we see in Magdalena's discourse, by a general accounting of hardship through a particular narrative plotline. This plotline involves recounting the events that have (through no fault of the individual's own) left a person in trying circumstances, which that person nevertheless endures (and sometimes perseveres).

This story arc is beautifully captured in Magdalena's description of her work experience, which portrays her Marian suffering. There she used to find herself buried under a mountain of white laundry, no doubt egregiously stained from meals enjoyed on *mesas esas pa'salón* (those dining room tables). Left to wash this mountain by hand in two days with one bar of soap—even though her employer owned a washing machine—Magdalena nevertheless always overcame the laundry-mountain, leaving it stain-free and "white, white!" "as she requested of me" (line 23). Magdalena thus represents her employer as irrationally demanding, even cruel: someone who created a context of suffering, for which Magdalena was not to blame but which she faced without faltering and without complaining—until now.

This exchange is the first of a series of narratives of personal hardship, all of which follow this type of plotline. After describing her experience with laundry mountain, Magdalena goes on to describe the back pain that forced her to stop working and her trip to city hall to request government assistance for the back surgery she now needs, which she was denied, and so on. The injustices and impossibilities of making life better unfurl in a seemingly endless list. Interwoven through these stories of her work life, poverty, and physical disability is an ever-more disturbing account of Magdalena's abandonment by her husband, which describes the emotional and physical abuse she suffered at the hands of this man before he left her and Rigoberto. These narratives are dense with reported conversations that transpose and enact the words of her husband, as in this brief excerpt:

Magdalena's Suffering in Marriage

1	M	Una vez, llevó una mujer en la casa, y yo lo hallé en mi casa con ella.	One time, he brought a woman home, and I found him in my house with her.
2	H	**Ugh.**	**Ugh.**
3	M	¿Hmm? {Raises her eyebrows at me}	Hmm? {Raises her eyebrows at me}
4	H	**¿¡Como . . . como es que cree que tiene licencia [pa'hacer eso!?]**	**How . . . why does he think he has the right [to do that!?]**
5	M	[Dijo, "Déjala—deja] esa muchacha, en el rincón . . . Déjela que se acueste y mañana se va."	[He said, "Leave her alone—leave] that girl in the corner . . . Let her sleep here and she'll leave tomorrow."

As in the other narratives of her abandonment, Magdalena's animating of this past conversation evocatively depicts her husband as a tyrant who violated the terms of traditional marriage. She forcefully emphasizes this point when she tells me that later that same night he kicked her out onto the street after she interrupted him and this woman having sex. This act was especially punishing not only because of his disregard for her feelings and obligation to her, but because to put a woman on the street at night is to place her virtue in distinct moral peril in full view of the neighborhood (see chapter 2). True to the discretion and deference that signal Marian womanhood, Magdalena uses her husband's words to convey her perspective. Instead of making an overt statement, such as "It is not my fault I was abandoned!" she depicts herself in a relationship with and subject to her husband, who fails her, violating the sanctity of *her* house. Note the use of "en mi casa" in line 1. This is a marked use of the pronoun *mi* (my)—normally a speaker would say "en la casa." Thus her use of the possessive pronoun here serves to highlight the intensity of her suffering. Through this she shows that it was her husband who failed to fulfill matrimonial obligations, not her.

Over the course of the recording Magdalena's troubles are laminated one on top of another, collectively producing her as a woman who has not only suffered but suffered more than enough. This self-portrait is conveyed not only through the plotlines of her narratives but also in patterns of response from the rest of us as we listened. That is, her becoming the suffering woman is an interactional accomplishment we collectively realize (cf. Briggs 2014; Urban 1996; Wilce 1998). First, it is apparent that a voicing of the *mujer sufrida* has occurred because of the shift in interaction that happens around it: not only Rigoberto excusing himself, which points to the gendered nature of this kind of interaction, but Belén's immediately becoming Magdalena's "yes woman," which prompted me also to become a supportive recipient of Magdalena's performance. Our respective responses were prompted by Magdalena's intonational pattern in line 3, where she says, "But that woman was nothing but difficult {about} her clothes!" Magdalena starts speaking with a measured pace in low volume and pitch, but by mid-sentence she rapidly increases her pace, volume, and pitch, as if the sentence were a whip she pulls back slowly and then suddenly releases. At this point Belén, struck by that verbal lashing, immediately responds "Ohhhhh!" (line 4) and Rigoberto leaves the interaction.

Belén's cry helps me discern that we have left the factual description of work life and begun an enactment of suffering in which my role, like

Belén's, is to utter statements of support. Throughout, we affirm Magdalena's portrayals with empathic sounds ("oh," "ay no," and so on) and statements such as mine in line 20: "Was she crazy!?" We did not do this during the exchange of facts that proceeded this excerpt. In this way we not only convey that we hear Magdalena and sympathize with her but help her elaborate the description of her suffering, as in lines 13 and 14. Together we produce not only the narration of Magdalena's humiliations but the intensity of her pain as she endured them. Enactments of the *mujer sufrida* thus are co-constructed across a pattern of interaction that emerges over several turns of talk, including that which proceeds and follows it.

The *Mujer Sufrida* and Appeals for Resources

But why do we engage in these enactments of suffering—what purpose do they serve interactionally? Though such enactments depict difficult personal events, among working-class Uriangatenses they are not typically a way to forge intimacy. While people in relationships of trust and confidence are of course familiar with and care about each other's struggles, blatant recountings of suffering are not central to how working-class Uriangatenses generate bonds of family and friendship. To be sure, while such recountings dominate my interaction with Magdalena and Belén, they were not at all characteristic of my interactions with people I knew well. In relationships between family or friends, the interactional cultivation of a stoic humor that mocks hardship is the key modality of intimacy (cf. Chávez 2015; Farr 2006; Mendoza-Denton 2008: chapter 6). For example, one afternoon at my friend Elena's house, her cousin Nicolás came to say good-bye. He was leaving the next day for the United States. Nicolás did not have authorization to cross the border legally and was therefore facing a dangerous journey that could easily result in his death: something Elena knew well, as her husband had been migrating without authorization for years. But instead of engaging in a tearful, sentimental farewell, Elena teased Nicolás, saying sarcastically that she would stay up every night worrying over him until he called to let her know he had arrived safely. They both laughed heartily and she refused to hug him—saying it wasn't such a big deal he was leaving. Nicolás squeezed her shoulder affectionately, giving her a brief look of warmth, and then walked out of the store, at which point Elena told me that Nicolás was her favorite cousin and she would miss him terribly.

By foregrounding and elegizing suffering, voicing the *mujer sufrida* breaks from the ideal of facing hardship with dignity and a sense of humor illustrated in the interaction between Elena and Nicolás. But rather than serving to resist these tenets of proper personhood, this practice brings into relief the individual's usual stoicism (cf. Abu-Lughod 1986). Therefore voicing the *mujer sufrida* is a form of anticipatory interpellation, in which women divert readings of their character as "immoral" and create positive alignments with the virtuous character of Mary. This dynamic occurs especially in "troubles talk" (Wilce 1998) aimed at moving listeners to be not just sympathetic but giving. When done successfully, voicing the *mujer sufrida* allows women to establish an ethicomoral personhood as being like Mary in order to convince someone that they are deserving of respect and support. Thus, this practice is not just expressive of self or identity but is also very potently a form of appeal (cf. Das 2006; Keane 2010, 2011; Napolitano 2002: 8, 184; Wilce 1998). Indeed voicing the *mujer sufrida* is related to and often embedded in quite overt requests for aid, such as *pidiendo limosnas* (asking for alms). Paradoxically, Magdalena and Belén's talk of their suffering comes to a halt three-fourths of the way into our interaction, when we are interrupted by a man who knocks on the door asking for money for medicine. This person's more evident suffering and degradation silences the women's talk of their own difficulties. After he leaves, we drop discussion of suffering all together.

The connection between suffering and resource allocation is also created in state-endorsed policies that encourage women to ask for resource based on performances of their suffering. Consider that Magdalena and Belén not only have more well-to-do family in the United States to whom they make requests for aid; they also collect *dispensas*—the Mexican equivalent of food stamps. Consequently, they are subject to routine interactions with family and municipal officials, who evaluate them to assess whether their need is legitimate—judgments that hinge on how well they enact suffering (cf. Behrman and Skoufias 2006; Dion 2009; Molyneux 2006). And, indeed, my conversation with Magdalena and Belén is rich in recountings of "request-for-aid encounters" with family and bureaucrats.

It is not unreasonable to propose that in my interaction with Magdalena and Belén there was carryover from these types of exchanges—that they were petitioning me for aid. This point is suggested by the increasing ferocity with which they trade tales of woe. Each tale is more devastating than the next, until they reveal extraordinarily intimate details of their lives to me, a relative stranger. Furthermore, recall that I met Magdalena while conducting survey interviews that in some ways resemble state needs-assessment interviews. For instance, they both gauge socioeconomic status through questions about the infrastructure of the home (does it have running water, electricity, tiled or dirt floors?). Moreover, my positioning as a person from the United States, understood as a place of deep resource, reinforces the likelihood that Magdalena and Belén are attempting to request aid.

A vision of the United States as a place of resource is invoked several times during our interaction through a contrast Magdalena and Belén repeatedly draw between the virtuous US government that helps and their *desobligada* Mexican family in the United States that does not help. Belén makes a point of situating me in this sociopolitical landscape by asking if I am from the United States. After clarifying my national origins, she proceeds to inquire why women in the United States go to bars, "just like men." She clearly thinks this activity is scandalous and is not too subtly assessing whether or not I am *that* kind of girl. It is plausible that the enactments of suffering in this exchange are efforts to figure out not only if I am moral but also if, as a moral person, I might be an obliging source of help. Upon relistening to this exchange, I came to the conclusion that Magdalena and Belén thought I was a social worker. This conclusion is supported not only by the resemblance between the survey and state needs-assessment interviews but also by the fact that I was a "trainee" the day I met Magdalena.

When I began the MMP survey, I was accompanied by a graduate student from the Universidad de Guadalajara, who taught me how to implement it and ran the first several survey interviews, including the one with Magdalena (see chapter 2). This lent a further air of institutional authority to the interaction, making me seem—perhaps—like a newly hired social worker. After listening to the recording, my research assistant Camilo, a native Spanish speaker, came to the same conclusion unprompted. Moreover, once I finished talking with the women that day, I went to visit Elena, who lived just down the street from Magdalena and Belén. When I told her I had come from interviewing these women, Elena cut me off—I know them, she said with a dismissive bite in her tone. Elena warned me against visiting them again because, as she put it, "all those women do is beg for money."

As voicing the *mujer sufrida* works as a form of appeal: it interpellates listeners: as potential sources of aid; as moral or immoral; and so forth. The interpellation of listeners can be observed in the boundaries around who is and is not welcome in the interaction (cf. Carr 2009; Dick

2017; Goffman 1974; Irvine 1996). Magdalena's shift into the narration of her suffering in the excerpt above, for example, positioned her son as an unwelcomed overhearer in a conversation in which he had—just a few moments before—been the center of attention. This reversal further genders the interaction, hailing Belén, Sofía, and me as women and Rigoberto as a man, a move amplified by his leaving the conversation to work on the repairs to his mother's gas stove. Rigoberto only returns to the front room when the beggar arrives and we stop voicing the *mujer sufrida*.

When Rigoberto departed the conversation to join the stove repair efforts, Magdalena and Belén interjected that they would not do such a dirty, elbow-grease job because it is men's work. At the same time, they highlighted Rigoberto and his friend's youth (and incomplete manhood) by chiding them that they'd better not blow us up (it was a gas stove): another example of forging intimacy through laughing at hardship. Rigoberto's departure also pulled into relief Sofía's continued (if relatively silent) presence. She may not have felt licensed to speak, but she was welcome to listen. Indeed her status as the youngest in the room, daughter to Belén, and fiancée to Rigoberto seemed to position her throughout the interaction as there to learn from her female elders—to hear their suffering, perhaps to avoid her own.

Silencing Suffering: (Not) Listening to Belén's Discourse

The role and positioning of the listener in enactments of suffering has been highlighted in work on the psychoanalytic dimensions of such events of interaction (Briggs 2014; Robben 1995, 1996). As this work suggests, the fate of enactments of suffering—whether or not they are successful moments of anticipatory interpellation that become intelligible and effective—rests within the interaction between the speaker and his or her listeners. For instance, Magdalena and Belén decide they should not give alms to the beggar at the door because he was clearly intoxicated and the "medicine" container he held looked like a bottle of cooking oil. They deduced that the man wanted money for more alcohol: a form of suffering that did not make them feel charitable. This determination unfurls in contrast to other instances of *pidiendo limosnas* that they describe during our conversation, such as a *mujer abandonada* they saw asking for alms for medicine at a pharmacy, to whom they did give money.

In comparing different performances of suffering, not only are the needs of some people situated as being more worthy than the needs of others; some people are also better at performing their suffering (and receiving aid). Therefore the interactional dimensions of expressions of suffering point to the politics of suffering because they shape the distribution of sympathies in ways that elevate the needs of some, while silencing those of others (cf. Das 2006; Robben 1995, 1996). Being attentive to the ways expressions of suffering can seduce, compel, or silence listeners—the ways they can, and cannot, make listeners complicit in the interests of the speaker—offers a window into these dynamics.

Consider an interactional pattern that emerges over the course of the recording: Belén and I are much more responsive to Magdalena's voicing of the *mujer sufrida* than Magdalena and I are to Belén's voicing of this figure. Evidence of this pattern can be found early in the conversation, as we see in the following exchange, which happens about ten minutes into the recording when Rigoberto is still present and we have not yet shifted into enactments of suffering. I have been asking my interlocutors what life is like in the United States:

Life Is Beautiful There: Belén's Failed Suffering

1	B	*[Está bonita {en los EEUU}.]*	*[It is beautiful {in the United States}.]*
2	R	*[Está mejor que acá.]*	*[It's better than here.]*
3	H	**{To R} ¿Por qué?**	**{To R} Why?**
4	B	*Que tienen las casas más amuebladas que aquí.*	*They have houses that are better furnished than here.*
5	R	*[Es que—]*	*[It's that—]*
6	M	[Aquí ves] no tiene ni pa'comer—	[You see,] here one doesn't even have food to eat—
7	B	*Aquí ves que no tiene uno ni que comer aquí, y aquí es más difícil que allá, así es que mejor {irse} allá.*	*You see, here one doesn't even have food to eat and here it's harder than there, therefore it's better {to go} there.*
8	M	No tengo ni estufa ni que hacer de comer.	I don't even have a stove for preparing food.
9	B	*Y allá ayuda mucho el gobierno y aquí no.*	*And there the government helps a lot and here, no.*
10	M	Ey.	Yeah.
11	B	*Si trabaja uno, comes.*	*If one works, you eat.*
12	H	**Sí.**	**Yes.**

13	B	*Y si no, no.*	*And if no {you don't work}, no {you don't eat}.*
14	H	**Sí.**	**Yes.**
15	B	*Eso es lo—y luce más el dinero pos de allá que el de aquí.*	*That is why—and the money from there is worth more than the money from here.*
16	M	*¡Oh sí!*	Oh, yes!
17	B	*Por eso se va todos: a aventonear, a trabajar, y a mandar dinero {aquí}—*	*That is why everyone goes there: to struggle, to work, and to send money {back here}—*
18	M	*Y ya a lo mejor se va a casar.*	And now most likely he's getting married.
19	B	*¡Se va a casar con mi hija! Por eso.*	*He's going to marry my daughter! For that {reason he'll migrate}.*
20	M	[To H] *¿Como ves?*	[To H] What do you think of that?
21	H	**[To R] ¿Sí? {M, B, and H laugh}**	**[To R] Yeah? {M, B, and H laugh}**

Belén articulates a litany of factors that construe migration as inexorable. At five different moments in the conversation she repeats this litany, each time adding an additional factor that makes life in Mexico impossible for her. This sort of migration discourse is a common strategy that working-class Uriangatense women use to maintain their Marian womanhood in the face of mobility to the immoral United States (cf. Dick 2010b). Such litanies position the desire to migrate not as a violation of Marianism (not as wanderlust) but as a manifestation of virtuous womanhood. Therefore, they convey suffering both as a causal force that shapes future events and as an ethical justification. As with *promesas*, voicing the *mujer sufrida* a radiating moral here, effectively saying: no matter where I go, I am grounded morally.

But Belén's attempt to voice the *mujer sufrida* is not as successful as Magdalena's. Although it does garner some sympathetic reaction from Magdalena and me (lines 10, 12, 14, and 16), overall Belén's litany does not spark the kind of interactional shift that Magdalena's story of laundry mountain does. For one thing, Rigoberto does not leave the room. There is also a marked difference in Magdalena's responses to Belén toward the end of the exchange. Take line 18: this statement comes on the heels of Belén's point in line 17, which is meant to summarize and complete her litany. Typically, listeners who are included in the interaction (as opposed to bystanders) follow such litany conclusions with an affirmative utterance (cf. Dick 2010b). But Magdalena interrupts Belén's conclusion and turns the focus to her family, saying: "And now most likely he's [Rigoberto] getting married." This statement diverts attention away from Belén's suffering, prompting me, Magdalena, and Belén to tease Rigoberto, who finally says he's migrating to escape the women in his life, inspiring hearty laughter and a bright blush of embarrassment on Sofía's face.

This moment is followed by a lull, during which I change the subject back to Rigoberto's migration experiences. At the same time, even as Belén tries to spotlight her suffering, she engages in substantial uptake of Magdalena's discourse. In line 6, for instance, Magdalena says, "You see, here one doesn't even have food to eat." In line 7 Belén begins her litany with a reiteration and elaboration of Magdalena's statement: "You see, here one doesn't even have food to eat and here it's harder than there." This pattern of greater uptake of Magdalena's words and topics by Belén continues throughout the conversation and effectively shines a brighter light on Magdalena's suffering, making it more worthy of our attention. Indeed, even when we are being fairly receptive to Belén, Magdalena is able to insert another injury of her own, saying she has no stove on which to prepare food (line 8): perhaps a pointed comment to Rigoberto and his friend as they try to repair the appliance.

These interactional patterns are joined with other features of Belén's enactment of the *mujer sufrida* that render it less compelling to her listeners than Magdalena's. Consider the patterns of pronominal usage and reference to personal experience in each woman's account. Magdalena, like Doña Cecilia in chapter 4, overwhelmingly grounds her suffering in tales with specific actors, usually herself and her family members— as she does above, when she references Rigoberto's impending marriage. As such, she cloisters her womanhood—and thus produces her likeness to Mary—through a domestic calibration (see chapter 4) that plants her views inside the personal experience of her family (cf. Dick 2010b, 2013; Farr 2006). In contrast, Belén tends to use impersonal pronouns and generalizing speech, as she does in the excerpt above, where she employs the general "you" and the impersonal "one" typical of men's migration discourse.

When men favor the use of impersonal pronouns in talk of migration, it generally helps them to take a stance of knowledgeable distance (see chapter 4). But it can have the opposite interactional effect for women, making them seem disconnected from the webs of family in which they are meant to ground their lives. Such a disconnect makes it harder for women to be received as sympathetic actors, as it seems to do here. The sense of disconnect in Belén's discourse is amplified about midway through the recording, when she starts using rapid-fire mumbling speech, which pulls her words so far inward that they become inaudible. This increasing disconnect happens just as Magdalena's stories of suffering reach a fever pitch through the articulate animation of past conversations between family members, which draw both me and Belén ever closer to her, only further highlighting the disparity in our responses to each woman's suffering.

But while this disparity is in part a product of Magdalena's superior discursive skill in performing the *mujer sufrida*, that alone does not explain why Belén's suffering becomes ignored and effectively silenced in this interaction. The disparity in our response to her continues even as Belén (again taking Magdalena's lead) begins to tell first-person narratives of hardship. On relistening, I have found many of these stories to be far more upsetting than Magdalena's, as they involve what appears to be the development of Belén's husband's mental illness and the severe physical abuse he inflicted on her as he became increasingly ill.

At the time not even these stories draw our focus to her: there is very little of the "yes-woman" affirmation that Belén and I give to Magdalena throughout. Magdalena never picks up Belén's topics, turns of phrase, or rhetorical strategies. In the most cringe-inducing example of this discrepancy, Belén turns to me after recounting an especially horrific incident when her husband tried to burn her to death because he was hallucinating that she was a demon. She pulls up her sleeve, shows me the burn scars on her forearms, and asks me if she should file for divorce (perhaps hailing me as a social worker). Not only do I not respond, but Magdalena and I actually change the subject. Belén persists, seeking recognition. She again returns to tales of her husband, at which point I vividly remember starting to feel exhausted and embarrassed because I was unable to take up her suffering or the role into which she was calling me. I can hear my own withdrawal from her in the recording after her last story, as I say over and over: "I'm so sorry. I don't know what to say."

I cannot speak in any substance to Magdalena's apparent disregard for her friend during this interaction, though it does not seem unreasonable to suggest that it was because she thought my greater attention to her might be useful as a gateway to resources. But I can address my own reaction. With Magdalena, while her stories were awful, they were fundamentally accounts of bad jobs and male betrayals. I had my own experience with such things and felt on some ground to address them, if only with affirmative utterances, which was after all the only immediate thing she really required of me. By contrast, Belén's endeavoring to interpellate me as someone able to help rectify her suffering overwhelmed me. I was shut down by the quantity of events of suffering she relayed; the rapid-fire speech in which she conveyed them, which I struggled to follow; the horror of her experiences; her directly asking my advice about divorce—as if I had any right to say what she should do about her marriage. Antonius Robben (1995, 1996), in his work on interviewing survivors of torture after Argentina's dirty war, describes a similar experience of overwhelm. Faced by the weight of the horrors described to him and the responsibility he carried to portray those horrors accurately, he felt at times incapable of processing the words uttered to him, unable to respond effectively—or at all. In my interactions with Belén, the interaction not only had the effect of shutting me down; it led me—in concert with Magdalena—to silence Belén. I effectively treated her suffering as less legitimate or compelling than Magdalena's, even though it may actually have been more severe. Thus, the legitimacy of someone's need is in part an outcome of interactions in which some people are better able to get listeners to ratify their self-presentation as a suffering person who deserves help. As such, suffering is a tenuous arrangement that shifts depending on audience and performance.

Saints and Suffering as Alternative Politics

The discussion above shows that women sometimes fail in their efforts to use the *mujer sufrida* to garner sympathy and resources. But these moments nevertheless also function as a form of calling back to and critique of their government and its forms of interpellation into Mexicanidad. This point is evident in Belén's litanies, which highlight a feature of the *seguir adelante* (to get ahead) proposition—the idea that working-class people cannot get ahead in Mexico but must migrate to gain access to the resources that will allow them to progress (see chapter 3). Like many other women—including Doña Cecilia in chapter 4—Belén portrays the US government as one that helps, providing a range of resources that safeguard and facilitate well-being and mobility, from food stamps to protection against spousal abuse. This image is placed in contrast to a disobliging Mexican government that abandons its people like an immoral, *desobligado* husband.

This contrast is widespread and familiar to working-class Uriangatenses. Given the level of US-bound migration from La Libertad, most people, even if they do not have migrants in their families, are aware of US government assistance programs. The image of the United States as "helpful" is not a description of the actual life of migrants in the United States. The vast majority of migrants never avail themselves of government assistance (Van Hook and Bean 2009). Moreover, working-class Uriangatenses are acutely aware (and critical) of the ways the US government is often hostile to migrants (cf. Chávez 2015; Dick and Arnold 2017a; Yeh 2017). Instead, talk about the US government expresses a critique of the Mexican government in an alternate vision for its future. It projects a time when Mexico will enforce its laws and rectify the vulnerabilities of working-class people so that they would no longer have to go to the United States in order to *seguir adelante*.

Similarly, the cultivation of relationships with divine figures (whether through *promesas* or the *mujer sufrida*) in turn authorizes Uriangatenses to construe an alternative imaginary of moral mobility as the basis of belonging in Mexico. This imaginary entails a consequentialist ethics that exists in a dialogue with the critique of the failures of progress produced through working-class Uriangatense migration discourse. Discourse such as the litanies produced by Belén inverts the terms of state-endorsed imaginings of moral mobility. It posits the government of the "immoral beyond" of the United States as more obliging—more communitarian—and thus more moral than their own government. In this way migration discourse and saintly relations refigure the "heres" that can enable the production of a moral life for Mexicans.

In one sense this enactment replicates the imaginary of state discourse, desiring religiously grounded, communitarian progress. But it also exposes that the resources that make such progress possible—obliging husbands, decent employers, government assistance—are unavailable to them through no fault of their own. Consequently, both migration discourse and relationships with divine figures condemn state-endorsed imaginaries, while affirming their producers' Mexican virtue and thus their legitimate national belonging. Through such practices, they construct an imaginary in which not only the Mexican government but also *desobligado* family members are exposed for being immoral, while also being—at least imaginatively—brought to account for their failures to meet their obligations. *Promesas* and accounts of suffering make people like vengeful saints pursuing supplicants who have not fulfilled their *commitments*. Therefore these practices highlight the ways that the production of social imaginaries not only maps out existing sociopolitical landscapes but can also generate possibilities that change such landscapes.

The use of relationships with the divine to critique and revise existing forms of inequality is a familiar tactic employed across a range of contexts (e.g., Abu-Lughod 1986; Bonfil Batalla 1990; Gálvez 2009; Lester 2005; Martín 2013; Mittermaier 2011; Peña 2011), from the piety movement in Egypt (Mahmood 2005) to the practices of care among heroin addicts in the United States (Garcia 2010). Mexico has a well-documented history of harnessing relationships with divine figures, especially the Virgin Mary, to programs of social reform, including—at times—a full-tilt revolution (see Napolitano 2016: chapter 5 for a review). And this tradition is carried on today. For example, some social movements use syncretic Indigenous-Catholic religious practice as part of a push for the recognition of the rights of Indigenous peoples. The role of the Virgin of Guadalupe as both symbol of colonial oppression and portal for liberation in the Zapatista movement is a case in point (Napolitano 2016: chapter 5; Martín 2013), but there are other examples as well (e.g., Faudree 2013). For Mexican migrants devotion to the Virgin of Guadalupe has also played an important role in the immigrant rights movement in the United States—by producing an infrastructure for political organizing; by cultivating contexts in which the lives of migrants are valorized and legitimated; and by providing the materials for imagining a different world (Baquedano-López 2001; Gálvez 2009; Peña 2011).

In these movements, relationships with divine figures (like the practices examined in this chapter) simultaneously highlight, elegize, critique, and transform the forms of variegation, co-optation, and occlusion endured by Mexicans abroad and by marginalized groups in Mexico. As I illustrate in this chapter, it is not only people actively involved in protest, rights organizing, or revolution who use the divine to critique and transform their world. This happens also in daily practices of prayer and self-presentation. It is not unreasonable to suggest that these quotidian rituals are a key source for the more overt forms of political protest such as testimonies (described above), helping create the conditions of possibility that make those protests legible, plausible, and effective.

As the analysis in this chapter demonstrates, these daily practices such as *promesas* and voicing the *mujer sufrida* are powerful because they involve multiple and overlapping forms of interpellation. Through them people can call upon and position themselves, each other, their nation, and the divine in potentially transformative ways—commanding children to remain true to parents across geopolitical borders; garnering resources that are otherwise denied to you by family or nation; and so forth. Therefore this chapter illustrates the central importance of the dynamics of particular moments of interaction in which people cultivate relationships with divine figures. It also highlights the ways such cultivation shapes people's relationship not only with themselves and their God but with their family and nation, wherever they may roam, creating a portable method of critical intervention into the injustices of political economic life.

Worlds of Passage:
Moral Mobility in Global Context

This ethnography has illuminated the many ways the imagined lives of migrants shape national belonging and resource access for working-class Uriangatenses whose lives are imbricated with migration to the United States. As *Words of Passage* shows, Uriangatenses live their lives in the company of imagined fellows. The unfolding of their present life is refracted through a prism of possible lives not only in the United States but in other interrelated places "beyond here" (in the ranchos, in heaven). These imagined lives influence a range of activities not directly related to migration, from the pressing concerns of family to those that help render the nation-state as a potent form of affiliation that makes people into distinct and hierarchically arranged types. Therefore the practices through which people link the unfolding of life in the here-and-now to the imagination of life beyond are of enormous consequence. They inform not only an individual's sense of belonging to a place but also the ability to access the resources that facilitate mobility: steady employment with benefits, social services, education, migrant remittances. In its exploration of national belonging and resource access, *Words of Passage* develops three central insights.

First, the depiction of lives in and out of migration is a core feature of the social imaginaries that organize the production of national (be)longing: who is and who is not seen to reside legitimately in a nation-state and to be deserving of access to its resources. Therefore the imagined lives of migrants enable and contour the variegation of belonging; determining who is and who is not included in the nation-state relies on ideas about who migrants are and what their role in the nation-state should be in both migrant-receiving and migrant-sending countries. Thus, this book lends credence to the idea that such variegation is a core feature of nation building more generally. While the cross-border movements of migrants are often depicted as threatening to the nation-state, they are in fact essential to the production of national belonging as well as the parameters of sovereignty. The representation of these movements helps define what it means to be properly Mexican and who can enjoy the fruits of the nation. This is true both in the elite spheres of people actively engaged in nation building and policy making (such as the architects of Mexican nationalism discussed in chapter 1) and in the milieu of people directly involved in migration, including the non-migrants whose lives are at the center of this book. In focusing on the experiences of nonmigrants, *Words of Passage* spotlights how imagined lives of migrants order social worlds long before and independent of actual movements abroad.

Second, this book demonstrates the absolutely central role that talk and writing about migration (migration discourse) plays in the production of imagined lives and their consequences. The words of passage through which images of migrant lives take form and become available for circulation are essential to the processes through which migration becomes actionable as a matter of nation-state building. Therefore this book illustrates that the imaginative practices that enable actors to create, form attachments to, and transform large-scale social formations like the nation-state are fundamentally discursive. Migration discourse is itself a widely accessible practice for the imagination of lives but it also frames and organizes the ways other semiotic processes, such as home-building and saintly relationships, become linked to national belonging. It does this primarily through generating chronotopic frameworks that organize times, places, and persons with respect to one another, as illustrated, in the discussion of the moral geography of rural and urban life that orders working-class Uriangatense understandings of progress.

As I elucidate throughout, migration discourse is never only about migration. It is also always about the promises, possibilities, and failures of life at home. The production of migration discourse is a common practice not only for people involved in migration but also for the politicians, policy makers, academics, and journalists on both sides of the Mexico-US border whose work contributes to the definition of national belonging and its relationship to the possibility of geographic and socioeconomic mobility. As such, this book is as much about a broader politics of mobility as it is about a particular history or context of migration (cf. Berg 2015; Salazar 2010).

Words of Passage explores two dimensions of migration discourse, which allow me to track the concrete practices through which people's present here-and-now becomes imbricated with counterpoint lives inhabitable elsewhere. While many scholars of globalization have remarked on this process, few have systematically examined how these lives are constructed and made consequential. The first dimension of migration discourse examined here involves the genealogical links that connect state-endorsed imaginaries of moral mobility across key moments of Mexican nation building, beginning in the late nineteenth century. The connections among state-endorsed imaginaries generated by nation-builders in the Porfirian, postrevolutionary, and neoliberal periods create an interdiscursive web that has naturalized some ways of being Mexican while making others unacceptable, abnormal, and immoral (chapter 1). These imaginaries contain a double-bind of moral mobility for working-class people, who are perpetually caught between being neither traditional nor modern enough. That positioning has repeatedly been used by state institutions to justify their exclusion from full membership in the polity. As social imaginaries move across contexts, they produce similarities and resonances but also points of contention and friction. As I demonstrate throughout the book, attending to both resonance and friction is essential to understanding how the imaginaries that variegate national belonging in Mexico shape the unfolding of social life in Uriangato.

The second dimension of migration discourse examined involves the practices of actual language use, such as stancetaking and pronominal patterns. Uriangatenses craft their own imaginaries of moral mobility through these practices, placing themselves and others inside those imaginaries. In so doing, they link their present world to lives modeled in state-endorsed imaginaries and to lives they envision beyond-here, taking positions on which lives are desirable and which are not. Analysis of this dimension of migration discourse links linguistic anthropological work on social indexicality (how language practices work to create difference between groups of people, thus rendering the social boundaries that enable processes of inclusion and exclusion) to the cultural anthropology of social imaginaries and their salience to nation building.

Finally, a key discovery of this book is that the production, replication, and revision of state-endorsed and Uriangatense imaginaries of moral mobility are motivated and linked through acts of interpellation: the processes of call-and-response through which people are hailed to be and see themselves as certain kinds of members of a polity. As shown, interpellation relies on more than literal calls-and-responses. The implementation and enactment of social imaginaries that model what it means to be a proper Mexican are also a form of interpellative call. These imaginaries create differences between types of Mexicans (working-class people versus elites; men versus women; migrants versus nonmigrants) and beckon people to these groups by naturalizing them as frames of reference for the interpretation of events, from homebuilding to migration. In producing their own imaginaries, Uriangatenses call back to those who produce state-endorsed imaginaries. These "call backs" critique and revise the terms of national belonging in Mexico, highlighting the marginalization of working-class people, the failures of progress in Mexico, and the asymmetrical relationship between Mexico and the United States. They also open up the possibilities of transformation and change.

Processes of interpellation matter because they not only reveal the terms and limits of who can lay claim to national belonging; they also establish what it means to live right. That is, the production and circulation of imaginaries are integral to the construction of ethico-moral life: what does it mean to be a good person or a bad one? Through what practices does an individual create ethico-moral personhood and signal it to others? Responses to the interpellative calls of imaginaries of national belonging are a form of ethico-moral work through which people attempt to enact themselves as right kinds of Mexicans who can demand full inclusion in the nation-state and access to its resources. Thus, the construal of ethico-moral life in Uriangato is nationally inflected, concerned with what it means to be Mexican and not, say, someone from the United States. Moreover, it is gendered: men and women become properly Mexican in distinct ways. And it is discursive, steeped in concepts of personhood, collectivity, and agency that emphasize the importance of verbal sociality in the creation of proper people and relationships. The discursive character of ethico-moral life in Mexico includes the cultivation of expertise about nation and migration, which influences what can and cannot constitute an "authoritative account." Therefore it is also deeply political, as it helps order interested regimes of governance over self and others, which separate people hierarchically and deny some the full privileges of belonging.

Overall, then, *Words of Passage* tells a story of national belonging rendered through the imagination of migration across and in between different places and people. In so doing, this ethnography does not take for granted or decide at the outset how and why such belonging comes to matter. It carefully documents the historical production and interactional accomplishment of national belonging and its variegation in particular contexts and at particular times. As such, the book pushes against what Andreas Wimmer and Nina Glick-Schiller (2002: 302) have called "methodological nationalism": the idea that the nation-state is the natural container of analysis for contemporary social life. Methodological nationalism produces scholarship that elides the pragmatics and politics that lead to the nation-state's emergence and continued salience, keeping us from interrogating how national belonging matters, who gets to say why it matters, and what practices enable someone to lay claim to it.

I counteract this tendency by exploring how national belonging matters—and how it does not. As I illustrate in chapters 3 to 5, national belonging in Mexico is not always the primary point of reference in the production of group inclusion and exclusion. The important roles played by both transnational migration and Catholicism in Uriangatense imaginaries of moral mobility reveal the ways that the forms of belonging examined in this book are never only about nationalism. At the same time, neoliberal globalization has inspired nation-states aggressively to assert their sovereign right to define and defend borders. This has helped make the nation-state a potent frame of reference for many migrants and nonmigrants, despite the dramatic predictions by some scholars in the early 1990s that the future viability of the nation-state was fundamentally threatened by contemporary globalization (Dick and Arnold 2017b; Werbner 2013). Thus, I conclude with a consideration of the resurgence of nationalism as revealed through contemporary reactions to the movement of people across settings, placing the analysis of moral mobility in global context, its worlds of passage.

Moral Mobility across Contexts

Words of Passage begins with a description of the day Pope John Paul II departed from Mexico for the final time. During that departure—and indeed during his entire trip—it seemed that the whole nation had stopped to behold this beloved pope, who called Mexico the most perfect of Catholic countries. In Uriangato his trip—which people watched on television throughout his visit—framed everyday life with a sense of grace: the possibilities for change modeled by Catholic sociality and transcendence, as exemplified in people's relationships with the saints (see chapter 5). In late September 2015 I experienced another papal visit, as Pope Francis spent the weekend in Philadelphia on the final leg of his first visit to the United States. Since Francis became pope in 2013, he has been crafting an imaginary that calls for transformation in ways that are confusing to the frames and positions of right-left politics in the United States: he is against abortion and against gay marriage but vociferous about confronting global climate change, poverty, and social inequality. While in Philadelphia, Pope Francis enacted this imaginary through the ways he conducted the visit. He followed a meeting with bishops about how the church can manage the "degradation" of the family after the US Supreme Court decision to legalize gay marriage with a visit to a local correctional facility. There he addressed the problem of mass incarceration, placing no uncertain blame on US policy. He lovingly acknowledged the incarcerated, greeting each prisoner individually, shaking every hand, and giving words of blessing to each inmate.

While Pope Francis's imaginary agitates the usual boundaries of political affiliation in the United States, his combination of traditional morality and progressive politics is familiar to Mexicans, for whom ideas about the integration of tradition and modernity are a familiar lynchpin of ethico-moral personhood and national belonging. In Uriangato, where the essences of nation and personhood are understood to be rooted in Catholicism, the acknowledgment of a pope carries special weight. This was true when Pope John Paul visited Mexico in 2002. Pope Francis's mode of engaging his worldwide flock is similarly meaningful, not only to Mexicans but to people from all over Latin America. One of the standout characteristics of Pope Francis's visit to Philadelphia was its powerful witness to the humanity of migrants living in the United States. This took the form of the pope's direct address to audiences in the United States, as when he implored members of the US Congress to "reject a mind-set of hostility" and embrace migrants. In a speech on religious freedom the pope introduced himself as "the son of an immigrant family" and as a "guest of this country, which was largely built by such families" (Corchado 2015).

In his many speeches touching on the human rights of migrants (in the United States and in public appearances in many other countries) the pope pushes against the pervasive imagining of migrants as threatening and Other. He asks his audiences to see the parallels between their own lives and those of migrants. The pope's witness of migrant humanity while in Philadelphia focused on the inclusion of Latin American migrants. This is not surprising, considering he is the first Latin American pope and was on his first papal visit to the Americas. But it is also because migrants from Mexico and other parts of Latin America have in recent decades been the object of the most vitriolic anti-immigrant rhetoric and policy in the United States (Chavez 2008; De Genova 2005; Dick 2011b; Santa Ana 2002).

Pope Francis's witness of Latin American migrants is especially potent in dialogue with US anti-immigrant imaginaries, proffered most recently by US president Donald J. Trump, who infamously described Mexicans as "drug dealers, rapists, and killers" when he announced his bid for office in June 2015. Trump's rhetoric and his proposed policy to deport all undocumented migrants in two years and "build that wall" garnered criticism from many, including several of the other Republican presidential candidates (Haddon 2015). His persistent popularity as a candidate and eventual victory, however, both relied on and reveal an ongoing history of criminalizing migrants from Mexico and increasingly from other parts of Latin America. Indeed Trump eventually extended his invectives against Mexicans to include migrants coming from Central America.

Such processes of criminalization, although well documented in the case of the United States (Abrego 2014; Chávez 2015; Coutin 2005, 2007; De Genova 2005; Dick 2012; Dick and Arnold 2017a; Ngai 2004), are not exclusive to the United States. They are found in a variety of places across the globe, in countries as diverse as South Africa, Sweden, and Australia. Likewise, the pope's inclusive imaginary, like other humanistic imaginaries of migration, is not only about Latin American migrants: it addresses the lives of all displaced and mobile populations.

As I argue throughout this book, the ways we imagine migrants in migration discourse and in related semiotic practices (such as how migrants are represented visually in the media: cf. Chavez 2001, 2008) shape the treatment of migrants and their loved ones. And how they are treated matters more and more, as human mobility becomes more the norm than human rootedness (Berg 2015; Urry 2007). Recent decades have seen staggering increases in the numbers of displaced and mobile populations worldwide (Marfleet 2006). According to a 2014 report by the United Nations' Refugee Agency, nearly 60 million people were forcibly displaced in that year, a number greater than the populations of two-thirds of the world's nation-states (UNHCR 2014: 2). And that number includes only people who fled from political conflicts, largely in Syria, Eritrea, Somalia, and Afghanistan (UNHCR 2014: 3). It does not count the hundreds of thousands of people who leave home due to economic distress and/or who are displaced within their own country.

Moreover, most mobile populations today cross national borders for a mixture of reasons that reveal the inaccuracy of the categories "voluntary economic migrant" and "involuntary political refugee" (Marfleet 2006). Think, for example, of the unaccompanied child migrants from Central America, whose unauthorized border crossings were a centerpiece of US migration politics in 2014 (Martínez 2014). These children, some as young as five years old, are fleeing gang violence in Central America and therefore partially fit the profile of what we might imagine a refugee to be. Yet they also move in search of parents and other relatives who went to the United States for economic reasons (Abrego 2014; Coutin 2007). Thus, their movements are also the product of desires to access greater socioeconomic opportunities associated with the image of the voluntary migrant, though some scholars and immigration rights activists question how voluntary economic migration actually is (see Andrijasevic 2003; Marfleet 2006).

Increases in cross-border movements are the result of long-term international conflicts and global economic policies, in which many migrant-receiving countries are complicit. Migration from Central America, for example, is a result of the ongoing legacies of three factors: US military intervention during the late twentieth century civil wars that plagued the region; a US refugee program that resettled people fleeing those conflicts in US cities; and the US-sponsored neoliberal economic reforms that followed the wars (Abrego 2014; Moodie 2010). And this is but one example. Almost every migration pathway has its roots in economic and political displacements rendered by the political, economic, and/or military intervention of foreign powers (Massey et al. 2005).

Yet, when faced with the movements of people that result from these displacements, the overwhelming response of governments and citizens in receiving countries in recent decades has been to support policies that "crack down" on cross-border movements. Receiving countries have placed tighter and tighter restrictions on access to legal migration and criminalized people who migrate without documents even when they seek political asylum (Abrego 2014; Coutin 2005; De Genova 2005; Dick 2011b, 2012; Marfleet 2006). These policies are made possible by, but also legitimate and codify, the ongoing production of imaginaries that represent migrants as Other: dangerous and unassimilable to society. And they authorize shocking approaches to managing migration, such as Australia's Operation Sovereign Borders, which ruthlessly refuses boatloads of migrants just as they reach shore (Sullivan 2015). As a result of such policies, many displaced people face harrowing life-and-death experiences as they move, from days crossing the Mexico-US border through the desert without water to dangerous sea voyages across the Mediterranean. The consequences of the hostile, inhumane imaginaries legitimated by draconian crackdowns on immigration are also evinced in extralegal responses, such as the violent antimigrant riots in South Africa in 2008 and 2015 (Lindow and Perry 2008; Patel 2015).

The criminalization and Othering of migrants matters not only because it enables violations of the human rights of migrants, but also because it occludes the way international conflict and global economic policies have also harmed nonmigrants. Scapegoating migrants for broad sociopolitical transformations obscures the fact that those transformations affect the lives of both migrants and people who may not physically move but are nevertheless displaced. This book considers this point from the perspective of nonmigrants in Uriangato, people who live close to and are often part of migration. *Words of Passage* documents their diaspora at home: the ways they are imaginatively and economically dislocated from the lives they feel a national and ethico-moral imperative to fulfill.

But displacement is a feature of life for many nonmigrants in the global economy. Neoliberal economic policies, such as the North American Free Trade Agreement (NAFTA), put workers across the globe in competition with each other (Harvey 2006; Wright 2006). Such competition not only uproots labor in migrant-sending countries, increasing transnational migration (Durand and Massey 2003; Massey 2007; Massey et al. 2005); it dramatically alters opportunities for native-born residents of migrant-receiving countries. These processes are felt in an especially tense way in places that are unaccustomed to receiving migrants and therefore do not have the imaginative or economic resources to integrate newcomers easily (Varsanyi 2010; Wortham et al. 2011). Take the case of Hazleton, Pennsylvania, which I have explored in other work (Dick 2011b).

Hazleton is an economically depressed and diminishing mining town in a part of Pennsylvania's once-booming anthracite coal region. This town is like many areas in western Pennsylvania that thrived during the pre-neoliberal era but are now part of what is known as the "rust belt," so named because of the collapse of the steel industry. The economic and social challenges faced by such towns are significant: high unemployment rates, dwindling tax bases, outmigration of people looking for better opportunities, increased drug abuse, and so on. In an attempt to foster economic development and job growth, the Pennsylvania state government designated Hazleton as a "Keystone Opportunity Zone" (KOZ), a status that allows the town to waive taxes on outside corporations.

The use of tax breaks to court outside investment is a common strategy for depressed rural areas in many US states, who compete with each other to attract businesses that largely create jobs in retail, meat packing, and prisons and typically do not match the salaries and benefits that people enjoyed in mid-twentieth-century manufacturing jobs (Fleury-Steiner and Longazel 2010; Thompson 2010). They also often do not employ exclusively (or even largely) local workers; Hazleton is a case in point. In 2001 Hazleton's Community Area New Development Organization (CAN DO) used the KOZ to attract a meat-packaging plant. The plant is run by Cargill Meat Solutions, a major national corporation that owns dozens of brands (such as Shady Brook Farms) and has an established record of hiring foreign-born migrant labor, especially people from Mexico and other parts of Latin America (De Jesús 2006). The foreign-born Latino/a population of Hazleton, composed especially of Mexicans and Dominicans, boomed shortly after the arrival of Cargill's plant (Dick 2011b). In 2000 "Latinos" (the US Census designation that includes Latin American immigrants) represented less than 5 percent of the population. By 2010 Latino/as represented close to 30 percent of the population in a town that was over 90 percent white in 2000 (Fleury-Steiner and Longazel 2010: 161). During the 2000s the Latino/a population in Hazleton increased at the fourth-fastest rate of all large US counties (El Nasser and Heath 2007).

The abrupt emergence of Latin American migrant communities in mostly white receiving areas with little experience of inmigration is a recent trend found across the country (Varsanyi 2010; Wortham et al. 2002). The swiftness with which these communities emerge understandably draws the attention of long-term residents and sparks public debate, as it did in Hazleton (cf. Massey and Sánchez 2010). However, rapid demographic shifts do not determine the character of emergent migration politics (Hopkins 2010). Some new migrant-receiving towns have declared themselves "sanctuary cities," where officials are not allowed to inquire about immigration status (Degnen 2007). But this was not the case in Hazleton. There—and in many other municipalities that have become migrant-receiving areas over the last two decades—the response has been to treat migration as a criminal justice problem (cf. Varsanyi

2010). In 2006 Hazleton passed the Illegal Immigration Relief Act. The act, which eventually failed in a years-long court battle, would have punished town employers and landlords for hiring or renting property to undocumented immigrants.[1]

This ordinance was part of a wave of nonfederal immigration laws that spiked in 2006, when the US Congress again failed to engage in immigration policy reform, something that it still has not yet managed to do over ten years later (Hopkins 2010; Varsanyi 2010). Such ordinances vary in aim and scope. Some, like those of the sanctuary cities, are aimed at integrating migrants, while others concentrate on finding ways to remove them. Consider policies of "self-deportation." Such policies endeavor to drive away migrants by creating material conditions so intolerable that they pressure migrants to leave or "self-deport": a paradoxical term first coined by political cartoonist Lalo Alcaraz, who used it to critique such policies (Dick 2012). This term has nevertheless been taken up in earnest by supporters of such policies; it even appeared in the 2012 US presidential election, when Republican candidate Mitt Romney called for federal self-deportation policies. The author of many of these policies, Republican strategist Kris Kobach (Dick 2011b), has advised both Romney and Trump on immigration policy.

Even when they are struck down in the courts—and they often are, as the creation of immigration policy is the purview of the federal government—policies of self-deportation have enduring effects. One particularly dangerous effect is that they occlude the global political economic transformations that have emptied both migrant-sending and migrant-receiving locations of stable, well-paid work, thereby encouraging migration. Instead of interrogating these processes and the policies that enable them, such as the KOZ that facilitated Hazleton's courting of Cargill Meat Solutions, policies of "self-deportation" blame these transformations on migrants. This was the case in Hazleton, where at least some of those concerned about the impact of the sudden influx of migrants decided to treat migration as a result of a moral failing on the part of migrants themselves. Those who passed and supported the Illegal Immigration Relief Act assumed that these migrants were in the town illegally and treated that putative illegality as evidence of their dangerous, criminal character—an assumption they used to justify the act (Dick 2011b). This response to migration is not particular to Hazleton.

As Benjamin Fleury-Steiner and Jamie Longazel (2010) argue, this is part of a broader political economic regime, wherein government and community organizations aggressively court industries with known histories of hiring foreign-born migrant labor, such as Cargill. Thus, they encourage that migration while they simultaneously criminalize migrants. As a result, any critique of state or industry action gets deflected onto migrants. What gets lost when migrants become the scapegoats for the political economic transformations to which we are all subjected is the humanity and vulnerability not only of migrants but also of long-term residents of migrant-receiving areas, especially the poor and working-class people who find themselves in increasingly deteriorating socioeconomic conditions across the globe. If we think of moral mobility in the broadest terms as the ability to engage in socioeconomic advancement and still be able to claim to be living an ethico-moral life, then the double-binds of belonging and their politics are an issue not only for Mexican migrants and their relations but for poor and working-class people more generally.

Both exclusionary imaginaries, such as those undergirding and codified in policies of "self-deportation," and inclusive imaginaries, such as those generated by Pope Francis and humanitarian migrant advocacy groups, are part of a politics of representation that pivot around the morality and ethics of mobility (cf. Mehan 1997). That is, they make assertions about the social good of mobility, about who should and should not benefit from it, and about how people should and should not engage in it. As this book shows, these assertions have long tendrils that affect migrants and nonmigrants alike. My examination of how imaginaries of moral mobility are generated and circulated, how they come to interpellate people in different ways, and how they inspire responses that potentially transform the terms of belonging is relevant to more than the specific case of Mexican nationalism and Mexican migration to the United States. It offers a window onto processes of call-and-response that are taking form in distinct ways across many settings, suggesting that we should examine migrations as part of the broader global dynamics of mobility and social differentiation. Situating migration as part of these dynamics can help denaturalize the populations, practices, and contexts conventionally associated with migration, helping place them in relation to other forms of movement made possible by various aspects of globalization, from tourism to terrorism (cf. Andrijasevic 2003; Berg 2015: Urry 2007).

At every turn, language practices play a crucial role in the construal and circulation of processes of mobility and social differentiation. They help determine the social categories and sociogeographical boundaries that organize the ethics, morality, and political economy of mobility.

The relationship between language and mobility has been a central concern of the anthropology of language from its beginnings. One key insight in this work is that language practices are essential to the formation of the sociocultural and political economic borders that produce nation-states (see Dick 2011a for a review—see also Dick 2011b; Gal 1989; Irvine and Gal 2000). At the same time, as Alexandre Duchêne and Monica Heller (2011: 4, 10) argue, neoliberalism disrupts the relationship between language and group formation that supports the nation-state form: it construes language practices as marketable skill sets that theoretically can be acquired by anyone. This disruption is heralded in utopian neoliberal discourses about increased freedom of mobility across geographical and social boundaries, which root the possibilities of movement not in belonging to a nation-state but in willingness to acquire new skills (Harvey 2006; Marfleet 2006; Wacquant 2009).

Such utopian visions obscure the harsh realities of border-crossing during the neoliberal period, which have produced two worlds of mobility. One is populated by authorized groups whose lives are valued and secured, while the other is populated by people treated as suspects, who lives are devalued and disposable (Amoore and de Goede 2008: 13). Therefore it is imperative to understand how "mobility" works as a social-semiotic process, rooted in particular contexts and historical moments and producing shifts in the constitution of mobility. These shifts can lead—and have led—to the exclusion and abandonment of those deemed unfit to belong. But they can also generate new horizons, alternative imaginaries that transform the boundaries of exclusion, inviting those who are rooted at home to see reflected in displaced peoples not an Other but ourselves.

Notes

Technical Note

1. The term *gringo/gringa* was originally used in Spain in the 1700s to denote any foreign, non-native speakers of Spanish. In Mexico and many other parts of Latin America it is most widely used to refer to people from the United States.

Introduction

1. Except for historical or public figures, all names are pseudonyms.

2. See Technical Note: Methodology and Methods for an accounting of my research methods.

3. Schmidt Camacho (2008) partially addresses this question but focuses on activists, artists, and public intellectuals—especially in the United States—and not on migrants and their relations in Mexico.

4. Contrary to many popular depictions of late nineteenth century and early twentieth century European migration, this was not primarily a settlement-oriented migration. Most of these migrants came with the desire to use migration to build a life in their country of origin: nearly half of them did in fact return home (Foner 2000).

5. The scholar most associated with this concept is Cornelius Castoriadis (1987), who developed it in *The Imaginary Institution of Society*. Castoriadis emphasized people's ability to make social worlds to resist what he saw as the "deterministic ontology" of Western thought, which he argued discounted the importance of creativity (Breckman 2013: 96–138; Gaonkar 2002). He did not focus on the conditions under which any particular sociohistorical world emerged, however, and argued that any given sociohistorical world is created *ex nihilo* in bursts of imagination (Gaonkar 2002: 6–7). Consequently, his theory is too ahistorical and decontextualized to be gratifying for an anthropology of imaginaries.

6. As Didier Fassin argues (2012a, 2012b), this means drawing another facet of Foucault's work into the study of ethico-moral life—the understanding of how techniques of self are part of larger regimes of governmentality through which relations of power are produced and have wide-reaching consequences.

7. In 2010 these municipalities sought to capitalize further on their influence by forming a joint metropolitan zone, which creates an infrastructure for the agencies and organizations that oversee the textile industry to combine forces in promoting their interest to the state and federal government and in the industry overall.

8. The following history is compiled from interviews I conducted with Uriangato's town archivist, two textile factory owners, and several textile employees.

9. Mushroom farming began in this area in the late nineteenth century as small family-run enterprises; in the 1920s the farms had expanded enough to merit the recruitment of outside labor sources. This outside labor has always been a migrant population—first Italians, recruited from South Philadelphia in the 1920s, who were replaced by Puerto Ricans in the 1940s and 1950s, who were then replaced by Mexicans in the 1970s.

10. There is a pattern of employers across the country pitting Puerto Rican and Mexican workers against each other in this way, which, not surprisingly, is a source of tension between these groups (cf. De Genova and Ramos-Zayas 2003).

11. This term is adapted from the related term "immigrant enclave" in sociology. Such enclaving involves the formation of a critical mass of migrants who create self-sufficient semiautonomous political economic units within the migrant-receiving country, with businesses, language practices, and forms of social difference that resemble life "at home" more than life in the host country (Portes and Wilson 1980).

Chapter 1

1. Recent anthropological literature on state practices has shown that "the state" is an after-the-fact reification; what we tend to refer to as "the state" is the output of a complex and often contradictory layering of processes (Herzfeld 1997; Riggan 2016). Any full accounting of "the Mexican state" would have to attend to such layering—a task that is outside the scope of this book, which focuses on working-class Uriangatenses' engagements with national belonging.

2. Many scholars make similar distinctions but refer to them using different versions of the term "citizenship" (e.g., Biolsi 2005; Ong 1999; Stack 2012a; Stephen 2004, 2007).

3. The idea that Mexicans are morally underdeveloped is a legacy of the Spanish colonial caste system, which not only privileged people of Spanish descent over people of other ethno-racial backgrounds; it created a ranked distinction between people of Spanish lineage born in Spain and those born in the New World, figuring racial mixing as a sign of moral corruption (Alonso 2004: 461; Young 1995).

4. Although the country's previous constitution contained similar anticleri-

cal provisions, Díaz did not enforce them and tacitly allowed the church's political economic power to remain intact, something that postrevolutionary leaders sought to counteract as part of undoing his interventionist policies.

5. Gamio (1964: 121) argued that Mexico's mestizos were "the real protagonist(s) of Mexico's 'second independence'" (its revolutionary overthrow of Porfirian elites). Like Vasconcelos, he posited that a fully sovereign Mexico would be forged in relation to both the external Other of the United States and the internal Other of nonmestizos (Alonso 2004: 466–467).

6. Gamio was one of the first great scholars of Mexico-US migration, spearheading the Social Science Research Council's early work on migration (Walsh 2008) and documenting the transnational lives of Mexican migrants decades before such research came into vogue in US anthropology (e.g., Gamio 1930).

7. Mexican candidates for office at the municipal, state, and federal levels from all parties now frequently include tours to migrant communities in the United States as part of their political campaigns, which would have been unheard of in previous eras (Goldring 2002: 57).

8. NAFTA is an agreement signed by Canada, Mexico, and the United States implemented in 1994. It created a trilateral trade bloc that limited barriers to trade and investment among these three countries.

9. http://siteresources.worldbank.org/INTMEXICOINSPANISH /Resources/c_capitulo_1.pdf.

Chapter 2

1. This is a pseudonym.

2. Butler uses John L. Austin's speech act theory to broaden analysis of the forms of interaction that interpellate beyond Althusser's paradigmatic call of the police officer. She underscores the idea that language is a form of social action that does not just reflect the world; it helps make it. At the same time, drawing from Jacques Derrida's philosophy of language, Butler critiques a tendency born from the speech act theory of John L. Austin and John R. Searle to treat the forms of personhood typical of Western social life as universal (cf. Duranti 1993; Rosaldo 1980). It follows, therefore, that to understand interpellative processes we must be open to cultural differences in personhood.

3. In other work (Dick 2010b, 2013) I describe this form of personhood as "role-constituted."

4. A key finding of *Return to Aztlán* is that migration is a social process shaped by household economics and family interaction, contrary to then-prevailing models of migration, which posited choices to migrate as outcomes of rational cost-benefit analyses made by individuals.

5. The so-called Minutemen were a vigilante group that apprehended people that they assumed were undocumented on Arizona's border with Mexico during most of the 2000s. Although their operation was shuttered in 2010, recent reports show that similar activities are still occurring (http://www.salon.com/2013/10/05 /vigilantes_patrolling_arizona_border_are_more_radical_than_ever_partner/).

6. According to Paz, Latino/a migrants describe themselves as *chismosos* be-

cause collectively they do not have the requisite social, cultural, or legal capital to utter speech that could be authoritative outside Latin American migrant enclaves in Israel. Consequently, they routinely framed Latino/a accounts of happenings as *chisme* in contrast to accounts produced by more authoritative sources located in the mainstream of Hebrew-speaking Israeli society.

Chapter 3

1. Other scholars (e.g., Eisenlohr 2006; Werbner 2002) have shown that diasporic imaginaries are as much about seeking political and sociocultural inclusion in the country of destination as they are about maintaining contact with the homeland. However, these works do not explore how diaspora is a process that begins at home, is experienced by those at home, and reveals the politics of belonging at home as well as abroad (Dick 2013).

2. Because such raids are rare, they provide electric content when they do happen. I was regaled more than once with stories of a raid in 2000, when federal officials confiscated pirated goods and shut down the factories where they were manufactured. This raid became a touchstone in conversations about the government's failure to protect working-class citizens. The Uriangatenses I knew understood the raid to have been primarily an effort to protect manufacturers, instead of a measure taken to enforce the country's labor and welfare laws.

3. Both Mexican and US scholars contribute to this assumption in their research, which overwhelmingly documents migration out of rural communities.

4. The average price for a completed home in Uriangato is between 250,000 and 300,000 pesos (25,000–30,000 US dollars), while a plot of land costs between 80,000 and 120,000 pesos (8,000–12,000 US dollars).

5. Initially a feature of the administration of Indigenous communities by Spanish colonialists, *ejidos* are a key point of intersection between Mexico's rural communities and its government. *Ejidos* were abolished in the mid-1800s as antithetical to the free-market ideologies of nineteenth-century liberalism and then reestablished in the decades following the 1910 Revolution. To protect the integrity of the *ejidos*, federal laws were passed in the early twentieth century making it illegal for *ejidatarios* to sell their land (Kourí 2004). This changed in the 1990s, thanks to laws passed by President Salinas to promote free-market principles, which prioritize private property rights (Gilbreth and Otero 2001).

6. Working with Latina gang girls in California, Norma Mendoza-Denton (1999, 2008) found that the high school students who are the focus of her work use *norteño/a* (northerner) in contrast with the designation *sureño/a* (southerner) to lay claim to a Mexican American identity within the racial politics of the United States. For her research participants these designations are different ways of embracing "Mexicanness" in a country marked by the hegemony of whiteness (see also Hill 2008) rather than a way of separating true Mexicans from false Mexicans.

7. Relationships of transnational obligation take on the asymmetrical interdependence that characterizes relationships between Mexico and the United States. In discussions of resources in Uriangatense migration discourse we see

this asymmetry reproduced in the balance of power—it is the family in the United States that should send gifts and money and should be calling, as the United States is the land of resources (cf. Arnold 2016; Dick and Arnold 2017a).

Chapter 4

1. The US Congress passed IRCA in an attempt to stop undocumented immigration to the United States. It increased border enforcement along the border with Mexico, made it illegal for employers to knowingly hire undocumented workers, and granted legal permanent residency visas to the 3 million people then believed to be working in the United States without authorization (Durand and Massey 2003).

2. The US visa allocation system, established by the 1965 Hart-Celler Act, allows US legal permanent residents (green card holders) to apply for green cards for their spouses and unmarried minor children.

3. This work is particularly indebted to M. M. Bakhtin for his concept of voicing and the "chronotope" (see Blommaert 2015; Dick 2010a; Lempert and Perrino 2007; Wirtz 2014, 2016).

4. Silverstein (1993) posits three kinds of calibration: reportive, reflexive, and nomic. Reportive calibration involves marking the present event as a representation of a previous event, as when someone reports words spoken earlier that day, importing into the present the words, images of personhood, and interactional dynamics of the original interaction (see also Irvine 1996). Reflexive calibration relates events through a recognizable poetic structure, as in routinized forms of interaction like greetings—here the relationship is not to a prior exchange but to a model type. Finally, nomic calibration refers to a relationship established between a present sign event and an event understood to have occurred in an ontologically distinct realm, like the world of myth or abstract generalization.

5. The idea that stance toward personae is an ethico-moral practice builds on an intellectual tradition rooted in the work of M. M. Bakhtin. Because figures of personhood have distinct moral freighting, the stances taken on them involve a choice between different ethico-moral possibilities (cf. Hill 1995; Keane 2010, 2011).

6. Secondary indexical effects allow speakers to make talk putatively about one topic also function as talk about another topic (Dick 2011b; Hill 2008).

7. This form of calibration can be likened to what Silverstein (1993) calls "nomic calibration," which refers to a relationship established between a present sign event and an event understood to have occurred in an ontologically distinct realm.

Chapter 5

1. Translations in this chapter were compiled collaboratively with research assistants Camilo López Delgado and Bryan Mier; all mistakes are my responsibility.

2. In Jewish, Christian, and Islamic religious texts, Michael is depicted as the angel who casts Satan from heaven. Michael was never a human, so he is not officially a saint. Nevertheless, Catholics often refer to him as "Saint Michael" and numerous shrines have been set up to venerate him, including in Uriangato. There is a long tradition of his being treated as an intercessor between humans and God, like a saint (Ingham 1986).

3. Linguistic anthropologists, drawing on Bakhtin (1996), call this phenomenon "double-voicedness" or double indexicality (Hill 2001).

Conclusion

1. In a ruling on a suit filed by the American Civil Liberties Union and other organizations, the ordinance was declared unconstitutional by a federal judge in 2007.

Bibliography

Abrego, Leisy J. 2014. *Sacrificing Families: Navigating Laws, Labor, and Love across Borders*. Stanford, CA: Stanford University Press.

Abu-Lughod, Lila. 1986. *Veiled Sentiments: Honor and Poetry in a Bedouin Society*. Berkeley: University of California Press.

Agha, Asif. 2007a. *Language and Social Relations*. New York: Cambridge University Press.

———. 2007b. "Recombinant Selves in Mass Mediated Spacetime." *Language and Communication* 27: 320–335.

Ahearn, Laura. 1999. "Agency." *Journal of Linguistic Anthropology* 9: 12–14.

Alarcón, Rafael. 1992. "Nortenización: Self-Perpetuating Migration from A Mexican Town." In *U.S.-Mexico Relations: Labor Market Interdependence*, edited by Jorge Bustamante and C. Reynolds Hinojosa, 302–318. Stanford, CA: Sanford University Press.

———. 2011. "U.S. Immigration Policy and the Mobility of Mexicans (1882–2005)." *Migraciones Internacionales* 6, no. 1: 185–217.

Alim, H. Samy. 2006. *Roc the Mic Right: The Language of Hip Hop*. New York: Routledge.

Alim, H. Samy, and Geneva Smitherman. 2012. *Articulate While Black: Barack Obama, Language, and Race in the U.S*. New York: Oxford University Press.

Alonso, Ana Maria. 1994. "The Politics of Space, Time, and Substance: State Formation, Nationalism and Ethnicity." *Annual Review of Anthropology* 23: 379–405.

———. 2004. "Conforming Disconformity: 'Mestizaje,' Hybridity, and the Aesthetics of Mexican Nationalism." *Cultural Anthropology* 19, no. 40: 459–490.

Althusser, Louis. 2001. *Lenin and Philosophy and Other Essays* (1971). London: Monthly Review Press.

Amoore, Louise, and Marieke de Goede. 2008. "Introduction: Governing by Risk in the War on Terror." In *Risk and the "War on Terror,"* edited by Louise Amoore and Marieke de Goede, 5–14. New York: Routledge.

Anders, Cindy. 1993. "Mushroom Workers Walk Off Job." *Philadelphia Inquirer*, April 2.

Anderson, Benedict. 1991. *Imagined Communities: Reflections on the Origin and Spread of Nationalism* (1983). London: Verso.

Anderson, Paul. 2011. "The Piety of the Gift: Selfhood and Sociality in the Egyptian Mosque Movement." *Anthropological Theory* 11, no. 1: 1–19.

Andrijasevic, Rutvica. 2003. "The Difference Borders Make: (Il)legality, Migration and Trafficking in Italy among Eastern European Women in Prostitution." In *Uprootings/Regroundings: Questions of Home and Migration*, edited by Sara Ahmed, Claudia Castada, Anne-Marie M. Fortier, and Mimi Sheller, 251–272. New York: Berg.

Appadurai, Arjun. 1996. *Modernity at Large: Cultural Dimensions of Globalization*. Minneapolis: University of Minnesota Press.

———. 2001. "Deep Democracy: Urban Governmentality and the Horizon of Politics." *Environment & Urbanization* 13, no. 2: 23-44.

———. 2006. *Fear of Small Numbers: Essay on the Geography of Anger*. Durham, NC: Duke University Press.

Aranda Ríos, Gerardo. 2000. *Monografía de Uriangato, GTO 2000*. Uriangato, Mexico: Municipal Government of Uriangato.

Arnold, Lynnette. 2016. "Communicative Care across Borders: Language, Materiality, and Affect in Transnational Family Life." PhD dissertation, Department of Linguistics, University of California, Santa Barbara.

Asad, Talal. 2003. *Formations of the Secular: Christianity, Islam, Modernity*. Stanford, CA: Stanford University Press.

Bakhtin, M. M. 1996. *The Dialogic Imagination: Four Essays* (1935). Edited by Michael Holquist. Translated by Caryl Emerson and Michael Holquist. Austin: University of Texas Press.

Balderrama, Francisco E., and Raymond Rodríguez. 1995. *Decade of Betrayal: Mexican Repatriation in the 1930s*. Albuquerque: University of New Mexico Press.

Baquedano-López, Patricia. 2001. "Creating Social Identities through Doctrina Narratives." In *Linguistic Anthropology: A Reader*, edited by Alessandro Duranti, 343–358. Malden, MA: Blackwell.

Bartra, Roger. 1992. *The Cage of Melancholy: Identity and Metamorphosis in the Mexican Character*. Translated by Christopher J. Hall. New Brunswick, NJ: Rutgers University Press.

Basch, Linda, Nina Glick Schiller, and Cristina Szanton Blanc. 1994. *Nations Unbound: Transnational Projects, Postcolonial Predicaments, and Deterritorialized Nation-States*. Amsterdam: Gordon and Breach.

Bauman, Richard. 2004. *A World of Others' Words: Cross-Cultural Perspectives on Intertextuality*. Malden, MA: Wiley-Blackwell.

Bauman, Richard, and Charles L. Briggs. 1990. "Poetics and Performance as Critical Perspectives on Language and Social Life." *Annual Review of Anthropology* 19: 59–88.

———. 2003. *Voices of Modernity: Language Ideologies and the Politics of Inequality*. New York: Cambridge University Press.

Baurers, Sandi. 1993. "Shirtsleeve Owners Have Roots in Picking." *Philadelphia Inquirer*, April 19.

Behrman, Jere R., and Emmanuel Skoufias. 2006. "Mitigating Myths about

Policy Effectiveness: Evaluation of Mexico's Antipoverty and Human Resource Investment Program." *Annals, AAPSS [American Academy of Political and Social Science]* 606: 244–275.

Bejarano, Cynthia. 2002. "Law Super Madres de Latino America: Transforming Motherhood by Challenging Violence in Mexico, Argentina, and El Salvador." *Frontiers: A Journal of Woman Studies* 23: 126-140.

Benhabib, Seyla. 2002. "Citizens, Residents, and Aliens in a Changing World: Political Membership in the Global Era." In *The Postnational Self: Belonging and Identity*, edited by Ulf Hedetoft and Mette Hjort, 85–119. Minneapolis: University of Minnesota Press.

Benjamin, Thomas, and Marcial Ocasio-Meléndez. 1984. "Organizing the Memory of Modern Mexico: Porfirian Historiography in Perspective, 1880s–1980s." *Hispanic American Historical Review* 64, no. 2: 323–364.

Benjamin, Walter. 1968. *Illuminations*. New York: Harcourt, Brace and World.

Benveniste, Émile. 1971. "The Nature of Pronouns" (1956). In *Problems in General Linguistics*, edited by Mary Elizabeth Meek, 217–222. Miami: University of Miami Press.

Berg, Ulla. 2015. *Mobile Selves: Migration, Race, and Belonging in Peru and the U.S.* New York: New York University Press.

Biolsi, Thomas. 2005. "Imagined Geographies: Sovereignty, Indigenous Space, and American Indian Struggle." *American Ethnologist* 32, no. 2: 239–259.

Blommaert, Jan. 2010. *The Sociolinguistics of Globalization*. Cambridge, UK: Cambridge University Press.

———. 2013. *Ethnography, Superdiversity and Linguistic Landscapes: Chronicles of Complexity*. Bristol: Multilingual Matters.

———. 2015. "Chronotopes, Scales, and Complexity in the Study of Language in Society." *Annual Review of Anthropology* 44, no. 1: 105–116.

Boehm de Lameiras, Brigitte, ed. 1987. *El municipio en México*. Zamora, MX: El Colegio de Michoacán.

Bonfil Batalla, Guillermo. 1990. *México profundo: Una civilización negada*. Mexico City: Consejo Nacional para la Cultura y las Artes.

Bonilla, Yarimar. 2015. *Non-Sovereign Futures: French Caribbean Politics in the Wake of Disenchantment*. Chicago: University of Chicago Press.

Bouvard, Marguerite. 1994. *Revolutionizing Motherhood: The Mothers of the Plaza de Mayo*. Wilmington, DE: Scholarly Resources.

Brah, Avtar. 1996. *Cartographies of Diaspora: Contesting Identities*. New York: Routledge.

Brandes, Stanley. 1998. "The Day of the Dead, Halloween, and the Quest for Mexican National Identity." *Journal of American Folklore* 111, no. 442: 359–380.

Breckman, Warren. 2013. *Adventures of the Symbolic: Post-Marxism and Radical Democracy*. New York: Columbia University Press.

Briggs, Charles. 1986. *Learning How to Ask: A Sociolinguistic Appraisal of the Role of the Interview in Social Science Research*. New York: Cambridge University Press.

———. 2007. "Anthropology, Interviewing, and Communicability in Contemporary Society." *Current Anthropology* 48, no. 4: 551–580.

———. 2014. "Dear Dr. Freud." *Cultural Anthropology* 29, no. 2: 312–343.

Briggs, Charles L., and Richard Bauman. 1992. "Genre, Intertextuality, and Social Power." *Journal of Linguistic Anthropology* 2, no. 2: 131–172.

Brown, Peter. 1981. *The Cult of the Saints: Its Rise and Function in Latin Christianity.* Chicago: University of Chicago Press.

Bucholtz, Mary, and Kira Hall. 2004. "Language and Identity." In *A Companion to Linguistic Anthropology,* edited by Alessandro Duranti, 369–394. Malden, MA: Blackwell Publishing.

Bucholtz, Mary, Audrey Lopez, Allina Mojarro, Elena Skapoulli, Chris Vander Stouwe, and Shawn Warner-Garcia. 2014. "Sociolinguistic Justice in the Schools: Student Researchers as Linguistic Experts." *Language and Linguistics Compass* 8, no. 4: 144–157.

Burawoy, Michael, Joseph A. Blum, Sheba George, Zsuzsa Gille, Teresa Gowan, Lynne Haney, Maren Klawiter, Steven H. Lopéz, Seán Ó. Riain, and Millie Thayer. 2000. *Global Ethnography: Forces, Connections, and Imaginations in a Postmodern World.* Berkeley: University of California Press.

Butler, Judith. 1993. *Bodies That Matter.* New York: Routledge.

———. 1997. *Excitable Speech: A Politics of the Performative.* New York: Routledge.

Butler, Matthew. 2004. *Popular Piety and Political Identity in Mexico's Cristero Rebellion: Michoacán, 1927–29.* New York: Oxford University Press.

Cardoso, L. A. 1980. *Mexican Emigration to the United States, 1897–1931: Socioeconomic Patterns.* Tucson: University of Arizona Press.

Carr, E. Summerson. 2009. "Anticipating and Inhabiting Institutional Identities." *American Ethnologist* 36, no. 2: 317–336.

———. 2011. *Scripting Addiction: The Politics of Therapeutic Talk and American Sobriety.* Princeton, NJ: Princeton University Press.

Carr, E. Summerson, and Michael Lempert. 2016. *Scale: Discourse and Dimensions of Social Life.* Berkeley: University of California Press.

Carris, Lauren Mason. 2011. "La voz gringa: Latino Stylization of Linguistic (In)Authenticity as Social Critique." *Discourse and Society* 22, no. 4: 474–490.

Castellanos, M. Bianet. 2010. *A Return to Servitude: Maya Migration and the Tourist Trade in Cancún.* Minneapolis: University of Minnesota Press.

Castoriadis, Cornelius. 1987. *The Imaginary Institution of Society* (1975). Cambridge, MA: MIT Press.

Cavanaugh, Jillian. 2007. "Making Salami, Producing Bergamo: The Production and Transformation of Value in a Northern Italian Town." *Ethnos* 72, no. 2: 114–139.

———. 2009. *Living Memory: The Social Aesthetics of Language in a Northern Italian Town.* Malden, MA: Blackwell Publishing.

Chasteen, John Charles. 2001. *Born in Blood and Fire: A Concise History of Latin America.* New York: W. W. Norton and Company.

Chávez, Alex. 2015. "So ¿te fuiste a Dallas? (So You Went to Dallas/So You Got Screwed?): Language, Migration, and the Poetics of Transgression." *Journal of Linguistic Anthropology* 25, no. 2: 150–172.

———. 2017a. "Intimacy at Stake: Migration and the Separation of Family." *Latino Studies* 15(1): 1–23.

———. 2017b. *Sounds of Crossing: Music, Migration, and the Aural Poetics of Hua-pango Arribeño*. Durham, NC: Duke University Press.

Chavez, Leo. 2001. *Covering Immigration: Popular Images and the Politics of the Nation*. Berkeley: University of California Press.

———. 2008. *The Latino Threat: Constructing Immigrants, Citizens, and the Nation*. Stanford, CA: Stanford University Press.

Christian, William. 1989. *Person and God in a Spanish Valley* (1972). Princeton, NJ: Princeton University Press.

Clark, A. Kim. 1998. "Racial Ideologies and the Question for National Development: Debating the Agrarian Problem in Ecuador (1930–1950)." *Journal of Latin American Studies* 30: 373–393.

Clifford, James. 1994. "Diasporas." *Cultural Anthropology* 9, no. 3: 302–338.

Cody, Francis. 2013. *The Light of Knowledge: Literacy Activism and the Politics of Writing in South India*. Ithaca, NY: Cornell University Press.

Collier, Stephen, and Aihwa Ong. 2005. "Global Assemblages, Anthropological Problems." In *Global Assemblages: Technology, Politics, and Ethics as Anthropological Problems*, edited by Stephen Collier and Aihwa Ong, 3–21. Malden, MA: Blackwell Publishing.

Comaroff, John L., and Jean Comaroff. 1992. *Ethnography and the Historical Imagination*. Boulder, CO: Westview Press.

Consulta Mitofsky. 2014. "México: Confianza en instituciones." On-line: Consulta Mitofsky: The Poll Reference, February 2014: http://www.consulta.mx/index.php/estudios-e-investigaciones/mexico-opina.

Corchado, Alfredo. 2015. "Where Freedom Rang, Immigrants Cheer Pope's Message." *Dallas Morning News*, September 26.

Coupland, Nicholas, ed. 2010. *The Handbook of Language and Globalization*. Malden, MA: Blackwell.

Coutin, Susan Bibler. 2005. "Contesting Criminality: Illegal Immigration and the Spatialization of Legality." *Theoretical Criminology* 9, no. 1: 5–33.

———. 2007. *Nations of Emigrants: Shifting Boundaries of Citizenship in El Salvador and the United States*. Ithaca, NY: Cornell University Press.

Coutin, Susan Bibler, and Phyllis Pease Chock. 1995. "'Your Friend, the Illegal': Definition and Paradox in Newspaper Accounts of U.S. Immigration Reform." *Identities* 2, no. 1–2: 123–148.

Crapanzano, Vincent. 2004. *Imaginative Horizons: An Essay in Literary-Philosophical Anthropology*. Chicago: University of Chicago Press.

Das, Sonia Neela. 2011. "Rewriting the Past and Reimagining the Future: The Social Life of a Tamil Heritage Language Industry." *American Ethnologist* 38, no. 4: 774–789.

———. 2016. *Linguistic Rivalries: Tamil Migrants and Anglo-Franco Conflicts*. New York: Oxford University Press.

Das, Veena. 2006. *Life and Words: Violence and the Descent into the Ordinary*. Berkeley: University of California Press.

Daswani, Girish. 2010. "Transformation and Migration among Members of a Pentecostal Church in Ghana and London." *Journal of Religion in Africa* 40, no. 4: 424–474.

———. 2013a. "The Anthropology of Transnationalism and Diaspora." In *A*

Companion to Diaspora and Transnationalism. Edited by Ato Quayson and Girish Daswani, 29–53. Malden, MA: Blackwell Press.

———. 2013b. "On Christianity and Ethics: Rupture as Ethical Practice in Ghanaian Pentecostalism." *American Ethnologist* 40, no. 3: 467–479.

Dave, Naisarge N. 2012. *Queer Activism in India: A Story in the Anthropology of Ethics*. Durham, NC: Duke University Press.

Dávila, Arlene. 2016. *El Mall: The Spatial and Class Politics of Shopping Malls in Latin America*. Berkeley: University of California Press.

De Fina, Ana. 2003. *Identity in Narrative: A Study of Immigrant Discourse*. Philadelphia: John Benjamins Publishing Company.

De Fina, Ana, and K. King. 2011. "Language Problem or Language Conflict?: Narratives of Immigrant Women's Experiences in the US." *Discourse Studies* 13, no. 2: 163–188.

De Fina, Ana, and Sabina Perrino. 2011. "Interviews versus 'Natural Contexts': A False Dilemma." *Language and Society* 40, no. 1: 1–11.

De Genova, Nicholas. 2002. "Migrant 'Illegality' and Deportability in Everyday Life." *Annual Review of Anthropology* 31: 419–447.

———. 2005. *Working the Boundaries: Race, Space, and "Illegality" in Mexican Chicago*. Durham: Duke University Press.

De Genova, Nicholas, and Ana Y. Ramos-Zayas. 2003. "Latino Racial Formations in the United States: An Introduction." *Journal of Latin American Anthropology* 8, no. 2: 2–17.

Degnen, Chris. 2007. "Documentary: Immigration on Main Street." *NOW*. Public Broadcasting Service, October 18.

De Jesús, José. 2006. "Employees at Meatpacking Plant Allege Mistreatment." *Des Moines Register*, April 12.

Delgado-Wise, Raúl. 2004. "The Hidden Agenda of Mexico's Fox Administration." *Latin American Perspectives* 31: 146–164.

Dick, Hilary Parsons. 2006a. "El Norte No Se Hizo Para Todos/The United States Wasn't Made for Everyone: Imagined Lives, Social Different, and Discourse in Migration." PhD dissertation, Department of Anthropology, University of Pennsylvania, Philadelphia.

———. 2006b. "What Do You Do with 'I Don't Know': Processes of Elicitation in Ethnographic vs. Survey Interviews." *Qualitative Sociology* 29, no. 1: 87–102.

———. 2010a. "Imagined Lives and Modernist Chronotopes in Mexican Nonmigrant Discourse." *American Ethnologist* 37, no. 2: 275–290.

———. 2010b. "No Option But to Go: Poetic Rationalization and the Discursive Production of Mexican Migrant Identity." *Language & Communication* 30, no. 2: 90–108.

———. 2011a. "Language and Migration to the United States." *Annual Review of Anthropology* 40: 227–240.

———. 2011b. "Making Immigrants Illegal in Small Town USA." Special issue: *Journal of Linguistic Anthropology* 21, no. S1: E35–E54.

———. 2012. "Self-Deportation as Neoliberal Cautionary Tale (Language and Culture, Immigration Discussion III)." *Anthropology News*. October 2012: anthropology-news.org.

———. 2013. "Diaspora and Discourse: The Contrapuntal Lives of Mexican Nonmigrants." In *A Companion to Diaspora and Transnationalism*, edited by Ato Quayson and Girish Daswani, 412–427. Malden, MA: Wiley-Blackwell.

———. 2017. "Una Gabacha Sinvergüenza/A Shameless White-Trash Woman: Moral Mobility and Interdiscursivity in a Mexican Migrant Community." *American Anthropologist* 119, no. 2: 223-235.

Dick, Hilary Parsons, and Lynnette Arnold. 2017a. "From South to North and Back Again: Making and Blurring Boundaries in Conversations across Borders." *Language & Communication* (in press). DOI: 10.1016/j.langcom.2017.02.005.

———. 2017b. "Multisited Ethnography in Studies of Language and Migration." In *The Routledge Handbook on Language and Migration*, edited by Suresh Canagarajah, 397–412. New York: Routledge.

Dion, Michelle. 2009. "Globalization, Democracy, and Mexican Welfare, 1988–2006." *Comparative Politics* 42, no. 1: 63–82.

Divita, David. 2014. "From Paris to Pueblo and Back: (Re)Emigration and the Modernist Chronotope in Cultural Performance." *Journal of Linguistic Anthropology* 24, no. 1: 1–18.

Donham, Donald L. 1999. *Marxist Modern: An Ethnographic History of the Ethiopian Revolution*. Berkeley: University of California Press.

Dowling, Julie. 2014. *Mexican Americans and the Question of Race*. Austin: University of Texas Press

Du Bois, John. 2007. "The Stance Triangle." In *Stancetaking in Discourse: Subjectivity, Evaluation, Interaction*, edited by Robert Englebretson, 139–182. Philadelphia: John Benjamins Publishing Company.

Duchêne, Alexandre, and Monica Heller. 2011. *Language in Late Capitalism: Pride and Profit*. Hoboken, NJ: Routledge.

Durand, Jorge. 1994. *Más allá de la línea: Patrones migratorios entre México y Estados Unidos*. Mexico City: Consejo Nacional para la Cultura y las Artes.

———. 2004. *From Traitors to Heroes: 100 Years of Mexican Migration Policies*. Washington, DC: Migration Policy Institute.

Durand, Jorge, and Douglas S. Massey. 1995. *Miracles on the Border: Retablos of Mexican Migrants to the United States*. Tucson, AZ: University of Arizona Press.

———. 2003. "The Costs of Contradiction: US Border Policy 1986–2000." *Latino Studies* 1: 233–252.

Durand, Jorge, and Jorge A. Schiavon, eds. 2010. *Perspectivas migratorias: Un análisis interdisciplinario de la migración internacional*. Mexico City: Centro de Investigación y Docencia Económica.

Duranti, Alessandro. 1993. "Intentions, Self, and Responsibility: An Essay in Samoan Ethnometapragmatics." In *Responsibility and Evidence in Oral Discourse*, edited by Jane H. Hill and Judith T. Irvine, 27–47. New York: Cambridge University Press.

———. 1997. "Indexical Speech across Samoan Communities." *American Anthropologist* 99, no. 2: 342–354.

Eisenlohr, Patrick. 2004. "Temporalities of Community: Ancestral Language,

Pilgrimage, and Diasporic Belonging in Mauritius." *Journal of Linguistic Anthropology* 14, no. 1: 81–98.

———. 2006. *Little India: Diaspora, Time, and Ethnolinguistic Belonging in Hindu Mauritius.* Berkeley: University of California Press.

El Nasser, Haya, and Brad Heath. 2007. "Hispanic Growth Extends Eastward." *USA Today*, August 9.

Escalante, Fernando G. 2006. "Anything But the People." *Public Culture* 18, no. 2: 265–269.

Escobar, Arturo. 1995. *Encountering Development: The Making and Unmaking of the Third World.* Princeton, NJ: Princeton University Press.

Farr, Marcia. 2006. *Rancheros in Chicagoacán: Language and Identity in a Transnational Community.* Austin: University of Texas Press.

Fassin, Didier. 2012a. "Introduction: The Moral Question in Anthropology." In *Moral Anthropology: A Critical Reader*, edited by Didier Fassin and Samuel Lézé, 1–11. New York: Routledge.

———. 2012b. "Introduction: Toward a Critical Moral Anthropology." In *A Companion to Moral Anthropology*, edited by Didier Fassin, 1–17. Hoboken, NJ: John Wiley and Sons.

Faudree, Paja. 2013. *Singing for the Dead: The Politics of Indigenous Revival in Mexico.* Durham: Duke University Press.

Fennel, Catherine. 2015. *Last Project Standing: Civics and Sympathy in Post-Welfare Chicago.* Minneapolis: University of Minnesota Press.

Ferguson, James. 2006. "Transnational Topographies of Power." In *Accelerating Possession: Global Futures of Property and Personhood*, edited by Bill Maurer and Gabriele Schwab, 76–98. New York: Columbia University Press.

Fernández-Kelly, María Patricia 1983. *For We Are Sold, I and My People: Women and Industry in Mexico's Frontier.* Albany, NY: University of New York Press.

Ffrench-Davis, Ricardo. 2005. *Reforming Latin America's Economies: After Market Fundamentalism.* New York: Palgrave MacMillan.

Fitzgerald, David. 2009. *A Nation of Emigrants: How Mexico Manages Its Migration.* Berkeley: University of California Press.

Fleury-Steiner, Benjamin, and Jamie Longazel. 2010. "Neoliberalism, Community Development, and Anti-Immigrant Backlash in Hazleton, Pennsylvania." In *Taking Local Control: Immigration Policy Activism in U.S. Cities and States*, edited by Monica W. Varsanyi, 157–172. Stanford, CA: Stanford University Press.

Flores, Nelson, and Jonathan Rosa. 2015. "Undoing Appropriateness: Raciolinguistic Ideologies and Language Diversity in Education." *Harvard Educational Review* 85, no. 2: 149–171.

Foner, Nancy. 2000. *Ellis Island to JFK: New York's Two Great Waves of Immigration.* New Haven, CT: Yale University Press.

Foucault, Michel. 1990. *The History of Sexuality, Vol. 2: The Use of Pleasure.* New York: Vantage Books.

———. 1997. *Ethics: Subjectivity and Truth.* New York: New Press.

Franklin, Stephen. 1993. "Mushroom Farming on Skillet." *Chicago Tribune*, April 25.

Friedman, Emil. 1998. "Paradoxes of Gendered Political Opportunity in the

Venezuelan Transition to Democracy." *Latin American Research Review* 33: 87–135.

Gal, Susan. 1989. "Language and Political Economy." *Annual Review of Anthropology* 18: 345–367.

———. 2002. "A Semiotics of the Public/Private Distinction." *Differences* 13, no. 1: 77–95.

———. 2005. "Language Ideologies Compared: Metaphors of Public/Private." *Journal of Linguistic Anthropology* 15: 23–37.

———. 2016. "Scale-Making: Comparison and Perspective as Ideological Projects." In *Scale: Discourse and Dimensions of Social Life*, edited by E. Summerson Carr and Michael Lempert, 91–111. Berkeley: University of California Press.

Gal, Susan, and Kathryn A. Woolard, eds. 2001. *Languages and Publics: The Making of Authority*. Manchester, UK: St. Jerome.

Gallo, Rúben. 2006. "Introduction: The First Published Review of Octavio Paz's 'Labyrinth of Solitude.'" *Modern Language Association* 121, no. 5: 1509–1513.

Gálvez, Alyshia. 2006. "La Virgen Meets Eliot Spitzer: Articulating Labor Rights for Mexican Immigrants." *Social Text* 24, no. 3: 99–130.

———. 2007. "'I Too Was an Immigrant': An Analysis of Differing Modes of Mobilization in Two Bronx Mexican Migrant Organizations." *International Migration* 45, no. 1: 87–120.

———. 2009. *Guadalupe in New York: Devotion and the Struggle for Citizenship Rights among Mexican Immigrants*. New York: New York University Press.

Gamio, Manuel. 1922. *La población del Valle de Teotihuacán*. Mexico City: Talleres Gráficos de la Nación.

———. 1924. *The Present State of Anthropological Research in Mexico and Suggestions Regarding Its Future Developments*. Washington, DC: Pan American Union.

———. 1930. *Mexican Immigration to the United States: A Study of Human Migration and Adjustment*. Chicago: University of Chicago Press.

———. 1931. "Migration and Planning." *Survey Geographic* 66: 174–175.

———. 1964. *Forjando patria: Pro-nacionalismo* (1916). Mexico City: Editorial Porrúa.

———. 1987. *Hacía un México nuevo: Problemas sociales* (1935). Mexico City: Instituto Nacional Indigenista.

Gaonkar, Dilip Parameshwar. 2002. "Toward New Imaginaries: An Introduction." *Public Culture* 14, no. 1: 1–19.

Garcia, Angela. 2010. *The Pastoral Clinic: Addiction and Dispossession along the Rio Grande*. Berkeley: University of California Press.

———. 2014. "The Promise: On the Morality of the Marginal and the Illicit." *Ethos* 42, no. 1: 51–64.

Garcia, Victor Q. 2005. "The Mushroom Industry and the Emergence of Mexican Enclaves in Southern Chester County Pennsylvania, 1960–1990." *Journal of Latino/Latin American Studies* 1, no. 4: 67–88.

———. 2008. "Silvia Tlaseca and the Kaolin Mushroom Workers Union: Women's Leadership in the Mexican Diaspora." *Signs: Journal of Women in Culture and Society* 34, no. 1: 42–47.

García-Sánchez, Inmaculada. 2014. *Language and Muslim Immigrant Childhoods: The Politics of Belonging.* Malden, MA: Wiley Blackwell.

Geertz, Clifford. 1998. "Deep Hanging Out." *New York Review of Books.* October 22: http://www.nybooks.com/articles/1998/10/22/deep-hanging-out/.

Gilbreth, Chris, and Gerardo Otero. 2001. "Democratization in Mexico: The Zapatista Uprising and Civil Society." *Latin American Perspectives* 28, no. 4: 7–29.

Goffman, Erving. 1974. *Frame Analysis.* New York: Harper.

Goldring, Luin. 2002. "The Mexican State and Transmigrant Organizations: Negotiating the Boundaries of Membership and Participation." *Latin American Research Review* 37, no. 3: 55–99.

Gonzalez, Gilbert G. 2004. *Culture of Empire: American Writers, Mexico, and Mexican Immigrants, 1880–1930.* Austin: University of Texas Press.

Gonzalez-Barrera, Ana. 2015. *More Mexicans Leaving Than Coming to the U.S.* Washington DC: Pew Hispanic Center.

González de la Rocha, Mercedes. 1994. *The Resources of Poverty: Women and Survival in a Mexican City.* Oxford: Blackwell.

———. 2001. "From the Resources of Poverty to the Poverty of Resources: The Erosion of a Survival Model." *Latin American Perspectives* 28: 72–100.

González Navarro, Moisés. 1994. *Sociedad y cultura en el Porfiriato.* Mexico City: Consejo Nacional para la Cultura y las Artes.

———. 2001. *Cristeros y agraristas en Jalisco.* Vol. 2. Mexico City: Colegio de México.

Good, Mary K. 2012. "Modern Moralities, Moral Modernities: Ambivalence and Change Among Youth in Tonga." PhD dissertation, Department of Anthropology, University of Arizona, Tucson.

Goodson-Lawes, Julie. 1993. "Feminine Authority and Migration: The Case of One Family from Mexico." *Urban Anthropology* 22: 277–297.

Graham, Laura R. 1995. *Performing Dreams: Discourses of Immortality among the Xavante Indians of Central Brazil.* Austin: University of Texas Press.

Guarnizo, Luis Eduardo. 1998. "The Rise of Transnational Social Formations: Mexican and Dominican State Responses to Transnational Migration." *Political Power and Social Theory* 12: 45–94.

Guerra, Juan C. 1998. *Close to Home: Oral and Literate Practices in a Transnational Mexicano Community.* New York: Teacher's College Press, Columbia University.

Gumperz, John J. 1982. *Discourse Strategies.* Cambridge, UK: Cambridge University Press.

Gupta, Akil. 1992. "The Song of the Nonaligned World: Transitional Identities and the Reinscription of Space in Late Capitalism." *Cultural Anthropology* 7, no. 1: 63–79.

Gutmann, Matthew. 2007. *The Meanings of Macho: Being a Man in Mexico City* (1996). Berkeley: University of California Press.

Habermas, Jürgen. 1989. *The Structural Transformation of the Public Sphere: An Inquiry into a Category of Bourgeois Society* (1962). Translated by Thomas Burger. Cambridge, MA: MIT Press.

Haddon, Heather. 2015. "Trump Says Immigration Deportations Done in Two Years." *Wall Street Journal,* September 11.

Hagan, Jacqueline M. 2008. *Migration Miracle: Faith, Hope, and Meaning on the Undocumented Journey.* Cambridge, MA: Harvard University Press.

Hall, Kathleen D. 2002. *Lives in Translation: Sikh Youth as British Citizens.* Philadelphia: University of Pennsylvania Press.

Hallett, Miranda Cady. 2012. "'Better Than White Trash': Work Ethic, Latinidad and Whiteness in Rural Arkansas." *Latino Studies* 10: 81–106.

Hallett, Miranda Cady, and Beth Baker-Cristales. 2010. "Diasporic Suffrage: Rights Claims and State Agency." *The Salvadoran Trans-Nation: Urban Anthropology and Studies of Cultural Systems and World Economic Development* 39, no. 1/2: 175–211.

Haney-López, Ian. 2006. *White by Law: The Legal Construction of Race.* New York: New York University Press.

Hannerz, Ulf. 1980. *Exploring the City: Inquiries toward an Urban Anthropology.* New York: Columbia University Press.

———. 2003. "Being There . . . and There . . . and There!: Reflections on Multi-Site Ethnography." *Ethnography* 4, no. 2: 201–216.

Harkness, Nicholas. 2014. *Songs of Seoul: An Ethnography of Voice and Voicing in Christian South Korea.* Berkeley: University of California Press.

Harvey, David. 2006. "Neoliberalism as Creative Destruction." Geografiska Annaler: Series B. *Human Geography* 88, no. 2: 145–158.

Hastings, Adi, and Paul Manning. 2004. "Introduction: Acts of Alterity." *Language and Communication* 24: 291–311.

Heller, Monica, ed. 2007. *Bilingualism: A Social Approach.* New York, NY: Palgrave Macmillan.

Hernández-León, Rubén, and Víctor Zúñiga. 2016. "Special Issue: Contemporary Return Migration." *Mexican Studies/Estudios Mexicanos* 32, no. 2.

Herrera-Sobek, María. 1993. *Northward Bound: The Mexican Immigrant Experience in Ballad and Song.* Bloomington, IN: Indiana University Press.

Herzfeld, Michael. 1997. *Cultural Intimacy: Social Poetics in the Nation-State.* New York: Routledge.

Hewitt de Alcántara, Cynthia. 1976. *Modernizing Mexican Agriculture: Socioeconomic Implications of Technological Change, 1940–1970.* Geneva: United Nations Institute for Social Development.

Hill, Jane H. 1995. "The Voices of Don Gabriel: Responsibility and Self in a Modern Mexicano Narrative." In *The Dialogic Emergence of Culture*, edited by Dennis Tedlock and Bruce Mannheim, 97–147. Chicago: University of Illinois Press.

———. 1998. "Today There Is No Respect: Nostalgia, 'Respect,' and Oppositional Discourse in Mexicano (Nahuatl) Language Ideology." In *Language Ideologies: Practice and Theory*, edited by Bambi B. Schieffelin, Kathryn A. Woolard, and Paul V. Kroskrity, 68–86. New York: Oxford University Press.

———. 2001. "Mock Spanish, Covert Racism, and the (Leaky) Boundary between Public and Private Spheres." In *Languages and Publics: The Making of Authority*, edited by Susan Gal and Kathryn A. Woolard, 83–102. Manchester, UK: St. Jerome.

———. 2008. *The Everyday Language of White Racism.* Malden, MA: Wiley-Blackwell.

Hill, Jane H., and Judith T. Irvine. 1993. *Responsibility and Evidence in Oral Discourse*. Cambridge: Cambridge University Press.

Hirsch, Jennifer S. 2003. *A Courtship after Marriage: Sexuality and Love in Mexican Transnational Families*. Berkeley: University of California Press.

Hirschkind, Charles. 2006. *The Ethical Soundscape: Cassette Sermons and Islamic Counterpublics*. New York: Columbia University Press.

Hondagneu-Sotelo, Pierrette. 1994. *Gendered Transitions: Mexican Experiences of Immigration*. Berkeley: University of California Press.

Hopkins, Daniel J. 2010. "Politicized Places: Explaining Where and When Immigrants Provoke Local Opposition." *American Political Science Review* 104, no. 1: 40–60.

Hyams, Melissa. 2003. "Adolescent Latina Bodyspaces: Making Homegirls, Homebodies, and Homeplaces." *Antipode* 35, no. 3: 536–558.

Iglesias Prieto, Norma. 1999. *Beautiful Flowers of the Maquiladora: Life Histories of Women Workers in Tijuana* (1985). Austin: University of Texas Press, Institute of Latin American Studies.

Ingham, John. 1986. *Mary, Michael, and Lucifer: Folk Catholicism in Central Mexico*. Austin: University of Texas Press.

Inoue, Miyako, ed. 2004. "The History of Ideology and the Ideology of History." Special issue: *Journal of Linguistic Anthropology* 14, no. 1.

Irvine, Judith T. 1989. "Strategies of Status Maintenance in the Wolof Greeting." In *Explorations in the Ethnography of Speaking*, edited by Richard Bauman and Joel Sherzer, 167–191. New York: Cambridge University Press.

———. 1996. "Shadow Conversations: The Indeterminacy of Participant Roles." In *Natural Histories of Discourse*, edited by Michael Silverstein and Greg Urban, 131–159. Chicago: University of Chicago Press.

———. 2009. "Stance in a Colonial Encounter: How Mr. Taylor Lost His Footing." In *Stance: Sociolinguistic Perspectives*, edited by Alexandra Jaffe, 53–71. New York: Oxford University Press.

Irvine, Judith T., and Susan Gal. 2000. "Language Ideology and Linguistic Differentiation." In *Regimes of Language: Ideologies, Polities, and Identities*, edited by Paul V. Kroskrity, 35–84. Santa Fe, NM: School of American Research Press.

Jacquemet, Marco. 2005. "Transidiomatic Practices: Language and Power in the Age of Globalization." *Language and Communication* 25: 257–277.

Jaffe, Alexandra. 2009. "Introduction: The Sociolinguistics of Stance." In *Stance: Sociolinguistic Perspectives*, edited by Alexandra Jaffe, 3–28. New York: Oxford University Press.

Jakobson, Roman. 1971. "Shifters, Verbal Categories, and the Russian Verb." In *Selected Writings, Vol. 2: Word and Language*, 130–147. The Hague: Mouton.

———. 1995. *On Language*. Edited by Linda R. Waugh and Monique Monville-Burston. Cambridge, MA: Harvard University Press.

Jameson, Fredrick. 2001. Introduction. In *Lenin and Philosophy*, vii–xiv. New York: Monthly Review Press.

Joseph, Gilbert M., and Timothy J. Henderson. 2002. *The Mexico Reader: History, Culture, Politics*. Durham, NC: Duke University Press.

Keane, Webb. 1995. "The Spoken House: Text, Act, and Object in Eastern Indonesia." *American Ethnologist* 22, no. 1: 102–124.

————. 2003. "Semiotics and the Social Analysis of Material Things." *Language and Communication* 23, no. 3–4: 409–425.

————. 2007. *Christian Moderns: Freedom and Fetish in the Mission Encounter.* Berkeley: University of California Press.

————. 2010. "Minds, Surfaces, and Reasons in the Anthropology of Ethics." In *Ordinary Ethics: Anthropology, Language, and Action*, edited by Michael Lambek, 64–83. New York: Fordham University Press.

————. 2011. "Indexing Voice: A Morality Tale." *Journal of Linguistic Anthropology* 21, no. 2: 166–178.

————. 2014. "Affordances and Reflexivity in Ethical Life: An Ethnographic Stance." *Anthropological Theory* 14, no. 1: 3–26.

Kearney, Michael. 1986. "From Invisible Hand to Visible Feet: Anthropological Studies of Migration and Development." *Annual Review of Anthropology* 15: 331–361.

Kelly, John, and Martha Kaplan. 2001. *Represented Communities: Fiji and World Decolonization.* Chicago: University of Chicago Press.

Keohane, Robert O., and Joseph S. Nye Jr. 1987. "Power and Interdependence Revisited." *International Organization* 41, no. 4: 725–753.

Kockelman, Paul. 2007. "Agency: The Relation between Meaning, Power, and Knowledge." *Current Anthropology* 48: 375–400.

Kourí, Emilio. 2004. *A Pueblo Divided: Business, Property, and Community in Papantla, Mexico.* Stanford, CA: Stanford University Press.

Koven, Michèle. 2004. "Transnational Perspectives on Sociolinguistic Capital among Luso-Descendants in France and Portugal." *American Ethnologist* 31, no. 2: 270–290.

————. 2007. *Selves in Two Languages: Bilinguals' Verbal Enactments of Identity in French and Portuguese.* Philadelphia: John Benjamins.

————. 2013a. "Antiracist, Modern Selves and Racist, Unmodern Others: Chronotopes of Modernity in Luso Descendants' Race Talk." *Language and Communication* 33, no. 4: 544–558.

————. 2013b. "Speaking French in Portugal: An Analysis of Contested Models of Emigrant Personhood in Narratives about Return Migration and Language Use." *Journal of Sociolinguistics* 17, no. 3: 324–354.

————. 2014. "Interviewing: Practice, Ideology, Genre, and Intertextuality." *Annual Review of Anthropology* 43: 499–520.

————. 2016. "Essentialization Strategies in the Storytellings of Young Luso-Descendant Women in France: Narrative Calibration, Voicing, and Scale." *Language and Communication* 46: 19–29.

Koven, Michèle, and Isabelle Simões Marques. 2015. "Performing and Evaluating (Non)modernities of Portuguese Migrant Figures on YouTube: The Case of Antonio de Carglouch." *Language in Society* 44, no. 2: 213–242.

Kroskrity, Paul V., ed. 2000. *Regimes of Language.* Santa Fe, NM: School of American Research Press.

Kurtz, Marcus J. 2002. "Understanding the Third World Welfare State after Neoliberalism: The Politics of Social Provision in Chile and Mexico." *Comparative Politics* 34, no. 3: 293–313.

Lambek, Michael, ed. 2010. *Ordinary Ethics: Anthropology, Language, and Action.* New York: Fordham University Press.

Larkin, Brian. 2002. "Indian Films and Nigerian Lovers: Media and the Creation of Parallel Modernities." In *Readings in African Popular Fiction*, edited by Stephanie Newell, 18–36. Bloomington: Indiana University Press.

Lattanzi Shutika, Debra. 2011. *Beyond the Borderlands: Migration and Belonging in the United States and Mexico*. Berkeley: University of California Press.

Lazar, Sian. 2015. "'This Is Not a Parade, It's a Protest March': Intertextuality, Citation, and Political Action on the Streets of Bolivia and Argentina." *American Anthropologist* 117, no. 2: 242–256.

Lempert, Michael. 2012a. *Discipline and Debate: The Language of Violence in a Tibetan Buddhist Monastery*. Berkeley: University of California Press.

————. 2012b. "Interaction Rescaled: How Monastic Debate Became a Diasporic Pedagogy." *Anthropology and Education Quarterly* 43, no. 2: 138–156.

————. 2013. "No Ordinary Ethics." *Anthropological Theory* 13, no. 4: 370–393.

Lempert, Michael, and Sabina Perrino. 2007. "Entextualization and the Ends of Temporality." Special issue: *Language and Communication* 27, no. 3: 205–211.

León-Portilla, Miguel. 1962. "Manuel Gamio, 1883–1960 (Obituary)." *American Anthropologist* 64, no. 2: 356–366.

Lester, Rebecca J. 2005. *Jesus in Our Wombs: Embodying Modernity in a Mexican Convent*. Berkeley: University of California Press.

Lewis, Laura. 2000. "Blacks, Black Indians, Afromexicans: The Dynamics of Race, Nation, and Identity in a Mexican 'Moreno' Community." *American Ethnologist* 27, no. 4: 898–926.

Lindow, Megan, and Alexandria Perry. 2008. "Anti-Immigrant Terror in South Africa." *Time*, May 20.

Lomnitz, Claudio. 2001a. *Deep Mexico, Silent Mexico: An Anthropology of Nationalism*. Minneapolis: University of Minnesota Press.

————. 2001b. "Modes of Citizenship in Mexico." In *Alternative Modernities*, edited by Dilip Parameshwar Gaonkar, 299–326. Durham, NC: Duke University Press.

————. 2001c. "Nationalism as a Practical System: Benedict Anderson's Theory of Nationalism from the Vantage Point of Spanish America." In *The Other Mirror: Grand Theory through the Lens of Latin America*, edited by Miguel Angel Centeno and Fernando López-Alves, 329–359. Princeton, NJ: Princeton University Press.

————. 2008. *Death and the Idea of Mexico*. New York: Zone Books.

————. 2009. "Chronotopes of a Dystopic Nation: The Birth of 'Dependency' in Late Porfirian Mexico." In *Clio/Anthropos: Exploring the Boundaries between History and Anthropology*, edited by A. Willford and E. Tagliacozzo, 102–138. Stanford, CA: Stanford University Press.

Lomnitz-Adler, Claudio. 1992. *Exits from the Labyrinth: Culture and Ideology in the Mexican National Space*. Berkeley: University of California Press.

Lopez, Sarah Lynn. 2015. *The Remittance Landscape: Spaces of Migration in Rural Mexico and Urban USA*. Chicago: University of Chicago Press.

Lund, Joshua. 2008. "The Mestizo State: Colonization and Indianization in Liberal Mexico." *PMLA: The Journal of the Modern Languages Association* 123, no. 5: 1418–1433.

Mahmood, Saba. 2005. *Politics of Piety: The Islamic Revival and the Feminist Subject*. Princeton, NJ: Princeton University Press.

Malkki, Liisa. 1992. "National Geographic: The Rooting of Peoples and the Territorialization of National Identity among Scholars and Refugees." *Cultural Anthropology* 7, no. 1: 24–44.

———. 1995. *Purity and Exile: Violence, Memory, and National Cosmology among Hutu Refugees in Tanzania.* Chicago: University of Chicago Press.

Marcus, George. 1995. "Ethnography in/of the World System: The Emergence of Multi-Sited Ethnography." *Annual Review of Anthropology* 24: 95–117.

Marfleet, Philip. 2006. *Refugees in a Global Era.* London: Palgrave.

Martín, Desirée A. 2013. *Borderlands Saints: Secular Sanctity in Chicano/a and Mexican Culture.* New Brunswick, NJ: Rutgers University Press.

Martínez, Óscar. 2001. *Mexican Origin People in the United States: A Topical History.* Tucson: University of Arizona Press.

———. 2014. "Why the Children Fleeing Central America Will Not Stop Coming." *Nation*, August 18–24.

Massey, Douglas S. 2007. *Categorically Unequal: The American Stratification System.* New York: Russell Sage Foundation.

Massey, Douglas S., Rafael Alarcón, Jorge Durand, and Humberto González. 1987. *Return to Aztlán: The Social Process of International Migration from Western Mexico.* Berkeley: University of California Press.

Massey, Douglas S., Joaquin Arango, Graeme Hugo, Ali Kouaouci, Adela Pellegrino, and J. Edward Taylor. 2005. *Worlds in Motion: Understanding International Migration at the End of the Millennium.* New York: Oxford University Press.

Massey, Douglas S., and M. R. Sánchez. 2010. *Brokered Boundaries: Creating Immigrant Identity in Anti-Immigrant Times.* New York, NY: Russell Sage Foundation.

Mehan, Hugh. 1997. "The Discourse of the Illegal Immigration Debate: A Case Study in the Politics of Representation." *Discourse and Society* 8, no. 2: 249–270.

Mendoza-Denton, Norma. 1999. "Fighting Words: Latina Girls, Gangs, and Language Attitudes." In *Speaking Chicana: Voice, Power, and Identity*, edited by D. Letticia Galindo and María Dolores Gonzales, 39–56. Tucson: University of Arizona Press.

———. 2008. *Homegirls: Language and Cultural Practice among Latina Youth Gangs.* Malden, MA: Blackwell.

Messing, Jacqueline. 2002. "Fractal Recursivity in Ideologies of Language, Identity and Modernity in Tlaxcala, Mexico." *Texas Linguistic Forum* 45: 95–105.

———. 2007. "Multiple Ideologies and Competing Discourses: Language Shift in Tlaxcala, Mexico." *Language in Society* 36: 555–577.

Miller, Daniel. 1994. *Modernity, an Ethnographic Approach: Dualism and Mass Consumption in Trinidad.* Providence, RI: Berg.

Mishler, Elliot G. 1986. *Research Interviewing: Context and Narrative.* Cambridge, MA: Harvard University Press.

Mittermaier, Amira. 2011. *Dreams That Matter: Egyptian Landscapes of the Imagination.* Berkeley: University of California Press.

Molyneux, Maxine. 2006. "Mothers at the Service of the New Poverty Agenda: Progresa/Oportunidades, Mexico's Conditional Transfer Program." *Social Policy and Administration* 40, no. 4: 425–449.

Moodie, Ellen. 2010. *El Salvador in the Aftermath of Peace: Crime, Uncertainty, and the Transition to Democracy.* Philadelphia: University of Pennsylvania Press.

Moreno Figueroa, Mónica. 2010. "Distributed Intensities: Whiteness, Mestizaje and the Logics of Mexican Racism." *Ethnicities* 10: 387–401.

———. 2013. "Displaced Looks: The Lived Experience of Beauty and Racism in Mexico." *Feminist Theory* 14, no. 2: 137–151.

Moreno Figueroa, Mónica, and Emiko Saldívar Tanaka. 2015. "'We Are Not Racists, We Are Mexicans': Privilege, Nationalism and Post-Race Ideology in Mexico." *Critical Sociology* 42, nos. 4–5: 515–533.

Muehlebach, Andrea. 2012. *The Moral Neoliberal: Welfare and Citizenship in Italy.* Chicago: University of Chicago Press.

Nájera-Ramírez, O. 2002. "Haciendo Patria: The Charreada and the Formation of a Mexican Transnational Identity." In *Transnational Latino/a Communities: Politics, Processes, and Cultures,* edited by Carlos G. Vélez-Ibáñez and Anna Sampaio, 167–180. New York: Rowman and Littlefield Publishers.

Napolitano, Valentina. 2002. *Migration, Mujercitas, and Medicine Men: Living in Urban Mexico.* Berkeley: University of California Press.

———. 2016. *Migrant Hearts and the Atlantic Return: Transnationalism and the Roman Catholic Church.* New York: Fordham University Press.

Ngai, Mae M. 2004. *Impossible Subjects: Illegal Aliens and the Making of Modern America.* Princeton, NJ: Princeton University Press.

Olcott, Jocelyn. 2005. *Revolutionary Women in Postrevolutionary Mexico.* Durham, NC: Duke University Press.

Ong, Aiwa. 1999. *Flexible Citizenship: The Cultural Logics of Transnationality.* Durham: Duke University Press.

———. 2000. "The Global Situation." *Cultural Anthropology* 15, no. 3: 327–360.

Orellana, MF. 2009. *Translating Childhoods: Immigrant Youth, Language, and Culture.* New Brunswick, NJ: Rutgers University Press.

O'Toole, Gavin. 2003. "A New Nationalism for a New Era: The Political Ideology of Mexican Neoliberalism." *Bulletin of Latin American Research* 22, no. 3: 269–290.

OXFAM. 2016. "OXFAM Briefing Paper (210)." Oxford, UK: OXFAM International.

Pader, Ellen. 1993. "Spatiality and Social Change: Domestic Space in Mexico and the United States." *American Ethnologist* 20, no. 1: 114–137.

Paley, Julia. 2001. *Marketing Democracy: Power and Social Movements in Post-Dictatorship Chile.* Berkeley: University of California Press.

Passel, Jeffrey S., and D'Vera Cohn. 2009. "A Portrait of Unauthorized Immigrants in the United States." Washington, DC: Pew Hispanic Center.

Pastor, Manuel, Jr. 1989. "Latin America, the Debt Crisis, and the International Monetary Fund." *Latin American Perspectives* 16, no. 1: 79–110.

Patel, Khadija. 2015. "Anti-Immigrant Violence Spreads in South Africa: Arrests Made in Gauteng Province Following Overnight Street Battles in Downtown Johannesburg." April: http://247newsportalz.blogspot.com/2015/04/anti-immigrant-violence-spreads-in.html.

Paz, Alejandro. 2009. "The Circulation of Chisme and Rumor: Gossip, Eviden-

tiality, and Authority in the Perspective of Latino Labor Migrants in Israel."
Journal of Linguistic Anthropology 19, no. 1: 117–143.

———. 2015. "Stranger Sociality in the Home: Register of the Israeli Street: In
Latino Domestic Interaction." In *Registers of Communication*, edited by Asif
Agha and Mister Frog, 150–164. Helsinki: Finnish Literature Society.

———. 2016. "Speaking like a Citizen: Public Opinion and the Biopolitics of
Recognizing Noncitizen Children in Israel." *Language and Communication*
48: 18–27.

Paz, Octavio. 1994. *The Labyrinth of Solitude* (1950). New York: Grove Press.

Peña, Elaine A. 2011. *Performing Piety: Making Space Sacred with the Virgin of
Guadalupe*. Berkeley: University of California Press.

Perrino, Sabina. 2011. "Chronotopes of Story and Storytelling Event in Interviews." *Language in Society* 40, no. 1: 91–103.

———. 2015. "Performing Extracomunitari: Mocking Migrants in Veneto Barzellette." *Language in Society* 44: 141–160.

Pew Research Center. 2014. "Mexican President Peña Nieto's Ratings Slip with
Economy: Mexico Survey Methods." New York: Pew Research Center. August 26: http://www.pewglobal.org/2014/08/26/mexican-president-pena
-nietos-ratings-slip-with-economic-reform/.

Phillips, Adam. 2013. *Missing Out: In Praise of the Unlived Life*. New York:
Picador.

Phillips, Lynn. 1997. *The Third Wave of Modernization in Latin America: Cultural
Perspective on Neo-Liberalism*. New York: Rowman and Littlefield.

Piore, Michael J. 1979. *Birds of Passage: Migrant Labor and Industrial Societies*.
New York: Cambridge University Press.

Pitt-Rivers, Julian. 2011. "The Place of Grace in Anthropology" (1992). *HAU:
Journal of Ethnographic Theory* 1, no. 1: 423–450.

Portes, Alejandro, and Kenneth Wilson. 1980. "Immigrant Enclaves: An
Analysis of the Labor Market Experiences of Cubans in Miami." *American
Journal of Sociology* 86, no. 2: 295–319.

Potter, Jonathan. 2002. "Two Kinds of Natural." *Discourse Studies* 4, no. 4:
539–542.

Quayson, Ato, and Girish Daswani. 2013. "Introduction—Diaspora and Transnationalism: Scapes, Scales, and Scopes." In *A Companion to Diaspora and
Transnationalism*, edited by Ato Quayson and Girish Daswani, 1–26. Malden, MA: Blackwell Press.

Ramos, Samuel. 1934. *El perfil del hombre y la cultura en México*. Mexico City:
Universidad Nacional Autónoma de México.

Reichert, J. S. 1982. "Social Stratification in a Mexican Sending Community:
The Effect of Migration to the United States." *Social Problems* 29: 422–433.

Reyes, Angela, and Adrienne Lo. 2009. *Beyond Yellow English: Toward a Linguistic Anthropology of Asian Pacific America*. New York: Oxford University Press.

Reynolds, Jennifer F., and Marjorie Faulstich Orellana. 2009. "New Immigrant
Youth Interpreting in White Public Space." *American Anthropologist* 111,
no. 2: 211–223.

Riggan, Jennifer. 2016. *The Struggling State: Nationalism, Mass Militarization,
and the Education of Eritrea*. Philadelphia: Temple University Press.

Riley, Kate, and Jillian Cavanaugh. 2017. "Tasty Talk, Expressive Food: Introduction to the Semiotics of Food-and-Language." *Semiotic Review* 5: online at https://www.semioticreview.com/ojs/index.php/sr/article/view/1.

Robben, Antonius C. G. M. 1995. "The Politics of Truth and Emotion among Victims and Perpetrators of Violence." In *Fieldwork under Fire: Contemporary Studies of Violence and Survival*, edited by Carolyn Nordstrom and Antonius C. G. M. Robben, 81–104. Berkeley: University of California Press.

———. 1996. "Ethnographic Seduction, Transference, and Resistance in Dialogues about Terror and Violence in Argentina." *Ethos* 24, no 1: 71–106.

Robbins, Joel. 2007. "Between Reproduction and Freedom: Morality, Value, and Radical Cultural Change." *Ethnos* 72, no. 3: 293–314.

Rodó, José Enrique, and Belén Castro Morales. 2000. *Ariel* (1900). Madrid: Cátedra.

Rojas Gutiérrez, Carlos. 1992. "Solidaridad, suma de voluntades." *Examen* 3, no. 36: 9–13.

Rosa, Jonathan. 2014. "Learning Ethnolinguistic Borders: Language and Diaspora in the Socialization of U.S. Latinas/os." In *Diaspora Studies in Education: Toward a Framework for Understanding the Experiences of Transnational Communities*, edited by Rosalie Rolón-Dow and Jason G. Irizarry, 39–60. New York: Peter Lang Publishing.

———. 2016. "Racializing Language, Regimenting Latinas/os: Chronotope, Social Tense, and American Raciolinguistic Futures." *Language and Communication* 46: 106–117.

Rosaldo, Michelle Zimbalist. 1980. *Knowledge and Passion: Ilongot Notions of Self and Social Life*. New York: Cambridge University Press.

Roth-Gordon, Jennifer. 2017. *Race and the Brazilian Body: Blackness, Whiteness, and Everyday Language in Rio de Janeiro*. Oakland: University of California Press.

Rouse, Roger. 1991. "Mexican Migration and the Social Space of Postmodernism." *Diaspora* 1, no. 1: 8–23.

———. 1992. "Making Sense of Settlement: Class Transformation, Cultural Struggle and Transnationalism among Mexican Migrants in the United States." *New York Academy of Sciences* 645: 25–52.

———. 1995. "Questions of Identity." *Critique of Anthropology* 15: 351–380.

Rus, Jan. 1994. "The 'Comunidad Revolucionaria Institucional': The Subversion of Native Government in Highland Chiapas, 1936–1968." In *Everyday Forms of State Formation: Revolution and Negotiation of Rule in Modern Mexico*, edited by Gilbert M. Joseph and Daniel Nugent, 265–300. Durham, NC: Duke University Press.

Salazar, Noel B. 2010. *Envisioning Eden: Mobilizing Imaginaries in Tourism and Beyond*. Oxford: Berghahn.

———. 2011. "The Power of Imagination in Transnational Mobilities." *Identities: Global Studies in Culture and Power* 18(6): 576–598.

Sánchez, George J. 1993. *Becoming Mexican American: Ethnicity, Culture, and Identity in Chicago Los Angeles, 1900–1945*. New York: Oxford University Press.

Santa Ana, Otto. 2002. *Brown Tide Rising: Metaphors of Latinos in Contemporary American Discourse*. Austin: University of Texas Press.

Sassen, Saskia. 1988. *The Mobility of Labor and Capital: A Study in International Investment and Labor Flow*. Cambridge: Cambridge University Press.

Schmid, Carol. 2001. *The Politics of Language: Conflict, Identity, and Cultural Pluralism in Comparative Perspective*. New York: Oxford University Press.

Schmidt, Henry C. 1976. "Antecedents to Samuel Ramos: Mexicanist Thought in the 1920s." *Journal of Interamerican Studies and World Affairs* 18, no. 2: 179–202.

Schmidt Camacho, Alicia. 2006. "Migrant Melancholia: Emergent Discourses of Mexican Traffic in Transnational Space." *South Atlantic Quarterly* 105, no. 4: 831–861.

———. 2008. *Migrant Imaginaries: Latino Cultural Politics in the U.S.-Mexico Borderlands*. New York: New York University Press.

Shankar, Shalini. 2008. "Speaking Like a Model Minority: 'FOB' Styles, Gender, and Racial Meanings among Desi Teens in Silicon Valley." *Journal of Linguistic Anthropology* 18, no. 2: 268–289.

———. 2015. *Advertising Diversity: Ad Agencies and the Creation of Asian American Consumers*. Durham, NC: Duke University Press.

Shankar, Shalini, and Jillian Cavanaugh. 2012. "Language and Materiality in Global Capitalism." *Annual Review of Anthropology* 41: 355–369.

Shoaps, Robin Ann. 2007. "'Moral Irony': Modal Particles, Moral Persons and Indirect Stance-Taking in Sakapultek Discourse." *Pragmatics* 17, no. 2: 297–335.

———. 2009. "Ritual and (Im)moral Voices: Locating the Testament of Judas in Sakapultek Communicative Ecology." *American Ethnologist* 36, no. 3: 459–477.

Sidorkina, Maria A. 2015. "'Shining a Light' on Us and Them: Public-Making in Ordinary Russia." *Ab Imperio* 2: 209–251.

Silverstein, Michael. 1976. "Shifters, Linguistic Categories, and Cultural Description." In *Meaning in Anthropology*, edited by Keith H. Basso and Henry A. Selby, 11–55. Albuquerque: University of New Mexico Press.

———. 1979. "Language Structure and Linguistic Ideology." In *The Elements: A Parasession of Linguistic Units and Levels*, edited by Paul R. Clyne, William F. Hanks, and Carol L. Hofbauer, 193–247. Chicago: Chicago Linguistic Society.

———. 1992. "The Indeterminacy of Contextualization: When Is Enough Enough?" In *The Contextualization of Language*, edited by Peter Auer and Aldo Di Luzio, 55–76. Philadelphia: J. Benjamins Publishing Company.

———. 1993. "Metapragmatic Discourse and Metapragmatic Function." In *Reflexive Language: Reported Speech and Metapragmatics*, edited by John A. Lucy, 33–58. Cambridge: Cambridge University Press.

———. 2003. "Indexical Order and the Dialectics of Sociolinguistic Life." *Language and Communication* 23: 193–229.

———. 2005. "Axes of Evals: Token versus Type Interdiscursivity." *Journal of Linguistic Anthropology* 15, no. 1: 6–22.

Silverstein, Michael, and Greg Urban. 1996. "The Natural Histories of Discourse." In *Natural Histories of Discourse*, edited by Michael Silverstein and Greg Urban, 1–17. Chicago: University of Chicago Press.

Silverstein, Paul A. 2000. "Sporting Faith: Islam, Soccer, and the French Nation-State." *Social Text* 65/18, no. 4: 25–53.

———. 2004. *Algeria in France: Transpolitics, Race, and Nation*. Bloomington: Indiana University Press.

Simpson, Audra. 2014. *Mohawk Interruptus: Political Life across the Borders of Settler States*. Durham, NC: Duke University Press.

Smith, Robert Courtney. 2006. *Mexican New York: Transnational Lives of New Immigrants*. Berkeley: University of California Press.

Stack, Trevor. 2012a. "Beyond the State?: Civil Sociality and Other Notions of Citizenship." *Citizenship Studies* 16, no. 7: 871–885.

———. 2012b. *Knowing History in Mexico: An Ethnography of Citizenship*. Albuquerque: University of New Mexico Press.

Stark, Oded and J. Edward Taylor. 1991. "Migration Incentives, Migration Types: The Role of Relative Deprivation." *Economic Journal* 101: 1163–1178.

Stepan, Nancy Leys. 1991. *"The Hour of Eugenics": Race, Gender, and Nation in Latin America*. Ithaca, NY: Cornell University Press.

Stephen, Lynn. 1995. "Women's Rights Are Human Rights: The Merging of Feminine and Feminist Interests among El Salvador's Mothers of the Disappeared (CO-MADRE)." *American Ethnologist* 22: 807–827.

———. 2004. "The Gaze of Surveillance in the Lives of Mexican Immigrant Workers." *Development* 47, no. 1: 97–102.

———. 2007. *Transborder Lives: Indigenous Oaxacans in Mexico, California, and Oregon*. Durham, NC: Duke University Press.

———. 2013. *We Are the Face of Oaxaca: Testimony and Social Movements*. Durham, NC: Duke University Press.

Sullivan, Michael. 2015. "Australia Uses Tough Measures to Keep Migrants Out." National Public Radio, September 7: http://www.npr.org/2015/09/07/438228413/australia-uses-tough-measures-to-keep-migrants-out.

Taylor, Charles. 2004. *Modern Social Imaginaries*. Durham, NC: Duke University Press.

Taylor, William. 1987. "The Virgin of Guadalupe in New Spain: An Inquiry into the Social History of Marian Devotion." *American Ethnologist* 14, no. 1: 9–33.

Teichman, Judith A. 2009. "Competing Visions of Democracy and Development in the Era of Neoliberalism in Mexico and Chile." *International Political Science Review* 30, no. 1: 67–87.

Tenorio-Trillo, Mauricio. 1993. "Review of *The Cage of Melancholy: Identity and Metamorphosis in the Mexican Character*." *Cultural Studies* 7, no. 3: 519–521.

———. 1996. *Mexico at the World's Fairs: Crafting a Modern Nation*. Berkeley: University of California Press.

Thompson, Heather Ann. 2010. "Why Mass Incarceration Matters: Rethinking Crisis, Decline, and Transformation in Postwar American History." *Journal of American History* 97, no. 3: 703–758.

Torres Pares, Javier. 1990. *La revolución sin frontera: El Partido Liberal Mexicano y las relaciones entre el movimiento obrero de México y el de Estados Unidos*. Mexico City: UNAM Ediciones Hispánicas.

Trejo, Guillermo, and Claudio Jones. 1998. "Political Dilemmas of Welfare Reform: Poverty and Inequality in Mexico." In *Mexico under Zedillo*, edited by Susan Kaufman Purcell and Luis Rubio, 67–100. London: Lynne Rienner.

Trouillot, Michel-Rolph. 1997. *Silencing the Past: Power and the Production of History*. Boston: Beacon Press.

United Nations-Habitat (UN-Habitat). 2011. *Housing Finance Mechanisms in Mexico*. Nairobi, Kenya: UN-Habitat: United Nations Human Settlements Programme.

United Nations High Commission on Refugees (UNHCR). 2014. *World at War: Global Trends, Forced Displacement in 2014*. New York: United Nations High Commission on Refugees.

Urban, Greg. 1989. "The 'I' of Discourse." In *Semiotics, Self and Society*, edited by Benjamin Lee and Greg Urban, 27–52. New York: Mouton de Gruyter.

———. 1991. *A Discourse-Centered Approach to Culture: Native South American Myths and Rituals*. Austin: University of Texas Press.

———. 1996. *Metaphysical Community: The Interplay of the Sense and the Intellect*. Austin: University of Texas Press.

———. 2001. *Metaculture: How Culture Moves through the World*. Minneapolis: University of Minnesota Press.

Urciuoli, Bonnie. 1993. "Representing Class: Who Decides?" *Anthropology Quarterly* 66, no. 4: 203–210.

———. 1996. *Exposing Prejudice: Puerto Rican Experiences of Language, Race, and Class*. Boulder, CO: Westview Press.

Urry, John. 2007. *Mobilities*. Malden, MA: Polity Press.

Van Hook, Jennifer, and Frank D. Bean. 2009. "Explaining Mexican-Immigrant Welfare Behaviors: The Importance of Employment-Related Cultural Repertoires." *American Sociology Review* 74, no. 3: 423–444.

Varsanyi, Monica W. 2010. "Immigration Policy Activism in U.S. States and Cities: Interdisciplinary Perspectives." In *Taking Local Control: Immigration Policy Activism in U.S. Cities and States*, edited by Monica W. Varsanyi, 1–30. Stanford, CA: Stanford University Press.

Vasconcelos, José. 1926. "The Latin-American Basis of Mexican Civilization." In *Aspects of Mexican Civilization*, edited by José Vasconcelos and Manuel Gamio, 3–102. Chicago: University of Chicago Press.

———. 1997. *The Cosmic Race/La Raza Cósmica* (1925). Translated by Didier T. Jaén. Race in the Americas. Baltimore, MD: Johns Hopkins University Press.

Vasconcelos, José, and Manuel Gamio, eds. 1926. *Aspects of Mexican Civilization*. Chicago: University of Chicago Press.

Vaughan, Mary K., and Stephen E. Lewis, eds. 2006. *The Eagle and the Virgin: Nation and Cultural Revolution in Mexico*. Durham, NC: Duke University Press.

Wacquant, Loïc. 2009. *Punishing the Poor: The Neoliberal Government of Social Insecurity*. Durham, NC: Duke University Press.

Walsh, Casey. 2004. "Eugenic Acculturation: Manuel Gamio, Migration Studies, and the Anthropology of Development in Mexico, 1910–1940." *Latin American Perspectives* 31, no. 5: 118–145.

———. 2008. *Building the Borderlands: A Transnational History of Irrigated Cotton on the Mexico-Texas Border.* College Station: Texas A&M University Press.

Warner, Michael. 2002. "Publics and Counterpublics." *Public Culture* 14, no. 1: 49–90.

Warren, Kay B. 2001. "Telling Truths: Taking David Stoll and the Rigoberta Menchú Exposé Seriously." In *The Rigoberta Menchú Controversy,* edited by Arturo Arias, 198–218. Minneapolis: University of Minnesota Press.

Werbner, Pnina. 2002. *Imagined Diasporas among Manchester Muslims.* Oxford: James Currey/Santa Fe, CA: School of American Research.

———. 2013. "Migration and Transnational Studies: Between Simultaneity and Rupture." In *A Companion to Diaspora and Transnationalism,* edited by Ato Quayson and Girish Daswani, 106–124. Malden, MA: Blackwell Press.

Wilce, James. 1998. *Eloquence in Trouble: The Poetics and Politics of Complaint in Rural Bangladesh.* New York: Oxford University Press.

Williams, Brackette F. 1989. "A CLASS ACT: Anthropology and the Race to Nation across Ethnic Terrain." *Annual Review of Anthropology* 18: 401–444.

Williams, Raymond. 1973. *The Country and the City.* London: Chatto and Windus.

Willis, Paul. 1981. *Learning to Labor: How Working Class Kids Get Working Class Jobs.* New York: Columbia University Press.

Wimmer, Andreas, and Nina Glick-Schiller. 2002. "Methodological Nationalism and Beyond: Nation-State Building, Migration and the Social Sciences." *Global Networks* 2, no. 3: 301–334.

Winegar, Jessica. 2006. *Creative Reckonings: The Politics of Art and Culture in Contemporary Egypt.* Stanford, CA: Stanford University Press.

Wirtz, Kristina. 2007. *Ritual, Discourse, and Community in Cuban Santería: Speaking a Sacred World.* Gainesville: University of Florida Press.

———. 2013. "A 'Brutology of Bozal': Tracing a Discourse Genealogy from Nineteenth-Century Blackface Theater to Twenty-First-Century Spirit Possession in Cuba." *Comparative Studies in Society and History* 55, no. 4: 800–833.

———. 2014. *Performing Afro-Cuba: Image, Voice, Spectacle in the Making of Race and History.* Chicago: University of Chicago Press.

———. 2016. "The Living, the Dead, and the Immanent: Dialogue across Chronotopes." *HAU: Journal of Ethnographic Theory* 6, no. 1: 343–369.

Woolard, Kathryn. 1990. "Voting Rights, Liberal Voters, and the Official English Movement: An Analysis of Campaign Rhetoric in San Francisco's Proposition 'O.'" In *Perspectives on Official English: The Campaign for English as the Official Language of the USA,* edited by Karen L. Adams and Daniel T. Brink, 125–138. New York: Mouton de Gruyter.

———. 2004. "Is the Past a Foreign Country? Time, Language Origins, and the Nation in Early Modern Spain." *Journal of Linguistic Anthropology* 14, no. 1: 57–80.

———. 2016. *Singular and Plural: Ideologies of Linguistic Authority in 21st Century Catalonia.* Oxford, UK: Oxford University Press.

Woolard, Kathryn, and Bambi B. Schieffelin. 1994. "Language Ideology." *Annual Review of Anthropology* 23: 55–82.

Wortham, Stanton, Elaine Allard, Kathy Lee, and Katherine Mortimer. 2011. "Racialization in Payday Mugging Narratives." *Journal of Linguistic Anthropology* 21: E56–E75.

Wortham, Stanton, Enrique G. Murillo, and Edmund T. Hamann. 2002. *Education in the New Latino Diaspora: Policy and the Politics of Identity*. Westport, CT: Ablex.

Wortham, Stanton, and Angela Reyes. 2015. *Discourse Analysis beyond the Speech Event*. New York: Routledge.

Wright, Melissa W. 2006. *Disposable Women and Other Myths of Global Capitalism*. New York: Routledge.

Yeh, Rihan. 2012. "Two Publics in a Mexican Border City." *Cultural Anthropology* 27, no. 4: 713–735.

———. 2017. "Visas, Jokes, and Contraband: Citizenship and Sovereignty at the Mexico–U.S. Border." *Comparative Studies in Society and History* 59, no. 1: 154–182.

Young, Robert J. C. 1995. *Colonial Desire: Hybridity in Theory, Culture and Race*. New York: Routledge.

Zentella, Ana Cecilia. 1990. "Returned Migration, Language, and Identity: Puerto Rican Bilinguals in Dos Worlds/Two Mundos." *International Journal of Sociology of Language* 84: 81–100.

Zigon, Jarrett. 2007. "Moral Breakdown and the Ethical Demand: A Theoretical Framework for an Anthropology of Moralities." *Anthropological Theory* 7, no. 2: 131–150.

———. 2008. *Morality: An Anthropological Perspective*. New York: Berg.

———. 2011. *"HIV Is God's Blessing": Rehabilitating Morality in Neoliberal Russia*. Berkeley: University of California Press.

Index

absentee ballots, 69–70
acts of appeal, 191, 192
Afro-Mexicans, 55–56, 66
agency: of divine figures, 194; and ethico-moral life, 229; and interpellation, 83; and *voluntad*, 86–87, 89
alienation, 118, 133, 142–143, 190. *See also* liminality
Althusser, Louis, 44, 241n2
Anderson, Benedict, 12, 46–47, 58, 196. *See also* nationalism
anthropology: and discourse, 22; and ethico-moral work, 19, 182; and Gamio's work, 64, 241n6; of imaginaries, 239n5; of nationalism, 12. *See also* cultural anthropology; linguistic anthropology
anticipatory interpellation: and acts of appeal, 191; and "bragging migrant," 111; and performance of suffering, 217; and personhood, 84, 88; and self-presentation, 93, 104; and voicing the *mujer sufrida*, 215
Archangel Michael, 194, 196, 201, 244n2
Ariel (Rodó 1900), 53
"Atención a migrantes" (Attention for Migrants), 126, 137
Austin, John L., 241n2

authority: and accounts of migration, 34–35; and "bragging migrant," 107–108; constitution of, 80; and divine figures, 198; and ethico-moral life, 229; and fatherhood, 128; and gender, 36, 102–103, 105, 152, 176; and generalizing speech, 201; of immigration lawyers, 96; and interviews, 82–83, 99–101, 106, 153; and masculinity, 177; and media citation, 97–99, 111–112; and Mexican state, 32; and migrant enclaves, 241–242n6; and migration discourse, 21, 63, 114; and motherhood, 204; performance of, 202; and social indexicality, 110; and state-endorsed accounts, 81; and storytelling, 113; and survey protocol, 94, 216; and traditional Mexican womanhood, 170
autonomous personhood, 86, 87, 88–89

Bajío (central Mexican region), 194, 197
Bakhtin, M. M., 208, 243n3, 243n5, 244n3
belonging: access to, 6; and diaspora at home, 119–120, 242n1; double-bind of, 52, 60, 118, 159, 190, 237;

imaginaries of moral mobility (*cont.*)
guage practices, 191–192, 228; and
mestizaje, 53–54; and migrants' national belonging, 70; and migration discourse, 32; and modernist
contrasts, 198; and national belonging, 144; and neoliberalism,
74; and the political, 22; and Porfiriato, 47–50, 59; in postrevolutionary era, 51–52; and progress, 119;
and *promesas*, 203; reformulation
of, 75; and religiosity, 197; and resource distribution, 18–19; and
tradition, 132, 157–158; and welfare programs, 124; and working-
class people, 21, 35–36, 182, 191.
See also imaginaries
Immaculate Conception, 194
immigrant rights movement, 224
immigration laws and policy: of Mexico, 49–50; and representation,
96–97; and scholar-politicians,
94–95; and seasonal migration,
157; and self-deportation, 236; and
state-led transnationalism, 70; of
United States, 66, 243ch4n1. *See
also* Bracero Accord; Illegal Immigration Relief Act; Immigration
Reform and Control Act
Immigration Reform and Control
Act (1986), 68, 147–148, 155, 156,
243ch4n1. *See also* immigration
laws and policy
indexical orders, 16, 17, 243n5
indigeneity, 54–55, 56
Indigenous groups: and *ejidos*, 242n5;
and imaginaries of moral mobility, 41; and mestizo imaginaries,
66; and postrevolutionary imaginaries, 51, 54–55; and Spanish racial project, 50; state construction
of, 9; and testimony, 207
industrialization, 24–25, 28, 121
informal economy, 124–125
interdiscursive webs, 43, 75–76, 228
interdiscursivity: defined, 43; and interpellation, 44; and national be-

longing, 61; and neoliberalism, 72;
and postrevolutionary imaginaries, 66
International Monetary Fund (IMF),
70
interpellation: and belonging, 8; and
corporatist governance, 59; and
counterpoint lives, 6; and cultural
differences, 241n2; and ethico-
moral work, 22; and family, 91–
92; and gracious personhood, 83;
and imaginaries of moral mobility, 48, 228–229; and imaginaries of national belonging, 14; and
interdiscursivity, 44; and intersubjectivity, 182; into Mexicanidad, 146–147; and Mexican
national identity, 17–18; and migration discourse, 34–36; and migration histories, 181; and national
belonging, 66–67; and pilgrimage,
196; and postrevolutionary imaginaries, 51; and progress versus tradition, 42; and *promesas*, 201; and
pronoun use, 151–152; and religiosity, 203; and religious nationalism, 189; and sidewalk sociality,
92–94; and state-endorsed imaginaries, 118, 149; Uriangatense
practices of, 10; and variegation of
national belonging, 119; and voicing the *mujer sufrida*, 216–217
intersubjectivity, 177, 180–181, 182
interviews: and authoritative discourse, 99–100; and discourse circulation, 82–83; and ethnographic
research, 103–104, 105–106; and
interpellation, 34–35; and MMP
survey protocol, 94, 95, 101, 102–
103, 153; and resource distribution, 216

Jakobson, Roman, 191
John Paul II (pope), 1–2, 11, 230
Juan Diego (saint), 1, 2

Kobach, Kris, 236

Francis, 231; and PTSD, 178; and social differentiation, 8; and state-endorsed imaginaries, 21; and temporary labor, 10; and US government assistance, 223; US settlement of, 163. *See also* Mexico-US migration

migration: authoritative accounts of, 96–99; and Catholic cult of the saints, 196; and class mobility, 30; criminalization of, 233, 234; disparate accounts of, 209; and egalitarian imaginaries, 62; and ethico-moral character, 127; and global economic processes, 237; and home ownership, 115–116; and imaginaries of moral mobility, 63, 230; and living standards, 141; and nonmigrants, 153–154; and progress, 144; as release valve, 65–66; and sending communities, 7; as social process, 241n4; and suffering, 163; and *una vida bonita*, 128; from Uriangato, 24; and vice, 201–203; of young people, 175–176. *See also* Mexico-US migration

migration discourse: authority of, 80, 81–82, 153; and "bragging migrant," 107–110, 111, 112–114; and chronotopic frameworks, 227; and class status, 31–32; contradictions within, 66; and contrast between Mexico and United States, 33–34; defined, 10–11; and enclaving, 31; and ethico-moral character, 161; and gender, 155, 165; and generalizing speech, 167–169, 201, 220–221; and getting ahead, 135, 143; and home ownership, 129–130; and imaginaries of moral mobility, 22–23; and indexical function of language, 191; and industrialization, 28; and interpellation, 18; and language practices, 16; and media, 99; and Mexicanidad, 15, 18, 21; and Mexican politics, 69; in migrant enclaves, 148–149; and

modernity versus tradition, 121; and *mujer sufrida*, 219–220; and personae creation, 152; and post-revolutionary imaginaries, 62; and progress, 45; and resource distribution, 17, 242–243n7; and rural-urban contrast, 242n3; and significance of home, 119, 127–128; as site of ethico-moral transformation, 182; temporal framework of, 139–140; and traditionalist imaginary, 176; and Uriangatense imaginaries, 76; and us-them contrasts, 160; and women, 170; and working-class people, 159

migration histories: construction of, 149, 150; and ethico-moral life, 181; and interpellation, 152

Minutemen Project, 112, 241ch2n5

"Mitos y realidades" (Myths and Realities), 111

mobility: and displaced people, 232; ethico-moral loading of, 139; and gender, 155; gendering of, 90–91, 162; and language practices, 237–238; and masculinity, 109; moralizing of, 42–43; and progress, 14; and social imaginary, 12; and women migrants, 164. *See also* moral mobility

modernist chronotopes, 47–48

modernity: and diaspora at home, 141; and Enlightenment thought, 42; and homebuilding, 137; and Mexicanidad, 128; and nuclear families, 138; in Porfirian imaginaries, 48; and public/private contrast, 89–90; and return migrants, 65

modernity-tradition contrast, 48–49, 132, 136

morality: defined, 19; and intersubjective agreement, 152; and Mexicanidad, 128, 203; and Mexican national identity, 15; political dimensions of, 88; and progress, 14; versus progress, 121; and progres-